With best wishes

Jim Swanton

# CRICKET FROM ALL ANGLES

# E. W. SWANTON

# Cricket from all Angles

*London*
MICHAEL JOSEPH

*First published in Great Britain by*
MICHAEL JOSEPH LTD
*26 Bloomsbury Street*
*London, W.C.*1
1968

© 1968 *by E. W. Swanton*

7181 0617 2

*Set and printed in Great Britain by*
*Tonbridge Printers Ltd, Peach Hall Works, Tonbridge, Kent,*
*in Baskerville eleven on twelve point, and bound by*
*James Burn at Esher, Surrey*

# Contents

CHAPTER FOUR: *Prophecies, Conclusions – And a Few Mis-hits*

CHAPTER FIVE: *Some First Impressions*

CHAPTER SIX: *Topical Essays*

CHAPTER SEVEN: *The Seamy Side*

CHAPTER EIGHT: *Tributes to the Great*

CHAPTER NINE: *Oddments from Everywhere*

# Illustrations

# INTRODUCTION

I joined *The Daily Telegraph* in June, 1946, and have been writing cricket for it, at home and abroad, ever since. This book comprises a selection from the several thousand pieces, long and short, reports, articles, commentaries, and notices of various kinds that have since appeared in the paper under my name. There is also an extract or two from *The Sunday Telegraph*, and in the case of both papers I am indebted to Mr H. M. Stephen, their Managing Director, for permission to re-print. He has also kindly allowed the publishers to print extracts from the prologues and introductions by the late Mr C. B. Fry, the late Lord Birkett, and Mr Bernard Hollowood to the collections of my Anglo-Australian Test reports which after four of the series were published in book form by *The Daily Telegraph*. I must also thank the Editor of *The Field*, Mr Wilson Stephens, for similar permission in respect of certain articles contributed to that paper.

The idea behind the book has been to pick out some of the most interesting and important of the material, and so to try and hold up some sort of mirror to English post-war cricket – and, to a lesser extent, that of England's chief opponents also. I am not sure how successfully this original aim has worked out, since there have been so many 'problems' surrounding the game these last twenty-odd years that to have attempted any sort of comprehensive coverage of them would have been almost to have been obliged to leave out the actual cricket altogether. Also it seems to me that such subjects, vital though they may have seemed when they were in the balance, tend to make dullish reading in retrospect. So there is not too much about experimental law changes and match regulations, and other hardy annuals, while I have, in the most cowardly way, steered absolutely clear of the Clark Report.

Readers will find, I hope, a fair quota of the exciting and

memorable happenings of the period 1946–1968. No picture of the period can avoid the seamy side – either on the field or off it: hence Chapters Three and Seven. However, they are at least just about the shortest chapters, and I believe there is scarcely anyone of those coming in for some criticism therein who is not to be seen in a favourable light elsewhere in the book.

I have always tried to give some prominence to cricket other than first-class in *The Daily Telegraph*, and have been grateful to have been allowed the space to do so, especially on Monday mornings – in days before the allotment of cricket space in Monday's paper had to be given over largely to reports of county games on Sundays. This 'other' cricket has provided enough material, and a sufficient diversity of topics, to make a book on its own. If there has not been room to include as much as I should like I hope enough will be found to justify the title of the book.

For most readers I suppose this will be a 'dip-in' book. On this assumption it has been freely sign-posted both in the Contents pages and in the Index, so that names and topics that appeal can be quickly picked out.

I must conclude by registering gratitude to Mr Irving Rosenwater, who has been largely responsible for the selection, as well as for the sub-editing and the checking of figures. I should pay tribute also to the work of many hands both in transmission and in the Sports Room of *The Daily Telegraph*. Considering with what speed nearly all this writing had to be dealt with, from the moment it reached the copy-taker on the telephone or the cable operator until it was locked away by 'the man on the stone', the number of errors has been remarkably few.

Finally I must say how lucky I count myself to have had access to the photography of Mr Patrick Eagar whose work has done so much these last few years to embellish the pages of *The Cricketer*.

E. W. SWANTON

February 1968
St James, Barbados

# CHAPTER ONE

# GREAT TEST DAYS

Great is an over-worked word, maybe, in the sporting sense but there have been many days nevertheless in the Test cricket of the post-war period that have aspired to be so described. What follows is a necessarily arbitrary selection, from which many memorable occasions had to be omitted. To give an instance that is at once obvious, I begin with the latter part of the second of Denis Compton's historic innings against the 1948 Australians, the 145 at Old Trafford scored after he had been cut over the eye and laid flat by Lindwall, rather than that wonderful 184 in a losing cause at Trent Bridge. It is a nice point which day rates the higher. One can only hope that those that have been picked out revive more happy recollections than the omissions induce disappointment.

I must note again the point already made in the Introduction regarding differing length standards over the years. In 1948, where the story starts so far as this chapter is concerned, the paper shortage restricted the most momentous reports to a few hundred words. Five years later an enthralling day such as both the two immediately following would have commanded double the space. Readers may perhaps amuse themselves deciding which of the two writing techniques they prefer.

## Compton in Clover

This was the second day of the Third Test, Compton having been forced to retire on the first morning when, in hooking at a fast no-ball from Lindwall, he diverted the ball on to his head. The wound having been stitched and some gentle practice taken at the nets, the bandaged hero returned in mid-afternoon with the England score showing 119 for five, and came home safely, 64 not out at the close.

I suppose that Compton's fame reached its highest peak at this point – before 'the knee' began to prove an ever-increasing handicap

13

– as may be gathered from the assessment that follows. Above Hammond even! Yes, and looking back I still think so: not perhaps as an all-round cricketer, but, for all Hammond's superb skill, *as a Test batsman* against the best bowling.

ENGLAND V AUSTRALIA, Old Trafford, 2nd day: July 9, 1948
*Score at start:* England 231 for 7
*Score at close:* England 363; Australia 126 for 3

Compton's innings of 145 not out at Old Trafford yesterday, continued from his 64 on Thursday, has saved the England team from the starkest failure. Who but the softest and silliest could have conceived Australia being still 237 behind this morning (with three batsmen out) when the fifth wicket fell at 119?

The whole morning Bedser stayed with Compton, and Compton once again batted with that suppression of his true aggressive inclinations which make these Test innings of his more than ever praiseworthy. In his last ten Tests now he has made eight hundreds, which is a thing only Bradman has ever done and it is time, I think, to express the view that since Hobbs, and with all possible respect to the greatness of Hammond, we have not seen an English batsman so thoroughly equipped for every sort of situation on every sort of pitch.

Unfortunately the second day, like the first, did not pass without accident. Barnes at short leg was hit a full-blooded blow on the left side below the ribs when Pollard met an off-break from Johnson in the middle of the bat.

He was carried in in the greatest pain, and, of course, could not bat but after a hospital X-ray which revealed no broken bones he was put to bed in his hotel, and the latest news of him is comparatively reassuring. It needs a brave man to field where Barnes does: just as it needs courage to stand firm to fast bowling, and the risk of accident must always be present.

The morning's cricket opened soberly, livened considerably in a spell which began with Compton off-driving Toshack for two fours in an over, and ended on a tense note with several very fast overs from Lindwall, against which Compton was several times in difficulty.

Ninety-two more runs had brought England's score from 231 to 323. Bedser, apart from a few streaky ones past the slips, had well justified the compliment his partner had paid him by making no particular effort to keep the bowling, and Compton himself, of course, had reached his hundred.

Compton began after lunch with some superb late-cutting off Lindwall and Johnson, and the eighth wicket seemed firmly re-established again when it was broken in a manner singularly futile from the English point of view.

Compton played the ball slowly between Bradman and Loxton on the off-side, and as the fielders incommoded one another the batsmen eventually decided to run. But Bedser is not very quick out of his holes, and in any case the golden rule had been ignored which warns against running for a misfield unless there is a two in it.

Now Compton tried his hardest to arrange to take the bowling, Bradman countering by setting a field in which, for Compton, no one was nearer than fifty yards from the bat until after the fourth ball of the over. Thus 26 came for the last two wickets, and if in this period Compton was not able to manoeuvre things quite as he generally does, he had surely achieved enough.

In Barnes' absence Johnson came in with Morris, but was soon beautifully caught by Evans standing up, shoulder high. Bradman was seeing the ball very large from the beginning, but at 13 Pollard beat him, and here was crisis right atop of the Australians who on Thursday afternoon had England at their mercy.

Pollard and Bedser bowled with accuracy and life, and the resistance of Morris and Hassett raised the play to a much higher plane than anything that had occurred previously, except when Compton was at the batting end.

Pollard, after a fine bowl of two hours less tea, had just given way to Young when Hassett suddenly went down the pitch to hit Young over mid-on and skied the ball to cover. Miller came in at 82 for three, with fifty minutes to go, and the batting was fully adequate to all demands.

Indeed there was some beautiful stroke-making, accepted by the crowd with a strange lack of audible appreciation. Morris's reputation grows with every match; he has not served Australia better than yesterday.

# England's Astonishing Ascendancy

This was a palpitating day by any standards, but it earns inclusion here for the good reason that by close of play England had reached (for the only time in the course of the first ten – no, the first *fourteen* – post-war Tests against Australia) a cast-iron match-winning position.

I can remember clearly enough the frustration brought by the heavy rain of the week-end that then proceeded to let Australia off the hook. On the fourth day no play; on the fifth a few hours after lunch with the pitch like a pudding. But the third day was a wonderful salve to English pride.

ENGLAND v AUSTRALIA, Old Trafford, 3rd day: July 10, 1948
*Score at start:* England 363; Australia 126 for 3
*Score at close:* England 363 and 174 for 3; Australia 221

A lead of 316 with seven wickets standing and two days to go is, by all the lessons of Test match history, a cast-iron position, and perhaps only those who followed England's struggles in the last series in Australia can fully enjoy the luxury of feeling that this time at least the tables are turned.

A combination of many things has brought this about, from the accident of numerous catches dropped by Australians who are normally as safe as the Bank to the brave design of the Washbrook–Edrich partnership.

On Saturday afternoon these two stood up unflinchingly to the utmost efforts of Lindwall and Miller, who by sheer speed strove to turn the situation which had so unexpectedly and suddenly developed with Australia's batting failure.

The extraordinary English recovery begun by Compton's innings had been supported by some wonderfully good bowling by Pollard and Bedser, but when Tallon made the magnificent low right-handed catch which sent back Emmett, in the first over of England's second innings the awful fear was in every heart that Lindwall and Miller might together run through the side as each, separately, had done before.

The next hour was epic, the climax of what surely was as stirring a day's cricket as has been seen in a Test at Old Trafford since the classic match of 1902.

There was a moment in mid-afternoon when, with the ball

flying round the batsmen's heads and some in the crowd calling their disapproval, the atmosphere threatened to grow too antagonistic to be pleasant, but the warm underlying friendliness existing between the two sides was proof against trouble.

For the English team (and, if they may be safely referred to, for the selectors also) the day's play was indeed a vindication. There was admirable determination in the bowling of Pollard and Bedser, as in the gallant partnership for the second wicket; nor should Crapp's good service be forgotten.

When Compton was out for none following the run-out of Edrich, and the new ball was only a few overs off, a solid partner for Washbrook was very urgently needed, and no one could have conveyed a demeanour more appropriate to the occasion than Crapp.

England's lead was 271 when he came in, and there was an hour to go. Two more wickets, making five, and the door would have been open. But it was not at Crapp's end that the vital chance for Australia was given, and if there was poetic justice in some good luck for Washbrook evening out the ill that followed him in the first two Tests the fact that it was Hassett who missed him at long leg twice in an afternoon was perhaps the most remarkable happening in an extraordinary day.

The remaining Australian batting was surprisingly fallible. The English new-ball bowling had Morris and Miller playing and missing frequently at the start of the day, and when Miller was leg-before and Morris caught at long-leg no one that followed seemed likely to stage a recovery except Loxton, who in his first Test against England showed a punch worthy of Gregory, or Victor Richardson, or many another tough Australian batsman in the middle of the order.

No praise can be too high for the partnership of Washbrook and Edrich. On his form at Nottingham and Lord's Edrich was lucky to be in the match but England was luckier in his performance.

Before he was run out (by a combination of Morris's quickness and his own hesitation) he was beginning to make strokes again, and quite recovering his touch.

Washbrook from the start had declined to be subdued. His on driving of the fast bowling was magnificent, and his square-cutting as good as ever. The crowd was quite transported by

the play of their own hero, and trekked home in a daze of
happiness.

## England

| | | | |
|---|---|---|---|
| C. Washbrook b. Johnston | 11 | — not out | 85 |
| G. M. Emmett c. Barnes b. Lindwall | 10 | — c. Tallon b. Lindwall | 0 |
| W. J. Edrich c. Tallon b. Lindwall | 32 | — run out | 53 |
| D. C. S. Compton not out | 145 | — c. Miller b. Toshack | 0 |
| J. F. Crapp lbw. b. Lindwall | 37 | — not out | 19 |
| H. E. Dollery b. Johnston | 1 | | |
| N. W. D. Yardley c. Johnson b. Toshack | 22 | | |
| T. G. Evans c. Johnston b. Lindwall | 34 | | |
| A. V. Bedser run out | 37 | | |
| R. Pollard b. Toshack | 3 | | |
| J. A. Young c. Bradman b. Johnston | 4 | | |
| B. 7, l.b. 17, n.b. 3 | 27 | B. 9, l.b. 7, w. 1 | 17 |
| | **363** | **Three wkts, dec.** | **174** |

## Australia

| | | | |
|---|---|---|---|
| A. R. Morris c. Compton b. Bedser | 51 | — not out | 54 |
| I. W. Johnson c. Evans b. Bedser | 1 | — c. Crapp b Young | 6 |
| D. G. Bradman lbw. b. Pollard | 7 | — not out | 30 |
| A. L. Hassett c. Washbrook b. Young | 38 | | |
| K. R. Miller lbw. b. Pollard | 31 | | |
| S. G. Barnes retired hurt | 1 | | |
| S. J. Loxton b. Pollard | 36 | | |
| D. Tallon c. Evans b. Edrich | 18 | | |
| R. R. Lindwall c. Washbrook b. Bedser | 23 | | |
| W. A. Johnston c. Crapp b. Bedser | 3 | | |
| E. R. H. Toshack not out | 0 | | |
| B. 5, l.b. 4, n.b. 3 | 12 | N.b. 2 | 2 |
| | **221** | **One wkt** | **92** |

## Australia Bowling

| | O. | M. | R. | W. | | O. | M. | R. | W. |
|---|---|---|---|---|---|---|---|---|---|
| Lindwall | 40 | 8 | 99 | 4 | — | 14 | 4 | 37 | 1 |
| Johnston | 45.5 | 13 | 67 | 3 | — | 14 | 3 | 34 | 0 |
| Loxton | 7 | 0 | 18 | 0 | — | 8 | 1 | 29 | 0 |
| Toshack | 41 | 20 | 75 | 2 | — | 12 | 5 | 26 | 1 |
| Johnson | 38 | 16 | 77 | 0 | — | 7 | 3 | 16 | 0 |
| Miller | | | | | | 14 | 7 | 15 | 0 |

## England Bowling

| | O. | M. | R. | W. | | O. | M. | R. | W. |
|---|---|---|---|---|---|---|---|---|---|
| Bedser | 36 | 12 | 81 | 4 | — | 19 | 12 | 27 | 0 |
| Pollard | 32 | 9 | 53 | 3 | — | 10 | 8 | 6 | 0 |
| Edrich | 7 | 3 | 27 | 1 | — | 2 | 0 | 8 | 0 |
| Yardley | 4 | 0 | 12 | 0 | | | | | |
| Young | 14 | 5 | 36 | 1 | — | 21 | 12 | 31 | 1 |
| Compton | | | | | | 9 | 3 | 18 | 0 |

## FALL OF WICKETS

ENGLAND – First Innings: 1—22, 2—28, 3—96, 4—97, 5—119, 6—141, 7—216, 8—337, 9—352.
ENGLAND – Second Innings: 1—1, 2—125, 3—129.
AUSTRALIA – First Innings: 1—3, 2—13, 3—82, 4—135, 5—139, 6—172, 7—208, 8—219, 9—221.
AUSTRALIA – Second Innings: 1—10.

Umpires: D. Davies and F. Chester.

Match drawn

# The West Indies Make History

This was the big break-through for the West Indies. Formidable in their islands, they had never threatened to match England at home. Earlier in June they had been beaten by 202 runs – on a horrible wicket – in the First Test at Old Trafford.

Shattering though this Lord's victory was, its full significance was not at once generally appreciated – certainly not by me. Yet it was the first of nine Test wins in England and the turning-point that led on to success in three rubbers out of four.

Incidentally, it inspired the calypso about 'those little pals of mine, Ramadhin and Valentine.'

ENGLAND v WEST INDIES, Lord's, final day: June 29, 1950
*Score at start:* West Indies 326 and 425 for 6 dec.; England 151
and 218 for 4
*Score at close:* West Indies 326 and 425 for 6 dec.; England 151
and 274

Soon after lunch today West Indies gained the victory that had seemed theirs from the time on Monday afternoon when England's batting failed against Ramadhin and Valentine. The difference was 326 runs. Thus West Indies follow South Africa, who not only chose Lord's as the scene of their first and only success in a Test in England 15 years ago, but also won by a handsome and conclusive margin.

There could be no possible question of the justice of today's result. The two young spin bowlers certainly were chiefly responsible, but Rae and Walcott, Worrell, Weekes and Gomez have distinguished deeds against their names in the score sheet. Indeed, every member of Goddard's team contributed, not least the captain himself, who made several shrewd assessments in the field as well as setting an admirable lead by his performance at silly mid-off and short-leg.

From first to last the England batting was thrown completely back on trepidant and unconvincing defence, whereas the West Indies, faced by spin bowlers whose performance certainly could be expected to lose little or nothing by contrast with their own, declined to be dictated to at the wicket.

The delightful innings of Worrell and Weekes on the first day had a significance not properly expressed in the score. When this game is looked back to it may always be used as the model illustration of the ancient axiom that bowlers bowl as well as they are allowed to.

I would not seem to detract from the merit of Ramadhin and Valentine. The former, especially, bowled magnificently, using the arts and subtleties of a spinner in a way extraordinary in one who had had not a scrap of experience before this tour. But more than one wise critic hit the nail on the head when they said they would like to see those two bowling to Worrell and Weekes. To find the ideal pair of batsmen among Englishmen of the last generation one need not go beyond Hendren and Ames. If they, or their like, had been playing it is quite certain that Valentine would not have bowled 116 overs without being hit over his head.

The most significant of all the statistics connected with the game, even making allowance for the fact that England were latterly playing for a draw, is that in the two innings West Indies received from England only 11 overs more than they bowled themselves and they scored 326 more runs.

From the English angle it is fair to add that the side was considerably weakened beyond the expected absence of Compton, who has been the focal point of all our post-war Test teams, by the injuries to Simpson and Bailey. The rubber is all square now, with two matches to come, and it would be a foolish prophet who plumped very strongly for either side finishing with a clear lead.

The analyses of Ramadhin and Valentine set many wondering what new 'records' could be unearthed to underline their performances. Alfred Shaw inevitably came to mind and Geary and J. C. White. In 1880 Shaw bowled 116 four-ball overs against Gloucestershire, and five years later W. G. Grace, who never liked to be outdone, returned the compliment against Notts. with 120 overs, which is the equivalent of 80 today.

Geary and White bowled 81 and 75.3 respectively, of six balls each, against Australia at Melbourne in 1929 and (this makes a gratifying memory) Fleetwood-Smith and O'Reilly bowled 87 and 85 against England at the Oval in 1938. Incidentally Fleetwood-Smith's analysis was one for 289.

So the 72 and 71 overs of Ramadhin and Valentine in this second innings are not beyond compare. Furthermore, White bowled 124.5 overs in all at Adelaide in the Fourth Test of 1929. But it is safe to say that Valentine's 116 overs are the most that ever have been bowled in a match in England and that the combined score of 231 out of 298.1 is assuredly unique.

No summing up of the game is complete without a special word about the wicket, which was as near ideal as could be imagined. In spite of the preceding rain it was reasonably quick, it always took a sensible amount of spin and it lasted just about as well as was needed. I hope Martin has many applications for the recipe.

The onus of spinning out the game when it was restarted this morning rested really on Washbrook giving a repeat performance. He began by playing six maiden overs from Ramadhin, who mostly was attacking his legs with, of course, a close field. Washbrook seemed to have got the measure of this when he apparently struck his boot and was bowled by a ball that pitched about his leg-stump and hit the middle. He had been in for five and a half long hours, fighting bravely.

Yardley alternated moments of difficulty with some clean hits off Valentine into the covers, but he lost Evans after 25 minutes from a half-hit sweep which Rae caught at the second attempt about mid-way between square-leg and the Mound.

Then Yardley, who played Ramadhin better than anyone but Valentine rather more sketchily, snicked the ball hard to the wicket-keeper, off whose gloves it bounced to slip.

It was now a matter of whether the end would be before lunch or afterwards. Thanks to Wardle, who seemed to find little difficulty in the two young heroes now both flagging slightly, one wicket remained at half past one. No sudden thunderstorm threatened to cloud the bright blue sky.

Wardle hit four rousing fours off Valentine which had the effect of causing the runs scored against him slightly to out-number his overs, and it was Worrell who finally despatched him, to the unbridled joy of his countrymen.

Some of them, armed with impromptu instruments, saluted the great occasion with strange noises, and a handful with their leader swayed round the field to give a faint reminder to those who know the West Indian Islands of the bands at carnival time.

One felt sorry that the august dignity of Lord's and perhaps the sight of many helmets and uniforms so subdued the rest. But, for them at least, it was a victory unforgettable.

## West Indies

| | | | | | |
|---|---|---|---|---|---|
| A. F. Rae c. and b. Jenkins | ... | ... 106 | — | b. Jenkins ... ... | 24 |
| J. B. Stollmeyer lbw. b. Wardle ... | | ... 20 | — | b. Jenkins ... ... | 30 |
| F. M. Worrell b. Bedser ... | ... | ... 52 | — | c. Doggart b. Jenkins | 45 |
| E. Weekes b. Bedser | ... ... | ... 63 | — | run out ... ... | 63 |
| C. L. Walcott st. Evans b. Jenkins | | ... 14 | — | not out ... ... | 168 |
| G. E. Gomez st. Evans b Jenkins | ... | 1 | — | c. Edrich b. Bedser ... | 70 |
| R. J. Christiani b. Bedser | ... | ... 33 | — | not out ... ... | 5 |
| J. D. Goddard b. Wardle | ... | ... 14 | — | c. Evans b. Jenkins ... | 11 |
| P. E. Jones c. Evans b. Jenkins ... | | ... 0 | | | |
| S. Ramadhin not out | ... ... | ... 1 | | | |
| A. L. Valentine c. Hutton b. Jenkins | ... | 5 | | | |
| B. 10, l.b. 5, w. 1, n.b. 1 | ... | ... 17 | | L.b. 8, n.b. 1 ... | 9 |
| | | 326 | | Six wkts, dec. | 425 |

## England

| | | | | | |
|---|---|---|---|---|---|
| L. Hutton st. Walcott b. Valentine | ... | 35 | — | b. Valentine ... ... | 10 |
| C. Washbrook st. Walcott b. Ramadhin | | 36 | — | b. Ramadhin ... ... | 114 |
| W. J. Edrich c. Walcott b. Ramadhin | ... | 8 | — | c. Jones b. Ramadhin | 8 |
| G. H. G. Doggart lbw. b. Ramadhin | | 0 | — | b. Ramadhin ... ... | 25 |
| W. G. A. Parkhouse b. Valentine | | 0 | — | c. Goddard b. Valentine | 48 |
| N. W. D. Yardley b. Valentine ... | | 16 | — | c. Weekes b. Valentine | 19 |
| T. G. Evans b. Ramadhin | ... | 8 | — | c. Rae b. Ramadhin ... | 2 |
| R. O. Jenkins c. Walcott b. Valentine | ... | 4 | — | b. Ramadhin ... ... | 4 |
| J. H. Wardle not out | ... ... | 33 | — | lbw. b. Worrell ... | 21 |
| A. V. Bedser b. Ramadhin | ... | 5 | — | b. Ramadhin ... ... | 0 |
| R. Berry c. Goddard b. Jones | ... | 2 | — | not out ... ... | 0 |
| B. 2, l.b. 1, w. 1 | ... ... | 4 | | B. 16, l.b. 7 ... | 23 |
| | | 151 | | | 274 |

England Bowling

| | | O. | M. | R. | W. | | O. | M. | R. | W. |
|---|---|---|---|---|---|---|---|---|---|---|
| Bedser | ... | 40 | 14 | 60 | 3 | — | 44 | 16 | 80 | 1 |
| Edrich... | ... | 16 | 4 | 30 | 0 | — | 13 | 2 | 37 | 0 |
| Jenkins | ... | 35.2 | 6 | 116 | 5 | — | 59 | 13 | 174 | 4 |
| Wardle | ... | 17 | 6 | 46 | 2 | — | 30 | 10 | 58 | 0 |
| Berry ... | ... | 19 | 7 | 45 | 0 | — | 32 | 15 | 67 | 0 |
| Yardley | ... | 4 | 1 | 12 | 0 | | | | | |

West Indies Bowling

| | | O. | M. | R. | W. | | O. | M. | R. | W. |
|---|---|---|---|---|---|---|---|---|---|---|
| Jones ... | ... | 8.4 | 2 | 13 | 1 | — | 7 | 1 | 22 | 0 |
| Worrell | ... | 10 | 4 | 20 | 0 | — | 22.3 | 9 | 39 | 1 |
| Valentine | ... | 45 | 28 | 48 | 4 | — | 71 | 47 | 79 | 3 |
| Ramadhin | ... | 43 | 27 | 66 | 5 | — | 72 | 43 | 86 | 6 |
| Gomez | | | | | | ... | 13 | 1 | 25 | 0 |
| Goddard | | | | | | ... | 6 | 6 | 0 | 0 |

## FALL OF WICKETS

WEST INDIES – First Innings: 1—37, 2—128, 3—233, 4—262, 5—273, 6—274, 7—320, 8—320, 9—320.

WEST INDIES – Second Innings: 1—48, 2—75, 3—108, 4—146, 5—199, 6—410.

ENGLAND – First Innings: 1—62, 2—74, 4—75, 5—86, 6—102, 7—110, 8—113, 9—122.

ENGLAND – Second Innings: 1—28, 2—57, 3—140, 4—218, 5—228, 6—238, 7—245, 8—258, 9—258.

Umpires: D. Davies and F. S. Lee.

West Indies won by 326 runs.

# Elusive Victory

No need to elaborate at length on the significance of this day which assuaged so much disappointment, not to say humiliation. Since England stepped on to the field at Brisbane in the first post-war Test against Australia they had lost eleven of the fourteen games played, and drawn the remaining three. It is the most disastrous cycle in all but a century of combat.

Note the turning of the tide. This English win at Melbourne was to be the first of seven, punctuated by only two defeats, before another ebb took control.

AUSTRALIA V ENGLAND, Melbourne, final day: February 28, 1951

*Score at start:* Australia 217 and 129 for 4; England 320

*Score at close:* Australia 217 and 197; England 320 and 95 for 2

This was the day of days, and the score tells the story of the decisiveness of the victory. It was an added pleasure, when the long run ended at last, that there was no question of luck with either the weather or the wicket. For England won inside four days of playing time on a wicket that played true from first to last and, which is the nub of the matter, after losing the toss. I confess that when Australia won the choice of innings I felt a surge of pessimism which there was no point in passing on to those at home. Since M.C.C. sent its first team to Australia under P. F. Warner in 1903 Australia had failed only twice to win the fifth Test, in 1912 and 1933. Normally a touring side is at its peak, as Brown's side was, about the Second and Third Tests. But this apart it was hard to visualise the present batting side, dependent as it had been on one man with only occasional and uncertain outside help, making a sizeable score in the last innings. Thanks to Simpson England gained a three-figure lead after all, and thanks to Hutton, though the runs had to be fought for sternly, there was no breathless palpitating struggle for the 95 which were needed to win.

But while these two heroes are being applauded for their part, another name must be added, and it is a matter of personal judgment whether he occupies the chief post of honour. When Bedser got the last Australian wicket he brought his number for the series to thirty. If bare fact does not sound sufficiently impressive it should be enough to quote from the records. Tom Richardson, likewise a native of Surrey, took 32 wickets in an Australian Test series in 1894–5. He was followed in the course of years by Rhodes, J. N. Crawford, F. R. Foster, Barnes, Tate, and Larwood. Thus Bedser makes the eighth of an illustrious line. All were great bowlers, and that overworked adjective can certainly be applied to Bedser at least on Australian wickets. In the whole series he was never collared and rarely played with much appearance of comfort, and in case any may have assumed he concentrated mainly on the in-swinger, which to some is an unpalatable form of attack, it may be as well to point to the number of wickets he got with slip catches. When the shine was on he frequently made the ball go the other way, and afterwards his chief weapon of destruction was the ball that he cut away towards the slips.

The efforts of Bedser, coupled with the limitations of the England batting, were chiefly responsible for the scoring in the

Tests being so low. An inspection of the statistics suggests many pertinent thoughts, but the one that looms most vital from the English viewpoint is that if Hutton in the batting had had the support that Bedser enjoyed at one time or another in the bowling from Brown, Bailey, and, in spite of adverse figures, from Wright, the battle might so easily have swayed the other way.

To make a final and significant comparison with history it will be noted that England have now put an end to a run of eleven Australian victories in three series. An exactly similar number were scored by Australia in the period after the first world war, and the success by A. E. R. Gilligan's team at Adelaide in 1925 paved the way for England winning the Ashes on Australia's next visit to England. If the right deductions are made from the results in 1950–1 the pattern might continue to run the same way.

Before this last day's play began the bulk of the Australian Press had more or less awarded the game to England. This may have been wishful thinking, but, considering that Hassett and Hole were to be followed by three batsmen who with them could be easily capable of setting England at least 200 or 250 in the last innings, it gave quite a false picture. In retrospect the bowling of Hassett by Wright was probably the vital incident. Hassett had held the fort for three hours and twenty minutes in all, and Hole had suggested that he might well proceed at any time to an aggressive counter-attack, as in fact he proceeded now to do. Since the new ball was due in eight overs Brown himself began the bowling with Wright, and it was after twenty-five minutes of quiet play that Wright's beautifully-pitched leg-break got past Hassett's bat. In the same over Johnson essayed an ambitious straight drive, and was caught at deep mid-on by Brown, who as he waited had plenty of time to reflect on the possible consequences of a miss.

Wright up to this point had bowled dangerously and not expensively, but now Lindwall with a lofty drive for three and Hole with three fours took 15 in the next over. Wright, one felt before this onslaught, might have swept through the remaining Australian batting, but his brilliance and his limitations were reflected in these two overs. The four strokes persuaded Brown to take the new ball, and Bedser and Bailey bowled until the innings ended. Lindwall stayed nearly an hour while Hole, aided with just a little luck, coped successfully with Bedser and Bailey. The shine was off some time before, in the last over before lunch, Lindwall played too late at Bedser and snicked the ball on. Hole had certainly shown his nerve and his quality and if Australia had gone in with three wickets standing in addition to his there would still have been the prospect of a longish score to chase. As it was, the stand of 50 between Hole and Lindwall had given England something to go for. After lunch Brown still persisted with Bailey, who was economical without looking particularly dangerous, at the other end to Bedser, and soon Hole was bowled as in the first innings aiming an on-drive. That was that, and it took Bedser the minimum time to pick up the last two wickets.

Hutton and Washbrook scored 32 for England's first wicket, half against Lindwall and Miller before they were quickly replaced by Iverson and Johnston. Washbrook cocked an easy catch to short-leg, whereupon Simpson, now of an entirely different stature after his first innings, played easily and well with Hutton. Just before tea Simpson was surprised by the exceptional speed of Harvey in the covers and was thrown out before he seemed to envisage the danger. The advent of Compton inevitably made for more tension, and another half-hour's struggle was needed before Hutton fittingly scored the final run. He as ever in this series had been the master, and one felt that perhaps the fact of Compton being with him at the end was the sign of better things to come against South Africa.

The result altered the whole aspect of this tour as it will be remembered by the players taking part, by those both at home and in Australia who followed the fortunes of the series in the press and over the air, and for that matter for those who in the future look back into cricket history. Moral victories and near-things and unlucky breaks are all very well but each reverse in these three series since the war made it harder for the English side to break through. Now the reproach is past and when the comedy of a last over by Hassett and three premature stump-grabbings by the players had culminated in Hutton making the winning stroke, one sensed the same emotion of relief and pleasure among the spectators as had marked a more domestic occasion just before the war when Harrow for the first time in forty years beat their rivals from Eton. The crowd here was more orderly and self-conscious than that which swarmed the field at Lord's in 1939, but they would not leave before Brown and Hassett had said their brief well-chosen words from the grand-stand balcony. As England's captain observed, it would have been nicer if this had been the match that had decided the Ashes. But at least the manner of the victory made it clear that if things had run differently it could have been.

## Australia

| | | | |
|---|---|---|---|
| J. Burke c. Tattersall b. Bedser ... ... | 11 | — c. Hutton b. Bedser ... ... | 1 |
| A. R. Morris lbw. b. Brown ... ... | 50 | — lbw. b. Bedser ... | 4 |
| A. L. Hassett c. Hutton b. Brown ... | 92 | — b. Wright ... ... | 48 |
| R. N. Harvey c. Evans b. Brown ... ... | 1 | — lbw. b. Wright ... | 52 |
| K. R. Miller c. and b. Brown ... ... | 7 | — c. and b. Brown ... | 0 |
| G. Hole b. Bedser ... ... ... | 18 | — b. Bailey ... ... | 63 |
| I. W. Johnson lbw. b. Bedser ... ... | 1 | — c. Brown b. Wright ... | 0 |
| R. R. Lindwall c. Compton b. Bedser ... | 21 | — b. Bedser ... ... | 14 |
| D. Tallon c. Hutton b. Bedser ... ... | 1 | — not out ... ... | 2 |
| W. A. Johnston not out ... ... ... | 12 | — b. Bedser ... ... | 1 |
| J. Iverson c. Washbrook b. Brown ... | 0 | — c. Compton b. Bedser | 0 |
| B. 2, l.b. 1 ... ... ... ... | 3 | — B. 2, l.b. 8, n.b. 1, w. 1 | 12 |
| | **217** | | **197** |

## England

| | | | |
|---|---|---|---|
| L. Hutton b. Hole ... ... ... | 79 | — not out ... ... | 60 |
| C. Washbrook c. Tallon b. Miller ... | 27 | — c. Lindwall b. Johnston | 7 |
| R. T. Simpson not out ... ... ... | 156 | — run out ... ... | 15 |
| D. C. S. Compton c. Miller b. Lindwall | 11 | — not out ... ... | 11 |
| D. S. Sheppard c. Tallon b. Miller ... | 1 | | |
| F. R. Brown b. Lindwall ... ... ... | 6 | | |
| T. G. Evans b. Miller ... ... ... | 1 | | |
| A. V. Bedser b. Lindwall ... ... | 11 | | |
| T. E. Bailey c. Johnson b. Iverson ... | 5 | | |
| D. V. P. Wright lbw. b. Iverson ... | 3 | | |
| R. Tattersall b. Miller ... ... | 10 | | |
| B. 9, l.b. 1 ... ... ... ... | 10 | L.b. 2 ... ... | 2 |
| | **320** | Two wkts | **95** |

## England Bowling

| | O. | M. | R. | W. | O. | M. | R. | W. |
|---|---|---|---|---|---|---|---|---|
| Bedser... ... | 22 | 5 | 46 | 5 | 20.3 | 4 | 59 | 5 |
| Bailey ... ... | 9 | 1 | 29 | 0 | 15 | 3 | 32 | 1 |
| Brown... ... | 18 | 4 | 49 | 5 | 9 | 1 | 32 | 1 |

| | O. | M. | R. | W. | O. | M. | R. | W. |
|---|---|---|---|---|---|---|---|---|
| Wright | ... 9 | 1 | 50 | 0 | — 15 | 2 | 56 | 3 |
| Tattersall | ... 11 | 3 | 40 | 0 | — 5 | 2 | 6 | 0 |

## Australia Bowling

| | O. | M. | R. | W. | O. | M. | R. | W. |
|---|---|---|---|---|---|---|---|---|
| Lindwall | ... 21 | 1 | 77 | 3 | — 2 | 0 | 12 | 0 |
| Miller ... | ... 21.7 | 5 | 76 | 4 | — 2 | 0 | 5 | 0 |
| Johnston | ... 12 | 1 | 55 | 0 | — 11 | 3 | 36 | 1 |
| Iverson | ... 20 | 4 | 52 | 2 | — 12 | 2 | 32 | 0 |
| Johnson | ... 11 | 1 | 40 | 0 | — 1 | 0 | 1 | 0 |
| Hole ... | ... 5 | 0 | 10 | 1 | — 1 | 0 | 3 | 0 |
| | | | Hassett | ... | 0.6 | 0 | 4 | 0 |

### FALL OF WICKETS

AUSTRALIA – First Innings: 1—23, 2—111, 3—115, 4—123, 5—156, 6—166, 7—184, 8—187, 9—216.

AUSTRALIA – Second Innings: 1—5, 2—6, 3—87, 4—89, 5—142, 6—142, 7—192, 8—196, 9—197.

ENGLAND – First Innings: 1—40, 2—171, 3—204, 4—205, 5—212, 6—213, 7—228, 8—236, 9—246.

ENGLAND – Second Innings: 1—32, 2—62.

Umpires: H. Elphinston and A. Barlow.

England won by 8 wickets

# Triumph for Alec Bedser

Herewith the more significant portions of two successive reports at Trent Bridge containing much exciting cricket. In particular, of course, they embody Alec Bedser's finest hour. The sad thing was that with the game so poised rain prevented any play on the fourth day, and allowed only a useless two hours at the end of the fifth. I hope these remarks may give to the younger generation an idea of what a tremendous bowler Bedser was in this his prime. As with others that follow these pieces have had to be condensed.

ENGLAND v AUSTRALIA, Trent Bridge, 2nd and 3rd days: June 12 and 13, 1953
*Score at start:* (2nd day): Australia 157 for 3
*Score at close:* (2nd day): Australia 249; England 92 for 6
*Score at close:* (3rd day): Australia 249 and 123; England 144 and 42 for 1

One must beware of saying that today's play in the first Test was among the most remarkable within memory, because the history of cricket is one long chronicle of the incredible coming to pass. I would say, though, that the happenings this afternoon and evening were particularly unusual, if not unique, in one regard. Between luncheon and the end at 6 o'clock, 12 wickets fell for 98 runs and yet the wicket was always completely placid and easy.

The mastery of Bedser and later of Lindwall was attributable not in any way to the turf but to the raw, damp atmosphere in which they swung the ball with extraordinary skill.

It is true, of course, that in both camps there is an unusual lack of technically sound, organised batsmen experienced in the highest class of Test cricket – which implies nothing except matches between England and Australia. Take away the innings of Morris, Hassett, Miller and Hutton and one might be regarding the score book of a village match.

England's position this evening is, of course, dire in the extreme, though not beyond all expectations of recovery – quite. Where for the purpose of winning the match there must have been hopes of a lead in the neighbourhood of 100, tonight there is even the threat of a follow-on. Of course it will not occur but England have still to score eight more.

There were two disastrous periods, the first brought about by Lindwall, the second by bowlers of lesser stature who had to thank some faultless catching and also not least a further deterioration in the light. There were no scapegoats among the English batsmen, none who succumbed to a specially unworthy stroke. In the first place, Lindwall bowled magnificently; in the second everything that went remotely to hand was snapped up.

May's wicket at the end might, without offence in any direction, be ascribed to the light. At the end of the over after he went the umpires conferred, since Bailey had made the one allowable appeal 20 minutes earlier; and they then took off the bails.

If it is permissible to give a personal view from the pavilion, it is that the light during the last half hour's cricket was worse than when the umpires brought the players in at 6 o'clock last evening.

The especial irony in England's score lies in that it is such a pitiful compliment to Bedser's magnificent bowling. This

morning he seemed not unnaturally a little stiff after yesterday's
great effort. He had bowled 30-odd overs at the Oval on
Tuesday. After luncheon he swept through the Australian
ranks in the manner of a truly great bowler.

With his last wicket he brought his number in Test matches
up to the 189 of Sydney Barnes, who was at hand spare,
straight, and fit at the age of 80 to make his congratulations.
Four for two in this last phase made his analysis for the innings
seven for 55.

The morning's play was a carry-over from the night before:
same wicket, same batting tempo, same hint of drizzle in the
damp breeze, same dim religious light. Again the bowlers had
to bowl with a wet ball which they tried to dry with towels and
sawdust. There are few more depressing handicaps than this.

Hutton did not give Bedser a protracted bowl, sensing,
maybe, that once Hassett and Miller had played themselves in
the critical phase might come with the new ball directly after
luncheon. Bedser had five overs first thing, then went to graze
until brought back on Benaud's arrival two overs before the
interval.

It was Wardle who eventually made the breach. Miller went
to sweep over square leg and skied high to mid-wicket. Bailey
turned and caught the ball on the run as it came over his
shoulder, an awkward catch perfectly judged.

The taking of the new ball plainly was going to be the
crucial event, but the complete sweeping away of the remaining
Australian batting in less than three-quarters of an hour was,
of course, beyond anyone's reckoning.

The catch with which Evans started the business will be
spoken of at Trent Bridge as long as George Parr's tree over-
shadows the square leg boundary. Benaud's stroke was a
genuine leg glance, and Evans, standing back, must have made
something like 10 feet before he took off and held the ball
left-handed as he hit the ground.

From that moment the Australian innings just folded up.
Bedser, with his second ball of the new over, delivered the
crowning blow when he bowled Hassett. This was a peach of
a ball, a peach or a pig according to the point of view. It
started about on the leg stump and it hit the top of the off.

Thus left Hassett, having been in possession a full 6½ hours.

His was a remarkable effort of sustained application and in view of the afternoon's events one may well wonder what might have happened had he gone early.

Tallon had to face Bedser in full career, four wickets in the bag already, and in no mood to be resisted by the tail. Tallon had three balls, any one of which might have been the last, before he succumbed to one only slightly less unpleasant than Hassett's.

Bailey next had Lindwall caught at the wicket, a nice gentlemanly sort of catch for Evans this time on the off side from the outside edge. Davidson batted with much more certainty than any of the others following Miller, but an inswinger soon finished Hill, and, with only Johnston left, Davidson had a Saturday afternoon dip and that was Bedser's seventh.

Even while these great events were in train a still small voice seemed to be saying: 'This is all very fine, but what will Lindwall do? He can swing the ball pretty well, too.'

*　　　*　　　*　　　*

A matter of 187 runs lies between England and what would be the fifth victory over Australia in this country in 40 years. There was solid rain in Nottingham this evening, and we must hope for a fine night, so that the wicket may remain as true and as placid as it has been, with just two or three momentary exceptions, since the long-ago of last Thursday morning. In these circumstances the prospect looks very favourable, bitterly though the Australian bowlers and fielders will contest every run.

Throughout the extraordinary cricket of the last three days the use of the new ball by Bedser and Lindwall has been the crucial factor. After 17 overs the gloss has gone from the present one, and another will not be due until after luncheon.

One's feeling on leaving the ground on Saturday evening was that the situation was altogether too good to be true. In the morning England's last four wickets made a further 52 runs, which was just about what could reasonably have been hoped for.

However, Australia's lead was 105, the wicket was behaving impeccably, and England had no relief bowling whatever to supplement Bedser and Bailey, who had bowled 82 overs between them in the first innings.

As the world knows, Bedser 'did it again', magnificently, incredibly. And in the fateful evening period England endured from five o'clock onwards for the cost of Kenyon's wicket.

One can look back on past struggles and sometimes say that the issue turned on one ball. Thus Fleetwood-Smith probably won the match and the rubber when he bowled Hammond at Adelaide one morning 16 years ago.

Here at Trent Bridge in 1930 England beat Australia when Copley, a young substitute from the ground staff, brilliantly caught McCabe. If the present match ends according to English hopes it will have been decided at the moment when a lifting ball from Bedser accounted for Hassett.

The ball did two things in one. It removed prop and stay of the Australian batting, and it sowed in Australian minds a distrust of the wicket which was reflected in all that happened subsequently.

From that moment, only Morris's batting, which proceeded on a plane far removed from that of any of his companions, held the slightest certainty of confidence. And as soon as Morris was gone, sixth out at 81, of which he had actually made 60, the Australians had no other thought than to make what they could as quickly as they could, and to get England in again at all costs.

Yet only about three balls bowled by Bedser in any way misbehaved. At the other end a few from Wardle turned a little and lifted a little, but he was bowling to a defensive field and they did no damage. Australians not unnaturally have never relished the ball that stops, for their wickets at home give them no experience in dealing with it.

On this occasion their apprehensions were founded on terribly slight evidence. What we saw was precious near a panic. Whatever uncomplimentary things may have been said of England's batting on Friday were infinitely more applicable to that of the Australians, Morris excepted, next day.

Hole had the unenviable task of facing Bedser's opening over with his 0 in the first innings behind him. If a Lock, an Ikin or a Sheppard had been at short leg he might have bagged a brace. As it was, from the first ball, he bisected the distance between the middle two fielders in the leg trap and was credited with four runs.

After luncheon Morris began with a series of brilliant strokes while Hole struggled to become acclimatised. He had added only one to his first involuntary four when Bedser got through his defence for the second time with another ball of full length.

As soon as Hassett arrived he took four off the edge past slip. Morris had little of Bedser and was accumulating readily off first Bailey and later Wardle. But while he did so the heart and middle of the Australian innings was destroyed by Bedser in the course of half an hour.

First Hassett got the nasty lifter, which with a hurried protective stab he could only push gently to short leg. Harvey was surrounded with a bristling hedge of fielders, with May at forward short leg as close as S. G. Barnes stood to English batsmen five years ago. Harvey immediately took one on the arm and was thereafter confined to keeping the ball out of his stumps. When at last Harvey got a shortish ball he leaped round, eager for the first opportunity to change the course of the battle. He hooked hard and true, straight at Graveney at backward short leg, and Graveney stood and took the catch brilliantly hip-high.

Miller was just as much pinned by Bedser as Harvey had been, and he likewise fell as soon as a loose one came. This time it was Bedser's slower ball, and a full pitch, and Miller with all the leg-side to choose from, hit it comfortably to deep mid-on.

After Bedser bowled Benaud behind his legs Tattersall came decisively into the game, and all the last five wickets fell by his agency. He bowled Morris behind his legs and had Davidson well taken by Graveney running in from mid-wicket. The most spectacular catch of a match of many fine catches came next. Tallon skied the ball high behind square leg. Simpson, giving chase at high speed, found in the end he had overrun the ball, but pulling up and stretching backwards he flung out an arm and clutched it.

After tea it was two high steepling catches at mid-wicket by Tattersall that completed Bedser's triumph. Thus, with 14 for 99, he joined the select company of three who have taken as many wickets or more in a Test between England and

B

Australia: Spofforth, Verity and one who was on the ground to hear of his success if not, alas, to see it. Wilfred Rhodes.

## Australia

| | | |
|---|---|---|
| G. B. Hole b. Bedser | 0 | b. Bedser ... ... 5 |
| A. R. Morris lbw. b. Bedser | 67 | b. Tattersall ... ... 60 |
| A. L. Hassett b. Bedser ... | 115 | c. Hutton b. Bedser ... 5 |
| R. N. Harvey c. Compton b. Bedser | 0 | c. Graveney b. Bedser 2 |
| K. R. Miller c. Bailey b. Wardle | 55 | c. Kenyon b. Bedser ... 5 |
| R. Benaud c. Evans b. Bailey | 3 | b. Bedser ... ... 0 |
| A. K. Davidson b. Bedser | 4 | c. Graveney b. Tattersall 6 |
| D. Tallon b. Bedser ... | 0 | c. Simpson b. Tattersall 15 |
| R. R. Lindwall c. Evans b. Bailey | 0 | c. Tattersall b. Bedser 12 |
| J. C. Hill b. Bedser ... | 0 | c. Tattersall b. Bedser 4 |
| W. A. Johnston not out ... | 0 | not out ... ... 4 |
| B. 2, l.b. 2, n.b. 1 ... | 5 | L.b. 5 ... ... 5 |
| | **249** | **123** |

## England

| | | |
|---|---|---|
| L. Hutton c. Benaud b. Davidson | 43 | not out ... ... 60 |
| D. J. Kenyon c. Hill b. Lindwall | 8 | c. Hassett b. Hill 16 |
| R. T. Simpson lbw. b. Lindwall... | 0 | not out ... ... 28 |
| D. C. S. Compton c. Morris b. Lindwall... | 0 | |
| T. W. Graveney c. Benaud b. Hill | 22 | |
| P. B. H. May c. Tallon b. Hill ... | 9 | |
| T. E. Bailey lbw. b. Hill ... | 13 | |
| T. G. Evans c. Tallon b. Davidson | 8 | |
| J. H. Wardle not out ... | 29 | |
| A. V. Bedser lbw. b. Lindwall ... | 2 | |
| R. Tattersall b. Lindwall... | 2 | |
| B. 5, l.b. 3 ... ... | 8 | B. 8, l.b. 4, w. 2, n.b. 2 16 |
| | **144** | **One wkt 120** |

## England Bowling

| | O. | M. | R. | W. | O. | M. | R. | W. |
|---|---|---|---|---|---|---|---|---|
| Bedser... | 38.3 | 16 | 55 | 7 | 17.2 | 7 | 44 | 7 |
| Bailey ... | 44 | 14 | 75 | 2 | 5 | 1 | 28 | 0 |
| Wardle ... | 35 | 16 | 55 | 1 | 12 | 3 | 24 | 0 |
| Tattersall ... | 23 | 5 | 59 | 0 | 5 | 0 | 22 | 3 |

| | O. | M. | R. | W. | O. | M. | R. | W. |
|---|---|---|---|---|---|---|---|---|
| Lindwall ... | 20.4 | 2 | 57 | 5 | 16 | 4 | 37 | 0 |
| Johnston ... | 18 | 7 | 22 | 0 | 18 | 9 | 14 | 0 |
| Hill ... | 19 | 8 | 35 | 3 | 12 | 3 | 26 | 1 |
| Davidson ... | 15 | 7 | 22 | 2 | 5 | 1 | 7 | 0 |
| Benaud | | | | | 5 | 0 | 15 | 0 |
| Morris | | | | | 2 | 0 | 5 | 0 |

## FALL OF WICKETS

AUSTRALIA – First Innings: 1—2, 2—124, 3—128, 4—237, 5—244, 6—244, 7—246, 8—247, 9—248.

AUSTRALIA – Second Innings: 1—28, 2—44, 3—50, 4—64, 5—68, 6—81, 7—92, 8—106, 9—115.

ENGLAND – First Innings: 1—17, 2—17, 3—17, 4—76, 5—82, 6—92, 7—107, 8—121, 9—136.

ENGLAND – Second Innings: 1—26.

Umpires: D. Davies and Harold Elliott (Lancashire).

Match drawn.

# The Famous Rearguard

No anthology of great days within the post-war period could be contemplated without including this one. But for the resistance of Watson and Bailey, of course, the triumph that lay ahead at the Oval would not have been possible.

ENGLAND v AUSTRALIA, Lord's, final day: June 30, 1953
*Score at start:* Australia 346 and 368; England 372 and 20 for 3
*Score at close:* Australia 346 and 368; England 372 and 282 for 7

There are excellent cricketers, and there are excellent Test match cricketers, and sometimes there is a great gulf dividing them. It was England's fortune today that there came together in the crisis two men who seemed to grow in stature with the fame of the opposition.

Watson, of Yorkshire, and Bailey, of Essex, became joined on this last morning of the second Test at 20 minutes to one, after Watson and Compton had withstood the Australian bowling for 70 minutes. Despite all the bowling variety that Hassett could call upon, despite the inevitable wear in the wicket, which operated particularly against the left-hander Watson, they declined to be separated until 10 minutes to six, by which time the prospect of an Australian victory, which had seemed when they became joined almost a matter of detail, of margin in time and runs, had receded almost to nothing.

In fact, the second hero, Bailey, followed Watson, the first, quickly into the pavilion, and so it needed another half-hour's resistance by Brown and Evans, who had waited all day in their pads, with feelings that are not difficult to imagine, to make the door almost, almost safe.

When Brown was caught at slip at 27 minutes past six, four balls of Benaud's over remained. An over once begun must be completed, and so technically Australia could still win without even recourse to a hat-trick. Wardle played those last four balls, or rather, he saw them out of harm's way, and so a great Test match ended.

The adjective I submit is admissible because though the level of the cricket waxed and waned, sometimes below the level to be expected of a Test between England and Australia, the match proceeded on a plane of interest and level grappling that was sustained over almost the entire five days.

The only period in which it seemed that one side must win was when England's first three second innings wickets toppled over one another last evening. Even then something suggested that this remarkable game could not end in capitulation and I hope to be excused from saying now that your correspondent did not leave his readers altogether without hope this morning. It is not the least satisfactory part of the occasion that the spectators who have much to endure in these days had ample value for their money from first to last. There were 137,915 of them in all, and the takings of £57,716 are by some £13,000 the largest at any cricket match anywhere.

The scorecard might possibly suggest that England's ambitions need not necessarily have been limited to a draw. But I think the most that the most optimistic patriot allowed himself was the occasional moment of regret that that estimable aggressive innings by Lindwall after tea yesterday had put victory out of reckoning.

Seen in retrospect, but for that England could, indeed one might say probably would, have won. As it is a draw will be held by both sides as a fair result, and for England to have achieved it after losing the toss and seeing Australia 190 on the first day before the second wicket fell should be satisfaction enough.

In the Australian camp they may well be asking themselves what more could have been done. Well, they have no reproaches in the field, for there seemed only two half chances in the whole English innings, each off Ring, to a backward short leg standing within such closeness to the batsman's legs that his grab could have been no more than a reflex action.

When Brown and Evans had the last half-hour to face one's thoughts turned inevitably and fearfully to Lindwall. Hassett must be wondering whether he should have given him a last fling. For myself I feel he should certainly have done so.

Nevertheless it has to be said that it was Ring, bowling down wind from Lindwall's end who had sent back both Watson and Bailey. Of course, if Australia had had Grimmett, that industrious gnome, to exploit the worn patches it must have needed even more than a Watson and a Bailey to have survived; but there is no end to speculation. If he by some magic could have been summoned back England must have called for Hobbs and Sutcliffe to assist them!

Whichever of the two possible objectives England might later choose there was from their point of view only one beginning to the day. The collection of runs was unimportant as compared with survival.

The first attack came from Lindwall, Johnston assisting, and Lindwall bowled fast and with all the subtlety that differentiates him from other great fast bowlers.

Compton had some fast balls on the body which he thrust down safely off his ribs. Watson one or two outside the off stump which he was lucky not to touch. This was the particular peril of the left-hander, that outside his off stump there lay a stretch of rough ground made by the bowlers' follow-through.

The batting proclaimed with every stroke that in the English camp the watchword was defiance. Yet no reasonable scoring opportunities were lost.

When the leg-spinners, Ring and Benaud, appeared the temperature dropped and the spectators enjoyed the luxury of applauding three fours in an over by Compton, the last an off-drive of the best 1947/8 vintage.

The narrowest squeak for England in the first hour was when Watson padded up and the ball falling rolled back towards the stumps. Watson kicked it away with only an inch or two to spare. The first hour brought 51 and for the erratic Benaud came back Johnston who at 20 minutes to one broke the partnership with a ball that skidded through to hit Compton's pad at ankle height. From the moment of his taking Hutton's place last evening Compton had not put a foot wrong.

The situation was hand-made for Bailey who expresses his true nature in a long defensive vigil. Never has the dead bat stroke, both forward and back, been played hour after hour with more evident relish. In some stages of his innings Bailey seemed to accept a single with reluctance, as though unwilling to be deprived even momentarily of the bowling. Bailey fitted straight away into the gap left by Compton.

Miller had a spell down wind, including one soaring bumper, and Davidson bowled one very good over just before luncheon to Watson. The two hours' play had fetched 96 runs, from 20-3 to 116-4.

Behind the playing-in period after luncheon lay the fundamental importance of both batsmen being still there when the new ball became due at 3 o'clock. Hence, 13 runs only in the first half-hour, 20 in the next 20 minutes, then Lindwall and Miller in full onslaught.

Watson and Bailey faced this test as they faced all else, with rigid composure, broken only twice when Bailey was hit painfully by Lindwall on the right hand. I cannot remember when a crowd so revelled in defence for defence's sake. As Bailey got right behind the ball immediately following those that hit him the crowd applauded with a fervour that in different circumstances might have greeted a six.

Lindwall and Miller bowled for 40 minutes, and if any super-sanguine person this afternoon had ever presumed to think in terms of victory their expectations must have been finally quenched when this period was withstood at a cost to Australia of only 12 runs. The hour between three o'clock and four, produced 23, including just five singles.

At tea the score stood at 183 for four, or 160 short of the target. Afterwards Watson and Bailey proceeded with the composure that had marked their whole stand. Temperamentally it seemed the ideal partnership. Hassett tried everyone, and it was his least considered bowler, Davidson, who came nearest to making the separation.

When Watson was 88 he snicked only just short of Hole at slip, and the next ball, pitching in that dangerous area outside the off stump beat him. In golfing circles it would have been marked off as Ground Under Repair.

# GREAT TEST DAYS # GREAT TEST DAYS 39

At twenty-five past five Watson went to his hundred sweeping Ring lustily to long leg and it was a sign of the zeal and skill the young Australian fieldsmen had shown throughout this game that Benaud leapt instinctively in to try to conjure a catch out of a ball going like smoke that pitched well in front of him and went smack against the railings in front of the Tavern.

The stand of four hours and 10 minutes ended when Watson apparently snicked a ball from Ring that he seemed not to play at, and which bounced off his pad to slip. A few minutes later Bailey, in his one departure from self discipline, cover-drove a widish ball into the hands of Benaud standing at cover point.

Ring now bowled to Brown and Evans with three slips, but Brown sensed that for him at least the best defence was attack and the rich forcing strokes he made on the off-side served to give the pent-up crowd something indeed to cheer. Further, it took time to fetch the ball back from the boundaries.

Thus no lapse from discretion marred the ending. England's performance all through the day had been alike full of spirit and of character.

## Australia

| | | | |
|---|---|---|---|
| A. L. Hassett c. Bailey b. Bedser | 104 | c. Evans b. Statham | 3 |
| A. R. Morris st. Evans b. Bedser | 30 | c. Statham b. Compton | 89 |
| R. N. Harvey lbw. b. Bedser | 59 | b. Bedser | 21 |
| K. R. Miller b. Wardle | 25 | b. Wardle | 109 |
| G. B. Hole c. Compton b. Wardle | 13 | lbw. b. Brown | 47 |
| R. Benaud lbw. b. Wardle | 0 | c. Graveney b. Bedser | 5 |
| A. K. Davidson c. Statham b. Bedser | 76 | c. and b. Brown | 15 |
| D. Ring lbw. b. Wardle | 18 | lbw. b. Brown | 7 |
| R. R. Lindwall b. Statham | 9 | b. Bedser | 50 |
| G. R. Langley c. Watson b. Bedser | 1 | b. Brown | 9 |
| W. A. Johnston not out | 3 | not out | 0 |
| B. 4, l.b. 4 | 8 | B. 8, l.b. 5 | 13 |
| | **346** | | **368** |

## England

| | | | |
|---|---|---|---|
| L. Hutton c. Hole b. Johnston | 145 | c. Hole b. Lindwall | 5 |
| D. Kenyon c. Davidson b. Lindwall | 3 | c. Hassett b. Lindwall | 2 |
| T. W. Graveney b. Lindwall | 78 | c. Langley b. Johnston | 2 |
| D. C. S. Compton c. Hole b. Benaud | 57 | lbw. b. Johnston | 33 |
| W. Watson st. Langley b. Johnston | 4 | c. Hole b. Ring | 109 |
| T. E. Bailey c. and b. Miller | 2 | c. Benaud b. Ring | 71 |

| | | | |
|---|---|---|---|
| F. R. Brown c. Langley b. Lindwall | ... | 22 | — c. Hole b. Benaud ... 28 |
| T. G. Evans b. Lindwall ... ... | ... | 0 | — not out ... ... 11 |
| J. H. Wardle b. Davidson | ... | 23 | — not out ... ... 0 |
| A. V. Bedser b. Lindwall... | ... | 1 | |
| J. B. Statham not out ... | ... | 17 | |
| B. 11, l.b. 1, w. 1, n.b. 7 | ... | 20 | B. 7, l.b. 6, w. 2, n.b. 6  21 |

372                         Seven wkts  282

## England Bowling

| | O. | M. | R. | W. | | O. | M. | R. | W. |
|---|---|---|---|---|---|---|---|---|---|
| Bedser... | ... 42.4 | 8 | 105 | 5 | — | 31.5 | 8 | 77 | 3 |
| Statham | ... 28 | 7 | 48 | 1 | — | 15 | 3 | 40 | 1 |
| Brown... | ... 25 | 7 | 53 | 0 | — | 27 | 4 | 82 | 4 |
| Bailey ... | ... 16 | 2 | 55 | 0 | — | 10 | 4 | 24 | 0 |
| Wardle | ... 29 | 8 | 77 | 4 | — | 46 | 18 | 111 | 1 |
| Compton | | | | | ... | 3 | 0 | 21 | 1 |

## Australia Bowling

| | O. | M. | R. | W. | | O. | M. | R. | W. |
|---|---|---|---|---|---|---|---|---|---|
| Lindwall | ... 23 | 4 | 66 | 5 | — | 19 | 3 | 26 | 2 |
| Miller ... | ... 25 | 6 | 57 | 1 | — | 17 | 8 | 17 | 0 |
| Johnston | ... 35 | 11 | 91 | 2 | — | 29 | 10 | 70 | 2 |
| Ring ... | ... 14 | 2 | 43 | 0 | — | 29 | 5 | 84 | 2 |
| Benaud | ... 19 | 4 | 70 | 1 | — | 17 | 6 | 51 | 1 |
| Davidson | ... 10.5 | 2 | 25 | 1 | — | 14 | 5 | 13 | 0 |
| Hole ... | ... | | 1 | | | 1 | 1 | 0 | 0 |

### FALL OF WICKETS

Australia – First Innings: 1—65, 2—190, 3—225, 4—229, 5—240, 6—280, 7—291, 8—330, 9—331.

Australia – Second Innings: 1—3, 2—168, 3—227, 4—235, 5—248, 6—296, 7—305, 8—308, 9—362.

England – First Innings: 1—9, 2—177, 3—279, 4—291, 5—301, 6—328, 7—328, 8—332, 9—341.

England – Second Innings: 1—6, 2—10, 3—12, 4—73, 5—236, 6—246, 7—282.

Umpires: F. S. Lee and H. G. Baldwin.

Match drawn.

# The Ashes Regained

Herewith the beginning and the end of an era. This series introduced four great cricketers to Tests between England and Australia: Peter May, Fred Trueman, Tony Lock and Tom Graveney. It also saw the retirement of Lindsay Hassett, the only survivor of Bradman's 1938 Australian side.

I do not seem to have made the point in this closing report, though I did when the side was chosen, that Australia handicapped themselves gravely by pinning all their hopes on speed at the expense of spin. Hassett remembered the Oval pitches of 1938 and 1948, but in the fifties they were vastly different – as witness England's wicket-takers in Australia's second innings.

Perhaps on the whole the balance of the luck in this series ran England's way – if it did it was certainly high time.

ENGLAND v AUSTRALIA, Oval, final day: August 19, 1953
*Score at start:* Australia 275 and 162; England 306 and 38 for 1
*Score at close:* Australia 275 and 162; England 306 and 132 for 2

The Fifth Test, which had seemed to turn so sharply England's way when Australia were battling against the spin bowlers yesterday, duly ended in victory here shortly before 3 o'clock this afternoon: that elusive victory which has been awaited ever since D. R. Jardine's side won the Ashes 20 years ago. The margin of eight wickets was conclusive enough, but the result was not gained without a fight to the last ball as between Edrich, May and Compton on the one hand, and Johnston, Lindwall and Miller, supported magnificently as ever in the field, on the other.

Johnston bowled today without respite until Hassett came on, as at Melbourne on a similar occasion in '51, to bowl a final comedy over at his end.

Lindwall, likewise, from the pavilion end kept up a ceaseless, fast and accurate attack, apart from five overs from Miller, until he gave the ball finally to Morris, off whom Compton hit the last four needed. It took two hours and 40 minutes of resolute batsmanship to make the final 94 runs, May's wicket being the Australians' only reward.

All this was as it should be, a hard struggle to the finish, and the final scenes were equally fitting. At the end some 15,000 clamoured in front of the pavilion. Hutton and Hassett obliged with speeches, and the players were cheered on their respective balconies.

It all took one back 27 years to the August evening when for the first time since the first war Australia's colours were lowered in a Test rubber, and the crowd let themselves go as though a reproach had been wiped away. Then, as now, England's side was a blend of the ages, from the youthful Chapman and Larwood to the grizzled Rhodes, and Strudwick playing, too, in his last match against Australia. It cannot be said that any of Hutton's present team are anywhere near the end of their tethers but certainly several are, or should be, at the beginnings of fine achievements. One thinks of the four in this team who were not born when Hobbs and Sutcliffe were fashioning that former victory on an Oval sticky-dog: Graveney, May, Trueman and Lock. The performance of the latter three over these last few days was rich in promise.

In 1926 it was universally said that the change in the tide would be all for the good of cricket in Australia. They had won three rubbers with consummate ease, and the keen edge of competition was worn blunt. Exactly the same situation exists, so our Australian friends assure us, in their country today. Three rubbers have been won against England, and now, after the warning jolt of the drawn series against Cheetham's admirable young South Africans in the last Australian summer, it is established that the supremacy has passed to other hands.

It will prove to be the spur that has been needed in Melbourne, Sydney and Adelaide, and one can almost savour the unholy relish with which the next M.C.C. side will be received at Perth in October next year.

It must be said at this crowning moment that the idea that the Australians were a weak side bears no close examination. Hassett had the finest fast bowler in the world, and support for him that was adequate in quantity if not powerful, as the old sides have been, on slow or spinning wickets.

The fielding of this side has scarcely ever been surpassed, and if the form of some of the more experienced batsmen has been erratic and unreliable is it not proper to give the chief credit to the English bowlers, and chiefly to Bedser, whose performance, of course, has been the outstanding event in the series. Against the run of our county sides Morris, Miller, Hole and the others have looked fine enough batsmen: and Harvey, with 10 centuries already, has been absolutely devastating.

Bedser must take the palm, but the honours of the series have not been monopolised by the captain and his foremost bowler. Everyone of today's XI has played a part at one time or another, along with several not called upon in this match: Watson, Wardle, Tattersall, Statham, Simpson, and not least, Brown.

Bailey's unique contribution will not quickly be forgotten, while in support of all the bowling Evans, apart from a few off-moments at Old Trafford, has been, as usual, quite admirable.

On Hutton has been the greatest strain. Anyone who has seen all five Tests, and who has realised how he has upheld the batting and appreciated the difficulties he has encountered in the field, three times with only four bowlers, almost always irked by the presence of a left-handed batsman and with several fieldsmen of limited mobility, will give him a high degree of praise for his efforts.

Edrich and May played with excellent poise and judgment when the last phase of the game began this morning. Australia, of course, desperately needed a quick break-through and though Compton and Graveney were waiting with their pads on, steeled no doubt to put right their contributions of Monday, no Englishman on the ground can have relished the thought of watching them doing so at the start of the day.

The crowd was hushed and still, bursting into a loud and fevered sort of applause whenever there was a specially good stroke. These, it may be added, very frequently produced no runs, for Harvey in the cover country was in the most scintillating order even by his own standards, and Davidson, as usual, was leaping about like a cat. He is not only a magnificent fieldsman close in but is extraordinarily quick on the chase and turn. So, again, is Archer, while the older brigade, Hassett, Miller and, despite his long bowl, Lindwall, more than once cut off hits that seemed certain to go through.

The milestones occurred slowly. At noon the overnight 38 had become 52. At half-past twelve it was only 63, an addition of 25. The intention to score was there, but at Johnston's end the wicket was not to be trusted, while Lindwall was too accurate to be forced away. He bowled two or three break-backs which needed a lot of stopping. May was applauded by the spectators behind the arm for keeping one venomous one out of his stumps.

Considering how often Lock and Laker were hitting the edge of the bat and passing it yesterday it was extraordinary how few streaky strokes there were this morning. Once May snicked four between the wicket-keeper and first slip off Johnston, who had changed to bowling over the wicket, and next over Edrich from a sharply spinning ball gave a very difficult low fast catch at second slip to Hole. This was the one and only catch missed by Hole in this series, and he has caught seven, including some wonderfully good ones.

May was out just after one o'clock. He had just hit the stroke of the innings, a thrilling cover drive off Miller. Then he glanced to leg firmly off the middle of the bat and Davidson, close though he was standing at leg slip, made the catch look simple.

For the second time in the match May had come through his trial in all ways. He is one of those blessed cricketers with whom rare gifts of temperament and of technique go hand-in-hand.

Compton this time caused no qualms while Edrich was impervious to error and temptation, batting slowly, resolutely on. When luncheon came with the score at 101 for two only 31 runs short of the goal, everyone knew the game was won. Still Johnston and Lindwall had a final fling and Edrich and Compton had to watch with all their eyes and wits.

The crowd relaxed now, cheered Edrich's 50, laughed as Hassett made great play breaking down the ridges of Johnston's bowling hole before delivering his over, and finally swarmed the field happy and exultant.

## Australia

| | | | |
|---|---|---|---|
| A. L. Hassett c. Evans b. Bedser... | 53 | lbw. b. Laker... | 10 |
| A. R. Morris lbw. b. Bedser | 16 | lbw. b. Lock ... | 26 |
| K. R. Miller lbw. b. Bailey | 1 | c. Trueman b. Laker... | 0 |
| R. N. Harvey c. Hutton b. Trueman | 36 | b. Lock | 1 |
| G. B. Hole c. Evans b. Trueman | 37 | lbw. b. Laker... | 17 |
| J. H. de Courcy c. Evans b. Trueman ... | 5 | run out | 4 |
| R. G. Archer c. and b. Bedser ... | 10 | c. Edrich b. Lock | 49 |
| A. K. Davidson c. Edrich b. Laker | 22 | b. Lock | 21 |
| R. R. Lindwall c. Evans b. Trueman | 62 | c. Compton b. Laker... | 12 |
| G. R. Langley c. Edrich b. Lock | 18 | c. Trueman b. Lock ... | 2 |
| W. A. Johnston not out ... | 9 | not out | 6 |
| B. 4, n.b. 2 | 6 | B. 11, l.b. 3 | 14 |
| | 275 | | 162 |

## England

| | | | |
|---|---|---|---|
| L. Hutton b. Johnston ... | 82 | run out | 17 |

| | | | |
|---|---|---|---|
| W. J. Edrich lbw. b. Lindwall ... ... | 21 | — not out ... ... | 55 |
| P. B. H. May c. Archer b. Johnston ... | 39 | — c. Davidson b. Miller | 37 |
| D. C. S. Compton c. Langley b. Lindwall | 16 | — not out ... ... | 22 |
| T. W. Graveney c. Miller b. Lindwall ... | 4 | | |
| T. E. Bailey b. Archer ... ... ... | 64 | | |
| T. G. Evans run out ... ... ... | 28 | | |
| J. C. Laker c. Langley b. Miller... ... | 1 | | |
| G. A. R. Lock c. Davidson b. Lindwall... | 4 | | |
| F. S. Trueman b. Johnston ... ... | 10 | | |
| A. V. Bedser not out ... ... ... | 22 | | |
| B. 9, l.b. 5, w. 1 ... ... ... | 15 | L.b. 1 ... ... | 1 |
| | 306 | Two wkts | 132 |

## England Bowling

| | O. | M. | R. | W. | O. | M. | R. | W. |
|---|---|---|---|---|---|---|---|---|
| Bedser ... | 29 | 3 | 88 | 3 — | 11 | 2 | 24 | 0 |
| Trueman ... | 24.3 | 3 | 86 | 4 — | 2 | 1 | 4 | 0 |
| Bailey ... ... | 14 | 3 | 42 | 1 | | | | |
| Lock ... ... | 9 | 2 | 19 | 1 — | 21 | 9 | 45 | 5 |
| Laker ... ... | 5 | 0 | 34 | 1 — | 16.5 | 2 | 75 | 4 |

## Australia Bowling

| | O. | M. | R. | W. | O. | M. | R. | W. |
|---|---|---|---|---|---|---|---|---|
| Lindwall ... | 32 | 7 | 70 | 4 — | 21 | 5 | 46 | 0 |
| Miller ... ... | 34 | 12 | 65 | 1 — | 11 | 3 | 24 | 1 |
| Johnston ... | 45 | 16 | 94 | 3 — | 29 | 14 | 52 | 0 |
| Davidson ... | 10 | 1 | 26 | 0 — | | | | |
| Archer ... | 10.3 | 2 | 25 | 1 — | 1 | 1 | 0 | 0 |
| Hole ... ... | 11 | 6 | 11 | 0 | | | | |
| Hassett ... | | | | | 1 | 0 | 4 | 0 |
| Morris ... | | | | | 0.5 | 0 | 5 | 0 |

## FALL OF WICKETS

AUSTRALIA – First Innings: 1—38, 2—41, 3—107, 4—107, 5—118, 6—160, 7—160, 8—207, 9—245.

AUSTRALIA – Second Innings: 1—23, 2—59, 3—60, 4—61, 5—61, 6—85, 7—135, 8—140, 9—144.

ENGLAND – First Innings: 1—37, 2—137, 3—154, 4—167, 5—170, 6—210, 7—225, 8—237, 9—262.

ENGLAND – Second Innings: 1—24, 2—88.

Umpires: F. S. Lee and D. Davies.
England won by 8 wickets.

# Salute to Keith Miller

This was a day that 'had everything' in the way of drama, and not least a performance by one of the supreme actors on the modern cricket stage, Keith Miller. He had responded to the special atmosphere of Lord's from his first appearance in the war-time matches. Now aged 36 this clearly was the curtain-call for him, so far as the great ground was concerned, and what a performance he gave! With ten for 152 in *seventy* overs he in the end was the prime match-winner for Australia.

But after this third day, thanks to the counter-attack by England in the field, the issue was still completely open.

ENGLAND V AUSTRALIA, Lord's, 3rd day: June 23, 1956
*Score at start:* Australia 285; England 74 for 3
*Score at close:* Australia 285 and 115 for 6; England 171

If there have been many days in modern Test cricket more highly charged with drama than Saturday at Lord's their recollection fades from the mind in face of the game at present being waged wherein fortune has fluctuated so very excitingly.

Soon after lunch Australia, in the commanding person of Miller, swept away the remnants of the England tail to give themselves a lead of 114. Around this time many reproachful things were being said, and not without fair cause, about the condition of England batsmanship. While allowing as generously as might be for Miller's bowling effort the picture of England at the wicket spoke for itself.

Cowdrey had batted excellently, May had fought tenaciously against indifferent form, and Bailey had shown his customary obduracy in defence. There commendation had perforce to end. But when Australia went in a second time, with the solid advantage in their grasp, the England XI, and especially two members of it, Bailey and Trueman, reacted wonderfully to the crowd's fervour.

The air was charged with an excitement and an enthusiasm more common to Melbourne, or to Port of Spain, so that the England bowlers were uplifted to regions of effort and inspiration normally outside their scope. The Australians must have felt, at times, as though they were indeed strangers in a foreign land.

Yet there were touches enough to illustrate that sportsmanship had been by no means outrun by patriotism. In particular there were the ovations to Miller, those that applauded his bowling, the reception he had when he came out to bat in the evening, and the acclamation that accompanied his return.

People will perhaps remember these salutes to a great and gay cricketer when the details of the play become blurred. For the present they will no doubt agree that it was good to have been at Lord's, or to have listened, or to have looked at the TV screen on Saturday, June 23, 1956.

Cricket is changing, maybe, and cricket can sometimes nowadays be dull and colourless. But a game between England and Australia on a good, fair wicket between well-matched sides is still a classic *par excellence*.

This morning, thanks to the finely sustained counter-attack made when Australia batted again, England will return to the field with the position largely rectified, though not completely redressed.

Having lost six wickets for 115 Australia are 229 runs on with a certain amount of solid defensive batting still to be shifted, apart from the presence of the incalculable Benaud, who has already made no mean mark on the game both as bowler and fielder.

I suppose the odds to be still slightly on Australia, but the accent is on the 'slightly': that is provided the weather holds. The wicket on Saturday surprised most people by playing faster than hitherto. Indeed, it was consistently lively, encouraging the quicker men, who did practically all the bowling, and by its pace giving full value for strokes played.

If hereafter it conforms to type the wicket may be somewhat milder, and accordingly more to the liking of the England batsmen when they face what is sure to be a taxing job in the fourth innings.

There will, however, be the hazard of the worn ground just outside the leg-stump, while the mat of grass is so full that the seam bowlers should always be able to move the ball a little off the ground.

When the third day's play began it at once struck the note of tension which was maintained without diminution over the whole six hours. May, it seemed, held the key to England's fortunes, Miller to those of Australia. The duel between these two gripped from the first ball a crowd most of whom had been in their places for an hour or more. (The gates were closed at half-past 10.)

At a quarter to 12, Miller had his first victim, Watson

playing the ball on to his pads whence it dollied off to Benaud in the gully. There was a touch of ill-luck about this dismissal which, of course, made May's function correspondingly more important.

Bailey at once dropped anchor, and it is sufficient tribute to his qualities to say that he did no more than everyone expected him to do. Inevitably most of the runs had to come from May who, in fact, in the hour they were together scored 29 against Bailey's 9.

Yet if May was always looking for the scoring opportunity, and making a number of handsome strokes, he also appeared the more vulnerable. One of the sages was certain he was picking up the bat too late. Certainly he was sometimes playing in a hurry. Once May snicked Miller involuntarily to first slip, where Archer would probably have taken the chance, shoulder-high to his right, if he had not seen second slip converging upon him.

With the new ball Archer and Miller settled the innings in a little over half an hour. Laker was bowled playing back to a ball of full length, and Wardle was caught finely on the leg-side first ball by Langley.

Trueman made a cover-stroke so thrilling that it seemed inevitably too good to last. He fell to the admirable Langley (victim number four), and finally Bailey himself. Bailey's wicket was Miller's fifth, and apart from seven overs he had bowled through the whole innings of four hours and three-quarters. Mostly his pace, from a quick, easy run of some nine paces, was a brisk fast-medium, but there was always the threat of the truly fast ball, there was the constant variation of pace, and there was movement both ways off the wicket, especially from leg to off down the hill.

Above all, the batsmen never knew when that flip of the loose wrist would bring the good length ball steeply up to the bat-handle. All in all it was a memorable performance.

## Benaud Rises to it

This was Richie Benaud's tenth Test against England, and for all the promise that his cricket held out in the preceding nine he had (fielding apart) accomplished astonishingly little. Now he rose to it with a vengeance, playing one of the most spectacular innings seen in Anglo-Australian Test cricket for many a day. It clinched the game. I wonder, by the way, why I wrote 'if not quite irrevocably' in the first paragraph. I suppose I was thinking back to Lord's in '53!

ENGLAND v AUSTRALIA, Lord's, 4th day: June 25, 1956
*Score at start:* Australia 285 and 115 for 6; England 171
*Score at close:* Australia 285 and 257; England 171 and 72 for 2

The fourth day of the Test match turned the game decidedly, if not quite irrevocably, towards Australia, whose position was lifted up this morning by a magnificent innings by Benaud.

By the time the teams were presented to the Queen and to the Dukes of Edinburgh and Gloucester in front of the pavilion at the tea interval England faced the prospect of making 372 to win, or alternatively to bat nigh on nine hours to save the game. They had then scored 26 for no wicket, and it was to be noticed that Her Majesty's Royal impartiality was strained to the point of having a special word to the two batsmen with their pads on. Of these Cowdrey, almost wholly passive henceforward, still remains, but Richardson is gone, and so is Graveney, and the remaining runs have been whittled painfully down to 300.

A very eminent person on leaving the ground this evening lamented that England, left with no more than 43 runs an hour to get, seemed to have decided they could do no better than a draw. He pointed to the fact that Cowdrey made only one scoring stroke in his last hour and a half at the wicket, and that a 4 off a slowish long-hop from Miller. He mentioned, too, the sending in of Watson, who saved the day here against Australia three years ago, this evening rather than May.

I hope and believe that England's ambitions may not have excluded a win, by any means. However, considering the uncertainty in the middle of the order and the weakness of the tail they may well have decided that runs were subsidiary this evening.

If Australia had Grimmett in their ranks, one would say that England had no hope. As it is the battle is uphill, but there are several players left whom such a situation shows at their best.

But enough of speculation. It is a greater pleasure to salute Benaud for a magnificent piece of batting. Many people must have begun to wonder whether 'the new cricket' held such hidden difficulties, undetectable to those whose playing days are past, that it was no longer 'on' to make attacking cricket in a Test match. Benaud, apart from all else, illustrated that that is far from being so. He batted for only two hours and 20 minutes, he hit a six and 14 fours, he gave no chance, and the number of false strokes was astonishingly few. It was a glorious piece of batsmanship, at a time when England had largely brought the situation back to parity.

Benaud proclaimed his intentions as soon as the day's play began. In the first two overs he made 11, with one false stroke, an attempted straight drive which swirled high and clear of cover-point.

The significance of these early manifestations by Benaud may have been noted only by the few. His Test record against England until today was so modest. Trueman and Statham no doubt, were warming up. Such seemed to be the feeling.

In fact, Benaud very soon warmed them up in no ordinary way. He hit Trueman high and handsomely for six into the crowd below the grandstand, and when Statham tried him likewise with a bumper he found himself hooked down to the Mound with a stroke of quelling velocity.

Four more came in the same way, and altogether Benaud showed such form that when May came to take stock after three-quarters of an hour, it was to find 45 runs scored, 42 by Benaud while Mackay acquitted himself precisely as he had on Saturday.

By now it looked that speed had tried and failed. The wicket seemingly (having been cut this morning) was plumb and took less movement from the seam than on Saturday. Moreover, Trueman, who needs to be fed by success, was not getting any.

One hoped for the spinners on every ground, not least because Mackay seems less happy against them than against the fast bowling: or, rather, the spinners induce some temptation in him to make a stroke or two, instead of either stopping, or deflecting, or, most often, letting the ball pass by. It is easy

to blame May for persisting with a fast attack long after it had
looked to be absolutely Benaud's and Mackay's handwriting.
The decision, of course, was his, and the responsibility therefore. At the same time he was merely following an old English
pattern.

For years in Test matches, English spin bowling has been
seen only as a defensive weapon, unless the ball has been
turning quite appreciably. May could be observed in conference
with the two senior members of his side, Evans and Bailey. I
should be very surprised to hear that either of them had
suggested putting on Wardle and/or Laker, each issuing his
invitations, and with traps concealed and duly baited. As
it was, England simply plugged doggedly away.

May's first reaction to Benaud's belligerence was to substitute Bailey for Statham, who had bowled five overs for 18
runs. At the other end Trueman bowled until half-past twelve:
seven overs for 34 runs. Statham then took a turn for a couple
of overs from the nursery before Wardle was brought on at ten
minutes to one. By this time Benaud was well in the sixties, having reached his first 50 against England with the first of three
successive fours off Bailey. These strokes apart, Bailey subdued
Benaud better than anyone, while he bowled four maiden
overs against Mackay.

Facetious people have suggested that someone should promote a single-wicket match between Bailey and Mackay. No
doubt it would attract the same sort of public as enjoy endless
bicycle races or gentlemen squatting interminably on poles.

When it seemed as though Bailey might bowl a maiden to
Benaud (no one in fact did so from start to finish of his innings),
he skied a four over slips. I counted only three false strokes all
morning by Benaud, this being one. Another was a slash
against Wardle which avoided connection. It was extraordinary,
considering his freedom of stroke, that Benaud looked so safe,
and his bat so broad.

Every cricketer will have been captivated by his innings, the
older school most of all. For he makes his strokes by swinging
from the shoulders, and he is happiest when driving. It was in
the character of his play that in Wardle's last over before lunch
Benaud took ten runs, six of them from true lofted hits to
mid-wicket. He came in having scored 87 in the two hours

out of the 106 scored and needing 10 for his century.

Of Mackay's part if there is little to be said its value was evident enough. Australia have scarcely sent a more disheartening player for fast bowlers to spend their energies on since Woodfull left the scene. In particular, he is an extraordinary judge of the ball that may safely be let pass.

May took the new ball 10 minutes after lunch, with Benaud 96. He got a single for a leg glance, then in the same over aimed to reach his hundred with a hook off a ball not all that short and skied it vertically off the top edge. Evans had plenty of time to get underneath, and so Benaud's innings failed to reach the goal it deserved, to the sorrow surely of all – provided, naturally, it could have been apprehended that he would get out immediately afterwards.

The rest of Australia's innings was inevitably anti-climax, though it had its value for Australia. In 50 minutes came another 24.

## Australia

| | | | | |
|---|---|---|---|---|
| C. C. McDonald c. Trueman b. Bailey | 78 | — | c. Cowdrey b. Bailey | 26 |
| J. W. Burke st. Evans b. Laker | 65 | — | c. Graveney b. Trueman | 16 |
| R. N. Harvey c. Evans b. Bailey | 0 | — | c. Bailey b. Trueman | 10 |
| P. Burge b. Statham | 21 | — | b. Trueman | 14 |
| K. R. Miller b. Trueman | 28 | — | c. Evans b. Trueman | 30 |
| K. Mackay c. Bailey b. Laker | 38 | — | c. Evans b. Statham | 31 |
| R. G. Archer b. Wardle | 28 | — | c. Evans b. Bailey | 1 |
| R. Benaud b. Statham | 5 | — | c. Evans b. Trueman | 97 |
| I. W. Johnson c. Evans b. Trueman | 6 | — | lbw. b. Bailey | 17 |
| G. R. Langley c. Bailey b. Laker | 14 | — | not out | 7 |
| P. Crawford not out | 0 | — | lbw. b. Bailey | 0 |
| L.b. 2 | 2 | | B. 2 l.b. 2 n.b. 4 | 8 |
| | 285 | | | 257 |

## England

| | | | | |
|---|---|---|---|---|
| P. E. Richardson c. Langley b. Miller | 9 | — | c. Langley b. Archer | 21 |
| M. C. Cowdrey c. Benaud b. Mackay | 23 | — | lbw. b. Benaud | 27 |
| T. W. Graveney b. Miller | 5 | — | c. Langley b. Miller | 18 |
| P. B. H. May b. Benaud | 63 | — | c. Langley b. Miller | 53 |
| W. Watson c. Benaud b. Miller | 6 | — | b. Miller | 18 |
| T. E. Bailey b. Miller | 32 | — | c. Harvey b. Archer | 18 |
| T. G. Evans st. Langley b. Benaud | 0 | — | c. Langley b. Miller | 20 |
| J. C. Laker b. Archer | 12 | — | c. Langley b. Archer | 4 |
| J. H. Wardle c. Langley b. Archer | 0 | — | b. Miller | 0 |
| F. S. Trueman c. Langley b. Miller | 7 | — | b. Archer | 2 |

| J. B. Statham not out | ... | ... | ... | 0 | — | not out | ... | ... | 0 |
| L.b. 14 ... | ... | ... | ... | ... | 14 | L.b. 5 | ... | ... | 5 |
| | | | | | 171 | | | | 186 |

## England Bowling

|  | | O. | M. | R. | W. | | O. | M. | R. | W. |
|---|---|---|---|---|---|---|---|---|---|---|
| Statham | ... | 35 | 9 | 70 | 2 | — | 26 | 5 | 59 | 1 |
| Trueman | ... | 28 | 6 | 54 | 2 | — | 28 | 2 | 90 | 5 |
| Bailey ... | ... | 34 | 12 | 72 | 2 | — | 24.5 | 8 | 64 | 4 |
| Laker ... | ... | 29.1 | 10 | 47 | 3 | — | 7 | 3 | 17 | 0 |
| Wardle | ... | 20 | 7 | 40 | 1 | — | 7 | 2 | 19 | 0 |

## Australia Bowling

| Miller ... | ... | 34.1 | 9 | 72 | 5 | — | 36 | 12 | 80 | 5 |
|---|---|---|---|---|---|---|---|---|---|---|
| Crawford | ... | 5 | 2 | 4 | 0 | | | | | |
| Archer | ... | 23 | 9 | 47 | 2 | — | 31.2 | 8 | 71 | 4 |
| Mackay | ... | 11 | 3 | 15 | 1 | | | | | |
| Benaud | ... | 9 | 2 | 19 | 2 | — | 28 | 14 | 27 | 1 |
| | | | | Johnson | ... ... | 4 | 2 | 3 | 0 | |

### FALL OF WICKETS

AUSTRALIA – First Innings: 1—137, 2—137, 3—151, 4—185, 5—196, 6—249, 7—255, 8—265, 9—285.

AUSTRALIA – Second Innings: 1—36, 2—47, 3—69, 4—70, 5—79, 6—112, 7—229, 8—243, 9—257.

ENGLAND – First Innings: 1—22, 2—32, 3—60, 4—87, 5—128, 6—128, 7—161, 8—161, 9—170.

ENGLAND – Second Innings: 1—35, 2—59, 3—87, 4—91, 5—142, 6—175, 7—180, 8—184, 9—184.

Umpires: E. Davies and F. S. Lee.

Australia won by 185 runs.

## "Fabulous"

Here is the culmination of the most remarkable turn-round in Test history. The West Indies were cruelly handicapped by injuries, while their tactics on the fourth day when still on top with the May-Cowdrey partnership in its infancy were vastly too defensive. Yet the performance remains staggering enough.

It might be said, without over-stretching the truth, that it took the West Indies ten Test Matches to recover from this set-back. At any rate of the nine intervening ones England won four, and were undefeated.

ENGLAND v WEST INDIES, Edgbaston, final day: June 4, 1957
*Score at start:* England 186 and 378 for 3; West Indies 474

*Score at close:* England 186 and 583 for 4 dec.; West Indies 474 and 72 for 7

This has been a fabulous Test Match. Writing a few moments after watching Goddard and young Smith fighting for their lives against Laker and Lock, with the English fieldsmen clustered round them like bees round a honeypot (and with the steel calypso band performing with smiles of relief on their faces in front of the pavilion), I cannot summon the memory or the knowledge of any previous game wherein the fortunes have changed with such utter completeness from one side to the other.

At noon yesterday May and Cowdrey came together, as they did at Sydney three years ago, knowing that only a day-long stand or thereabouts could bring England back into the match. A day and a half later West Indies surveyed a scoreboard showing 62 for 7, thanking their stars for an escape from defeat which could surely be measured only in terms of minutes.

Laker and Lock did not have the sort of wicket to bowl on which filled the Australians with dread last summer. Each is a master of using what little help a wearing wicket affords. They set the West Indies batsmen indeed a testing problem enough. The root of the collapse this evening was, however, psychological. The change in events, catastrophic from their angle combined with the long weary spell in the field, made them always likely victims. In such circumstances two hours and 40 minutes can seem an eternity.

The scoresheet will make it seem that England declared too late and I believe they could have come in with complete safety half-an-hour earlier than they did, in fact when Cowdrey was out.

At this point West Indies could have been asked to bat for just over three hours, with 237 runs standing between themselves and victory. Yet in retrospect a draw seems perhaps the fairest answer, bearing in mind the various West Indian injuries which dislocated them so seriously at the crucial time. For instance they bowled with the same ball for more than seven hours since they had no one left to use a new one. In any case no one who has any conception of the strain imposed by an innings of 10 hours will be disposed to blame May himself for not declaring earlier. With him I daresay times and figures were a blur in the mind.

May's batting, taking all the circumstances into consideration, deserves all the superlatives so sadly overworked which are part and parcel of a modern Test. It was an excellent innings from the technical viewpoint, an exemplary one in point of responsibility. This is the aspect, of course, which merits most praise.

George Geary at Charterhouse taught May the basic things of batsmanship and so made the sound foundations of his cricket. But the self-discipline which schools and directs his play is something he had to develop himself, albeit with the example of others to help. Here the name that suggests itself naturally is Hutton, on whom May has based not only his batting on these occasions, but to a considerable extent his uncompromising philosophy of Test cricket. It may be added that only four Englishmen have played bigger Test innings than this 285: Hutton, Hammond, Sandham and R. E. Foster, the latter by two runs. As a captain's effort, needless to say, it stands alone.

As to Cowdrey's innings, it had all the attributes of his captain in an only slightly less degree. His qualities have been known and his potentialities realised ever since his notable exploits in Australia. Now that this remarkable innings has come in a Test at home he must surely take the unquestioned place in the England side for which his talents qualify him. English prospects in the series are that much the better for his success.

When the morning began the point of consuming interest was, of course, what effect the rain would have on the wicket. There had not been a great deal, but it was enough at any rate to persuade May to use the heavy roller before the start.

Goddard started with Sobers bowling an exploratory over to see whether the left-arm spin would bite and the ball lift. However, after he had bowled a harmless over outside the off stump and Atkinson from the other end had suggested that the odd one might cause trouble, Ramadhin took over from his usual end into the breeze. In successive overs Ramadhin beat both men with leg-breaks. And when he turned the off-break he several times found the inside edge of the bat. However, since Ramadhin had neither a gully on the one side or any short legs either in front or behind on the other, the batsmen were spared the dangers of the cocked defensive stroke. Atkinson did have a slip, a backward short leg and a short mid-on, the latter not dangerously close.

Of course Ramadhin and Atkinson were both desperately tired men when the day started and their bowling gave signs of it, even if their accuracy still demanded respect. At both ends the performance was almost mechanical.

The several moments of difficulty which both May and Cowdrey encountered were a mere fraction of what a fresh Laker and Lock might have achieved with the faint vestige of help from the wicket, which is all they ever need.

May and Cowdrey both settled in as though they were simply continuing their great effort of yesterday, apparently quite fresh: two remarkably fit, strong, temperate young men. The only difference in the picture was that now Cowdrey played at least an equal part in the scoring. To be precise he went slightly the faster. In the first half-hour, which might have been such a nervous time, they scored 20; in the second half-hour 20 more. In the second hour the speed was slightly stepped up. All the time Ramadhin and Atkinson bowled. By now the former's field consisted of a circle of nine men, all more or less equidistant both from the bat and from each other.

It was just after one o'clock when Cowdrey reached his hundred. May immediately went up to him and presumably either propounded or agreed to Cowdrey pushing along faster. We now had some handsome off-side strokes from Cowdrey, in celebration of his first Test 100 in England and his third in all. Before lunch the stand exceeded the 338 which Worrell and Weekes hammered out of a precisely identical England attack on the jute mat of Trinidad three years ago.

When lunch gave everyone pause to examine the situation of the match England were 179 runs ahead with the same number of wickets intact as they had had at noon yesterday. In other words it was a question of when May would cry 'Enough'. A general estimate seemed to be around three o'clock, if not before, leaving the England bowlers a full three hours' work and the West Indies out of any practicable hope of getting the runs.

But May wanted a lot yet. In fact England batted a further
70 minutes, until twenty past three, thrashing 116 runs in this
time of which the captain himself summoned the energy to hit
54. Ramadhin still went through the motions of bowling,
floating about for all the world like a sleepwalker.

Cowdrey arrived at 150, May at 250, the 500 appeared, the
partnership became 400. At last, soon after Ramadhin had
handed the ball to Smith, Cowdrey on-drove the latter into
the hands of one of Goddard's three substitutes, Asgarali, at
deep mid-wicket. Thus ended the partnership for England's
fourth wicket, 40 runs short of the 451 that Bradman and
Ponsford picked up off England at the Oval in 1934. If May
and Cowdrey had been interested in such things they could
have buckled to and eclipsed this particular figure without
trouble. They had been in together eight hours and 20 minutes;
500 minutes wherein supreme concentration, good judgment
and strength of purpose had never wavered.

Evans was promoted now and he and May did more or less
what they liked with the flagging bowlers. May's activities
included two long, soaring sixes to wide long-on off Sobers.
Evans cut and carved and ran for everything, and hard though
the West Indies still strove in the field they could not staunch
the flow.

Just before he declared May hit a stinging chance off a long
hop to Alexander, fielding substitute at square-leg. Apart from
a half-chance which flew off deep mid-on's fingers just after
lunch this was only the second catch to go to hand from May's
bat, a difficult catch behind the wicket when he had made 119
being the other.

When the bowling figures were announced at the end of the
holocaust Ramadhin's analysis was revealed as two for 179 in
98 overs. In other words, he had bowled more balls than any
man ever in an innings before. I feel he should have been
spared the utterly deflating experience of his in the last two
hours when time, not runs, were the crucial thing for West
Indies. However, let it be recorded he did not wilt, even
though the power of spin had inevitably grown weak.

The West Indies second innings started on a note of disaster
and continued in suspense and uncertainty. Where a sober
start was necessary both openers were back before the shine

was off the ball. Kanhai got a bouncer in Trueman's first over
which he tried to hook. He hit the ball high towards long-leg
and Close, coming in fast, made a very good catch about knee
high.

Immediately Trueman hit Pairaudeau amidships with a fast
full-toss. Pairaudeau took a moment to collect himself, but in
the same over was bowled by a fast yorker. One could not
dissociate the one happening from the other. Trueman down
wind was bowling with speed and hostility, but he soon gave
way to Laker, Lock having already taken over from Statham.

Having been beaten twice by Lock, Sobers clumped him
twice bravely for four. He at least was prepared to keep trouble
at arm's length. But Sobers is young in this sort of situation and
presently he was caught at short-leg off bat and pads.

Tea came at 26 for 3 after 50 minutes' batting, with Weekes
undefeated and looking resourceful and determined. In turn
he saw both his distinguished colleagues depart. Each fell to
the bristling short-leg field which only Weekes from now
onwards sought to disperse. Both Worrell and Walcott were
lame and the batting of each naturally suffered.

Smith, the hero of the first innings, now joined Weekes and
for half an hour the sixth wicket stood. Then at 10 minutes to
six Weekes got a brute of a ball from Lock, bowling as he did
from each end in turn over the wicket, pitching in the footmarks
of the follow through.

Weekes tried to whip his bat away from one that spun
viciously across him only to see Trueman make a fine catch
within three yards of the bat in the gully.

Now came Goddard to face Lock, his left-handedness
helping him in that Lock was spinning in to him and by going
forward he could stave off a lot of trouble with his pads. This
Goddard proceeded to do to the extent of being appealed
against four times for lbw in the first over he received. Thereafter Goddard used his bat a little more frequently, while
Smith, facing Laker, also used the left foot right forward to
pad off the off-breaks.

There was much appealing. There were also two chances in
one over. Smith being missed off Laker at deep mid-on high
up by May and very close indeed by Trueman in the middle of
the leg trap.

It was almost 25 past six when young Smith tried his tactic once too often. He had batted over an hour for five, an innings less glamorous than his first, indeed, but of infinite value. Atkinson, in what must have been the last over, relieved his feelings with a four to long-on off Laker and a few moments later walked in with his captain, the latter after 40 minutes still not out. If the result was appropriate it was fitting, too, that the West Indies captain should be there at the death.

## England

| | | |
|---|---|---|
| P. E. Richardson c. Walcott b. Ramadhin | 47 — | c. sub b. Ramadhin ... 34 |
| D. B. Close c. Rohan Kanhai b. Gilchrist | 15 — | c. weekes b. Gilchrist 42 |
| D. J. Insole b. Ramadhin ... ... | 20 — | b. Ramadhin ... ... 0 |
| P. B. H. May c. Weekes b. Ramadhin ... | 30 — | not out ... ... 285 |
| M. C. Cowdrey c. Gilchrist b. Ramadhin | 4 — | c. sub b. Smith ... 154 |
| T. E. Bailey b. Ramadhin ... ... | 1 | |
| G. A. R. Lock b. Ramadhin ... ... | 0 | |
| T. G. Evans b. Gilchrist ... ... ... | 14 — | not out ... ... 29 |
| J. C. Laker b. Ramadhin ... ... | 7 | |
| F. S. Trueman not out ... ... ... | 29 | |
| J. B. Statham b. Atkinson ... ... | 13 | |
| B. 3, l.b. 3 ... ... ... ... | 6 | B. 23, l.b. 16 ... 39 |
| | **186** | **Four wkts, dec. 583** |

## West Indies

| | | |
|---|---|---|
| Rohan Kanhai lbw. b. Statham ... ... | 42 — | c. Close b. Trueman ... 1 |
| B. H. Pairaudeau b. Trueman ... ... | 1 — | b. Trueman ... ... 7 |
| C. L. Walcott c. Evans b. Laker ... | 90 — | c. Lock b. Laker ... 1 |
| E. D. Weekes b. Trueman ... ... | 9 — | c. Trueman b. Lock ... 33 |
| G. Sobers c. Bailey b. Statham ... | 53 — | c. Cowdrey b. Lock ... 14 |
| O. G. Smith lbw. b. Laker ... | 161 — | lbw. b. Laker ... ... 5 |
| F. M. Worrell b. Statham ... | 81 — | c. May b. Lock ... 0 |
| J. D. Goddard c. Lock b. Laker ... | 24 — | not out ... ... 0 |
| D. Atkinson c. Statham b. Laker ... | 1 — | not out ... ... 4 |
| S. Ramadhin not out ... ... ... | 5 | |
| R. Gilchrist run out ... ... ... | 0 | |
| B. 1, l.b. 6 ... ... ... ... | 7 | B. 7 ... ... ... 7 |
| | **474** | **Seven wkts 72** |

## West Indies Bowling

| | | O. | M. | R. | W. | O. | M. | R. | W. |
|---|---|---|---|---|---|---|---|---|---|
| Worrell | ... | 9 | 1 | 27 | 0 | | | | |
| Gilchrist | ... | 27 | 4 | 74 | 2 — | 26 | 2 | 67 | 1 |
| Ramadhin | ... | 31 | 16 | 49 | 7 — | 98 | 35 | 179 | 2 |
| Atkinson | ... | 12.4 | 3 | 30 | 1 — | 72 | 29 | 137 | 0 |
| Sobers | ... | | | | | 30 | 4 | 77 | 0 |
| Smith | ... | | | | | 26 | 4 | 72 | 1 |
| Goddard | ... | | | | | 6 | 2 | 12 | 0 |

England Bowling

|  | O. | M. | R. | W. | O. | M. | R. | W. |
|---|---|---|---|---|---|---|---|---|
| Statham | ... 39 | 4 | 114 | 3 | — 2 | 0 | 6 | 0 |
| Trueman | ... 30 | 4 | 99 | 2 | — 5 | 3 | 7 | 2 |
| Bailey ... | ... 34 | 11 | 80 | 0 | — | | | |
| Laker ... | ... 54 | 17 | 119 | 4 | — 24 | 20 | 13 | 2 |
| Lock ... | ... 34.4 | 15 | 55 | 0 | — 27 | 19 | 31 | 3 |
| | | | Close ... | | ... 2 | 1 | 8 | 0 |

## FALL OF WICKETS

ENGLAND – First Innings: 1—32, 2—61, 3—104, 4—115, 5—116, 6—118, 7—121, 8—130, 9—150.

ENGLAND – Second Innings: 1—63, 2—65, 3—113, 4—524.

WEST INDIES – First Innings: 1—4, 2—83, 3—120, 4—183, 5—197, 6—387, 7—466, 8—469, 9—474.

WEST INDIES – Second Innings: 1—1, 2—9, 3—25, 4—27, 5—43, 6—66, 7—68.

Umpires: E. Davies and C. S. Elliott.

Match drawn.

# The Most Exciting Draw

This report seems complete enough as it stands, without additional comment or notation. What a finish!

ENGLAND V WEST INDIES, Lord's, final day: June 25, 1963
*Score at start:* West Indies 301 and 229; England 297 and 116 for 3
*Score at close:* West Indies 301 and 229; England 297 and 228 for 9

Writing as one whose lasting regret is that he was not at Brisbane for the tie, I have never seen a more exciting culmination to a Test match than this. Durban in 1948, when England won by two wickets off the last ball – and with a leg bye at that – was, I suppose, a close parallel.

When the last over started with Shackleton receiving from Hall, Allen at the bowler's end and Cowdrey plastered from left wrist to elbow waiting in the pavilion, eight runs were needed. Shackleton swung prodigiously at the first ball and missed, and took a single for a little tap for the second. Allen played a third nicely to long-leg for one. The next ball was decisive so far as an England win went. Shackleton missed a widish one which Murray took and, as Allen charged down to sneak a bye, threw underhand at the stumps.

Shackleton was slow to respond and so we had Worrell taking Murray's throw at the near stumps, and these two senior cricketers racing towards the bowler's end, Worrell with ball in hand. It was a tight thing with Worrell the winner.

If Shackleton had made his ground Allen, having crossed to the batting end, would have had two balls in which to make five with two wickets standing. As it was Allen, with six to win in two balls and Cowdrey now at the safe end unable to do more than defend, played them quietly and that was that.

So ended a classic game and perhaps some neutral arbiter (if there were any such cold-blooded being present) would say that this was the right result. Obviously but for a little, a slip here an edge there, some quickening of the over-rate giving more time, the score in the rubber might tonight be either one all or two nil. What we must be thankful for at all events, is that the miserable English weather, which interrupted the action from mid-afternoon yesterday until after lunch today, did not have the final word.

In today's cricket there were two heroes, one on either side. For a physical feat comparable to that of Hall, who, apart from the tea interval, bowled non-stop fast and furiously from 2.20 to six o'clock, cricket history shows no parallel, so far as I know, since Tom Richardson slaved away unrelieved for much the same sort of stretch at Old Trafford in 1896. Richardson saw Australia scrape home narrowly in the end. As for Hall, he must know that but for him England in all probability would have won.

For England, Close batted with courage and versatility, first withstanding the fast onslaught while he played himself thoroughly in, and in the later stages taking the battle into the enemy camp in the most exciting way.

Certainly he gave his own side and their supporters agonies of anxiety as he chanced his arm and his eye after tea.

But the West Indies must have been equally at their wits' end knowing that if the luck held and Titmus stayed firm they faced defeat. Lucky were the West Indies now that they had so cool a head in charge. There was not an overthrow, scarcely a miss of any kind in the field. Every chance was taken. The only qualification I must reluctantly make is that even with fast bowling holding the stage the whole time, apart from five overs by Gibbs, an over-all rate of 14 overs an hour is tedious slow. This brings me to Griffith, whose support of Hall, into the wind for 19 overs with only two brief breaks, was of the utmost value to his captain. But now to the story in some detail.

After yesterday's frustrations, today's: a spitting rain, now quite heavy, now scarcely a trickle, kept the pitch and surrounding square under covers all morning. When the apparatus could be removed the umpires announced that though the ground was firm the light was not. (Before play begins they arbitrate on the light as well as the ground.)

From breakfast there had been a waiting queue outside but in the dismal weather most had melted away before at twenty past two it became clear enough to start. After the crowded tiers of the first four days, the off-white expanse of vacant stands induced an anti-climax, which for a long time the cricket did nothing to dissolve.

Worrell began with Gibbs, but although the wind had so dried the turf that neither he nor the fast bowlers needed sawdust, Worrell removed Gibbs after a single over and relied on Hall down wind from the Pavilion end, Griffith from the Nursery. Both batsmen naturally took time to settle in and in due course Close seemed fairly acclimatised. Barrington by contrast had seemingly used up all his virtue yesterday and looked wretchedly ill at ease.

When he did make a good hook that was worth four it was finely fielded. At last after three-quarters of an hour Barrington got an involuntary single off his glove from a ball from Hall that flew wickedly. Barrington raised hopes with a nice four off his legs, but was then caught behind trying to make room to cut.

At this point in 52 minutes today 14 runs had come from the 13 overs bowled. Hall, very fast, variable both in length and direction and straying quite often to leg, was desperately hard to score from and Close took most of him. Indeed, when the tally was counted up at tea, out of Hall's 14 successive overs Close had received 65 balls – all but 11 of them. When Hall was short and on line Close often preferred to take the ball on the body anywhere between the top of the pads and the shoulder, doing his best to ride the blow. As an example of pluck it could not be improved on.

The only respect wherein Close fell short was in failing to take a number of safe short runs. Since time was obviously likely to be a factor, this disregard was irritating to watch.

Parks is a facile scorer by nature, and with him we saw runs coming off the front foot. Parks twice cover-drove Griffith handsomely for four, but immediately after the second stroke aimed to force Griffith to leg off the back foot, was beaten by the break-back and went lbw.

The advent of Titmus led to a much greater sense of urgency in the running, perhaps in response to captain's order. Before tea Gibbs had one over to relieve Griffith.

The over rate at the interval worked out at 14 per hour, and the score of 171 for five meant that if the same rate obtained to the end England would need to score a full three runs an over to make the 63 runs they needed.

So far as Hall was concerned, Worrell was stony-hearted – or perhaps who knows, Hall would not countenance the idea of coming off.

After tea Griffith, having bowled two overs more, was rested in favour of Gibbs. But Hall kept on, and at long-leg still had the suppleness and energy to make an amazing swoop and stop a hit that looked four runs all the way.

Close after tea grew more free, while Titmus played staunchly and sensibly giving Close all the bowling he could. Close swung the ball for four with a fine flowing hit, then missed a hook. An appeal for lbw. rent the heavens in vain. Close rubbed his thigh vigorously, which indicated the ball was going over the stumps. But I would not be prepared to swear it.

At 5 o'clock 48 were needed. A few moments later Close reached his 50 with his favourite stroke then repeated it off Gibbs, who had now relieved Griffith. At this point England were in their best situation: 50 minutes left 31 needed and five wickets still in hand. But a fine catch by McMorris at short-leg changed the picture. Titmus thrust the ball firmly off his body yet McMorris, not much further away than Stewart yesterday, when he caught Worrell, clung on at the first attempt.

What now would Hall serve up to Trueman? Would the

cause of the brotherhood survive so volatile a situation? Hall's first ball was an extremely fast, good length one, just outside the off stump. Trueman groped, tickled and was gone: another good catch by Murray.

Joined by Allen, Close grew bolder to the extent of walking down the pitch at Hall who, puzzled, ran on to meet him without delivering. Close did this twice more without either being killed or causing Hall a thrombosis or indeed making contact.

Close interspersed improbable strokes with several brilliant hits until with 20 minutes to go and 15 only wanted he swung to leg for the last time. Little Murray made a good catch and this talented but hitherto ill-starred Test cricketer walked in with the applause of the crowd making no doubt the sweetest music in his ears.

There was a peculiarity now in that though the new ball was due Worrell preferred the old one. There were to be five more overs. Allen and Shackleton batted coolly and picked up singles where they could. There was never more than one to be had with the field either up to catch or back to save fours. Seven runs accrued or were scrambled in four overs and then came the final one.

What palpitations! What a pulling at the heart-strings! And at the close the best sight ever to be seen on a cricket field, the crowd besieging the pavilion and its heroes coming out, tired but happy, to make their bows.

## West Indies

| | | |
|---|---|---|
| C. C. Hunte c. Close b. Trueman ... 44 | — | c. Cowdrey b. Shackleton 7 |
| E. D. McMorris lbw. b. Trueman ... 16 | — | c. Cowdrey b. Trueman 8 |
| G. S. Sobers c. Cowdrey b. Allen ... 42 | — | c. Parks b. Trueman... 8 |
| R. B. Kanhai c. Edrich b. Trueman ... 73 | — | c. Cowdrey b. Shackleton 21 |
| B. F. Butcher c. Barrington b. Trueman... 14 | — | lbw. b. Shackleton ... 133 |
| J. S. Solomon lbw. b. Shackleton ... 56 | — | c. Stewart b. Allen ... 5 |
| F. M. Worrell b. Trueman ... ... 0 | — | c. Stewart b. Trueman 33 |
| D. L. Murray c. Cowdrey b. Trueman... 20 | — | c. Parks b. Trueman... 2 |
| W. W. Hall not out ... ... 25 | — | c. Parks b. Trueman... 2 |
| C. C. Griffith c. Cowdrey b. Shackleton... 0 | — | b. Shackleton... ... 1 |
| L. R. Gibbs c. Stewart b. Shackleton ... 0 | — | not out ... ... 1 |
| B. 10, l.b. 1 ... ... ... ... 11 | | B. 5, l.b. 2, n.b. 1 ... 8 |
| 301 | | 229 |

Graeme Pollock; power and grace. As fine a model for the straight hit as could be found. Occasion: Hampshire v South Africa at Southampton, August 1965

PHOTOGRAPH: PATRICK EAGER

Sydney: Leaving Lord's apart, this for me is the ideal Test ground. The light is perfect, there is plenty of 'air' while the high pinnacled stands hold a multitude of memories. The famous 'hill' is at bottom left

## England

| | | | | | | |
|---|---|---|---|---|---|---|
| M. J. Stewart c. Kanhai b. Griffith | ... | 2 | — | c. Solomon b. Hall | ... | 17 |
| J. H. Edrich c. Murray b. Griffith | ... | 0 | — | c. Murray b. Hall | ... | 8 |
| E. R. Dexter lbw. b. Sobers | ... | ... | 70 | — | b. Gibbs ... ... | 2 |
| K. F. Barrington c. Sobers b. Worrell | ... | 80 | — | c. Murray b. Griffith... | 60 |
| M. C. Cowdrey b. Gibbs | ... | ... | 4 | — | not out ... ... | 19 |
| D. B. Close c. Murray b. Griffith | ... | 9 | — | c. Murray b. Griffith... | 70 |
| J. M. Parks b. Worrell ... ... | ... | 35 | — | lbw. b. Griffith | ... | 17 |
| F. J. Titmus not out ... ... | ... | 52 | — | c. McMorris b. Hall ... | 11 |
| F. S. Trueman b. Hall ... | ... | 10 | — | c. Murray b. Hall | ... | 0 |
| D. A. Allen lbw. b. Griffith | ... | ... | 2 | — | not out ... ... | 4 |
| D. Shackleton b. Griffith | ... | ... | 8 | — | run out ... ... | 4 |
| B. 8, l.b. 8, n.b. 9 ... | ... | ... | 25 | | B. 5, l.b. 8, n.b. 3 ... | 16 |

297        Nine wkts 228

## England Bowling

| | | O. | M. | R. | W. | | O. | M. | R. | W. |
|---|---|---|---|---|---|---|---|---|---|---|
| Trueman | ... | 44 | 16 | 100 | 6 | — | 26 | 9 | 52 | 5 |
| Shackleton | ... | 50.2 | 22 | 93 | 3 | — | 34 | 14 | 72 | 4 |
| Dexter... | ... | 20 | 6 | 41 | 0 | | | | | |
| Close | ... | 9 | 3 | 21 | 0 | | | | | |
| Allen ... | ... | 10 | 3 | 35 | 1 | — | 21 | 7 | 50 | 1 |
| Titmus | | | | | | ... | 17 | 3 | 47 | 0 |

## West Indies Bowling

| | | O. | M. | R. | W. | | O. | M. | R. | W. |
|---|---|---|---|---|---|---|---|---|---|---|
| Hall ... | ... | 18 | 2 | 65 | 1 | — | 40 | 9 | 93 | 4 |
| Griffith | ... | 26 | 6 | 91 | 5 | — | 30 | 7 | 59 | 3 |
| Sobers... | ... | 18 | 4 | 45 | 1 | — | 4 | 1 | 4 | 0 |
| Gibbs ... | ... | 27 | 9 | 59 | 1 | — | 17 | 7 | 56 | 1 |
| Worrell | ... | 13 | 6 | 12 | 2 | | | | | |

### FALL OF WICKETS

WEST INDIES – First Innings: 1—51, 2—64, 3—127, 4—145, 5—219, 6—219, 7—263, 8—297, 9—297.

WEST INDIES – Second Innings: 1—15, 2—15, 3—64, 4—84, 5—104, 6—214, 7—224, 8—226, 9—228.

ENGLAND – First Innings: 1—2, 2—20, 3—102, 4—115, 5—151, 6—206, 7—235, 8—271, 9—274.

ENGLAND – Second Innings: 1—15, 2—27, 3—31, 4—130, 5—158, 6—203, 7—203, 8—219, 9—228

Umpires: J. S. Buller and W. E. Phillipson.
Match drawn.

# West Indies Make History

After the best of all Test series – between Australia and the West Indies in 1960–61 – which, alas! I did not see, the return visit was one obviously not to be missed. Sir Frank Worrell, captain in Australia and since retired, now managed the West Indies, Sobers taking on their captaincy. Hall's fast bowling was the match-winning factor, but it was his partner, Griffith, on whom an unenviable spotlight fell when Benaud, Australia's former captain, now in the Press-box, announced his opinion before this last day, that Griffith threw. I refer in a later chapter to this episode, and would only note here that from the moment Benaud's words were read the tour as a great sporting event was ruined irretrievably.

WEST INDIES V AUSTRALIA, Kingston, final day: March 8, 1965
*Score at start:* West Indies 239 and 373; Australia 217 and 42
        for 2
*Score at close:* West Indies 239 and 373; Australia 217 and 216

The West Indies in the first game of this fifth Test series between the two countries gained their fourth victory over Australia but their first in their own islands.

The margin of runs brooks little argument. The West Indies won despite disappointing batting in their first innings largely because of the superiority of their opening attack and in particular because of the sustained excellence of Hall. He has never bowled better, nor has his unflagging spirit been more abundantly manifest. Griffith supported him well in spurts without being consistently so fast or so accurate.

It has been an absorbingly interesting game all through, ruggedly contested yet with good feeling between the sides despite the excitable atmosphere of this cockpit arena of Sabina Park.

After a Sunday of unusual cloud and drizzle which would have prevented much cricket, Australia, facing their formidable task, had an early set-back. Hall, their scourge of the first innings, had Cowper walking into a fast ball right up to him in his second over, and O'Neill came in to join Hawke at 43 for three.

O'Neill quickly struck form, while Hawke, whose Sheffield Shield figures for the season just ended stamp him as a genuine all-rounder, put up a staunch front. The bowling of Hall and Griffith was fast and accurate except for occasional overstepping of the front line.

O'Neill lasted the opening onslaught, but when Gibbs relieved Griffith O'Neill, aiming to off-drive, edged him fast to slip, where Nurse made a lovely catch. So after an hour

Australia were 75 for four. Things then stepped up considerably, with Sobers bowling his spinners instead of Hall. It was mostly Booth who profited from five erratic overs that cost 29 runs.

It was clear that Sobers could not bring the weight forward on to his injured front leg. Sobers after lunch preferred to hold his speed in reserve, using White and himself. At the interval one learned that Gibbs' bruised fingers prevented his giving the ball its usual tweak, so the West Indies really were under a handicap.

White settled into a highly economical length, and kept his end tight-pinned, but Sobers was only half himself, and after a while called on Solomon's very occasional leg-breaks. A few cheap runs followed, but lo and behold, Solomon tempted Hawke into a liberty that the more reputable bowlers had never induced. He hooked across a short one that came through a little low, and so the long stand ended.

Promptly now, Sobers brought back Griffith with immediate result. Booth, who had played with much style and facility against the slower men, was promptly yorked exactly as he had been in the first innings: 167-6-56. The writing now was clear on the wall, and Hall was also brought back instead of White, who had bowled 12 overs in succession at the cost of four singles. There was some temporary hubbub when Griffith was called six times in his first two overs for cutting the front line.

Thomas made a spectacular hook off Hall to the square-leg boundary, then, as he tried the stroke again, Hall even more spectacularly ripped out his off-stump.

Grout went lbw., and then the crowd had the crowning pleasure of seeing Sobers getting his 100th Test wicket. No one has come near his performance of taking 100 wickets and scoring 4,000 runs. But let us not forget Walter Hammond, who took 83 wickets as well as making 7,249.

Just before four o'clock it was all over with a day and a bit to spare. Sobers and his side ran for shelter to escape the jubilant attentions of their admirers.

## West Indies

| | | | | |
|---|---|---|---|---|
| C. C. Hunte c. Grout b. Philpott | ... 41 | — | c. Simpson b. Mayne | 81 |
| S. M. Nurse c. Grout b. Hawke | ... 15 | — | run out ... ... | 17 |
| R. B. Kanhai c. Philpott b. McKenzie | ... 17 | — | c. and b. Philpott ... | 16 |

| | | | | |
|---|---:|---|---|---:|
| B. F. Butcher b. Mayne ...   ...   ... | 39 | — | c. Booth b. Philpott ... | 71 |
| G. S. Sobers lbw. b. Simpson   ...   ... | 30 | — | c. Simpson b. Philpott | 27 |
| J. S. Solomon c. Grout b. Mayne   ... | 0 | — | c. Grout b. Mayne   ... | 76 |
| J. L. Hendriks b. Philpott   ...   ... | 11 | — | b. O'Neill   ...   ... | 30 |
| W. W. Hall b. Hawke   ...   ... | 9 | — | b. Mayne   ...   ... | 16 |
| A. W. White not out   ...   ... | 57 | — | st. Grout b. Philpott ... | 3 |
| C. C. Griffith b. Mayne ...   ... | 6 | — | not out   ...   ... | 1 |
| L. R. Gibbs b. Mayne   ...   ... | 6 | — | b. Mayne   ...   ... | 5 |
| B. 4, l.b. 3, w. 1   ...   ...   ... | 8 | | B. 20, l.b. 7, n.b. 2, w. 1 | 30 |
| | 239 | | | 373 |

## Australia

| | | | | |
|---|---:|---|---|---:|
| W. M. Lawry lbw. b. Hall   ...   ... | 19 | — | b. Griffith   ...   ... | 17 |
| R. B. Simpson c. Kanhai b. Hall   ... | 11 | — | c. Hendriks b. Hall ... | 16 |
| R. M. Cowper c. Nurse b. Hall ...   ... | 26 | — | lbw. b. Hall ...   ... | 2 |
| N. C. O'Neill c. Butcher b. White   ... | 40 | — | c. Nurse b. Gibbs   ... | 22 |
| B. C. Booth b. Griffith   ...   ... | 2 | — | b. Griffith   ...   ... | 56 |
| G. Thomas b. Griffith   ...   ... | 23 | — | b. Hall   ...   ... | 15 |
| P. Philpott c. White b. Hall   ... | 22 | — | c. Kanhai b. Sobers ... | 9 |
| N. J. N. Hawke not out ..   ...   ... | 46 | — | b. Solomon   ...   ... | 33 |
| A. T. W. Grout c. Nurse b. Hall   ... | 5 | — | lbw. b. Hall ...   ... | 2 |
| G. D. McKenzie b. White   ...   ... | 0 | — | c. Hall b. White   ... | 20 |
| L. Mayne b. Sobers   ...   ... | 8 | — | not out   ...   ... | 11 |
| B. 2, l.b. 8, n.b. 5   ...   ... | 15 | | N.b. 13   ...   ... | 13 |
| | 217 | | | 216 |

## Australia Bowling

| | O. | M. | R. | W. | | O. | M. | R. | W. |
|---|---:|---:|---:|---:|---|---:|---:|---:|---:|
| McKenzie   ... | 20 | 2 | 70 | 1 | — | 33 | 7 | 56 | 0 |
| Hawke   ... | 14 | 4 | 47 | 2 | — | 18 | 5 | 25 | 0 |
| Mayne   ... | 17.2 | 2 | 43 | 4 | — | 23.4 | 5 | 56 | 4 |
| Philpott   ... | 14 | 2 | 56 | 2 | — | 47 | 10 | 109 | 4 |
| Simpson   ... | 4 | 2 | 15 | 1 | — | 15 | 2 | 36 | 0 |
| Cowper | | .. | 9 | 1 | | | | 27 | 0 |
| O'Neill | | .. | 7 | 0 | | | | 34 | 1 |

## West Indies Bowling

| | | | | | | | | | |
|---|---:|---:|---:|---:|---|---:|---:|---:|---:|
| Hall   ...   ... | 24 | 0 | 60 | 5 | — | 19 | 5 | 45 | 4 |
| Griffith   ... | 19 | 2 | 59 | 2 | — | 14 | 3 | 36 | 2 |
| Sobers ...   ... | 20.4 | 7 | 30 | 1 | — | 17 | 2 | 64 | 1 |
| Gibbs ...   ... | 16 | 8 | 19 | 0 | — | 9 | 1 | 21 | 1 |
| White ...   ... | 15 | 3 | 34 | 2 | — | 14.5 | 8 | 14 | 1 |
| Solomon | | .. | | | | 4 | 0 | 23 | 1 |

## FALL OF WICKETS

West Indies – First Innings: 1—48, 2—70, 3—82, 4—149, 5—149, 6—149, 7—181, 8—211, 9—229.

West Indies – Second Innings: 1—50, 2—78, 3—194, 4—211, 5—226, 6—247, 7—311, 8—314, 9—372.

AUSTRALIA – First Innings: 1—32, 2—39, 3—42, 4—80, 5—96, 6—136, 7—176, 8—192, 9—193.

AUSTRALIA – Second Innings: 1—39, 2—40, 3—43, 4—75, 5—144, 6—157, 7—180, 8—184, 9—192.

Umpires: O. Davies and D. Sang-Hue.

West Indies won by 179 runs

# Barber's 185

Among all the innings played for England since the war, for the sheer enjoyment of watching I place this by Barber at the top of the list. It was appropriate that it should have paved the way for what at the moment of writing is England's last victory over Australia – and by an innings at that.

AUSTRALIA V ENGLAND, Sydney, 1st day: January 7, 1966
*Score at close:* England 328 for 5

There is no game like cricket for throwing up surprises of the most dramatic kind – a banal observation, it may be thought, but on the spur of the moment I can offer nothing more original.

Consider the situation here today where 40,000 spectators, after seeing their attack reduced to an unholy tangle by Barber, enjoyed the startlingly unexpected spectacle of this same attack rescuing the situation in the last hour or so of the day. To be exact Barber played on, a stroke made more from fatigue than anything else, at 4.55, making the score 303 for two. Less than three-quarters of an hour later, with Barrington, Cowdrey and Smith back in the pavilion for seven runs between them, it was 317 for five.

Smith had been signalling to the dressing room before this trying to indicate whom he wanted next. The man who emerged was Brown who promptly gave a slip catch to Walters off McKenzie that was grassed. Otherwise it would have been 318 for six. Thereupon Brown stuck his bat there and survived. The most charitable explanation of this manoeuvre is that Smith was misunderstood and merely intended Titmus to come in ahead of Parks which would have been thoroughly under-standable.

Hawke bowled with splendid hostility in this new-ball spell –

8-3-14-4 and all credit to him and indeed to McKenzie, who bowled for an hour mostly to Edrich with tremendous verve and no luck.

But let not these events dim the glory of Barber's innings or of the third-highest opening stand in the story of England-Australia Tests.

Hobbs and Rhodes (323) and Hobbs and Sutcliffe (283), the time they batted all day, alone stand in the book above the 234 of Barber and Boycott at Sydney on January 7, 1966.

Barber's part in the English batting effort on this tour has been second to none but he needed perhaps one outstanding Test innings to establish a position at the top of the tree. Now he has played it and, in five hours less a few minutes, written a new, bold, clear page in cricket history. Only eight Englishmen have made more in an innings against Australia, household names all of them: Hammond (three times!), Hobbs, Leyland, Paynter, Sutcliffe, Barrington and, of course, the leaders in the field, Hutton and R. E. Foster. Only one of these innings, Barrington's 256 at Old Trafford on the last Australian tour, has been played since the war.

Barber's conversion from a sticky, often frankly boring, batsman to his present status is a story to which one can think of no close parallel. His migration to Warwickshire three years ago had much to do with it and so I think did the aggressive requirements of the Gillette Cup. His eyes were opened and a new man appeared with something of the suddenness with which Saul saw the light on the road to Damascus.

The omens for England on the morning of this match were in stark contrast to Melbourne. Everyone now was fit while Australia had to bear the loss of Simpson. What is more, this time Smith won a priceless toss.

One was surprised at the preference of Jones over Higgs in the England side, not that Jones might not be the more likely to get rid of a good player, but because Higgs's stamina and steadiness would have been much the safer insurance against any further breakdown on the part of Brown.

However the decision was at least as aggressive a one as could have been made and as such had as much merit in that respect as Australia's choice of both wrist-spinners to the exclusion of Veivers. But as the game unfolded, English bowling considerations were soon far out of mind.

Barber and Boycott's opening had little of the flamboyance of the second Test but there was a measured tread about it that their opponents might have found just as disconcerting. Among the 23 runs of the first half hour were two cover boundaries of good pedigree by Barber who in general seemed to be weighing up the bowling and the wicket which seemed not unlike that whereon he had played his brilliant innings against New South Wales.

With 31 runs on the board Australia had their one palpable chance of nipping this stand in the bud. Boycott gave a very fast chance chest high to Sincock at backward short-leg off McKenzie. It was more or less off the face of the bat – a tough catch.

By the time the first drinks came Walters had had a turn at both ends and had bowled very presentably. In a rather sticky patch, Barber made two edged strokes through the slips and when Philpott first appeared at 64 he was dealt with more decorously than at Melbourne. The burning question was at what point would Booth introduce Sincock? Booth did so for the last over before lunch, an edgy time. But there were no English edges and England came in at 93 for no wicket.

The period that really stressed the possible dimensions of the England score was the hour after lunch wherein came no fewer than 75 runs, bringing Barber from 59 to 99 and Boycott from the 30s into the 60s.

McKenzie was punished in this time for 30 in four overs, while Sincock's length was such that it was impossible for Booth to set him an economical field.

Barber, it so happened, had to wait for 10 minutes when 99 without getting a ball but with a firm off-drive he reached the goal at last, his umpteenth fine Test innings but first Test hundred, in three hours 10 minutes.

In mid-afternoon Booth tried his sixth bowler, Cowper the off-spinner, and when Cowper turned a couple beating Barber each time the knowing ones found the sight almost as significant as the freedom of the batting. What might Titmus and Allen do after the week-end?

They say the ball generally turns here, but I must add it

looks as solid as could be and too well grassed, one would have thought, to develop the cracks that give encouragement to all sorts of bowlers late in a match. At all events Barber was soon cracking Cowper with great force for successive fours to the sight-screen and in so doing bringing the score above the 219 that Hutton and Barnett made together at Trent Bridge.

The partnership ended in the last over before tea when Boycott, playing firmly forward, was caught and bowled by Philpott low down. Barber afterwards lasted nearly an hour and made a further 38 runs.

Not unnaturally he showed some signs of tiredness and was beaten a couple of times by Philpott. But while Edrich was settling in, he continued to pile on the agony, taking two lovely fours square of the wicket on either side in McKenzie's first over with the new ball.

He was out at last, cutting a short ball on to his stumps and the crowd rose in salute – and perhaps some physical relief.

### England

| | |
|---|---:|
| G. Boycott c. and b. Philpott ... ... ... | 84 |
| R. W. Barber b. Hawke ... ... ... ... | 185 |
| J. H. Edrich c. and b. Philpott ... ... ... | 103 |
| K. F. Barrington c. McKenzie b. Hawke ... | 1 |
| M. C. Cowper c. Grout b. Hawke ... ... | 0 |
| M. J. K. Smith c. Grout b. Hawke ... ... | 6 |
| D. J. Brown c. Grout b. Hawke ... ... ... | 1 |
| J. M. Parks c. Grout b. Hawke ... ... ... | 13 |
| F. J. Titmus c. Grout b. Walters ... ... | 14 |
| D. A. Allen not out ... ... ... ... | 50 |
| I. J. Jones b. Hawke ... ... ... ... | 16 |
| B. 3, l.b. 8, w. 2, n.b. 2 ... ... ... | 15 |
| | ——— |
| | 488 |

### Australia

| | | | | |
|---|---:|---|---|---:|
| W. M. Lawry c. Parks b. Jones ... ... | 0 | — | c. Cowdrey b. Brown | 33 |
| G. Thomas c. Titmus b. Brown ... ... | 51 | — | c. Cowdrey b. Titmus | 25 |
| R. M. Cowper st. Parks b. Allen ... | 60 | — | c. Boycott b. Titmus... | 0 |
| P. J. Burge c. Parks b. Brown ... ... | 6 | — | run out ... ... | 1 |
| B. C. Booth c. Cowdrey b. Jones ... | 8 | — | b. Allen ... ... | 27 |
| D. J. Sincock c. Parks b. Brown... ... | 29 | — | c. Smith b. Allen ... | 27 |
| K. D. Walters st. Parks b. Allen ... | 23 | — | not out ... ... | 35 |
| N. J. N. Hawke c. Barber b. Brown ... | 0 | — | c. Smith b. Titmus ... | 2 |
| A. T. W. Grout b. Brown .. ... | 0 | — | c. Smith b. Allen ... | 3 |
| G. D. McKenzie c. Cowdrey b. Barber... | 24 | — | c. Barber b. Titmus ... | 12 |

| P. I. Philpott not out | ... | ... | ... | 5 | — | lbw. b. Allen ... | ... | 5 |
| B. 7, l.b. 8 | ... | ... | ... | 15 | | B. 3, l.b. 1 ... | ... | 4 |
| | | | | 221 | | | | 174 |

## Australia Bowling

| | | | O. | M. | R. | W. |
|---|---|---|---|---|---|---|
| McKenzie | ... | ... | 25 | 2 | 113 | 0 |
| Hawke | ... | ... | 33.7 | 6 | 105 | 7 |
| Walters | ... | ... | 10 | 1 | 38 | 1 |
| Philpott | ... | ... | 28 | 3 | 86 | 2 |
| Sincock | ... | ... | 20 | 1 | 98 | 0 |
| Cowper | ... | ... | 6 | 1 | 33 | 0 |

## England Bowling

| | | O. | M. | R. | W. | | O. | M. | R. | W. |
|---|---|---|---|---|---|---|---|---|---|---|
| Jones ... | ... | 20 | 6 | 51 | 2 | — | 7 | 0 | 35 | 0 |
| Brown | ... | 17 | 1 | 63 | 5 | — | 11 | 2 | 31 | 1 |
| Boycott | ... | 3 | 1 | 8 | 0 | | | | | |
| Titmus | ... | 23 | 8 | 40 | 0 | — | 17.3 | 4 | 40 | 4 |
| Barber... | ... | 2.1 | 1 | 2 | 1 | — | 5 | 0 | 16 | 0 |
| Allen ... | ... | 19 | 5 | 42 | 2 | — | 20 | 8 | 47 | 4 |

## FALL OF WICKETS

ENGLAND – First Innings: 1—234, 2—303, 3—309, 4—309, 5—317, 6—328, 7—358, 8—395, 9—433.

AUSTRALIA – First Innings: 1—0, 2—81, 3—91, 4—105, 5—155, 6—174, 7—174, 8—174, 9—203.

AUSTRALIA – Second Innings: 1—46, 2—50, 3—51, 4—86, 5—86, 6—119, 7—131, 8—135, 9—140.

Umpires: C. Egar and L. Rowan.

England won by an innings and 93 runs.

# CHAPTER TWO

# — AND OTHERS

A few famous feats are here perpetuated, and a (very) brief selection from the classic Lord's matches, a great Roses finish, another county game or two, and a couple of lively examples of that phenomenon of the 'sixties, the Gillette Cup. From somewhere around fifteen hundred days' watching (Test Matches excluded) one can only make an occasional arbitrary pick. This round dozen answer at least one test – where most of the cricket one has seen is either completely forgotten or at best a blur these days still stand out clear in the memory after, in most cases, a good many years.

## Donnelly's Classic

Martin Donnelly shares with another great left-hander, the late Percy Chapman, a Lord's record that must now stand for ever. He made a hundred in the University Match (142 for Oxford in 1946), a hundred for the Gentlemen described here, and a hundred in a Test Match (206 for New Zealand in 1949). In the immediately post-war years before he left the scene for a prosperous business life in Australia there was scarcely a batsman in the world better worth watching. Any anthology of the cricket of the period should accord him a prominent place, and I am only sorry this paltry account – paper restrictions were at their worst – does his innings such poor justice.

GENTLEMEN v PLAYERS, Lord's, 1st day: July 16, 1947
*Score at close:* Gentlemen 302; Players 67 for 2

There were 17,000 at Lord's today for Gentlemen and Players, a fact that is a sufficient answer in itself to any foolish and perverse suggestions that the match has outlived its fame. And the day was made for ever memorable for them by Donnelly, who played one of the classic innings of modern cricket history.

From lunch until the innings ended he batted, scoring 162 out of 240 in 175 minutes, and at the end the members in the pavilion seats all rose to give the innings its final hall-mark. This has not happened at Lord's since Hammond made 240 against Australia nine years ago.

It is remarkable how in so short a time Donnelly has been accepted quite universally by cricketers as comparable to the best left-handers who ever played, that is, of course, to Woolley and Clem Hill. Today he showed all the strokes, except, possibly, the leg glide, so that even Ames's ingenuity in setting a field went for very little. His special delight was the ball just barely short of a length on the middle and leg.

Wright was the only bowler to whom Donnelly accorded anything approaching respect. The rest he deposited hither and thither in the most arbitrary way and none more nonchalantly than Walsh, whose left-arm googlies were apt to puzzle everyone else. Butler was the better of the opening Players' bowlers, and both opening batsmen should have fallen to him, but Willatt was missed at leg slip. Willatt stayed long enough to justify his place in this distinguished company, and would be a better batsman if he could reassemble his stance, which at present precludes his swinging the bat straight to the on-side ball.

Edrich's confidence set the Gentlemen's innings on a profitable course on a good wicket, and 37 of the score of 64 for two at lunch were his. Afterwards Donnelly pulverised Walsh and the quicker bowlers, until Wright settled down to a long and admirable steady bowl, during which no doubt he thinned the ranks of his detractors. Edrich, who seemed the master of everyone else, was anything but confident against him, and justice was served when he was lbw. for 79.

The rest of the Gentlemen's innings, apart from Donnelly, contained much rather paltry cricket with a strange disregard for the text-book. But Simpson stayed long enough to show a pleasing similarity to Hardstaff's better method, and Cranston played some good strokes.

The Players batted in a poor light. Bailey bowled fairly quickly but rather short, and Mallett perhaps looked just the more dangerous. Robertson showed many a cultivated stroke, and when he left it was a pity that Ames, coming in to save a younger player, should not have had his proper reward.

## Gentlemen

| | | | |
|---|---:|---|---:|
| G. L. Willatt b. Walsh ... ... ... | 23 | — c. Fletcher b. Gladwin ... | 5 |
| H. A. Pawson c. Evans b. Butler | 4 | — lbw. b. Gladwin ... | 5 |
| W. J. Edrich lbw. b. Wright ... | 79 | — c. Gladwin b. Butler | 5 |
| M. P. Donnelly not out ... ... | 162 | — c. Compton b. Butler | 6 |
| R. T. Simpson c. Ames b. Walsh | 4 | — b. Gladwin .. ... | 0 |
| N. W. D. Yardley b. Gladwin ... ... | 9 | — lbw. b. Barnett ... | 46 |
| K. Cranston c. Evans b. Butler ... | 16 | — c. Walsh b. Butler ... | 47 |
| T. E. Bailey lbw. b. Walsh ... | 0 | — st. Evans b. Walsh ... | 1 |
| F. R. Brown b. Butler ... ... | 0 | — b. Walsh ... ... | 35 |
| S. C. Griffith lbw. b. Butler ... | 2 | — not out ... ... | 39 |
| A. W. H. Mallett b. Wright ... | 0 | — c. Wright b. Compton | 14 |
| B. 1, l.b. 1, n.b. 1 ... ... ... | 3 | — B. 5, l.b. 1 .. .. | 6 |
| | 302 | | 209 |

## Players

| | | | |
|---|---:|---|---:|
| C. Washbrook b. Edrich ... ... ... | 101 | — not out ... ... | 3 |
| J. D. Robertson lbw. b. Cranston ... | 28 | — not out ... ... | 0 |
| L. E. G. Ames c. Mallett b. Cranston ... | 6 | | |
| D. Compton c. Griffith b. Bailey ... | 11 | | |
| C. J. Barnett c. Simpson b. Mallett ... | 39 | | |
| D. G. W. Fletcher c. Griffith b. Bailey ... | 77 | | |
| T. G. Evans lbw. b. Brown ... | 22 | | |
| C. Gladwin not out ... ... ... | 31 | | |
| J. E. Walsh c. Griffith b. Bailey... ... | 2 | | |
| D. V. P. Wright not out ... ... ... | 0 | | |
| B. 11, l.b. 6 ... ... ... | 17 | | |
| Eight wkts, dec. | 334 | No wkt | 3 |

H. J. Butler did not bat.

## Players Bowling

| | O. | M. | R. | W. | | O. | M. | R. | W. |
|---|---|---|---|---|---|---|---|---|---|
| Butler ... ... | 24 | 4 | 91 | 4 | — | 21 | 4 | 56 | 3 |
| Gladwin ... | 20 | 3 | 66 | 1 | — | 17 | 7 | 36 | 3 |
| Barnett ... | 6 | 1 | 20 | 0 | — | 3 | 0 | 5 | 1 |
| Wright ... | 14.2 | 1 | 40 | 2 | — | 9 | 1 | 33 | 0 |
| Walsh ... ... | 18 | 0 | 82 | 3 | — | 11 | 0 | 67 | 2 |
| | | | | | Compton .. | 1.1 | 0 | 6 | 1 |
| Bailey ... ... | 25 | 3 | 83 | 3 | | | | | |
| Edrich... ... | 19 | 4 | 48 | 1 | | | | | |
| Mallett ... | 23 | 5 | 56 | 1 | | | | | |
| Brown... ... | 21 | 2 | 62 | 1 | — | 2 | 0 | 3 | 0 |
| Cranston ... | 20 | 4 | 61 | 2 | | | | | |

|          | O. | M. | R. | W. | O. | M. | R. | W. |
|----------|----|----|----|----|----|----|----|----|
| Donnelly ... | 2 | 0 | 7 | 0 |    |    |    |    |
| Yardley  |    |    |    |    | 1.5 | 1 | 0 | 0 |

Umpires: J. Smart and A. Skelding.
Match drawn.

## Golden Day at Lord's

There has been nothing in my time to compare with the hold that
Denis Compton had over crowds everywhere, and at Lord's most
of all. Here he is celebrating his benefit with a vintage innings before
a full house in blazing sunshine. It was characteristic of him that
he should choose the best sort of weather, and that he should make
the utmost out of the occasion in all respects. Note the size of the
crowd. It is personalities who bring people to cricket – and, for the
most part, batting personalities at that.

MIDDLESEX v SUSSEX, Lord's, 2nd day: June 6, 1949
*Score at start:* Sussex 251 for 8
*Score at close:* Sussex 269; Middlesex 420 for 7

Middlesex established a position this afternoon and evening
which gives them a sporting chance of forcing a win against
Sussex, and makes a full and interesting day certain tomorrow
in Denis Compton's benefit match. They are 151 runs on, the
pitch is a beauty, and further, it is fully covered and so cannot
be harmed by the weather.

For the crowd which packed every inch of Lord's it was a
day in a lifetime. They sat under a blue sky in the sunshine in
their shirt sleeves and blouses, and saw their hero make 182
runs in his own uniquely magnetic way. He began soberly,
launched gradually into his full range of strokes, and when
both his 100 and the Sussex score were left behind blossomed
forth into one of those dazzling exhibitions which are so
difficult for the bowler to compete with and so impossible to
describe.

Compton's last 82 were made in a few minutes over three-
quarters of an hour by a bewildering mixture and variety of the
drive, the cut, the hook and the pull, with the delayed wristy
drive to either side of cover point as the favourite and most
perfect stroke of all.

The Sussex bowlers could say, as the old Yorkshireman said of W. G. Grace: 'I put 'un where I like and he put 'un where he likes.' But the tempo of this final storming assault was considerably more rapid than any recorded effort by the champion.

With his score at 52 Compton had sliced a very wide half-volley from Wood straight into gulley's hands and out again. It was his first and last mistake.

When Denis Compton walked back at last his brother Leslie walked in, and in the last three-quarters of an hour made a very powerful and excellent 59, including some off-drives of a quality not a whit below those we had been enjoying earlier. Where else, as someone remarked, could a man get such value for eighteenpence as he had at Lord's today?

In the Sussex cricket there was a great deal to admire. The bowling of Cornford, Wood, James and Charles Oakes, supported most admirably both in the field and by Griffith behind the wicket, kept Middlesex down to 36 in the first hour and 66 in the hundred minutes before lunch.

They had their slice of luck when Edrich chopped the ball off the middle of the bat plumb on to Griffith's foot, whence it bounced into John Langridge's hands at slip. But it was a catch in a thousand by Jack Oakes that sent back Brown, who jumped out to James Langridge and hit the ball like a bullet to silly mid-off, where Oakes took it as it flew at his head with a force that knocked him on to his back. No one remembered a finer catch of its type, either at Lord's or anywhere.

Sussex, apart from the one dramatic miss, continued to field well to the end, and their bowling weathered its hammering as well as could be. Not the least brilliant thing was Griffith's lightning stumping of Thompson when the shadows were falling. Brown must be mentioned for a steady opening innings, Mann for a short but rousing one, and Sharp for playing the always difficult part of an unobtrusive partner to the great.

This was Compton's 77th hundred and his 53rd in the three years since cricket began again after the war. He has a position apart from all others, and if any tangible illustration of this were needed it was felicitously supplied by the crowd, which filled the subscription boxes this afternoon with the amount unprecedented at a single collection of £618. Over 30,000 were present, 27,818 paying at the gates. Receipts for the two days have brought in £2,838, and a Saturday collection amounted to £220.

## Sussex

| | | | |
|---|---|---|---|
| John Langridge lbw. b. Gray ... ... | 1 | c. L. Compton b. Sims | 139 |
| D. V. Smith b. Young ... ... ... | 85 | b. Edrich ... ... | 0 |
| C. Oakes b. Young ... ... | 25 | c. L. Compton b. Young | 52 |
| H. T. Bartlett c. Young b. Edrich ... | 4 | c. Edrich b. Young ... | 31 |
| G. Cox c. Edrich b. D. Compton ... | 17 | lbw. b. Young ... | 20 |
| James Langridge b. Gray ... ... | 40 | lbw. b. D. Compton ... | 20 |
| S. C. Griffith not out ... ... ... | 68 | c. L. Compton b. Sims | 5 |
| J. Oakes c. D. Compton b. Young ... | 1 | st. L. Compton b. Sims | 53 |
| A. E. James c. L. Compton b. Young ... | 7 | not out ... ... | 31 |
| J. Cornford run out ... ... ... | 14 | not out ... ... | 15 |
| J. Wood b. Sims ... ... ... ... | 0 | | |
| B. 2, l.b. 5 ... ... ... ... | 7 | B 5, l.b. 3 ... ... | 8 |
| | **269** | Eight wkts | **374** |

## Middlesex

| | |
|---|---|
| J. D. Robertson b. Cornford ... ... ... | 1 |
| S. M. Brown c. J. Oakes b. James Langridge ... | 66 |
| W. J. Edrich c. John Langridge b. James ... | 21 |
| D. C. S. Compton c. Bartlett b. Cornford ... | 182 |
| F. G. Mann b. Cornford ... ... ... | 26 |
| H. Sharp c. James Langridge b. Wood ... | 35 |
| A. Thompson st. Griffith b. Wood ... ... | 3 |
| L. Compton not out ... ... ... ... | 59 |
| J. Sims not out ... ... ... ... ... | 19 |
| B. 7, w. 1 ... ... ... ... ... | 8 |
| Seven wkts, dec. | **420** |

J. A. Young and L. Gray did not bat.

## Middlesex Bowling

| | O. | M. | R. | W. | | O. | M. | R. | W. |
|---|---|---|---|---|---|---|---|---|---|
| Edrich ... ... | 16 | 2 | 39 | 1 | — | 18 | 3 | 65 | 1 |
| Gray ... ... | 22 | 7 | 32 | 2 | — | 16 | 7 | 28 | 0 |
| Young ... ... | 30 | 9 | 69 | 4 | — | 31 | 11 | 123 | 3 |
| Sims ... ... | 14 | 0 | 58 | 1 | — | 38 | 3 | 111 | 3 |
| D. Compton ... | 17 | 3 | 64 | 1 | — | 13 | 3 | 39 | 1 |

## Sussex Bowling

| | O. | M. | R. | W. |
|---|---|---|---|---|
| Cornford ... ... | 26 | 9 | 71 | 3 |
| Wood ... ... | 24 | 7 | 82 | 2 |
| James ... ... | 32 | 8 | 85 | 1 |
| C. Oakes ... ... | 29 | 3 | 98 | 0 |

|  | O. | M. | R. | W. |
|---|---|---|---|---|
| John Langridge ... | 1 | 0 | 4 | 0 |
| James Langridge ... | 11 | 0 | 56 | 1 |
| Cox    ...    ... ... | 4 | 0 | 16 | 0 |

Umpires: A. Skelding and H. Elliott.
Match drawn.

## New Zealand Victory

When I went to New Zealand with the M.C.C. team in 1950–51 I was astonished at the number of people who recalled the exciting climax to this game. It so happened I was broadcasting it, and it seemed as though cricket followers identified me as the voice behind the last day at Southampton rather than with the four Test Matches, which as it happendd were all drawn.

Note, please, one statistical point. Despite the furious run-rate, and the fact of three wickets having fallen, in the 28 minutes that the New Zealand innings lasted Hampshire bowled 11.5 overs. How foolish of them: they had only to have a few consultations, do up a couple of bootlaces, and practise one or two more little tricks, and they would have saved the day!

HAMPSHIRE v NEW ZEALANDERS, Southampton, final day: June 17, 1949
*Score at start:* Hampshire 129 and 120 for 3; New Zealanders 430 for 5 dec.
*Score at close:* Hampshire 129 and 409; New Zealanders 430 for 5 dec. and 109 for 3

The New Zealanders beat Hampshire here this evening by seven wickets. That prosaic fact conceals the most spectacular piece of cricket I have had the pleasure and the thrill of watching for many a long day.

Hampshire won for themselves all honour and glory by batting nearly all through the day, and taking their 120 for three overnight to 409, the largest score made by any side against the New Zealanders in England so far. When they were out at last the clock showed a quarter to six, so that by taking the extra half-hour the New Zealanders had only 35 minutes in which to make 109.

Hadlee sent in Sutcliffe and Donnelly, and lucky is the captain who can call upon two such cricketers for such a task.

These two left-handers trusted their eye with a sequence of glorious strokes which must have made Ransom and Shackleton despair of where to pitch the next ball.

The first over produced 11 runs and the following four 11, 14, 13 and 10 respectively, before Sutcliffe was caught off the last ball of the fifth over for 46. The innings had then lasted 13 minutes. Of the 30 balls bowled he had received 20, and had hit a six over long-off, another over mid-wicket, a third over extra cover, and four fours, all brilliant and powerful hits that left the field standing.

The total then was 59. Smith heightened the drama by being yorked first ball by Shackleton, then Reid hit a few and snicked a few while Donnelly took charge. In the seventh over Reid was bowled, also by Shackleton (77-3-9), and in the ninth over Hampshire had their last chance when Donnelly gave a nasty running catch to long-on, but it was put on the floor.

Hadlee now was with him, running like a stag, so that Donnelly, having expended a great deal of energy, was utterly outpaced. From the start the New Zealanders had been running for everything. Together Donnelly and Hadlee saw the thing through comfortably, Donnelly bringing the scores level with a vast six to square-leg, and leaning elegantly on the next, which flew to long-on for a single and victory. The time taken was 28 minutes.

I have never seen more glorious striking than Sutcliffe's: the only innings at all comparable was one of 50 odd, off something just over 20 balls, made by Constantine against M.C.C. at Lord's in 1933. That was tremendous, too, but with the important difference that time was not then of the essence.

Hampshire's part in the last phase should not go unrecorded. Ransom and Shackleton, both fast-medium, withstood the hurricane pretty well, and the fieldsmen were so quick to change over that the 11th over was being bowled well inside the half-hour.

The Hampshire innings will give vast pleasure to those who had hoped for great things from their side this summer, and who had been downcast by a succession of low scores. Eagar played extraordinarily well, lasting almost until lunch, and relaxing from dead-bat defence to make many beautiful strokes, notably two splendid sixes to long-on.

Arnold, having given a difficult caught and bowled chance before he had scored, batted admirably for his first hundred of the season. It completed for him an unusual and significant performance, since he now has made a century against all the teams from overseas. As of Eagar it can be said of Arnold that with his quick eye and footwork he seems to deserve more runs than he habitually scores. Hill, hitherto quite out of form, also played well, and, all in all, it was a day that satisfied everyone.

## Hampshire

| | | | | | |
|---|---|---|---|---|---|
| N. McCorkell lbw. b. Cresswell ... | ... | 11 | — | c. Reid b. Burtt ... | 67 |
| N. H. Rogers st. Reid b. Cresswell | ... | 1 | — | b. Hayes ... ... | 4 |
| D. R. Guard c. Rabone b. Hayes | ... | 6 | — | b. Hayes ... ... | 12 |
| J. Bailey c. Rabone b. Cresswell... | ... | 4 | — | c. Rabone b. Burtt ... | 13 |
| E. D. R. Eagar b. Burtt ... ... | ... | 16 | — | b. Burke ... ... | 82 |
| J. Arnold c. Hayes b. Cresswell ... | ... | 16 | — | c. Cresswell b. Burtt ... | 110 |
| D. Shackleton b. Burke ... ... | ... | 16 | — | b. Burtt ... ... | 21 |
| C. Walker b. Hayes ... ... | ... | 20 | — | b. Burtt ... ... | 16 |
| G. Hill c. Reid b. Burke ... ... | ... | 0 | — | not out ... ... | 49 |
| V. J. Ransom c. Sutcliffe b. Burke | ... | 19 | — | c. Rabone b. Burke ... | 9 |
| C. J. Knott not out ... ... | ... | 9 | — | c. Cresswell b. Burtt ... | 0 |
| B. 2, l.b. 1, n.b. 8 ... ... | ... | 11 | | B. 15, l.b. 10, w. 1 | 26 |
| | | 129 | | | 409 |

## New Zealanders

| | | | | | |
|---|---|---|---|---|---|
| V. J. Scott c. Walker b. Bailey ... | ... | 129 | | | |
| B. Sutcliffe b. Knott ... ... | ... | 71 | — | c. Eagar b. Ransom ... | 46 |
| W. A. Hadlee c. Rogers b. Knott | ... | 33 | — | not out ... ... | 9 |
| J. R. Reid b. Knott ... ... | ... | 50 | — | b. Shackleton... ... | 9 |
| M. P. Donnelly not out ... ... | ... | 100 | — | not out ... ... | 39 |
| F. B. Smith st. McCorkell b. Eagar | ... | 23 | — | b. Shackleton... ... | 0 |
| G. O. Rabone not out ... ... | ... | 15 | | | |
| B. 4, l.b. 5 ... ... ... | ... | 9 | | L.b. 5, w. 1 ... | 6 |
| Five wkts, dec. | | 430 | | Three wkts | 109 |

T. B. Burtt, C. C. Burke, J. A. Hayes and G. F. Cresswell did not bat.

## New Zealand Bowling

| | | O. | M. | R. | W. | | O. | M. | R. | W. |
|---|---|---|---|---|---|---|---|---|---|---|
| Hayes ... | ... | 17.5 | 3 | 45 | 2 | — | 33 | 5 | 108 | 2 |
| Cresswell | ... | 26 | 14 | 28 | 4 | — | 16 | 4 | 42 | 0 |
| Burke ... | ... | 13 | 3 | 40 | 3 | — | 29 | 9 | 65 | 2 |
| Rabone | ... | 1 | 1 | 0 | 0 | — | 27 | 9 | 65 | 0 |
| Burtt ... | ... | 11 | 7 | 5 | 1 | — | 42.2 | 19 | 76 | 6 |
| Hadlee | ... | | | | | | 2 | 0 | 12 | 0 |
| Smith | ... | | | | | | 1 | 1 | 0 | 0 |
| Sutcliffe | ... | | | | | | 3 | 0 | 15 | 0 |

Hampshire Bowling

| | | | | | | | | | |
|---|---|---|---|---|---|---|---|---|---|
| Ransom | ... | 23 | 3 | 51 | 0 | — | 6 | 0 | 47 | 1 |
| Shackleton | ... | 18 | 2 | 58 | 0 | — | 5.5 | 0 | 56 | 2 |
| Knott ... | ... | 34 | 3 | 109 | 3 | | | | |
| Bailey ... | ... | 33 | 9 | 88 | 1 | | | | |
| Hill ... | ... | 17 | 4 | 66 | 0 | | | | |
| Walker | ... | 11 | 1 | 42 | 0 | | | | |
| Eagar ... | ... | 1 | 0 | 7 | 1 | | | | |

Umpires: H. Baldwin and D. Hendren.
New Zealand won by 7 wickets.

## Thrills at Bramall-Lane

Though I watched one of the two Roses matches every year from 1946 to the late 'fifties I was unlucky in the number of good matches I saw. This however was an exception; the first result since the war after eight draws.

I always enjoyed broadcasting from the old position at Bramall Lane – a table, unenclosed, and in full sight and sound of the Yorkshire members. It kept one up to the mark, and in every sense *live*. On this occasion, with one innings apiece not yet completed on the third morning, the gate when play began was, if I remember aright, a rather disappointing eight thousand or so.

My advice to all within range of Sheffield whenever I came on the air was to come and see for themselves. Over lunch the crowd all but doubled itself, to the Secretary's great pleasure. We were both surprised at this evidence of the degree of the influence of the B.B.C.

Talking of the B.B.C., I suppose the average young follower thinks of Norman Yardley as a Test summariser. This report will bring to his notice the fact that he was a remarkably good cricketer.

YORKSHIRE v LANCASHIRE, Sheffield, final day: May 30, 1950
*Score at start:* Lancashire 257; Yorkshire 185 for 6
*Score at close:* Lancashire 257 and 117; Yorkshire 193 for 8 dec. and 167

Lancashire beat Yorkshire here this afternoon by 14 runs after a day of agonising excitement which, many a year from now, will set tingling the blood of all those – and there were some 16,000 of us – who were lucky enough to have been present at Bramall Lane.

After the Yorkshire innings this afternoon had gone through

many palpitating changes of fortune, Wardle, at number nine, came in to join his captain, Yardley, with only 125 on the board of the 182 needed, and, with respect to Brennan, no substantial batting to follow. The wicket was spasmodically spiteful still, though scarcely the venomous, treacherous thing on which Lancashire had been bowled out for 117 in the morning.

The odds seemed long, but Yardley was playing most admirably, and whatever impious critics may say of certain technical limitations on faster wickets, he is, as he has always been, an excellent batsman when the turf is taking the spin. No one who saw his partnership with Hammond on that evil day at Brisbane in the first Test of 1946 could doubt that.

The mood of the whole day's cricket had been to 'get at him before he gets at you'. Only Hutton with his superb method, had been above and beyond the necessity of chancing his arm. Wardle was the last man to close up at such a moment, and in hardly more than a quarter of an hour 27 more came for the eighth wicket, mostly runs truly made against bowling that remained steady and fielding that took inspiration from the occasion. This was a moment, almost the only one in the match, when Yorkshire seemed really on top. And then, when another four or two would have counted beyond price, Wardle drove Berry hard off the meat of the bat straight back.

Berry clung safely to the ball, and in that there was poetic justice since the game from its beginning had developed largely into a duel between these two left-arm bowlers and the Lancastrian had proved a clear and worthy winner. With 30 needed Brennan took Wardle's place and began with a fine snick for four past the wicket-keeper to a roar that must have been heard far away in the heart of the city.

Yardley now monopolised the situation, drawing everything off his stumps with an easy dexterity that made it all look almost safe. His 50 arrived to a crescendo of cheering and then Brennan swung at an off-break and Wharton held a good, hard hit chest-high at short mid-wicket.

Now it was simply Yardley or no one. He declined single runs from each of the first three balls of Berry's next over, tried for the last time to flick the fourth off his wicket round the corner and so get the next over, and the ball, lifting, lobbed gently in the air to within reach of any of three men round the bat. Thus it ended and Lancashire had beaten their ancient enemies for the first time since on this same ground Iddon's fine bowling had won the day 13 years before. Since the war all the eight matches before this had been drawn, but in the late thirties Yorkshire had usually won with conclusive emphasis, and in recent times Lancashire has a long leeway to make up.

This has not been a happy match for young Close, but he had his brief moments of glory, pulling his first ball, from outside the off stump, for a thrilling six to square-leg, sending Berry whistling over extra cover to the boundary, and giving his captain cause to hope that the improbable might after all be brought to pass. The manner of his end was a tragedy for Yorkshire. Yardley declined a youthfully optimistic call for a second run. Close turned, and could no doubt have made his ground, but slipped up badly (was he properly studded?) and a quick pick up by Berry, followed by the slickest of returns ran him out.

In a match of this kind there are always many 'might-have-beens', and it seems hard after such a struggle that either side should have to lose, but tolerably composed afterthoughts emphasize that justice was certainly done in the result.

On Saturday Yardley gave Lancashire a more vicious wicket to bat on than Yorkshire themselves found yesterday; and when he declared after three overs this morning 64 behind with two wickets left including his own, he obliged them to bat on the unpleasantest one of all. I wrote last evening that a further judicious fall of rain might make for a battle, and so indeed it proved. Lancashire had a desperately sticky time of it this morning, and how few they might have been skittled for but for Grieves no one can say.

The first three wickets had gone for 35 when he came to the crease, and he made 52 out of the next 76 in well under the hour. As with Yardley, it was a case of a fine eye and quickness of judgment overcoming the attack against all the odds. As ever, when an Australian is assaulted, he hits back good and hard.

Wardle at any rate, though still inclined to drop short on the leg stump, bowled a fuller length than in the first innings, yet

Grieves found a variety of strokes with which to belabour him and to put heart into a succession of young partners at the other end. Grieves batted grandly, and it was not the least thing about this happy day for Lancashire that nearly everyone in the team contributed something notable to the success. For this critical enthusiast it was the best day, and the most exciting finish, since England won off the last ball at Durban 18 months ago.

## Lancashire

| | | | |
|---|---|---|---|
| W. Place c. Coxon b. Wardle ... ... | 15 | b. Close ... ... | 18 |
| J. T. Ikin c. Halliday b. Close ... ... | 19 | c. Brennan b. Wardle | 3 |
| G. A. Edrich c. Coxon b. Trueman ... | 70 | c. Coxon b. Close ... | 2 |
| K. Grieves c. Hutton b. Wardle ... | 1 | b. Wardle ... | 52 |
| A. Wharton c. Lester b. Wardle ... | 93 | c. Hutton b. Wardle... | 11 |
| N. D. Howard c. Brennan b. Trueman... | 11 | b. Wardle ... ... | 5 |
| J. G. Lomax c. Trueman b. Coxon ... | 27 | c. Wilson b. Close ... | 6 |
| D. Stone not out ... ... ... ... | 9 | b. Wardle ... | 0 |
| R. Tattersall c. Hutton b. Close ... | 2 | c. Lester b. Close ... | 14 |
| A. Barlow lbw. b. Coxon ... ... | 1 | c. Brennan b. Wardle | 5 |
| R. Berry c. Yardley b. Close ... ... | 3 | not out ... ... | 0 |
| B. 1, l.b. 5 ... ... ... ... | 6 | B. 1 ... ... ... | 1 |
| | 257 | | 117 |

## Yorkshire

| | | | |
|---|---|---|---|
| L. Hutton c. Grieves b. Tattersall ... | 39 | c. Ikin b. Tattersall ... | 45 |
| F. A. Lowson b. Grieves ... ... | 49 | b. Berry ... ... | 3 |
| H. Halliday c. Grieves b. Berry ... | 10 | c. Howard b. Tattersall | 9 |
| E. Lester c. Place b. Grieves ... | 16 | c. Grieves b. Tattersall | 2 |
| J. V. Wilson b. Grieves ... ... | 14 | b. Berry ... ... | 9 |
| N. W. D. Yardley not out ... ... | 27 | c. Ikin b. Berry ... | 51 |
| D. B. Close b. Berry ... ... | 22 | run out ... ... | 17 |
| A. Coxon c. Ikin b. Tattersall ... | 6 | b. Tattersall ... ... | 1 |
| J. H. Wardle b. Berry ... ... | 0 | c. and b. Berry ... | 13 |
| D. V. Brennan (did not bat) | | c. Wharton b. Tattersall | 5 |
| F. S. Trueman (did not bat) | | not out ... ... | 0 |
| B. 1, l.b. 8, n.b. 1 ... ... | 10 | B. 5, l.b. 6, w. 1 ... | 12 |
| Eight wkts, dec. | 193 | | 167 |

## Yorkshire Bowling

| | | O. | M. | R. | W. | O. | M. | R. | W. |
|---|---|---|---|---|---|---|---|---|---|
| Trueman | ... | 15 | 4 | 39 | 2 | 4 | 1 | 4 | 0 |
| Coxon | ... | 20 | 8 | 38 | 2 | 2 | 1 | 2 | 0 |
| Wardle | ... | 41 | 17 | 77 | 3 | 21.2 | 9 | 44 | 6 |
| Close | .. | 30.2 | 10 | 66 | 3 | 20 | 4 | 66 | 4 |
| Halliday | ... | 7 | 2 | 15 | 0 | | | | |
| Yardley | ... | 4 | 0 | 16 | 0 | | | | |

Lancashire Bowling

| | | | | | | | | |
|---|---|---|---|---|---|---|---|---|
| Lomax | ... | 7 | 3 | 11 | 0 | | | |
| Stone ... | ... | 4 | 0 | 5 | 0 — | 1. | 0 | 4 | 0 |
| Berry ... | ... | 36.3 | 17 | 50 | 3 — | 22.4 | 8 | 67 | 4 |
| Grieves ... | ... | 18 | 2 | 51 | 3 — | 9 | 2 | 24 | 0 |
| Tattersall | ... | 43 | 15 | 66 | 2 — | 30 | 11 | 60 | 5 |

Umpires: D. Davies and A. Lockett.
Lancashire won by 14 runs.

# F. R. Brown Concludes the Matter

In the last days of July, 1950, English cricket stock was terribly low in the market. The Test team had just suffered two overwhelming defeats at the hands of the West Indies, which was then thought a terrible affront. Ahead lay an M.C.C. tour of Australia for which both N. W. D. Yardley and F. G. Mann had declined the captaincy. Len Hutton, with Denis Compton recovering from a knee operation, was the one high-ranking batsman on the scene – and though he had done great things it happened that much of his best cricket for England (as also Alec Bedser's) lay in the immediate future.

But who was to lead in Australia? Freddy Brown, when the match between the Gentlemen and Players started at Lord's, was probably favourite in a very open field. Yet he was all but 40, had played only four times for England since the age of 23.

Such was the background to an innings which swiftly dispelled all doubts. It gives one quite a thrill at this distance of time to live it over again. Incidentally by 1950 double-column headings were back again, and one was being given a good deal more elbow-room!

GENTLEMEN v PLAYERS, Lord's, 1st day: July 26, 1950
*Score at close:* Gentlemen 325; Players 1 for 0

A memorable innings was played for the Gentlemen this afternoon by F. R. Brown. He made 122 in an hour and three-quarters out of the last 131 runs scored, bringing the Gentlemen's score to 325, an eminently satisfactory reply to Dollery's gesture in sending them in to bat. There was time for three overs of the Players' innings, and they produced one bye.

The Gentlemen's effort was the work of three batsmen of Cambridge origin. Brown, Dewes and Doggart. Dewes played one of his best innings, and Doggart supported him and, later, Brown quite admirably in a secondary part foreign to his normal style. But Brown stole the whole day with a piece of forcing cricket of a quality that enthused everyone, old and young.

The more elderly were reminded of how cricket used to be played and especially how the ball used to be driven before the game's descent, as many would lament, to an age of over-sophistication and a dreary philosophy of safety first.

As to the new post-war generation, their reaction was probably summed up by an intelligent young player, perhaps a little weary of hearing from his seniors of the glorious adventures of the past.

'I have a fair idea now,' he said, 'of how some of the great ones used to play.' And he spoke as a convert who hitherto had been a little uncertain as to how much to believe.

Brown's batting has been matched in this fixture of late only by M. P. Donnelly in 1947 and H. T. Bartlett in 1938. Both of these men also played great and historic innings at Lord's in the amateur tradition, and the significance of what we saw today was that it was the product of a style of play which is essentially that of a cricketer not under the restraints and taboos of one who plays the game for his living.

The first-class system as we know it has been built up by a fusion of two differing and equally valuable approaches to the game; and both must survive if cricket is to keep its character.

I doubt whether Dollery expected much positive help from the wicket when he put his opponents in. He saw three University names at the beginning of the order and perhaps reflected that they are not normally happy against the best spin bowling when the ball is not coming through.

He took a chance, and no one can say it might not have turned out well but for the partnership of Dewes and Doggart, which gave a solid foundation to the innings after Simpson had been caught and bowled pushing out too soon at Bedser's slower ball.

Dewes played in one of the less inhibited of his several styles. He left his crease occasionally to drive the slower bowlers, and when he did so he generally took four for a good strong punch either through the covers or, if he got to the ball on the full, somewhere on the leg side. Once when Wright bowled a no-ball he swung at it without any great effort and the ball comfortably cleared the stand at long on. This was a most impressive hit.

Occasionally, as at Nottingham, he played across the flight of the ball on or round the leg stump, and his calling was often eccentric to a degree.

One projected run to cover-point declined by Doggart would probably have been the end of Dewes, for the batsmen could hardly have crossed. Later he sent back Doggart for a hit that was almost worth two.

But until he pushed forward at Tattersall without any appropriate movement of the feet and gave a soft catch to cover-point he had not often looked in difficulty, and his power of concentration at least never had seemed likely to fail him.

Doggart, on coming in, was at once confronted by Hollies, who has often been his master, but today he played all the slow bowling carefully and, on the whole, convincingly. This must be qualified slightly as regards the leg-stump for he, too, was sometimes guilty of playing towards square-leg instead of mid-on.

People often foolishly are inclined to discount the runs made at Fenner's. But it does seem to have encouraged dangerous habits in this particular direction.

The bowler who gave most bother to Doggart was Shackleton, who, with an action suggesting the in-swing, often seems to move the ball away off the wicket towards the slips, in this case up the hill.

Apart from several balls played at and missed from Shackleton, Doggart batted with a restraint partly induced by the needs of the situation and partly perhaps due to the fact that this game, indirectly and incidentally, is being played for big stakes so far as several individual cricketers are concerned. Doggart's stroke-making is not suspect, but his ability to last through a long defensive innings against the best bowling had not previously been proved.

After the partnership of 140 between Dewes and Doggart had been broken there was a sad slide of wickets until Brown's arrival. Carr was bowled first ball playing back rather than forward to a good, quicker ball from Tattersall, and Insole was caught at the wicket playing forward to a good-length break.

Yardley was run out from cover-point answering his partner's call, presumably by the barest margin and to the surprise of all sitting square with the wicket. Bailey, rather unluckily, was caught beautifully low down by Parkhouse on the leg side from a genuine glance.

There was less than a quarter of an hour to tea when Brown arrived and the ball was new. He had scored 20 by the interval from a succession of drives, which must have suggested to anyone just arrived that he had been batting since lunch. Afterwards he continued to play in the same free, delightful way, hitting powerfully off the back leg when the bowlers dropped short, but always especially looking for the over-pitched one and driving it beautifully with a long, sweeping follow-through.

When Doggart was bowled at last by Wright, and Warr had failed to survive, Brennan remained for 35 minutes while 35 were scored, all by Brown. Knott came in when his captain needed seven for his 100, and survived five balls to the mounting delight of the crowd before Brown took two savage fours to leg off Wright and the deed was done. He then hit five rapid and bewildering fours to bring the performance to a fitting climax.

Considering that county bowlers are not accustomed to being treated in this manner, except, of course, by teams from abroad, they stood up well to the attack today. There was little really inaccurate stuff, Wright being the most dangerous, Hollies the steadiest, according to character, and Tattersall anything but a failure. To complete the picture, the day was sunny and genial and there were 17,000 to see the fun.

### Gentlemen

| | | | | | |
|---|---:|---|---|---|---:|
| R. T. Simpson c. and b. Bedser ... | 10 | — | lbw. b. Hollies | .. | 69 |
| J. G. Dewes c. Washbrook b. Tattersall | 94 | — | b. Tattersall ... | ... | 48 |
| G. H. G. Doggart b. Wright ... | 75 | — | lbw. b. Wright | ... | 36 |
| D. B. Carr b. Tattersall ... | 0 | — | c. Bedser b. Wright | ... | 17 |
| D. J. Insole c. Evans b. Wright ... | 4 | — | not out | ... | 38 |
| N. W. D. Yardley run out ... | 5 | | | | |
| T. E. Bailey c. Parkhouse b. Bedser ... | 5 | | | | |
| F. R. Brown b. Tattersall ... | 122 | — | not out | ... | 22 |
| J. J. Warr b. Wright ... | 2 | | | | |
| D. V. Brennan b. Hollies ... | 0 | | | | |
| C. J. Knott not out ... | 1 | | | | |
| B. 5, l.b. 2 ... | 7 | | B. 1, l.b. 3, n.b. 1 ... | | 5 |
| | 325 | | Four wkts, dec. | | 235 |

## Players

| | | | | | | |
|---|---|---|---|---|---|---|
| H. Gimblett lbw. b. Brown | ... | ... 23 | — | c. Knott b. Bailey | ... | 14 |
| C. Washbrook c. Insole b. Bailey | | ... 0 | — | c. and b. Brown | ... | 43 |
| W. G. A. Parkhouse b. Brown | ... | ... 29 | — | c. Brown b. Knott | ... | 81 |
| D. J. Kenyon lbw. b. Brown | ... | ... 5 | — | c. Brennan b. Bailey | ... | 54 |
| H. E. Dollery c. Brennan b. Doggart | | ... 123 | — | c. Yardley b. Knott | ... | 20 |
| T. G. Evans b. Bailey | ... ... | ... 19 | — | st. Brennan b. Knott... | | 9 |
| D. Shackleton c. Simpson b. Knott | | ... 25 | — | c. Insole b. Knott | ... | 2 |
| A. V. Bedser c. Dewes b. Knott... | | ... 59 | — | b. Bailey | ... ... | 10 |
| R. Tattersall lbw. b. Doggart | ... | ... 12 | — | st. Brennan b. Knott... | | 0 |
| D. V. P. Wright not out ... | ... | ... 6 | — | not out.. | ... ... | 2 |
| W. E. Hollies not out | ... ... | ... 1 | — | not out.. | ... ... | 0 |
| B. 2, l.b. 4 | ... ... ... | ... 6 | | B. 2, l.b. 5 ... | ... | 7 |

Nine wkts, dec. 308          Nine wkts 242

## Players Bowling

| | | O. | M. | R. | W. | | O. | M. | R. | W. |
|---|---|---|---|---|---|---|---|---|---|---|
| Bedser | ... | 23 | 2 | 77 | 2 | — | 12 | 0 | 41 | 0 |
| Shackleton | ... | 18 | 3 | 51 | 0 | — | 13 | 0 | 60 | 0 |
| Tattersall | ... | 16.4 | 6 | 38 | 3 | — | 10 | 0 | 35 | 1 |
| Hollies | ... | 23 | 8 | 49 | 1 | — | 12 | 1 | 43 | 1 |
| Wright | ... | 25 | 4 | 103 | 3 | — | 9 | 0 | 51 | 2 |

## Gentlemen Bowling

| | | O. | M. | R. | W. | | O. | M. | R. | W. |
|---|---|---|---|---|---|---|---|---|---|---|
| Bailey ... | ... | 25 | 6 | 65 | 2 | — | 14 | 2 | 59 | 3 |
| Warr ... | ... | 21 | 5 | 66 | 0 | — | 8 | 1 | 38 | 0 |
| Yardley | ... | 10 | 1 | 23 | 0 | — | 4 | 0 | 13 | 0 |
| Brown | ... | 28 | 3 | 63 | 3 | — | 10 | 0 | 59 | 1 |
| Knott ... | ... | 21 | 2 | 63 | 2 | — | 11 | 0 | 66 | 5 |
| Carr ... | ... | 2 | 0 | 11 | 0 | | | | | |
| Doggart | ... | 4 | 1 | 11 | 2 | | | | | |

Umpires: K. McCanlis and A. Skelding.
Match drawn.

## Ames' Hundredth Hundred

Only one wicket-keeper has made as many as a hundred hundreds – if it comes to that no other has got as many as fifty of them. Les Ames chose the Canterbury week to reach his target, and the match against Middlesex which around that time on that most idyllic ground was apt to show county cricket at its very best.

Apart from this particular distinction it was a supremely good match. It so happened that, as at Southampton and Sheffield in preceding reports, I was on the air at the crucial moment: a great and memorable pleasure.

KENT V MIDDLESEX, Canterbury, final day: August 11, 1950

*Score at start:* Middlesex 249 and 140 for 3; Kent 254 for 6 dec.
*Score at close:* Middlesex 249 and 241 for 3 dec.; Kent 254 for
6 dec. and 239 for 6

Test matches can be tiresome intruders, for today the stories dwarfing all others should truly be those from Birmingham and Hastings, and not least that of a match well won and gallantly lost on the St Lawrence ground here and of a notable feat by a great English cricketer.

Kent, after they had been set by Middlesex to score 237 in two hours and a half, reached their target with three effective wickets and seven minutes to spare and Ames, whose innings was the inspiration of the whole effort, became the twelfth batsman in the game's history to score a hundred hundreds.

It was Clark's declaration as soon as the Middlesex score was passed on Thursday afternoon that invigorated the game to the degree of ensuring a combative last day. Edrich, who has led his side with a sure and easy touch in this match, was not the man to decline a challenge. This morning he himself batted in his best vein. To come into the ground soon after 11 o'clock and hear the sound of bat on ball a couple of times was all the assurance one needed on the matter. In 70 minutes Edrich added 54 to his score. With Brown also pushing along well runs came so quickly that Edrich could declare soon after noon, leaving Kent to make their runs at a rate of 95 an hour to win.

Fagg left at once and Clark very quickly, Warr, after much empty grasping at the ball, picking it up eventually and running him out at the bowler's end with a second run uncompleted.

Before lunch Ames had to do all the scoring himself and so Kent did not progress at anything like the required speed, Edrich finding it expedient to feed them an over of donkey-drops to increase their ardour. The arrival of Pawson coincided with a spate of fours by Ames, now in punishing form. It was a delight to see him cracking away in very much the old style. No one seems to play with a better bat than Ames when he is in full cry. His hundred was rapturously greeted, after which he flung away all care and bombarded the president's tent and that of the Band of Brothers, just to the on-side of the sight screen, with a series of the grandest on-drives.

Pawson, too, flung his bat at anything and everything, and

in the 35 minutes he and Ames were together the score leapt by 85. Mallett helped Pawson when Ames went at last, and so Kent coasted to a victory which had seemed almost a forlorn hope an hour earlier. Thus Ames joins a glorious band.

Since at the age of 21 he played first for Kent in only two matches in 1926, he has reached his milestone after 18 English seasons. In all he has scored 36,371 runs, which gives him an average in the neighbourhood of 44. From his batting yesterday one would imagine, as all Kent will hope, that these figures are due to be considerably augmented before he puts his pads on for the last time.

## Middlesex

| | | | | |
|---|---|---|---|---|
| J. D. Robertson st. Evans b. Wright | 40 | — | b. Dovey | 54 |
| J. G. Dewes c. Evans b. Wright | 60 | — | c. Pawson b. Dovey | 32 |
| W. J. Edrich b. Ridgway | 6 | — | not out | 77 |
| H. P. Sharp b. Dovey | 62 | — | c. Clark b. Wright | 21 |
| S. M. Brown b. Wright | 19 | — | not out | 51 |
| L. H. Compton b. Wright | 7 | | | |
| F. J. Titmus c. Evans b. Ridgway | 9 | | | |
| J. M. Sims c. Fagg b. Ridgway | 13 | | | |
| J. J. Warr b. Wright | 4 | | | |
| J. A. Young b. Dovey | 14 | | | |
| A. E. Moss not out | 7 | | | |
| B. 4, l.b. 4 | 8 | | B. 6 | 6 |
| | 249 | | Three wkts, dec. | 241 |

## Kent

| | | | | |
|---|---|---|---|---|
| A. E. Fagg run out | 88 | — | c. L. Compton b. Warr | 0 |
| D. G. Clark c. L. Compton b. Warr | 6 | — | run out | 3 |
| L. E. G. Ames c. L. Compton b. Warr | 4 | — | c. Moss b. Young | 131 |
| P. Hearn st. L. Compton b. Sims | 17 | — | b. Young | 30 |
| H. A. Pawson not out | 103 | — | b. Warr | 57 |
| T. G. Evans c. Sims b. Warr | 6 | | | |
| A. Woollett c. Young b Warr | 10 | — | not out | 0 |
| A. W. H. Mallett not out | 15 | — | b. Warr | 9 |
| R. R. Dovey (did not bat) | | — | not out | 5 |
| L.b. 4, w. 1 | 5 | | B. 4 | 4 |
| Six wkts, dec. | 254 | | Six wkts | 239 |

D. V. P. Wright and F. Ridgway did not bat.

## Kent Bowling

| | O. | M. | R. | W. | O. | M. | R. | W. |
|---|---|---|---|---|---|---|---|---|
| Ridgway | 31 | 9 | 86 | 3 — | 22 | 8 | 59 | 0 |
| Mallett | 20 | 5 | 58 | 0 — | 27 | 8 | 65 | 0 |

|          | O.   | M. | R. | W. |   | O.  | M. | R. | W. |
|----------|------|----|----|----|---|-----|----|----|----|
| Dovey... | 19.5 | 4  | 36 | 2  | — | 20  | 4  | 64 | 2  |
| Wright   | 30   | 8  | 61 | 5  | — | 11  | 2  | 47 | 1  |

Middlesex Bowling

|        | O. | M. | R. | W. |   | O.  | M. | R. | W. |
|--------|----|----|----|----|---|-----|----|----|----|
| Warr...  | 26 | 8 | 67 | 4 | — | 11  | 1 | 57 | 3 |
| Moss...  | 21 | 4 | 76 | 0 | — | 5   | 2 | 18 | 0 |
| Sims...  | 16 | 2 | 53 | 1 | — | 14  | 1 | 53 | 0 |
| Young... | 14 | 8 | 15 | 0 | — | 19  | 3 | 90 | 2 |
| Titmus...| 11 | 2 | 38 | 0 | — | 0.5 | 0 | 4  | 0 |
| Edrich |    |    |    |    |   | 1   | 0 | 13 | 0 |

Umpires: J. T. Bell and H. Elliott.
Kent won by 4 wickets.

# Cambridge Win on the Post

There have been some exciting draws, but this was much the closest finish to the University Match in my time. The Cambridge second innings took a curious, even at times inexplicable, course. However, Dennis Silk at the final moment of crisis took the bull by the horns while Robin Marlar, his captain (who had bowled so extremely well), was waving what could only be described as a very pale pink cape at the other end. But read on!

OXFORD v CAMBRIDGE, Lord's, final day: July 7, 1953
*Score at start:* Oxford 312 and 101 for 5; Cambridge 191
*Score at close:* Oxford 312 and 116; Cambridge 191 and 238 for 8

Cambridge won the University match here this evening by two wickets at 27 minutes past six, a statement that may picture, to those who have ever watched the matches between Oxford and Cambridge, something of the tenseness and excitements of the scene. The way the result was achieved, however, was something that defied imagination, for in cold truth it defeated all logical analysis.

The facts were these: Cambridge went in at 10 minutes past 12 to score 238 runs to win in 5 hours 20 minutes, a rate of 45 an hour. Despite a fair start, which by luncheon had produced 57 in an hour and 20 minutes for the loss of Bushby's wicket, they scarcely kept pace even with this sluggish tempo, although until after tea wickets fell at irregular intervals.

At tea Cambridge had six wickets in hand and needed to

make 93. An hour later they still needed 66 with only three wickets left, including certainly that of Silk, who had been batting from the beginning.

Silk, as he had from the start, was going with the utmost sedateness, while Crookes, his partner, who batted 35 minutes for five, was making no apparent effort to push the score along. In the first innings while making 25 in three-quarters of an hour Crookes had revealed himself as a somewhat cross-bat hitter. The only inference was that Cambridge by then were not prepared to embark on what had become a pretty sizeable order, and that the limit of their ambition was a draw. The next 23 minutes produced 14 runs in an air of sorry anti-climax.

These thoughts, with all their depressing implications so far as cricket generally is concerned, persisted until suddenly Crookes left his ground to hit Allan and was stumped. By now only some 37 minutes remained, and the last two Cambridge wickets needed to make 52. Marlar's dilatory stroll to the crease, which was received with some ironic hand clapping, seemed only to underline the Cambridge tactics. He walked to the far end to speak to Silk. And one recalled the captain's advice in A. G. Macdonell's immortal cricket match: 'Play carefully, Bobby. Keep your end up. Runs don't matter.' 'Very well, Bill,' replied Mr Southcott sedately, and proceeded to deliver such an assault on the bowling as the village of Fordenden had not seen in many a long year.

Silk did not quite take the bull by the horns in the manner of Mr Southcott, but he began to hit the ball in a way that everyone, I verily believe of whatever persuasion, had been hoping and praying to see for hours past. At Marlar's arrival Silk's score, after more than four and three-quarter hours' batting, stood at 77. A quarter of an hour later we were applauding his 100, having in the meantime seen some admirable straight hitting in the arc between extra cover and mid-on. The fast bowlers, Fasken and McKinna, and the slow left-arm Allan came alike to him, and Silk chose the ball to hit with such discretion that he scarcely made a false stroke.

His running between wickets had never been a strong point, and when at a quarter past six, there being only 10 to make, he took a particularly dangerous single, Marshall's throw from short extra cover hit the bowler's wicket, and he must have been only just home. That, as it turned out, was Oxford's last chance.

Once more the batsmen conferred, and again the scene of Macdonell came to mind. 'You needn't play safe any more, Bob. Play your own game.' A maiden played by Marlar from Allan between 6.20 and 6.22, the score then being 232, roused visions of a further crescendo of drama if anything happened to either batsman.

But at 6.25 Silk late-cut Allan for four down to the Clock Tower boxes (which were by no means the calmest places on the ground), and the scores were level. Off the fourth ball of the over he had to make a last-second dive into his crease when the winning run was projected and turned down, off the fifth the single came and all was over. Thus ended the closest finish to the University match since 1908 when at the climax C. E. Hatfield was the hero for Oxford and the margin was the same as this.

It scarcely needs emphasising that Cambridge should never have got themselves into the position they did. All through the match they had made runs at an inordinately slow pace despite the fact that the field was generally set for all-out attack.

A cold, neutral adjudicator, if such a one could be found, might have decided at the end that justice had been derided. Oxford almost all through had seemed the better as a team, and they held the initiative almost unchallenged until just before six o'clock this evening.

It could fairly be said that Cambridge might have won the game by a more purposeful plan, by half-past five or very soon after. At the same time, whatever may be remarked about the Cambridge tactics, Marlar's bowling was the outstanding piece of cricket in the match, overshadowing perhaps even Cowdrey's fine innings on Saturday. And there must be much praise for the steadfast effort of Silk. We saw little of his true batting qualities until he had been altogether nearly seven hours at the wicket. Then he revealed another nature and a skill one had had little reason to suspect. At a quarter past three he put up a catch to short leg off Jowett, and it went down. That was the only chance he gave, so far as could be detected,

The dust flies as Gary Sobers hits off the back foot during his innings of 161 v England at Old Trafford in 1966. It is an unusual 'live' picture in that no other figure is to be seen.

ABOVE: Bradman at Worcester. The phrase evokes the memory of four opening appearances there: three ended in double hundreds, on this the fourth time in his first innings in England for 10 years he was satisfied with 107. The keeper is Hugo Yarnold. BELOW: End of an innings. The late Sir Frank Worrell comes in from one of his last games in England: at Stanmore in 1964

over the whole of his two innings. It was a notable effort of application.

Cambridge made a quite satisfactory start to their effort to make the 238 needed to win, by putting on 40 for the first wicket. Bushby's method was approved by the older judges, until he tried to force a well-pitched ball square, instead of in the mid-on area, and was bowled.

Lumsden, as in the first innings, seemed intent on hitting the ball, but he misdrove the first ball after luncheon and skied a catch to short-leg, running back. Much rested on Subba Row, to whom Jowett bowled with particular accuracy. He batted an hour and 10 minutes for 28, showing just occasional flashes of his ability, and was then lbw. to a ball that straightened. It is a strange thing how, broadly speaking, the foremost Cambridge batsmen have recently not done themselves full justice against Oxford.

Alexander was well caught by Marshall, diving forward, at backward short-leg from a ball that went with Allan's arm, and Cambridge, at 20 minutes to four were 125-4. By now Silk had survived his chance, and caution was the watchword in the 35 minutes that spanned the time until tea.

Knightley-Smith left soon afterwards, caught at backward short leg, and Hayward, promoted no doubt to hasten matters, became involved in a hopeless muddle of calling and counter-calling and was run out. It would need a court of inquiry finally to fix the blame, but the one certain thing was Cambridge's misfortune. Lewis was most unhappy against the faster bowling, and was caught at square leg, fending off an in-swinger.

There followed the further period of stagnation described, and the final rousing ending. Inevitably, Oxford will have come in wondering what could have been done to stem Silk's belated assault. It may be the captain should have called again on Jowett, who did not bowl at all after the second new ball came at four o'clock. Perhaps at the end the field, which had been crouching close for hours, was a little slow to spread out.

However, regrets there must always be, and in any case Oxford kept them to themselves as they shook Silk by the hand and clapped him right the way into the pavilion.

D

## Oxford

| | | |
|---|---|---|
| H. B. Birrell (St Andrews, South Africa, and Lincoln) c. Alexander b. Hayward | 6 | — b. Hayward ... ... 0 |
| J. C. Marshall (Rugby and Brasenose) c. Alexander b. Marlar ... ... ... | 21 | — c. Alexander b. Dickinson 26 |
| C. C. P. Williams (Westminster and Christ Church) lbw b. Marlar ... | 40 | — c Hayward b Marlar 5 |
| M. C. Cowdrey (Tonbridge and Brasenose) c. Silk b. Marlar ... ... ... | 116 | — c. Alexander b. Marlar 0 |
| A. L. Dowding (St Peter's, Adelaide, and Balliol) lbw. b. Marlar ... ... | 7 | — c. Subba Row b. Marlar 9 |
| J. P. Fellows-Smith (Durban High School and Brasenose) b. Dickinson .. .. | 33 | — c. Alexander b. Marlar 49 |
| J. M. Allan (Edinburgh Academy and Worcester) run out ... ... ... | 2 | — c. Lumsden b. Marlar 7 |
| A. P. Walshe (Milton, Rhodesia, and Wadham) c. Marlar b. Dickinson ... | 29 | — b. Marlar ... ... 2 |
| G. H. McKinna (Manchester G.S. and Brasenose) c. Crookes b. Hayward ... | 0 | — c. Bushby b. Marlar ... 3 |
| D. K. Fasken (Wellington and Trinity) b. Marlar ... ... ... ... | 20 | — c. Lumsden b. Hayward 3 |
| D. C. P. R. Jowett (Sherborne and St John's) not out ... ... ... ... | 6 | — not out ... ... 0 |
| B. 18, l.b. 12, n.b. 2 ... ... ... | 32 | — B. 8, l.b. 2, n.b. 2 ... 12 |
| | 312 | 116 |

## Cambridge

| | | |
|---|---|---|
| M. H. Bushby (Dulwich and Queen's) c. Dowding b. Allan ... ... ... | 10 | — b. Jowett ... ... 21 |
| D. R. W. Silk (Christ's Hospital and Sidney Sussex) c. Fellows-Smith b. Allan | 22 | — not out ... ... 116 |
| V. R. Lumsden (Munro College, Jamaica, and Emmanual) c. Fellows-Smith b. Fasken ... | 16 | — c. Williams b. Fasken 14 |
| R. Subba Row (Whitgift and Trinity Hall) c. Marshall b. Jowett ... ... | 6 | — lbw. b. Jowett ... 28 |
| F. C. M. Alexander (Wolmer's College, Jamaica, and Caius) b. McKinna ... | 31 | — c. Marshall b. Allen ... 7 |
| W. Knightley-Smith (Highgate and St John's) c. Cowdrey b. McKinna ... | 20 | — c. Williams b. Fasken 10 |
| L. K. Lewis (Taunton and Pembroke) b. Jowett ... | 22 | — c. Williams b. McKinna 2 |
| D. V. Crookes (Michaelhouse, South Africa, and Jesus) c. Fasken b. Cowdrey | 25 | — st. Walshe b. Allan ... 5 |
| W. I. D. Hayward (St Peter's, Adelaide, and Jesus) not out ... ... ... | 6 | — run out ... ... 6 |
| D. C. Dickinson (Clifton and Trinity Hall) b. Jowett ... ... ... ... | 0 | |
| R. G. Marlar (Harrow and Magdalene) b. Allan ... ... ... ... ... | 11 | — not out ... ... 9 |
| B. 16, l.b. 3, w. 2, n.b. 1 ... ... | 22 | — B. 19, l.b. 1 ... 20 |
| | 191 | Eight wkts 238 |

## Cambridge Bowling

|  | | O. | M. | R. | W. | | O. | M. | R. | W. |
|---|---|---|---|---|---|---|---|---|---|---|
| Hayward | ... | 34 | 11 | 88 | 2 | — | 22.4 | 10 | 27 | 2 |
| Dickinson | ... | 21.5 | 4 | 58 | 2 | — | 5 | 1 | 10 | 1 |
| Marlar | ... | 37 | 14 | 94 | 5 | — | 25 | 8 | 49 | 7 |
| Lumsden | ... | 3 | 1 | 6 | 0 | | | | | |
| Subba Row | ... | 6 | 0 | 26 | 0 | — | 6 | 3 | 18 | 0 |
| Crookes | ... | 1 | 0 | 8 | 0 | | | | | |

## Oxford Bowling

|  | | O. | M. | R. | W. | | O. | M. | R. | W. |
|---|---|---|---|---|---|---|---|---|---|---|
| McKinna | ... | 17 | 9 | 14 | 2 | — | 20 | 4 | 45 | 1 |
| Fasken | ... | 17 | 7 | 28 | 1 | — | 22 | 5 | 48 | 2 |
| Jowett | ... | 31 | 11 | 57 | 3 | — | 32 | 15 | 50 | 2 |
| Allan ... | ... | 30.3 | 13 | 65 | 3 | — | 33.5 | 12 | 61 | 2 |
| Cowdrey | ... | 2 | 1 | 3 | 1 | | | | | |
| Fellows-Smith | | 2 | 1 | 2 | 0 | — | 1 | 0 | 3 | 0 |
| | | | | Birrell | ... | | 5 | 2 | 11 | 0 |

### FALL OF WICKETS

OXFORD UNIVERSITY – First Innings: 1—18, 2—57, 3—121, 4—150, 5—223, 6—241, 7—254, 8—259, 9—300.

OXFORD UNIVERSITY – Second Innings: 1—5, 2—18, 3—18, 4—29, 5—74, 6—101, 7—110, 8—115, 9—116.

CAMBRIDGE UNIVERSITY – First Innings: 1—19, 2—46, 3—66, 4—66, 5—115, 6—125, 7—167, 8—174, 9—174.

CAMBRIDGE UNIVERSITY – Second Innings: 1—40, 2—57, 3—114, 4—125, 5—155, 6—164, 7—167, 8—186.

Umpires: F. Chester and H. G. Baldwin.

Cambridge won by 2 wickets.

# Win for Harrow

The Eton and Harrow match is only belittled by those who know about it at second hand and/or by adherents to that sadly popular cult, inverted snobbery. For myself, uncommitted, neutral, and with friends equally in both camps, I can only say that the game has afforded me more comedy, perhaps even more pathos, at any rate more uproarious wit and humour than any other in the season. Alas, that nowadays it generally coincides with a Test Match!

This Harrow victory was their third only against Eton since 1908 – an occasion not to be passed over lightly.

ETON V HARROW, Lord's, final day: July 10, 1954
*Score at start:* Eton 168; Harrow 160 for 4
*Score at close:* Eton 168 and 119; Harrow 221 and 69 for 1

The light blue flag of Eton was lowered from the pinnacle of

Lord's pavilion at quarter past five on Saturday evening. It was a premature action inspired by caution and prompted, no doubt, by the memory of the flag that went mysteriously astray two years ago. The lowering was, however, also symbolic, for though the game was still in progress Harrow's second-wicket pair needed only a handful more for the *coup de grâce*.

Presently Miller off-drove the winning hit in the direction of the Nursery, and next moment the field was full of young figures with cornflowers in their buttonholes unleashing their spirits in a mad dash to the pavilion.

Harrow were not an outstanding side, but they held altogether too many guns for Eton, who will no doubt be put on their mettle by the knowledge that Neame, Harrow's captain and virtual match-winner, plus five more including the two left-handers who were not out, Parker and Miller, will be back next year.

Eton were served well by Hill-Wood, who looked a cricketer in all he did, and by Pugh; and Winter, the captain, did a gallant best to rally his forces when Neame's slow spinners were finding yawning gaps in the defences.

Up to a point Eton did every bit as well as their talents allowed; but once again the later batting failed, and failed almost without a flourish. Neame is a subtle off-spinner in pace, though not in quality, about akin to R. G. Marlar. Further, he had a helpful wicket to exploit. But it was a melancholy sight to see him bowling away without ever a man in the cow-country at mid-wicket. Only Winter at the end with a few pull-drives scattered the grazing pigeons. One might as well have been at Southampton, or – well, on recent evidence Old Trafford.

A lot of rain on Friday night restricted Harrow's lead but when Eton batted again the bowler could make the odd ball lift and turn spitefully. On balance probably the weather was a neutral agent.

Harrow, beginning the second morning eight runs behind with six wickets in hand, promptly lost their anchor, Neame, and generally made heavy going of the rest of the innings. Their prospect of a sizeable lead quickly gathered faded when Strang pushed out early and was caught at mid-on. His batting had been the pleasantest to watch in a game in which the rackets players had taken many of the honours: Strang, Bloomfield and Pugh. Among the later batsmen Aldous, chiefly a promising-looking wicketkeeper, played freely.

Eton's reply against a deficit of 53 on a wicket that could not quite be trusted began confidently. Stoddart, a left-hander, stayed long enough to attract favourable notice, and then Pugh and Hill-Wood tided over luncheon, and continued afterwards to bat rationally and with some authority.

By the time these two had put Eton level it began to seem that Harrow had spent too long over their first innings. But in an over and a bit Neame proceeded to win the match. First Pugh was caught behind and then Porter bowled first ball.

The hat-trick ball was a full pitch that Gibson hit gratefully away to the pavilion to escape his pair. In Neame's next over Hill-Wood, as in the first innings, was out playing back to him: 68 for four. That was really that, and Eton's hopes were turned on the weather.

A dean's prayers for rain were requested and when he turned an abstracted look on the petitioner it was assumed he was already in supplication.

The captain thrust away defiantly until he allowed his last partner to jockey him into a fourth run that had been better not attempted, and Harrow were left ages to score a mere 69. That indeed was 14 more than Harrow needed in Fowler's year, and 24 more than they got, but though the situation may have recalled poignant memories to the two eminent Harrovian Cabinet Ministers present who were concerned in that match of all matches, Eton knew they had no Fowler this time.

When Harrow won two years ago the Eton boys were confined to school in quarantine. Now Harrow could savour the triumph more fully. An Etonian attempt on the flag hanging from Harrow's balcony had to be frustrated. Minor skirmishes broke out sporadically for some while, and altogether Lord's has not been so agreeably woken up since the calypso-band celebrated West Indies' victory in the Test match.

The two Harrow cabinet ministers? Sir Walter Monckton, Minister of Labour, and Field-Marshal Lord Alexander of Tunis, Minister of Defence.

## Eton

| | | | | |
|---|---|---|---|---|
| C. T. M. Pugh c. Bloomfield b. Neame | 76 | — | c. Aldous b. Neame ... | 23 |
| D. R. Stoddart b. Davies-Barker ... | 9 | — | c. Aldous b. Davies-Barker ... ... | 17 |
| P. D. Hill-Wood lbw. b. Neame ... ... | 35 | — | b. Neame ... ... | 25 |
| J. M. Porter lbw. b. Bloomfield ... ... | 20 | — | b. Neame ... ... | 0 |
| N. A. J. Winter lbw. b. Neame ... ... | 12 | — | run out ... ... | 37 |
| C. H. Gibson b. Neame ... ... ... | 0 | — | b. Neame ... ... | 6 |
| A. M. Wolfe-Murray b. Bloomfield ... | 5 | — | lbw. b. Neame ... | 5 |
| C. P. de Laszlo lbw. b. Bloomfield ... | 1 | — | c. Massy b. Neame ... | 0 |
| J. A. Wolfe-Murray b. Bloomfield ... | 0 | — | lbw. b. Bloomfield ... | 1 |
| R. V. Craig not out ... ... ... | 1 | — | c. Parker b. Neame ... | 0 |
| Sir G. C. J. Palmer b. Bloomfield ... | 0 | — | not out ... ... | 0 |
| B. 6, l.b. 1, n.b. 2 ... ... ... | 9 | | B. 2, l.b. 1, n.b. 2 ... | 5 |
| | **168** | | | **119** |

## Harrow

| | | | | |
|---|---|---|---|---|
| J. M. Parker c. Hill-Wood b. J. Wolfe-Murray ... ... ... ... ... | 3 | — | not out ... ... | 32 |
| A. R. B. Neame lbw. b. Hill-Wood ... | 49 | — | c. de Laszlo b. J. Wolfe-Murray ... ... | 1 |
| R. S. Miller b. Hill-Wood ... ... | 9 | — | not out ... ... | 30 |
| T. J. E. Lardner c. A. Wolfe-Murray b. Palmer ... ... ... ... ... | 36 | | | |
| G. D. Massy c. A. Wolfe-Murray b. Palmer ... ... ... ... ... | 4 | | | |
| C. A. Strang c. J. Wolfe-Murray b. Winter | 52 | | | |
| W. Aldous c. Pugh b. Palmer ... ... | 23 | | | |
| R. J. L. Sidley c. and b. Winter ... | 18 | | | |
| R. B. Bloomfield c. and b. Hill-Wood ... | 3 | | | |
| N. Davies-Barker b. Winter ... ... | 0 | | | |
| G. W. H. Stevenson not out ... ... | 0 | | | |
| B. 14, l.b. 5, w. 2, n.b. 3 ... ... | 24 | | B. 4, n.b. 2 ... ... | 6 |
| | **221** | | One wkt | **69** |

## Harrow Bowling

| | O. | M. | R. | W. | | O. | M. | R. | W. |
|---|---|---|---|---|---|---|---|---|---|
| Sidley ... ... | 9 | 3 | 8 | 0 | — | 4 | 1 | 12 | 0 |
| Davies-Barker | 14 | 3 | 36 | 1 | — | 9 | 0 | 28 | 1 |
| Bloomfield ... | 11.5 | 2 | 27 | 5 | — | 16 | 5 | 30 | 1 |
| Stevenson ... | 3 | 0 | 24 | 0 | | | | | |
| Parker ... | 8 | 2 | 17 | 0 | — | 6 | 2 | 14 | 0 |
| Neame ... | 20 | 5 | 47 | 4 | — | 13.5 | 6 | 30 | 7 |

## Eton Bowling

| | O. | M. | R. | W. | | O. | M. | R. | W. |
|---|---|---|---|---|---|---|---|---|---|
| Hill-Wood ... | 24 | 7 | 42 | 3 | — | 4 | 2 | 6 | 0 |
| J. Wolfe-Murray | 16 | 4 | 45 | 1 | — | 4 | 0 | 9 | 1 |
| Winter ... | 32 | 9 | 39 | 3 | — | 5.2 | 0 | 15 | 0 |
| Palmer ... | 21 | 5 | 51 | 3 | — | 9 | 1 | 23 | 0 |
| de Laszlo ... | 5 | 1 | 20 | 0 | — | 3 | 1 | 10 | 0 |

FALL OF WICKETS

ETON – First Innings: 1—17, 2—76, 3—117, 4—144, 5—145, 6—166, 7—166, 8—167, 9—168.

ETON – Second Innings: 1—28, 2—61, 3—61, 4—68, 5—74, 6—93, 7—95, 8—102, 9—107.

HARROW – First Innings: 1—3, 2—16, 3—76, 4—84, 5—163, 6—177, 7—200, 8—221, 9—221.

HARROW – Second Innings: 1—2.

Umpires: W. Harrinton and L. D'Arcy.

Harrow won by 9 wickets.

# Dexter's Best

There has been nothing better in post-war cricket – no, nothing – than Ted Dexter at his best. This innings was his warning to Australia in 1962–63 after his ill-starred first appearance there (when called for in mid-tour) four years earlier.

By reason of the class of the bowling, and because the occasion was in the nature of a rehearsal, it can scarcely be ranked with some of his Test hundreds – or with his two great seventies, at Old Trafford in '61 and at Lord's in '63. But I guarantee that no-one who was at Melbourne that day will ever forget this piece of batsmanship.

AN AUSTRALIAN XI v M.C.C., Melbourne, 1st day: November 9, 1962
*Score at close:* M.C.C. 458 for 5

It is just 100 years since a team of English cricketers first stepped on to this Melbourne field and it is safe to say that rarely if ever in the intervening century have their descendants given Australian bowling a worse hammering. Dexter showed the way with the innings of a lifetime and this was the opening act of a drama that reached a climax in the last hour, wherein Knight punished the tired bowling for 57 out of an unbroken partnership with Barrington of 92.

It was all invigorating to a degree and the lift that has been given to the tour by the events of today is prodigious. There were 15,000 present – a good gate for a Friday – and it is now to be expected that everyone will want to see M.C.C. bat, especially, of course, Dexter. After a good many years of watching, relatively few innings stand out sharply in the mind above hundreds of others that become distinct again when one refers to them in books or in coversation.

Before today one has connected four pieces of English batsmanship with this vast and somewhat awesome arena. There were the hundreds by Compton and Hutton on the first appearance here of M.C.C. since the war. There was Simpson's 156 not out that brought England's first post-war Test victory and there was Cowdrey's first Test hundred against Australia made a few days after his 22nd birthday. Dexter's innings today brings the number as far as I am concerned to five. It was in every sense a *tour de force* that had the crowd humming with excitement and the Englishmen basking happily in reflected glory.

Dexter came in when M.C.C., after three-quarters of an hour had reached a rather uncomfortable 26 for one. The authority and power he immediately brought to the scene were remarkable. He began so audaciously in fact that one felt it was all rather too good to last. But last it did and that with the very minimum of false hits. He sliced a four over slips in the 20s and went slightly off the boil as it were in the 90s when Simpson bowled a couple of very good overs of leg-spin to him and both he and Veivers appealed vehemently for lbw.

These small items apart his stroke-play was not only extraordinarily powerful but practically devoid of mistake. He hit 13 fours and two sixes and reached his hundred in 106 minutes. It was one of the fastest seen in recent years in Australia and it was assuredly the hardest hit. Walcott is the name that one thinks of in terms of muzzle velocity, but I never remember seeing the ball travel faster even when there was a pile of runs on the board, let alone at the start of a game with the bowlers theoretically fresh.

Dexter having taken the Australian attack apart, the following M.C.C. batting on a wicket now mild after its fretful first period took full toll. Everyone made runs and made them attractively, though, of course, the innings that mattered most was Cowdrey's. He had at first the ideal role for a batsman out of luck – that of playing second fiddle to one in full command. By the time Dexter left Cowdrey was playing easily and well, and in that vein he continued drawing the short ball at the angles he wanted on the leg-side and thrusting the fuller-pitched ones through the covers with that final persuasion of the wrists that those at home know so well.

He had left his bad form behind him long before he got out, having incidentally batted only two hours 10 minutes for his 88. His falling just short of three figures was, indeed, the only minor disappointment of a wonderfully good day.

The Australian bowling was somewhat thin on paper and it never recovered from Dexter. In particular he murdered Martin, whose first four overs of left-arm wrist spin cost 34, and Veivers, whose first spell of off-breaks was almost as expensive.

By the time Sheppard was out, Dexter was in imperial control. Two straight drives off Veivers, each of which must have carried well over 100 yards into the crowd, were no more remarkable than certain off-drives that neither extra-cover nor mid-off could make a yard to even had they wished, which they certainly didn't.

When Dexter's driving invited a shorter length he punished just as prolifically with cutting and hooking. In this mood he is the most restless fellow, pacing around with a frown if he has allowed three or four balls to go unscored from. He fell at last to a strange flick straight down square-leg's throat, mentally perhaps, if not physically, exhausted.

## M.C.C.

| | | | | |
|---|---|---|---|---|
| G. Pullar c. Harvey b. Misson | 16 | — | b. Misson | 3 |
| Rev. D. S. Sheppard c. Martin b. Guest | 31 | — | c. Misson b. Guest | 1 |
| E. R. Dexter c. Veivers b. Simpson | 102 | — | c. Harvey b. Guest | 4 |
| M. C. Cowdrey lbw. b. Misson | 88 | — | c. Cowper b. Guest | 3 |
| K. F. Barrington not out | 219 | — | c. Misson b. Veivers | 19 |
| F. J. Titmus c. Harvey b. Simpson | 37 | — | not out | 14 |
| B. R. Knight c. Guest b. Simpson | 108 | — | not out | 10 |
| D. A. Allen b. Misson | 11 | | | |
| J. T. Murray not out | 9 | | | |
| B. 2, l.b. 8, w. 2 | 12 | | B. 9, l.b. 2, w. 3 | 14 |

Seven wkts, dec. 633    Five wkts, dec. 68

F. S. Trueman and J. D. F. Larter did not bat.

## Australian XI

| | | | | |
|---|---|---|---|---|
| G. Thomas c. Murray b. Knight | 27 | — | c. Barrington b. Larter | 1 |
| R. B. Simpson b. Trueman | 130 | — | c. Murray b. Larter | 9 |
| R. N. Harvey c. and b. Titmus | 51 | — | c. Murray b. Titmus | 21 |

| | | | | | |
|---|---|---|---|---|---|
| B. Shepherd run out ... ... | ... 114 | — | not out | ... ... | 91 |
| I. McLachlan c. Murray b. Dexter | ... 55 | — | run out | ... ... | 68 |
| F. M. Misson c. Allen b. Titmus | ... 19 | | | | |
| R. Cowper c. Dexter b. Larter | ... 17 | — | not out | ... ... | 0 |
| T. Veivers c. Cowdrey b. Larter | ... 9 | | | | |
| J. Martin c. Titmus b. Trueman | ... 4 | | | | |
| B. N. Jarman not out ... ... | ... 0 | | | | |
| C. Guest c. Murray b. Larter ... | ... 12 | | | | |
| B. 5, l.b. 5, w. 1, n.b. 2 ... | ... 13 | | B. 6, l.b. 4, n.b. 1 ... | | 11 |
| | 451 | | | Four wkts | 201 |

## Australian XI Bowling

| | | O. | M. | R. | W. | | O. | M. | R. | W. |
|---|---|---|---|---|---|---|---|---|---|---|
| Misson | ... | 24 | 3 | 103 | 3 | — | 6 | 2 | 13 | 1 |
| Guest ... | ... | 27 | 1 | 113 | 1 | — | 4 | 0 | 22 | 3 |
| Veivers | ... | 27 | 1 | 146 | 0 | — | 2 | 0 | 19 | 1 |
| Martin | ... | 12 | 0 | 101 | 0 | | | | | |
| Simpson | ... | 33 | 3 | 153 | 3 | | | | | |
| Cowper | ... | 1 | 0 | 1 | 0 | | | | | |
| Harvey | ... | 0.3 | 0 | 4 | 0 | | | | | |

## M.C.C. Bowling

| | | O. | M. | R. | W. | | O. | M. | R. | W. |
|---|---|---|---|---|---|---|---|---|---|---|
| Trueman | ... | 21 | 2 | 90 | 2 | — | 3 | 0 | 16 | 0 |
| Larter ... | ... | 17.3 | 1 | 83 | 3 | — | 3 | 0 | 16 | 2 |
| Knight | ... | 16 | 1 | 70 | 1 | — | 9 | 0 | 45 | 0 |
| Dexter ... | ... | 4 | 1 | 20 | 1 | — | 9 | 0 | 47 | 0 |
| Allen ... | ... | 30 | 3 | 95 | 0 | | | | | |
| Titmus | ... | 26 | 4 | 80 | 2 | — | 8 | 1 | 33 | 1 |
| Pullar | | | | | ... | | 8 | 0 | 33 | 0 |

### FALL OF WICKETS

M.C.C. – First Innings: 1—26, 2—110, 3—183, 4—272, 5—366, 6—575, 7—600.

M.C.C. – Second Innings: 1—10, 2—19, 3—19, 4—28, 5—58.

AUSTRALIAN XI – First Innings: 1—72, 2—172, 3—239, 4—354, 5—377, 6—415, 7—341, 8—436, 9—437.

AUSTRALIAN XI – Second Innings: 1—9, 2—18, 3—61, 4—201.

Umpires: W. Smyth and I. Stuart.

Match drawn.

# Gillette for Yorkshire

In five years the Gillette one-innings sixty-over Knock-out Cup has brought a new zest to the season and, I believe, has attracted back many old faithfuls for whom the championship nowadays is too sticky an affair. The Finals at Lord's on the first Saturday of September are sure sell-outs. This one in 1965 was the third, following wins in the first two years by Sussex. It showed Boycott in a new, almost unbelievable rôle – his innings being one of several lessons to be drawn for cricket generally.

YORKSHIRE V SURREY, Lord's (Gillette Cup Final): September 4, 1965 (One-day match)

Yorkshire's victory at Lord's in the Knock-out Cup could scarcely have been more conclusive: nor could it have been won by more admirable or spectacular batting. Yet more remarkable than anything was the fact that the game could be both begun and ended.

Thanks to the new drains, the field absorbed the solid, relentless rain of Friday quite astonishingly. But for them, those who know the ground best say that cricket would have been doubtful even on Sunday. Also the weather forecast turned out overwhelmingly wrong. Instead of wet and cloudy we had it dry, sunny and warm. So the Gillette Cup of joy was unexpectedly filled for a crowd of 24,000 – or at least for all those who were not of too strong a Surrey persuasion.

For them the chagrin must have been hard to bear as, watching Boycott and Close build with the most brilliant stroke play the partnership which clinched the result, they reflected that it might have been Edrich and Barrington, or Stewart and Smith who were doing something similar for them.

For Surrey won the toss and, as the jargon of the public address system has it, they 'elected' to field. Poor Stewart! He must be rueing his decision sadly enough, and hindsight makes wiseacres of us all.

But if one starts on a wet wicket on a fresh, drying day is it not better every single time to bat before the top becomes damaged? When one cannot start until a quarter past 12 of a bright September morning is it not certain that the side batting first will have vastly the better of the light?

If Surrey had lasted their allotted 60 overs the game must either have dragged on until well past 8 o'clock or extended into Monday. In any case, who would not rather have the runs in the book and set the enemy to chase them? Looked at thus, the victory was won for orthodox convention over modern theory, as also it was in the fact of Yorkshire fielding a balanced attack wherein Illingworth, Wilson and Close played their part whereas Surrey had left their young spin bowlers at home.

In a broader sense the occasion was a victory for *cricket*. Yorkshire won by underlining its traditional virtues in a way that did the heart good. In particular by batting as they did on a pitch which in a championship match would have been peered at and prodded with the deepest suspicion – probably until the innings ended around 6 o'clock for a score of 150 – they made nonsense of the notion that modern 'seam' bowling is fatal to stroke-play.

Boycott was a revelation. His 146, the only Knock-out hundred this summer as well as his own first century of the summer, was the highest score in the Cup's three-year existence. It began with a thorough appraisal of the pitch that lasted a dozen overs. (When Taylor was caught at slip trying to run Sydenham down to third man Yorkshire's score was only 22, Boycott 11).

Boycott thereupon greeted his captain by hitting Arnold for 11 handsome runs on the off side in three balls. From that moment he did not look back, while Close quickly found his touch.

If the chief honours went obviously to Boycott – no adjudicator can have had an easier job than D. J. Insole in naming him the Man of the Match – a considerable share is due to Close, both for the innings he played and for his decision to promote himself three places up the order at the fall of the first wicket. Five overs after he arrived Yorkshire had reached 55. At this point Close offered a nasty catch to Sydenham at long leg off Gibson, the ball going for four. That was one chance, and another behind the wicket, also difficult, came soon after lunch when Close was 32.

These items apart, the batting had all the virtues of cool, calculated, well-executed assault. When, in the 42nd over, with Boycott 93 and Close 70, a dramatic one-handed stop by Smith at cover found both batsmen in mid-pitch, Surrey's plight would have been lessened if anyone could have got to the stumps to take the throw-in. But with 180 for one on the board and 18 overs to go Yorkshire were then almost beyond catching. The second wicket in fact put on 192 in 35 overs, and long before the end of it, what with the vigour of the assault and the presence of a left-hander, Surrey (Storey's bowling excepted) were looking ragged to a degree.

Frankly I had no idea Boycott was such an exemplary front-foot driver, or that he boasted such a wealth of strokes. Perhaps the selectors who dropped him for the last Test can share with the sponsors of the Cup the credit for this agreeable revelation. If in Australia his captain or manager ever has cause to lament Boycott's slowness he has only to whisper in his ear the one word 'Gillette'.

When Close was finely picked up almost on the floor by Edrich at mid-wicket, first Trueman and then Hampshire hit hard and often. Hampshire's 38 in the last seven overs contained some of the strokes of the day.

Surrey's task of maintaining a scoring rate of more than five an over was hopeless from the start, and to this extent an air of inevitability overhung the play after tea.

Edrich and Stewart proceeded to 27 after eight overs, whereupon Trueman in the course of four balls made it sure that a Monday anti-climax would be avoided.

Edrich got one that stopped a bit and pushed a catch to mid-on. Smith was lbw., and a very good one that left him had Barrington caught at the wicket.

Stewart and Tindall, who played better than anyone, added 48, latterly against Illingworth and Wilson whose first six overs, three apiece, yielded only 16 runs.

Then Wilson had Stewart stumped by yards, whereupon Illingworth, like Trueman, had three wickets in an over, those of Storey, Edwards and Gibson.

The wicket was never difficult, but Illingworth got more out of it than anyone all day, as a good off-spinner so often will. One would have liked to see him operating against the top Surrey batsmen when the issue was still open, early in the day.

Yorkshire

| | |
|---|---|
| G. Boycott c. Storey b. Barrington... ... 146 |
| K. Taylor c. Barrington b. Sydenham ... ... 9 |
| D. B. Close c. Edrich b. Gibson... ... ... 79 |
| F. S. Trueman b. Arnold... ... ... ... 24 |
| J. H. Hampshire not out ... ... ... ... 38 |

D. Wilson not out ... ... ... ... 11
B. 3, l.b. 4, n.b. 3 ... ... ... ... 10

Four wkts (after 60 overs) 317

D. E. V. Padgett, P. J. Sharpe, R. Illingworth, R. A. Hutton and J. G. Binks did not bat.

## Surrey

| | | |
|---|---|---:|
| M. J. Stewart st. Binks b. Wilson | ... ... | 33 |
| J. H. Edrich c. Illingworth b. Trueman | ... | 15 |
| W. A. Smith lbw. b. Trueman | ... | 0 |
| K. F. Barrington c. Binks b. Trueman | ... | 0 |
| R. A. E. Tindall c. Wilson b. Close | ... | 57 |
| S. J. Storey lbw. b. Illingworth | ... ... | 1 |
| M. J. Edwards b. Illingworth | ... ... | 0 |
| D. Gibson lbw. b. Illingworth | ... ... | 0 |
| A. Long b. Illingworth | ... ... | 17 |
| G. Arnold not out | ... ... | 3 |
| D. A. D. Sydenham b. Illingworth | ... | 8 |
| B. 4, l.b. 4 | ... ... ... | 8 |
| | | 142 |

## Surrey Bowling

| | | O. | M. | R. | W. |
|---|---|---|---|---|---|
| Arnold | ... ... | 13 | 3 | 51 | 1 |
| Sydenham | ... ... | 13 | 1 | 67 | 1 |
| Gibson | ... ... | 13 | 1 | 66 | 1 |
| Storey .. | ... ... | 13 | 2 | 33 | 0 |
| Tindall | ... ... | 3 | 0 | 36 | 0 |
| Barrington | ... ... | 5 | 0 | 54 | 1 |

## Yorkshire Bowling

| | | O. | M. | R. | W. |
|---|---|---|---|---|---|
| Trueman | ... ... | 9 | 0 | 31 | 3 |
| Hutton | ... ... | 8 | 3 | 17 | 0 |
| Wilson | ... ... | 9 | 0 | 45 | 1 |
| Illingworth | ... ... | 11.4 | 1 | 29 | 5 |
| Close ... | ... ... | 3 | 0 | 12 | 1 |

### FALL OF WICKETS

YORKSHIRE: 1—22, 2—214, 3—248, 4—292.

SURREY: 1—27, 2—27, 3—27, 4—75, 5—76, 6—76, 7—76, 8—130, 9—132.
Umpires: J. S. Buller and C. S. Elliott.
Yorkshire won by 175 runs.

# Roy Marshall in the Groove

Another Gillette game wherein an opening batsman, none other than Roy Marshall, swung the day for his side. The mention of

Barbados at Lord's, by the way, referred to the great stand of 274 for the sixth wicket by Sobers and Holford which had turned the Second Test Match just previously.

HAMPSHIRE v SURREY, Bournemouth (Gillette Cup, third round match): June 22, 1966 (One day match)

Hampshire made their way into the semi-final of the Gillette Cup today for the first time, thanks to an innings of characteristic sparkle by Marshall, whose 85 made the job of Ian Thomson, in adjudicating the Man of the Match, a pure formality. Marshall and Reed had scored 128 for the first wicket in 29 overs when Marshall left, and though his partner soon followed him Hampshire still had half their overs in hand.

The later stages therefore were too foregone to provide much in the way of excitement, but the home crowd (some 4,000 paying around £700) were happy enough to see their side cantering home in the evening sunshine.

Altogether the day, after a drizzly start, was a success in all respects, this being due not least to the true wicket, not devoid of pace, provided here at Dean Park. Give the cricketers that and the rest can surely be left to them. I make no apology for harping again on the old theme.

After Barbados at Lord's, Barbados at Bournemouth: Marshall was in peerless form, driving the faster men, pulling them, and as soon as they dropped short cutting and hooking with time to spare. In other words he is a complete batsman, and in good conditions there is no holding him once he is in flow. He very nearly was not, and what would have happened if Stewart had held on to a diving catch at short mid-wicket off Jefferson in the second over of the innings there is no telling, for Hampshire's regular batting, Marshall apart, does not normally scintillate.

This, by the way, was Marshall's first 50 in the Knock-out Competition which no doubt explains why the side have not done better therein.

Marshall had admirable support from Reed, who in the Surrey innings had much distinguished himself in the field. Reed naturally took the minor part, but as he became set he disclosed a very good off-drive and effective hooking powers. He also hit a pulled six over mid-wicket that would have done credit to Marshall himself.

The Surrey bowlers were unlucky one might say in finding a batsman of such class in such form. They could not subdue him, and one wonders who would have been able to.

There was, however, one admirable and significant performance for Surrey, and that was the off-spin bowling of Pocock. He was presumably the 'spare' bowler, only to be used in extremity, but the fact was that with his spin and flight he caused far more bother than anyone else, and was also infinitely the least expensive.

Pocock has an easy controlled action in which it is not difficult to detect the influence of Jim Laker, and he also fielded well clinging on to a hot chance offered, albeit too late, by the match-winner.

The best innings for Surrey was Edrich's. After a shocking start to the season he is now playing in his most fluent form, and even Marshall's bat when Hampshire went in did not make a more mellow ring. Edrich, like Stewart, fell to Ingleby-Mackenzie, standing up behind the stumps, by the way, to the medium pace. Hampshire's former captain was not infallible but he held the chances and made some leg-side takes with much panache.

At the half-way mark Surrey were 87 for two and by lunch after 36 overs 102 for three. Barrington was in occupation, but he then quickly lost Willett to the steadiness of Gray while Storey, who probably represented Surrey's best prospect of a real windfall was caught with great brilliance by Barnard at slip. Barnard jumped and caught a proper flyer very high left-handed – it was one of the slip catches of the season.

Jefferson used his great reach to drive the fast bowling, a sight for sore eyes, while Barrington accumulated steadily until he lost his off stump making room for a square cut. If the tail had done better Surrey would have given themselves at least a chance of pulling the game round after Marshall left. But as it was they never seemed likely on so good a wicket to have sufficient runs to fight with.

## Surrey

| | |
|---|---|
| M. J. Stewart c. Ingleby-Mackenzie b. Shackleton | 0 |
| J. H. Edrich c. Ingleby-Mackenzie b. Gray ... | 37 |
| W. A. Smith c. Barnard b. Gray ... ... | 33 |
| K. F. Barrington b. White ... ... ... | 46 |
| M. D. Willett b. Gray ... ... ... ... | 1 |
| S. J. Storey c. Barnard b. Cottam ... ... | 10 |
| R. I. Jefferson b. Cottam... ... ... ... | 21 |
| P. I. Pocock not out ... ... ... ... | 7 |
| G. R. J. Roope b. White... ... ... ... | 2 |
| D. J. Taylor b. Cottam ... ... ... ... | 2 |
| G. Arnold b. White ... ... ... ... | 1 |
| B. 6, l.b. 3, n.b. 4 ... ... ... | 13 |
| | 173 |

## Hampshire

| | |
|---|---|
| R. E. Marshall c. Pocock b. Jefferson ... ... | 85 |
| B. L. Reed b. Arnold ... ... ... ... | 46 |
| H. Horton c. Stewart b. Pocock... ... ... | 15 |
| D. A. Livingstone not out ... ... ... | 14 |
| H. M. Barnard not out ... ... ... ... | 2 |
| L.b. 7, n.b. 5 ... ... ... ... ... | 12 |
| Three wkts | 174 |

A. C. D. Ingleby-Mackenzie, P. J. Sainsbury, J. R. Gray, D. Shackleton, D. W. White and R. M. Cottam did not bat.

## Hampshire Bowling

| | O. | M. | R. | W. |
|---|---|---|---|---|
| Shackleton ... ... | 12 | 4 | 22 | 1 |
| White ... ... ... | 10.1 | 1 | 41 | 3 |
| Gray ... ... ... | 12 | 4 | 28 | 3 |
| Cottam ... ... | 11 | 0 | 40 | 3 |
| Sainsbury ... ... | 12 | 3 | 29 | 4 |

## Surrey Bowling

| | O. | M. | R. | W. |
|---|---|---|---|---|
| Arnold ... ... | 12 | 2 | 38 | 1 |
| Jefferson ... ... | 9 | 0 | 43 | 1 |
| Storey... ... ... | 7 | 1 | 36 | 0 |
| Roope ... ... | 5 | 0 | 27 | 0 |
| Pocock ... ... | 10 | 1 | 18 | 1 |

### FALL OF WICKETS

SURREY: 1—0, 2—65, 3—102, 4—110, 5—126, 6—160, 7—162, 8—165, 9—168.
HAMPSHIRE: 1—128, 2—138, 3—166.

Umpires: L. H. Gray and A. E. Alderman.
Hampshire won by 7 wickets.

## Milburn Sparkles

The Saffrons ground, where I played a lot of cricket in the 'thirties, has a special place in my affections. This visit, considering that the first day of the match had been a blank, was made rather more for the sake of old associations than in the expectation of outstanding cricket. However I drew lucky, with an admirable day's play and in particular an innings by Milburn right out of the top drawer which no doubt helped to clinch his place – if it needed clinching – in the M.C.C. team for the West Indies.

Sussex v Northamptonshire, Eastbourne, final day: August 21, 1967
*Score at start:* Sussex 192 for 6 dec.; Northamptonshire 79 for 4
*Score at close:* Sussex 192 for 6 dec. and 180 for 6 dec.; North-
amptonshire 174 for 9 dec. and 201 for 0

Sparkling batsmanship on the usual serene Saffrons wicket, and in particular an innings of peculiar power by Milburn; a hot sun shining on the cricket: all in all, today was a timely antidote to the ugly and the boring things.

Everyone in Sussex is pleased with Parks's attitude to the job in his first year of captaincy, and he found a match here in Prideaux, who also was prepared to enthuse his side with the gusto necessary to compensate for the wet, blank Saturday. It was Prideaux's declaration this morning, 18 runs behind with one wicket in hand, following Parks's yesterday, that made room for the spirited cricket this afternoon. There was no collusion: it was simply that each captain trusted the other to accept the challenges held out.

In the end Parks's declaration setting Northampton to score 85 an hour for two hours and a quarter was made to seem all too generous, and Prideaux and Milburn actually reached their target with 20 minutes to spare. Yet so admirable was the batting that no one begrudged the result, and the biggest third-day crowd that the locals could remember went home more than content.

But Milburn! He began almost sedately, before, having got the measure of the wicket and the bowling, the fours simply flowed. It was one of those innings of which one might say one scarcely had to watch, only to listen. Wilfred Rhodes would have enjoyed it.

Milburn played all the strokes, but his signature, so to speak, is the square hit on the off side, played with the utmost felicity of timing off either foot. Of his 24 fours (to say nothing of a six) most flowed in that direction. Like Denis Compton in his day Milburn is a great teaser of cover-point. His hundred, in 78 minutes, was much the fastest scored this season in the championship, and second only to Majid Jehangir's 61-minute effort at Swansea. Incidentally it was just one minute slower than his 100 before lunch for Western Australia at Adelaide which was reputedly the fastest made in Australia since the war.

In this form, it is hard to think that there is no room for Milburn in the England XI. Today, despite the speed of his scoring, he needed to take no extravagant risks. His weighty strokes fairly scorched the turf.

Prideaux (still not 100 per cent fit after his attack of shingles) naturally gave Milburn his head, and played a perfect second-string innings. His driving, as always, gave most pleasure. It was not the least of the attractions of the batting all day that the best innings were generally founded on an orthodox method. I cannot think, by the way, that there is a better opening partnership on current form than Prideaux and Milburn.

The morning began with some pleasant stroke-play by Crump and Johnson, Keith Andrew's successor as 'keeper; also an effective spell by Michael Buss, who had in all six for 58 in 25 overs. But there is a wry note to add in respect of Buss. Until last month he bowled slow left arm. Now, after the experience of the single-wicket competition, he has quickened to medium and operates the everlasting seam. Ah well! But he is a more promising batsman anyway.

The features of the Sussex second innings were a typically free piece of batting by Parks, and a highly auspicious first championship appearance by Racionzer, a young man of 23 of Polish extraction, born in England, who learned his cricket in, and has played for, Scotland. Racionzer made his 60 in an hour and three-quarters, with the assurance of a practised hand. Watching from behind the bowler, one sees the full blade of the bat from the top of the swing thereafter. He made most of his runs in the arc between mid-off and wide mid-on, and I am only sorry that Milburn's innings must deprive him of a longer notice.

There was a special aptness in the quality of the cricket today, for the players were commemorating, whether they knew it or not, exactly a century of county cricket. It was 100 years ago tomorrow that Kent were the first visitors to this same field, which nowadays sees perhaps more games in a season – something around 170 including schoolboys' – than any other in England.

## Sussex

| | | | | | | |
|---|---|---|---|---|---|---|
| K. G. Suttle lbw. b. Crump | ... | ... | 5 | — | b. Sully ... ... | 31 |
| D. J. Semmence b. Crump | ... | ... | 7 | — | lbw. b. Kettle... ... | 1 |
| A. W. Greig b. Crump | .. | ... | 77 | — | c. Steele b. Kettle ... | 5 |
| M. G. Griffith lbw. b. Mushtaq | ... | ... | 10 | | | |
| J. M. Parks c. Sully b. Mushtaq | ... | ... | 49 | — | not out ... ... | 65 |
| M. A. Buss st. Johnson b. Mushtaq | ... | 3 | — | b. Kettle ... ... | 2 |
| T. B. Racionzer not out ... | ... | ... | 16 | — | c. and b. Kettle ... | 60 |
| G. C. Cooper not out ... | ... | ... | 16 | — | c. Johnson b. Kettle ... | 4 |
| A. Buss (did not bat) | | | | — | not out ... ... | 1 |
| B. 3, l.b. 3, n.b. 3 | ... | ... | 9 | | B. 6, l.b. 4, n.b. 1 ... | 11 |

Six wkts, dec. 192　　　　　　　　Six wkts, dec. 180

E. Lewis and D. L. Bates did not bat.

## Northamptonshire

| | | | | | |
|---|---|---|---|---|---|
| C. Milburn lbw. b. M. A. Buss ... | ... | 36 | — | not out ... ... | 141 |
| R. M. Prideaux lbw. b. M. A. Buss | ... | 25 | — | not out ... ... | 51 |
| D. S. Steele c. Greig b. Lewis | ... | 7 | | | |
| Mushtaq Mohammed b. M. A. Buss | ... | 11 | | | |
| A. Lightfoot b. M. A. Buss | ... | ... | 26 | | | |
| B. Crump c. Greig b. A. Buss | ... | ... | 34 | | | |
| M. E. Scott b. M. A. Buss | ... | ... | 8 | | | |
| M. K. Kettle b. M. A. Buss | ... | ... | 0 | | | |
| L. A. Johnson not out ... | ... | ... | 19 | | | |
| H. Sully b. A. Buss | ... | ... | 0 | | | |
| A. J. Durose not out | ... | ... | 6 | | | |
| L.b. 2 ... ... | ... | ... | 2 | | B. 1, l.b. 7, n.b. 1 .. | 9 |

Nine wkts, dec. 174　　　　　　　　No wkt 201

## Northamptonshire Bowling

| | | | | | | | | | |
|---|---|---|---|---|---|---|---|---|---|
| Crump | ... | 14 | 4 | 24 | 3 | | | | |
| Durose | ... | 11 | 2 | 38 | 0 | — | 13 | 2 | 34 | 0 |
| Mushtaq | ... | 17 | 4 | 63 | 3 | — | 10 | 1 | 27 | 0 |
| Sully ... | ... | 10 | 2 | 36 | 0 | — | 7 | 0 | 29 | 1 |
| Kettle ... | ... | 6 | 1 | 22 | 0 | — | 15 | 2 | 58 | 5 |
| | | Steele... | | ... | | 6 | 0 | 21 | 0 |

## Sussex Bowling

| | O | M | R | W | | O | M | R | W |
|---|---|---|---|---|---|---|---|---|---|
| A. Buss ... | 10 | 1 | 36 | 2 | — | 14 | 1 | 50 | 0 |
| Bates ... | 7 | 0 | 34 | 0 | — | 8 | 1 | 45 | 0 |
| M. A. Buss ... | 25 | 11 | 58 | 6 | — | 2 | 0 | 19 | 0 |
| Lewis ... | 16 | 4 | 44 | 1 | — | 3 | 0 | 17 | 0 |
| Suttle... | | | | | ... | 5.4 | 0 | 28 | 0 |
| Greig | | | | | ... | 6 | 0 | 30 | 0 |
| Cooper | | | | | ... | 2 | 0 | 3 | 0 |

### FALL OF WICKETS

SUSSEX – First Innings: 1—12, 2—15, 3—48, 4—154, 5—156, 6—167.
SUSSEX – Second Innings: 1—12, 2—26, 3—55, 4—159, 5—166, 6—171.
NORTHAMPTONSHIRE – First Innings: 1—60, 2—61, 3—79, 5—131, 6—143, 7—143, 8—161, 9—161.

Umpires: J. F. Crapp and F. Jakeman.
Northamptonshire won by 10 wickets.

# CHAPTER THREE

# A FEW CALAMITIES

Sad days, these – but from a certain angle. It has been said in relation to golf that there are few strokes which don't give pleasure to someone. By this token most of the days' play that follow must have afforded satisfaction to England's opponents. To that extent I must plead guilty to a no doubt deplorable insular prejudice. Yet several of them point cricket morals, and in any case if this book is to be in any sense representative of the post-war scene one cannot pretend that all has been sunshine and light. So let us get these worst calamities over quickly – or, if you like, skip them and pass on to the next chapter.

## A Brisbane "Sticky"

Calamitous is the only word to describe this fourth day of the first post-war Test between England and Australia. The Australian first innings had been concluded on the third morning for the highest score ever made by either side in Australia. After England had then made 21 for the loss of Hutton's wicket in reply, the first of two cataclysmic thunderstorms obliterated play for the day.

Astonishing to relate, cricket was possible on time next morning; whereupon the England batsmen gave an object-lesson in batting in horrible conditions, until an even more violent storm again cut short the day. On the fifth and last day, the Australian bowling was rather better, and England subsided into inevitable defeat. I suppose that if the boot had been on the other leg, England would probably have bowled out their opponents twice for something under 70 a time. A more sombre reflexion is that, if English claims for a catch against Bradman had been upheld, making Australia 74 for three instead of 322, the chances were that it would have been the enemy who would have been batting on the 'stickies', or at any rate one of them.

A profitless reflexion, of course, but in view of subsequent history it is permissible surely to stress that in this crucial first encounter the luck did not run kindly for England.

AUSTRALIA V ENGLAND, Brisbane, 4th day: December 3, 1946
*Score at start:* Australia 645; England 21 for 1
*Score at close:* Australia 645; England 117 for 5

The history of Test cricket is well furnished with occasions of high drama, and, perhaps if one had seen Jessop's innings at the Oval in 1902 or the last-wicket stand between Barnes and Fielder that drew victory out of the very jaws of defeat at Melbourne a few years later, one would write down today's play at Brisbane merely as one of the more interesting and significant of one's experience. But, right on top of the events, it seems to be one that will linger in the mind when the result of this rubber demands a moment's computation to recall.

Contrary to all reports and predictions, play began at noon. The parched field within a few hours absorbed more moisture than even Old Trafford can readily digest in a fortnight. With a scorching sun playing on the drying turf England batted for two hours 50 minutes on a pitch that was at first next to unplayable and ended just plainly unpleasant, and they lost precisely four wickets.

That is the plain story, and no censure of the Australians' bowling or of Bradman's strategy can withhold from Edrich and Compton, Hammond and Yardley the highest praise for this achievement.

One knew before the match that a wet wicket would confer on England a considerable technical advantage, but hardly that batsman and bowler would then be seen in the perspective of master and pupil. Until tea the duel went on, whereafter, following thunderous warnings, occurred a storm more mighty and violent than I have beheld ever before.

Thousands of hailstones, the size of golf balls, bounced upon the field and hurled themselves against the iron roof of the stand under which we huddled, our eyes blinded by lightning and our ears deafened by claps like the crack of doom. We saw the white-fenced oval swiftly assume the properties of a lake. The lake did preserve some little green island, and as a patriot one intensely resented any islands. Never, surely, had water fallen so solidly!

They say there will be no cricket tomorrow, but after today's experience I accept local pronouncements with reserve, including that of our Australian neighbour who, at the tempest's height, cupped his hands and bellowed, 'We *often* get it worse than this!' Now, indeed, it seems as though England may have several fewer than 10 hours' batting ahead in order to earn their draw and some moderate Australians are already persuading themselves that they would be happier if the luck of the weather did not, in these circumstances, give them victory.

Australia's bowling on this terrible wicket, Miller excepted, was inadequate and unintelligent. Bradman gave the first over of the day to Toshack, who theoretically should have assumed the role of an Ironmonger. But Toshack, though tried three times, could neither bowl the ball straight nor pitch it up, whether bowling over or round the wicket.

Conceive a slow bowler even considering bowling over the wicket in such a case! Putting on Toshack was equivalent to giving the batsmen a mental, almost a physical, siesta.

Miller did aim to hit the bat and realised that a four or two did not matter an iota. He began by scoring four hits on Edrich's body and one to Washbrook's head in his first over. Thereafter he decreased his pace – I hope in order to make it more difficult to leave the ball alone rather than from any qualms about hitting the batsmen, all of whom accepted their stripes willingly.

Lindwall found it difficult to avoid sending the ball high above all danger and Bradman is to be criticised for not quickly seeing what use Johnson could make of the pitch. It is generally good policy in such cases to try out all your bowling and see who responds best to the needs of the moment. Johnson, bowling his off-spinners, would at least have aimed at the stumps and thrown the ball well up. As it was, he had no over all day.

McCool had one, and a very short, bad one it was. Tribe bowled some dangerous balls in the afternoon if no really testing overs. Someone to push the ball along a little more quickly was needed.

Washbrook lasted 20 minutes this morning before failing

quite to get over the ball in a forward stroke. Edrich from the
start had shown an instinctive appreciation of how the bowling
must be played. He took his bat out of the path of everything
that was going over or to the side of the stumps.

The model innings was that of Compton who, during 40
minutes, played every ball he aimed at plumb in the middle of
the bat and, further, carried the game to the enemy by going
out of his ground and jostling the bowlers out of their length.

Hammond is an old hand at this sort of game and with the
pitch improving he looked as though he could have survived a
much more testing proposition. From the second ball after
lunch Edrich was caught at slip, and Ikin snicked the third to
the keeper standing back and to leg.

Hammond will go down in history as one of the classic
players on bad wickets. I remember an innings at Horsham
when he made 100 before lunch while the rest of Gloucestershire were got out for one's and two's. His innings was that of
an indulgent instructor surrounded by a not very gifted class.

Yardley's reputation is in the making and it was, therefore,
heartening to observe the skill and restraint with which he
batted during the sixth-wicket stand. If the Australians could
have got one more wicket England might have been quickly
dismissed. But of this there never seemed any real fear, and
when the captain and his deputy finally came in in the darkness
preceding the storm the honour and glory were England's
indisputably. The drill for play on wet wickets is not included
in the Australians' manual of instruction.


Australia

| | | | |
|---|---|---|---|
| S. G. Barnes c. Bedser b. Wright | ... | ... | 31 |
| A. Morris c. Hammond b. Bedser | ... | ... | 2 |
| D. G. Bradman b. Edrich ... | ... | ... | 187 |
| A. L. Hassett c. Yardley b. Bedser | ... | ... | 128 |
| K. R. Miller lbw. b. Wright ... | ... | ... | 79 |
| C. McCool lbw. b. Wright ... | ... | ... | 95 |
| I. W. Johnson lbw. b. Wright ... | ... | ... | 47 |
| D. Tallon lbw. b. Edrich ... | ... | ... | 14 |
| R. Lindwall c. Voce b. Wright ... | ... | ... | 31 |
| G. Tribe c. Gibb b. Edrich ... | ... | ... | 1 |
| E. Toshack not out ... | ... | ... | 1 |
| B. 5, l.b. 11, w. 2, n.b. 11 ... | ... | ... | 29 |

645

## England

| | | | | |
|---|---|---|---|---|
| L. Hutton b. Miller | ... | ... | ... | 7 |
| C. Washbrook c. Barnes b. Miller | | ... | | 6 |
| W. J. Edrich c. McCool b. Miller | | ... | | 16 |
| D. Compton lbw. b. Miller | | ... | ... | 17 |
| W. R. Hammond lbw. b. Toshack | | | ... | 32 |
| J. T. Ikin c. Tallon b. Miller | ... | ... | | 0 |
| N. W. D. Yardley c. Tallon b. Toshack | | ... | | 29 |
| P. A. Gibb b. Miller | ... | ... | ... | 13 |
| W. Voce not out | ... | ... | ... | 1 |
| A. V. Bedser lbw. b. Miller | | ... | ... | 0 |
| D. V. P. Wright c. Tallon b. Toshack | | ... | | 4 |
| B. 8, l.b. 3, w. 2, n.b. 3 | | ... | ... | 16 |

| | | | |
|---|---|---|---|
| c. Barnes b. Miller | ... | | 0 |
| c. Barnes b. Miller | | ... | 13 |
| lbw. b. Toshack | | ... | 7 |
| c. Barnes b. Toshack | | ... | 15 |
| b. Toshack | ... | ... | 23 |
| b. Tribe | ... | ... | 32 |
| c. Hassett b. Toshack | | | 0 |
| lbw. b. Toshack | | ... | 11 |
| c. Hassett b. Tribe | | ... | 18 |
| c. and b. Toshack | | ... | 18 |
| not out | ... | ... | 10 |
| B. 15, l.b. 7, w. 1, n.b. 2 | ... | ... | 25 |

141                  172

## England Bowling

| | O. | M. | R. | W. |
|---|---|---|---|---|
| Voce | 28 | 9 | 92 | 0 |
| Bedser | 41 | 4 | 159 | 2 |
| Wright | 43.6 | 4 | 167 | 5 |
| Edrich | 25 | 2 | 107 | 3 |
| Yardley | 13 | 1 | 47 | 0 |
| Ikin | 2 | 0 | 24 | 0 |
| Compton | 6 | 0 | 20 | 0 |

## Australia Bowling

| | O. | M. | R. | W. | O. | M. | R. | W. |
|---|---|---|---|---|---|---|---|---|
| Lindwall | 12 | 4 | 23 | 0 | | | | |
| Miller | 22 | 4 | 60 | 7 | 11 | 3 | 17 | 2 |
| Toshack | 16.5 | 11 | 17 | 3 | 20.7 | 2 | 82 | 6 |
| McCool | 1 | 0 | 5 | 0 | | | | |
| Tribe | 9 | 2 | 19 | 0 | 12 | 2 | 48 | 2 |
| Barnes | 1 | 0 | 1 | 0 | | | | |

### FALL OF WICKETS

AUSTRALIA – First Innings: 1—9, 2—46, 3—322, 4—428, 5—465, 6—596, 7—599, 8—629, 9—643, 10—645.

ENGLAND – First Innings: 1—10, 2—25, 3—49, 4—56, 5—56, 6—121, 7—134, 8—136, 9—136, 10—141.

ENGLAND – Second Innings: 1—0, 2—13, 3—33, 4—62, 5—65, 6—65, 7—112, 8—114, 9—143, 10—172.

Umpires: J. D. Scott and G. Borwick.
Australia won by an innings and 332 runs.

# Most Crushing Day

No discredit maybe at Brisbane '46 but Leeds '48 is a different and

more melancholy story, told relatively briefly here since 1948 was
a year of thin newspapers. Until this final day England had held
their own remarkably well against this formidable Australian side.
When on the fifth morning Australia went in, following Yardley's
declaration, to make 404 to win on a dusty, wearing pitch all the
odds were on England winning this Fourth Test and so giving themselves a chance of squaring the rubber at the Oval.

Morris and Bradman were in palpable difficulties in the early
part of their second-wicket stand, each giving chances before they
decided to hit their way out of trouble. The England effort dis-
integrated under their assault, in all respects. Five chances at least
were unaccepted, four off Compton, whose left-arm wrist-spin was
ideally suited to the wicket. To see the moral balance shifting, over
by over, in the light of these mistakes, made one of the saddest day's
watching in my experience. It was a wonderful coup on the part
of Morris and Bradman; but one spectator at least could not bring
himself to appreciate it!

ENGLAND v AUSTRALIA, Headingley, final day: July 27, 1948
*Score at start:* England 496 and 362 for 8; Australia 458
*Score at close:* England 496 and 365 for 8 dec.; Australia 458
and 404 for 3

At a quarter past six this evening Harvey hit Cranston past
mid-on for four, and Australia had won the fourth Test by
seven wickets, and brought the score in this rubber to three
victories to none with one game drawn.

Just five hours earlier Compton had been in the middle of a
dangerous spell of bowling from the Kirkstall end of the ground.
He had caught and bowled Hassett brilliantly, picking up the
ball very low with his left hand when following up half-way
down the pitch. Now he lured Morris out of his ground and
Evans might have made a stumping, but the ball came
awkwardly to the keeper.

Changed over to the other end, Compton beat Bradman,
who snicked to first slip a chest-high catch which Crapp,
perhaps the safest short fieldsman in English cricket, put down.
Bradman had then made 22. We deplored these chances
missed, but felt that they were ominously indicative from the
Australian point of view. The heavy motor roller which
Yardley, following Bradman's example yesterday, to quote no
earlier precedents, had ordered first thing, had dusted the

pitch, even if it had not crumbled it. Spin plus length would surely do the trick this afternoon.

The addition of Hutton to the attack at the other end to Compton was a dampener at this time, both on the general principle that it betrayed our limitations as regards spin and because Hutton pushed up five innocent, amiable full pitches in his first two overs, from which Bradman and Morris flicked five fours with lazy strokes over this glassy outfield. This interlude, received with a pointed silence by the Yorkshire crowd, proved to be the portent rather than the other.

As the afternoon wore on Morris and Bradman took an ever firmer grip of the situation as regards both the opposition and the ratio between runs and minutes. The English bowling declined in length, and the English effort in the field both in management and physical accuracy, to say nothing of apparent zeal. Hard chances were offered and put to grass. At half-past five Morris hit Yardley hard and low to Pollard at mid-off, and Australia's second wicket fell for 358, after the stand had made 301. Soon after six Miller was leg before, and so it was the youngest member of the team who joined the oldest to complete the business.

The Australian victory, when it came, was greeted quietly by the crowd, not because they were unappreciative of the splendid batsmanship of Morris and Bradman, but for sheer sickening disappointment and because Yorkshiremen, even more than most, despise long-hops and full pitches.

But no emphasis on English short-comings must dim the recognition of a remarkable Australian victory. For the first time since the first of all Tests at Melbourne in 1877 a team had won against a declaration, and in doing so they had scored, for three wickets, only seven runs fewer than any team had ever scored in the fourth innings.

A century by Bradman in a Test generally means an Australian victory, and the corollary of this is just as true. Thus it must be registered that this was his 19th against England, and that when his score reached 145 he had scored a little matter of 5,000 against us in Tests. In his four Tests at Leeds he has made four hundreds, 334, 304, 103 and 173 not out. Many other statistical milestones were doubtless passed. Certainly the crowd of 158,000 in all was a record for any match in England, and the aggregate of runs (1,723) easily exceeded the 1,610 which the two teams made in the glorious match at Lord's in 1930.

Morris's innings gives another lift to a reputation which has soared amazingly since it seemed even doubtful whether he might make the team for the first Test at Nottingham less than two months ago. Technically, he is wonderfully sound, with a supreme watchfulness and a knack of playing every stroke when beautifully balanced. But with great batsmen, and Morris now deserves to be ranked in that small, illustrious army, a temperament is even more than technique, and here Morris's steadfastness and concentration present a strong wall to the enemy.

Bradman, like Morris, had his lucky moments. After his chance to Crapp, Yardley missed him at cover off Cranston when 59, a brute of a low catch but the sort that decide Tests one way or the other. A nasty chance of stumping off Laker seemed from the stand to occur soon after, while when he wanted eight for his 100 only his abnormally swift reaction to danger saved him from playing on to Pollard.

It was sad indeed, after England's noble effort on the first day and again especially on the fourth, that things went so badly at the finish. Pollard and Bedser were unsuited by the pitch which cried aloud for a Verity or a Wright. The fast bowlers kept steady, while Compton, though that adjective can never be applied to a left-arm googly bowler, bowled dangerously enough to give England a winning chance if the ball had run differently.

Yardley under-bowled himself, and I felt his tactics should have been to partner Compton with length and an always defensive field at the opposite end. But there it is, regrets we must have, but, after all, it was indeed a grand match, and all honour to Australia.

### England

| | | | |
|---|---|---|---|
| L. Hutton b. Lindwall ... ... ... | 81 | — c. Bradman b. Johnson | 57 |
| C. Washbrook c. Lindwall b. Johnston ... | 143 | — c. Harvey b. Johnston | 65 |
| W. J. Edrich c. Morris b. Johnson ... | 111 | — lbw. b. Lindwall ... | 54 |
| A. V. Bedser c. and b. Johnson ... ... | 79 | — c. Hassett b. Miller ... | 17 |
| D. C. S. Compton c. Saggers b. Lindwall | 23 | — c. Miller b. Johnston... | 66 |

| | | | | | | |
|---|---|---|---|---|---|---|
| J. F. Crapp b. Toshack ... ... ... | 5 | — | b. Lindwall ... ... | 18 |
| N. W. D. Yardley b. Miller ... | 25 | — | c. Harvey b. Johnston | 7 |
| K. Cranston b. Loxton ... ... | 10 | — | c. Saggers b. Johnston | 0 |
| T. G. Evans c. Hassett b. Loxton | 3 | — | not out ... ... | 47 |
| J. C. Laker c. Saggers b. Loxton | 4 | — | not out ... ... | 15 |
| R. Pollard not out ... ... ... | 0 | | | |
| B. 2, l.b. 8, w. 1, n.b. 1 ... ... | 12 | | B. 4, l.b. 12, n.b. 3 | 19 |

496

Eight wkts, dec. 365

## Australia

| | | | | | | |
|---|---|---|---|---|---|---|
| A. R. Morris c. Cranston b. Bedser | 6 | — | c. Pollard b. Yardley... | 182 |
| A. L. Hassett c. Crapp b. Pollard | 13 | — | c. and b. Compton ... | 17 |
| D. G. Bradman b. Pollard ... | 33 | — | not out ... ... | 173 |
| K. R. Miller c. Edrich b. Yardley | 58 | — | lbw. b. Cranston ... | 12 |
| R. N. Harvey b. Laker ... ... | 112 | — | not out ... ... | 4 |
| S. J. Loxton b. Yardley ... ... | 93 | | | |
| I. W. Johnson c. Cranston b. Laker | 10 | | | |
| R. R. Lindwall c. Crapp b. Bedser | 77 | | | |
| R. A. Saggers st. Evans b. Laker | 5 | | | |
| W. A. Johnston c. Edrich b. Bedser | 13 | | | |
| E. R. H. Toshack not out ... ... | 12 | | | |
| B. 9, l.b. 14, n.b. 3 ... ... | 26 | | B. 6, l.b. 9, n.b. 1 .. | 16 |

458

Three wkts 404

## Australia Bowling

| | O. | M. | R. | W. | | O. | M. | R. | W. |
|---|---|---|---|---|---|---|---|---|---|
| Lindwall ... | 38 | 10 | 79 | 2 | — | 26 | 6 | 84 | 2 |
| Miller .. ... | 17.1 | 2 | 43 | 1 | — | 21 | 5 | 53 | 1 |
| Johnston ... | 38 | 13 | 86 | 1 | — | 29 | 5 | 95 | 4 |
| Toshack ... | 35 | 6 | 112 | 1 | — | | | | |
| Loxton ... | 26 | 4 | 55 | 3 | — | 10 | 2 | 29 | 0 |
| Johnson ... | 33 | 9 | 89 | 2 | — | 21 | 2 | 85 | 1 |
| Morris.. ... | 5 | 0 | 20 | 0 | | | | | |

## England Bowling

| | O. | M. | R. | W. | | O. | M. | R. | W. |
|---|---|---|---|---|---|---|---|---|---|
| Bedser.. ... | 31.2 | 4 | 92 | 3 | — | 21 | 2 | 56 | 0 |
| Pollard ... | 38 | 6 | 100 | 2 | — | 22 | 6 | 55 | 0 |
| Cranston ... | 14 | 1 | 51 | 0 | — | 7.1 | 0 | 28 | 1 |
| Edrich.. ... | 3 | 0 | 19 | 0 | | | | | |
| Laker .. ... | 30 | 8 | 113 | 3 | — | 32 | 11 | 93 | 0 |
| Yardley ... | 17 | 6 | 38 | 2 | — | 13 | 1 | 44 | 1 |
| Compton ... | 3 | 0 | 15 | 0 | — | 15 | 3 | 82 | 1 |
| | | | | | Hutton .. | 4 | 1 | 30 | 0 |

### FALL OF WICKETS

ENGLAND – First Innings: 1—168, 2—268, 3—423, 4—426, 5—447, 6—473, 7—486, 8—490, 9—496.

ENGLAND – Second Innings: 1—129, 2—129, 3—232, 4—260, 5—277, 6—278, 7—293, 8—330.

AUSTRALIA – First Innings: 1—13, 2—65, 3—68, 4—189, 5—294, 6—329, 7—344, 8—355, 9—403.
AUSTRALIA – Second Innings: 1—57, 2—358, 3—396.
Umpires: F. Chester and H. G. Baldwin.
Australia won by 7 wickets.

# England Plumb the Depths

Not much to add to this sombre tale, behind which was a philosophy, such as I never heard expressed by responsible cricketers before or since, of *wearing down* spin bowling. What was worn down was the patience of all – spectators, critics, and ultimately in some cases the batsmen themselves.

England had allowed themselves to be confined to their creases in the First Test and had lost it handsomely. The same happened here. The extraordinary thing was that after two such shattering rebuffs Hutton and his side recovered sufficiently to square the rubber.

It would be untrue to say that the over-riding reason was a sharp change in batting policy. The break-throughs were initially made by the bowlers, by Statham at Georgetown, Bailey at Kingston. But while Hutton in each case contributed a monumental innings the rest of the batting followed a more fluent natural course.

WEST INDIES v ENGLAND, Bridgetown, 3rd day: February 9, 1954
*Score at start:* West Indies 383; England 53 for 2
*Score at close:* West Indies 383; England 181 for 9

England finished the third day of the second Test here 202 runs behind with their last pair together. The performance can only be described as the weakest by an English side in many Test matches – at least since West Indies enjoyed their triumphs in England four years ago. In a full day's play of five hours only 128 runs were scored.

All one can say is that unless there is a radical change in heart as well as in method over these next three days West Indies will have virtually clinched the rubber. They will certainly have deserved to do so, for their cricket has been infinitely better in every respect.

One can but have sympathy for Hutton, whose side have lost form in the most mysterious way. Today he batted away for four hours and a half, a mere shadow of his best self, apparently seeing only one way of coping with a situation that pressed more heavily with every maiden over bowled.

I wrote yesterday that the crux of the match and therefore of the series must come today, with the success or otherwise of the English batsmen against Ramadhin and Valentine. Well, the engagement has been fought, and, as at Kingston in the first innings, it has been won conclusively by the bowlers.

Indeed, today's failure was in a sense more complete and significant than the former one. On that occasion England's batsmen just had a bad day and got out. This time they stayed in, almost interminably and got precious few more runs.

West Indians will excuse my analysing the matter from the English angle. It is not in belittlement of their splendid pair of bowlers, Ramadhin and Valentine. Their excellence in this innings is brought home by the score-sheet. But against batting of a different temper they might on such a wicket have bowled no less well for a vastly different return.

A between-the-wars cricketer of high achievement and, it may be added, a singularly punishing manner of play, has summed up the present-day English approach to spin bowling with an apt parody of Ranjitsinhji's famous dictum. Referring to my recent remarks about the almost universal tendency to play slow bowling from within the crease, he writes: 'The Jam Sahib said, "See the ball, go there, and hit it!" The modern English players say "See the ball, stay there, and sit on it." '

This is a cruel comment but it absolutely hits the bull's eye. One has been writing to this effect to the weariment of all since a sad afternoon at Sydney in '46 when McCool and Ian Johnson threw the ball ever higher and higher against our foremost batsmen on a wicket as good as today's and in a bowling spell after the Ramadhin-Valentine order won the first post-war rubber for Australia.

The morning's play was at once the grimmest, the tensest and the slowest imaginable. It lasted an hour and a half and in that time England made 27 for the loss of Compton's wicket. He had made eight more in 35 minutes, Graveney in just under the hour made four, and Hutton increased his score from 34 to 48.

At lunch the two slow bowlers had these figures: Ramadhin,

Lord's: England v India in 1967. As seen from the top storey of the new flats on the corner of St John's Wood Road and Grove End Road

27-17-25-2; Valentine, 27-16-17-1. They had settled right away into their length of last evening; they had above all bowled to their field and that field, cleverly set by Stollmeyer, acquitted itself extremely well.

Before the start of this series critics over here all thought that England would show up West Indies in fielding. So far the evidence is contrary. They may have fielded indifferently against India last year, but to the moment of writing they have looked agile and full of anticipation and that has been at least a subsidiary cause of the slow scoring.

At the lunch score of 80, Stollmeyer called for the new ball that had been due 20 minutes before. When, incidentally, has the new ball been claimable at 77?

The general noise now dissolved into an occasional chant of, 'We want our money back,' and 'We want cricket.' The situation was no less embarassing to an English watcher in that he must have had considerable sympathy for those who protested. When the first concerted barracking occurred England had batted four hours in all for 97, the day's cricket had lasted two hours 20 minutes for 44 and three boundaries had been hit.

But soon now the crowd had other excitements to divert their attention. Ramadhin against these anchored English batsmen is throwing an occasional ball very high indeed. May yesterday had two such, the second fatal. One of these to Graveney was a full-pitch and Graveney, who might have hit it anywhere, stepped back in an attempt apparently to play a flat-bat stroke over mid-on and merely lobbed it back to the bowler. It was the sort of stroke that completed what Graveney, I imagine, will look back upon as a regular nightmare of an innings. For just over two hours he had struggled away without really making a single well-timed stroke.

When Palmer faced Ramadhin he found himself hedged round by most of the West Indies team within a few yards of the bat. The situation demanded a good deal of him. He was playing in his first Test match and he had merely one first-class innings on the tour a month ago.

His first ball beat him and hit the pads outside the off-stump, his second he cover-drove for four with just about the best stroke of the innings.

Colin Cowdrey: while making 78 in the semi-final of the Gillette Cup against Sussex at Canterbury, July 1967. (Kent went on to win the final).

PHOTOGRAPH: PATRICK EAGER

But it was at this juncture that something in Hutton's mind seemed to snap. He could not have felt with No. 6 at the wicket that the time had come to go for everything, yet that is what he suddenly did. He pulled Valentine for four, then two balls later careered out and hit him, high over extra cover, for four more.

He seemed to decide to hit the next before it was out of the bowler's hand and lofted it high over mid-on. At first it looked that he might be lucky but Ramadhin at mid-on had moved deeper and Hutton's hit was plumb into the wind. The ball was blown back as Ramadhin ran towards it and finally he held a very difficult catch. Thus ended Hutton's innings of four and a half hours, during all of which he seemed quite overborne by the responsibility on his shoulders.

The tail subsided, playing much the same sort of cricket as those that came earlier. Gomez and Atkinson took over now from Ramadhin and Valentine who had bowled 100 overs between them. Evans did make one cheering drive over Gomez's head for four. But in the next over he hooked over a straight one and was bowled.

Bailey, who had played stubbornly as usual and without much apparent discomfort from his fractured finger, was caught at the wicket. Laker pushed a half-volley to short-leg and when No. 11 came in it was still a matter of whether the third innings might have to be begun tonight.

Stollmeyer did not seem in a hurry to capture the last wicket, preferring perhaps to have the evening to decide the same problem as he had been confronted with in the first Test, whether to make England follow on. It was a situation that before the series started he could hardly have visualised in his wildest dreams.

## West Indies

| | | | | |
|---|---|---|---|---|
| J. K. Holt c. Graveney b. Bailey | ... 11 | — | c. and b. Statham | ... 166 |
| J. B. Stollmeyer run out ... ... | ... 0 | — | run out ... ... | ... 28 |
| F. M. Worrell b. Statham ... | ... 0 | — | not out ... ... | ... 76 |
| C. L. Walcott st. Evans b. Laker | ... 220 | — | not out ... ... | ... 17 |
| B. Pairaudeau c. Hutton b. Laker | ... 71 | | | |
| G. E. Gomez lbw. b. Statham ... | ... 7 | | | |
| D. Atkinson c. Evans b. Laker ... | ... 53 | | | |
| C. McWatt lbw. b. Lock ... | ... 11 | | | |
| S. Ramadhin b. Statham ... | ... 1 | | | |

F. King b. Laker ... ... ... ... 5
A. L. Valentine not out ... ... ... 0
 L.b. 2, n.b. 2 ... ... ... ... 4    B. 4, n.b. 1 ... ... 5

          383     Two wkts, dec. 292

## England

| | | |
|---|---|---|
| L. Hutton c. Ramadhin b. Valentine ... 72 | — | c. Worrell b. Ramadhin 77 |
| W. Watson st. McWatt b. Ramadhin ... 6 | — | c. McWatt b. King ... 0 |
| P. B. H. May c. King b. Ramadhin ... 7 | — | c. Walcott b. Gomez... 62 |
| D. C. S. Compton c. King b. Valentine... 13 | — | lbw. b. Stollmeyer ... 93 |
| T. W. Graveney c. and b. Ramadhin ... 15 | — | not out ... ... 64 |
| C. H. Palmer c. Walcott b. Ramadhin ... 22 | — | c. Gomez b. Atkinson 0 |
| T. E. Bailey c. McWatt b. Atkinson ... 28 | — | c. sub b. Stollmeyer ... 4 |
| T. G. Evans b. Gomez ... ... 10 | — | b. Ramadhin ... 5 |
| J. C. Laker c. Gomez b. Atkinson ... 1 | — | lbw. b. Ramadhin ... 0 |
| G. A. R. Lock not out ... ... 0 | — | b. King ... ... 0 |
| J. B. Statham c. Holt b. Valentine ... 3 | — | b. Gomez ... ... 0 |
|  B. 2, l.b. 1, n.b. 1 ... ... ... 4 | | B. 5, l.b. 2, w. 1 ... 8 |

          181          313

## England Bowling

| | O. | M. | R. | W. | | O. | M. | R. | W. |
|---|---|---|---|---|---|---|---|---|---|
| Statham | 27 | 6 | 90 | 3 | — | 15 | 1 | 49 | 1 |
| Bailey | 22 | 6 | 63 | 1 | — | 12 | 1 | 48 | 0 |
| Lock | 41 | 9 | 116 | 1 | — | 33 | 7 | 100 | 0 |
| Laker | 30.1 | 6 | 81 | 4 | — | 30 | 13 | 62 | 0 |
| Compton | 5 | 0 | 29 | 0 | — | 1 | 0 | 13 | 0 |
| Palmer | | | | | .. | 5 | 1 | 15 | 0 |

## West Indies Bowling

| | O. | M. | R. | W. | | O. | M. | R. | W. |
|---|---|---|---|---|---|---|---|---|---|
| King | 14 | 6 | 28 | 0 | — | 18 | 6 | 56 | 2 |
| Gomez | 13 | 8 | 10 | 1 | — | 13.4 | 3 | 28 | 2 |
| Worrell | 9 | 2 | 21 | 0 | — | 1 | 0 | 10 | 0 |
| Atkinson | 9 | 7 | 5 | 2 | — | 23 | 23 | 35 | 1 |
| Ramadhin | 53 | 30 | 50 | 4 | — | 37 | 17 | 71 | 3 |
| Valentine | 51.5 | 30 | 61 | 3 | — | 39 | 18 | 87 | 0 |
| Stollmeyer | 1 | 0 | 2 | 0 | — | 6 | 1 | 14 | 2 |
| Walcott | | | | | .. | 2 | 0 | 4 | 0 |

### FALL OF WICKETS

WEST INDIES – First Innings: 1—11, 2—11, 3—25, 4—190, 5—226, 6—319, 7—352, 8—372, 9—378.

WEST INDIES – Second Innings: 1—51, 2—273.

ENGLAND – First Innings: 1—35, 2—45, 3—70, 4—107, 5—119, 6—158, 7—176, 8—176, 9—177.

ENGLAND – Second Innings: 1—1, 2—108, 3—181, 4—258, 5—259, 6—264, 7—281, 8—281, 9—300.

Umpires: H. Walcott and C. Jordan.

West Indies won by 181 runs.

# The Ultimate in Boredom

The cricket after lunch on the first day of the Third Test was the dullest of a singularly dull series. England, as events proved, paid dearly for their failure to build on to their successful batting of the morning. They let a favourable situation slip in an inexplicable way, allowing South Africa to fight back so strongly that on the last day they had a definite chance of victory.

The key to the cricket from the English viewpoint apparently was that they were two up in the rubber, and therefore put first priority on *not losing*. However this philosophy, if such it was, repaid them ill, since in the Fourth Test England were narrowly beaten, while in the Fifth, on a very poor wicket at Port Elizabeth, winning the toss almost meant winning the match – and England lost it.

Thus the series was halved after all, the decline in English fortunes stemming clearly from the change in batting tactics after lunch on this first day at Durban. What an obvious moral the story holds!

SOUTH AFRICA v ENGLAND, Durban, 1st day: January 25, 1957
*Score at close:* England 184 for 4

If ever a joyful, sunny morning gave way to toil and gloom, this first day of the third Test has seen that sad transformation here at Kingsmead. That states the matter from an English angle obviously, since from 103 for none at lunch the score had crawled to 184 for four when bad light brought the end of play twenty-five minutes early. It also states the matter pretty well, I think, as the South African spectators saw it, and the significant thing was that the crowd was a mere eight thousand odd. There had been half as many again for the Friday of M.C.C.'s first match against Natal.

The inference is obvious. The spectator always has one privilege, if no other, the privilege of staying away if he thinks the cricket unworthy of his attention. Thus, perhaps, he may have the final say in putting an end to this ultra-defensive cricket, which, nine times out of ten, is furthermore bad cricket.

There were extenuating things which in some degree accounted for the extraordinary contrast in the scoring rate before lunch and after. The fall of wickets at the other end put an added onus on Bailey, though it may well be argued that the strokes whereby both Compton and Cowdrey lost their wickets might not have been made if their partner, then well set, had been making better headway. In the last three-quarters of an hour, too, the light was as murky as the play was dull. Last but not least, South Africa made a staunch recovery once the first-wicket partnership was ended, and their cricket gained both in determination and accuracy.

The balance may be made, of course, according to taste. If the strokes are not forthcoming any bowler worth his salt will bowl well. Today the man who exploited the changed situation to the utmost advantage was Tayfield, who, when he was at length rested after a bowl of some two and a half hours, had just completed his fourteenth consecutive maiden.

What can be said of Bailey's innings? In its first part it fulfilled requirements admirably. Two and a half hours for 50 is slow, but with runs coming well at the other end perhaps not inordinately so. A full three hours for a further 21 on a good wicket and with the men at the other end out of touch has no justification technically and precious little morally, unless it be thought that for the prize of 'safety' in the rubber no price is too high. Possibly, but not certainly, today's batting may prove the cornerstone of the culminating victory in the series. If that is so the price has still to be considered – the alienation of the cricket public here.

It is possible that Bailey was playing to particularly stringent orders to keep up his wicket absolutely regardless of runs. I have not been able to ascertain that at the moment of writing, but if it is so I will report the fact on Monday. For the present I can only say I have never known an English professional, let alone an amateur (if that old-fashioned word has any relevance nowadays) so apparently cynical towards the idea that cricket is a game to be enjoyed, both by those who play and those who watch. Bailey at Lord's, staying in all day to save a Test against Australia, is admirable. Bailey at Durban exploiting a favourable situation with England on top . . . well!

Bailey did a little driving, for ones and twos, but Richardson chiefly held the eye with various deflections and some nice off-side hits off the back foot. The only irritations from the English standpoint were several good runs declined by Bailey on his partner's call. There was more than a hint that he was calling to keep the strike. As the slower partner, and other things being equal, he should, if anything, be anxious to concede it. However, Richardson, despite moments when his recently broken finger seemed to be irking him, continued to go well. He had his 50 in one hundred minutes out of 83 and at lunch had made 62 to Bailey's 36.

Compton was in good fettle, but inclined to find the fielders. Bailey, instead of accelerating, went more slowly. Thus, as the afternoon wore on, the morning's credit balance, so to speak, gradually whittled away. The bowlers, of course, had no small say in this. The fast bowlers' direction improved, Goddard was as tight as usual, while Tayfield, on changing to the river end, started bowling maidens. The breeze had shifted so that he was now flighting more or less into it, as he did at the Cape. From now onwards Tayfield controlled the play.

It was from this point that South Africa's fortunes changed for the better. The score was 148. It was the same when, at the other end, Compton moved too far across to glance Heine and was bowled behind his legs. Heine always girds his loins at the sight of May, and his first ball, a fast one and shortish, all but got through, May nicking it off the inside edge past the off-stump to leg-slip. Ten minutes later May, pushing out at the ball Tayfield tends to make go with his arm, edged it on to Waite's pads, whence Goddard, at slip, threw himself forward and just reached the ball one-handed.

There are many parallels of famous players having a low run of scores in Tests: the names of Compton and Hammond come quickly to mind. What we did not know at the time was the present cost to the spectators in terms of enjoyment; Cowdrey from first to last, was out of touch. A spell in bed and the loss of eight pounds in weight are not the best prelude to a Test match, especially one played in this humidity and heat. When a dozen runs had come in an hour, of which he had scored six, Cowdrey, losing patience, swung a wild sort of hook and was lbw.

Insole, in worsening light, struggled away, while Bailey, at the sound of a few mild jeers and claps, leant on his bat until the noise subsided. Heine, in desperation, bowled a slow leg-break which pitched half-way and was also a no-ball. This Bailey hooked for four, his second scoring stroke only in more than an hour. Van Ryneveld tested Insole to the hilt with two overs of leg-breaks; and then mercifully the umpires called it a day.

## England

| | | | | |
|---|---|---|---|---|
| P. E. Richardson lbw. b. Adcock | ... 68 | — | b. van Ryneveld ... | 32 |
| T. E. Bailey c. Keith b. Adcock ... | ... 80 | — | c. van Ryneveld b. Tayfield .. ... | 18 |
| D. C. S. Compton b. Heine ... | ... 16 | — | c. Keith b. Tayfield ... | 19 |
| P. B. H. May c. Goddard b. Tayfield ... | 2 | — | lbw. b. Tayfield ... | 2 |
| M. C. Cowdrey lbw. b. Goddard | ... 6 | — | lbw. b. Heine ... | 24 |
| D. J. Insole b. van Ryneveld ... | ... 13 | — | not out ... ... | 110 |
| T. G. Evans st. Waite b. van Ryneveld... | 0 | — | c. Waite b. Tayfield ... | 10 |
| J. H. Wardle b. Heine ... ... | ... 13 | — | c. Waite b. Tayfield ... | 8 |
| J. C. Laker not out ... ... | ... 0 | — | c. Goddard b. Tayfield | 6 |
| P. J. Loader c. Waite b. Adcock | ... 1 | — | lbw. b. Tayfield ... | 3 |
| J. B. Statham b. Adcock ... ... | ... 6 | — | c. van Ryneveld b. Tayfield ... ... | 9 |
| B. 2, l.b. 4, w. 5, n.b. 2 ... | ... 13 | | B. 8, l.b. 4, n.b. 1 ... | 13 |
| | **218** | | | **254** |

## South Africa

| | | | | |
|---|---|---|---|---|
| A. Pithey st. Evans b. Wardle ... | ... 25 | — | b. Statham ... ... | 0 |
| T. L. Goddard lbw. b. Statham ... | ... 69 | — | c. Cowdrey b. Wardle | 18 |
| H. J. Keith c. Evans b. Loader ... | ... 6 | — | c. sub b. Laker ... | 22 |
| W. R. Endean c. sub b. Wardle | ... 5 | — | c. and b. Laker ... | 26 |
| R. A. McLean c. Insole b. Bailey | ... 100 | — | b. Wardle ... ... | 4 |
| K. J. Funston b. Wardle ... ... | ... 19 | — | b. Loader ... ... | 44 |
| J. H. B. Waite b. Statham ... | ... 12 | — | not out ... ... | 1 |
| C. B. van Ryneveld c. Cowdrey b. Loader | 16 | — | not out ... ... | 14 |
| H. Tayfield not out ... ... | ... 20 | | | |
| P. S. Heine b. Wardle ... ... | ... 6 | | | |
| N. A. T. Adcock lbw. b. Wardle | ... 3 | | | |
| L.b. 2 ... ... ... ... | ... 2 | | B. 5, l.b. 6, n.b. 2 .. | 13 |
| | **283** | | Six wkts | **113** |

## South Africa Bowling

| | O. | M. | R. | W. | | O. | M. | R. | W. |
|---|---|---|---|---|---|---|---|---|---|
| Heine ... ... | 16 | 2 | 65 | 2 | — | 22 | 3 | 58 | 1 |
| Adcock ... | 15.3 | 3 | 39 | 4 | — | 21 | 7 | 39 | 0 |
| Goddard ... | 25 | 11 | 42 | 1 | — | 13 | 5 | 26 | 0 |
| Tayfield ... | 24 | 17 | 21 | 1 | — | 37.7 | 14 | 69 | 8 |
| van Ryneveld... | 14 | 4 | 38 | 2 | — | 14 | 2 | 49 | 1 |

## England Bowling

| | O. | M. | R. | W. | | O. | M. | R. | W. |
|---|---|---|---|---|---|---|---|---|---|
| Statham ... | 22 | 4 | 56 | 2 | — | 11 | 0 | 32 | 1 |
| Loader ... | 25 | 6 | 79 | 2 | — | 8 | 2 | 21 | 1 |
| Bailey ... ... | 17 | 3 | 38 | 1 | | | | | |

| | | | | | | | | | | |
|---|---|---|---|---|---|---|---|---|---|---|
| Wardle | ... | 20.2 | 6 | 61 | 5 | — | 20 | 7 | 42 | 2 |
| Laker ... | ... | 12 | 1 | 47 | 0 | — | 18 | 7 | 29 | 2 |
| | | | | Compton | ... | 1 | | 0 | 5 | 0 |

## FALL OF WICKETS

ENGLAND – First Innings: 1—115, 2—148, 3—151, 4—163, 5—186, 6—186, 7—202, 8—210, 9—212.

ENGLAND – Second Innings: 1—45, 2—77, 3—79, 4—144, 5—167, 6—192, 7—203, 8—220, 9—230.

SOUTH AFRICA – First Innings: 1—65, 2—76, 3—81, 4—145, 5—199, 6—225, 7—241, 8—264, 9—279.

SOUTH AFRICA – Second Innings: 1—0, 2—39, 3—45, 4—49, 5—124, 6—124.

Umpires: W. Marais and B. V. Malan.

Match drawn.

# Sterility Unlimited

In the last episode Trevor Bailey was the anti-hero, as alas! he is here. (Admirers are advised to omit what follows, turning back if they like to the story of his defence in an infinitely better cause on page 35).

This was a period of English Test history when the ancient axioms were thought to be outmoded, and several of the foremost players followed misguided theoretical notions. Not least among them was the idea that on one wicket after another the ball didn't 'come on to the bat'. In this instance O'Neill in his first Test Match exploded any such theory the following day in a match-winning innings of 71 not out made in less than two hours. In the press-box at any rate the ranks of Tuscany cheered every bit as loudly as the rest.

The series thus inauspiciously launched from the English point of view went from bad to worse. With four defeats in five Tests it was the most disappointing since 1920–21.

AUSTRALIA v ENGLAND, Brisbane, 4th day: December 9, 1958
*Score at start:* England 134 and 92 for 2; Australia 186
*Score at close:* England 134 and 198; Australia 186

Yesterday 122 in the day, today 106. Last evening one reported the slowest day's cricket in the history of England v Australia, or indeed of any Test where England have been concerned. Today's was slower by 16 runs.

At the end of it all Australia are left with 147 to make to win on a wicket which is still playing true. Laker and Lock certainly are apt to extract more from any wicket than anyone else in the later stages of a match. It scarcely needs saying that Australia will be made to fight terribly hard to win the match.

I dare say that to cricketers and followers of the game equally it scarcely needs stressing that the question is whether victory, if it should come, is worth the cost in terms of sterile boring play that made one sick at heart to watch. Let me try to imagine the feelings behind the mystification at home and answer a few of the questions which I suppose are being asked.

In the first place, were the Australian bowling and general tactics unduly defensive? Answer: No.

Benaud and Davidson were the chief bowlers. Indeed they shouldered almost the entire attack. As for Benaud, no leg-spin bowler, by the nature of his craft, can be a negative agent; quite the reverse.

Davidson certainly bowled a good many balls rather wider of the off-stump than he can have intended. But if they are only a little short of a length what better does a batsman want if his eye is in!

Was the wicket unduly sluggish so that the ball did not come up to the driving part of the bat? Again: No. The pace and bounce of the wicket seemed regular and comfortable.

Was the outfield unusually slow and difficult to pierce? quite the contrary.

If things were as you say how was it that over the time he was at the wicket the men at the other end did not score so very much more quickly than Bailey? The facts here are these: Bailey batted for seven hours 38 minutes and while he made 68, the rest of the England team scored 92.

On the face of it these figures argue something towards the merit of Bailey's innings. In this respect I can only say that practically every good batsman will want to be in with someone who is playing his fair part in subduing the opposition attack by making strokes and scoring runs.

To be saddled with a completely defensive player, who, if one takes a single off an early ball of an over will, as like as not, play out the remainder of it without scoring is a burden that in normal circumstances makes the job half as hard again. Further, in such a situation the run-getting settles into a sticky groove which is terribly hard to get out of. The bowlers have got on top and it is extremely difficult to wrest back the initiative.

Did the tactical situation justify England occupying the wicket for the longest possible time? Again I do not think so. Run-scoring was in England's interest much more than time. The extra wear in the wicket implied in batting eight and a half hours for 198 is a negligible factor compared with the extra runs that might have been expected to accrue by normal methods.

Finally, even if the conduct of the England innings could be justified on tactical grounds what was its effect on the spectators, and how is it likely to affect the public reception of the subsequent Tests at Melbourne, Sydney and Adelaide? There were rather fewer than 9,000 spectators today as against 14,000 yesterday and on every hand one heard derogatory remarks about the cricket. The public are gravely disappointed with it here and I believe they would have shown their dissatisfaction more pointedly in the more sophisticated arenas of Sydney and Melbourne.

It may be said to be outside the functions of the critic to express his personal hopes and fears. His job, I dare say, is to convey the fullest possible picture and leave it to his readers to form conclusions.

However, I will take the risk of censure from people far away, who, other things being equal, are naturally and properly anxious to see England win, and say I think it would be much better for the game of cricket if England were to be beaten than to succeed at the expense of the spectators on whose support and goodwill the game ultimately depends. I will only add to this that this is the 135th Test match that I have described and that I have never before held similar feeling so far as an England victory was concerned.

The bare facts of the morning's play were these. After four runs had been scored against Benaud and Davidson in 25 minutes Graveney pushed gently into the covers and called Bailey for a run.

Bailey started and then when Graveney was some six or seven yards down the wicket stopped and said No. Graveney did his best to get back, but Harvey, who was sauntering in slowly in acceptance of the run, accelerated when he saw the confusion and flicked the ball in too quickly for him. If he had gone one's impression was he would have got in comfortably. In any case the first axiom for the non-caller is that if he is going to refuse he must do so loudly and at once.

May came in to face Benaud and was promptly beaten and survived a piercing appeal for lbw. In Benaud's next over May on-drove him beautifully for 4 wide of mid-on. Then he went forward with the front leg and made no stroke with the bat, as though he had read the leg-break. It looked to be either the googly or top-spinner and this time May did not get the benefit of the doubt. So departed England's captain and leading batsman and Cowdrey appeared with nearly an hour to go before lunch.

The same pair of bowlers carried on until ten minutes before the interval, when Kline relieved Davidson. At lunch England were 111 for four. Cowdrey was 4 not out and in the 90 minutes of the morning Bailey had made 8. There had been 21 eight-ball overs and from these came 19 runs.

Bailey went to 48 – his first scoring stroke for three-quarters of an hour – with a single to square-leg from an intended off-drive. This got Cowdrey to the fast bowling end from which he was dismissed.

Cowdrey's end was one of those unsatisfactory affairs wherein some element of doubt seemed to be registered by both fielders and batsmen. Kline, at backward short-leg, some 12 yards distant and at an angle of 45 degrees, elongated himself forward and scooped the ball, almost, if not quite, off the floor.

Cowdrey hesitated and then walked out when he saw the signal from umpire McInnes at the bowler's end. Benaud ran up from mid-on and apparently inquired of the fielder and square-leg umpire as to the legitimacy of the catch and umpire Hoy finally walked across and spoke to his colleague.

The official explanation, ascertained during the tea interval, was that McInnes had not given Cowdrey out in the first place until he had had a sign and a nod from Hoy, who was, of course, not only closer but in a perfect position to make a decision. If he had had any doubt McInnes should have left the decision to his partner. However, according to him, Hoy was merely confirming the opinion he had formed himself. So the malign afternoon pursued its interminable course.

Bailey, at Lock's dismissal, was in the fifties. When he had made exactly 50 he had a clear escape from a run-out. Harvey, whose brilliant fielding along with O'Neill's, did something to supply the crowd with action, threw in like a bullet to the top of the stumps and the ball went clean through Grout's gloves with Bailey far from home.

The final denouement was spiced with a cynical flavour that a dramatist could hardly have contrived. At ten minutes past five Benaud, for the first time today, brought on Mackay, the super 'shut-up' bowler, who would allow no runs before the close.

Yesterday, it will be recalled, he had bowled six maidens out of seven overs. Bailey, however, seeing his natural opposite in action, suddenly threw all caution to the winds and, advancing towards him at the gallop, swung wildly and was bowled. There could, of course, have been no more ironical climax.

## England

| | | | |
|---|---|---|---|
| P. E. Richardson c. Mackay b. Davidson | 11 | — c. and b. Benaud ... | 8 |
| C. A. Milton b. Meckiff ... ... ... | 5 | — c. Grout b. Davidson | 17 |
| T. W. Graveney c. Grout b. Davidson ... | 19 | — run out ... ... | 36 |
| P. B. H. May c. Grout b. Meckiff ... | 26 | — lbw. b. Benaud ... | 4 |
| M. C. Cowdrey c. Kline b. Meckiff ... | 13 | — c. Kline b. Meckiff ... | 28 |
| T. E. Bailey st. Grout b. Benaud ... | 27 | — b. Mackay ... ... | 68 |
| T. G. Evans c. Burge b. Davidson ... | 4 | — lbw. b. Davidson ... | 4 |
| G. A. R. Lock c. Davidson b. Benaud ... | 5 | — b. Meckiff ... ... | 1 |
| J. C. Laker c. Burke b. Benaud ... ... | 13 | — b. Benaud ... ... | 15 |
| J. B. Statham c. Grout b. Mackay ... | 2 | — c. McDonald b. Benaud | 3 |
| P. J. Loader not out ... ... ... | 6 | — not out ... ... | 0 |
| L.b. 1, n.b. 1, w. 1 ... ... ... | 3 | B. 10, l.b. 4 ... | 14 |
| | 134 | | 198 |

## Australia

| | | | |
|---|---|---|---|
| C. C. McDonald c. Graveney b. Bailey... | 42 | — c. Statham b. Laker ... | 15 |
| J. W. Burke c. Evans b. Loader ... ... | 20 | — not out ... ... | 28 |
| R. N. Harvey lbw. b. Loader ... ... | 14 | — c. Milton b. Lock ... | 23 |
| N. C. O'Neill c. Graveney b. Bailey ... | 34 | — not out ... ... | 71 |
| P. J. Burge c. Cowdrey b. Bailey ... | 2 | | |
| K. D. Mackay c. Evans b. Laker ... | 16 | | |
| R. Benaud lbw. b. Loader ... | 16 | | |
| A. K. Davidson lbw. b. Laker ... ... | 25 | | |
| A. T. W. Grout b. Statham ... ... | 2 | | |
| I. Meckiff b. Loader ... ... ... | 5 | | |
| L. Kline not out ... ... ... | 4 | | |

B. 4, l.b. 1, n.b. 1 ... ... ... 6        B. 2, l.b. 3, n.b. 5 .. 10

186                                    Two wkts 147

## Australia Bowling

| | | O. | M. | R. | W. | | O. | M. | R. | W. |
|---|---|---|---|---|---|---|---|---|---|---|
| Davidson | ... | 16 | 4 | 36 | 3 | — | 28 | 12 | 30 | 2 |
| Meckiff | ... | 17 | 5 | 33 | 3 | — | 19 | 7 | 30 | 2 |
| Mackay | ... | 8 | 1 | 16 | 1 | — | 9 | 6 | 7 | 1 |
| Benaud | ... | 18.4 | 9 | 46 | 3 | — | 39.2 | 10 | 66 | 4 |
| Kline | | | | | | ... | 14 | 4 | 34 | 0 |
| Burke.. | | | | | | ... | 10 | 5 | 17 | 0 |

## England Bowling

| | | O. | M. | R. | W. | | O. | M. | R. | W. |
|---|---|---|---|---|---|---|---|---|---|---|
| Statham | ... | 20 | 2 | 57 | 1 | — | 6 | 1 | 13 | 0 |
| Loader | ... | 19 | 4 | 56 | 4 | — | 9 | 1 | 27 | 0 |
| Bailey ... | ... | 13 | 2 | 35 | 3 | — | 5 | 1 | 21 | 0 |
| Laker ... | ... | 10.1 | 3 | 15 | 2 | — | 17 | 3 | 39 | 1 |
| Lock ... | ... | 10 | 4 | 17 | 0 | — | 14.7 | 5 | 37 | 1 |

### FALL OF WICKETS

ENGLAND – First Innings: 1—16, 2—16, 3—62, 4—75, 5—79, 6—83, 7—92, 8—112, 9—116.

ENGLAND – Second Innings: 1—28, 2—34, 3—96, 4—102, 5—153, 6—161, 7—169, 8—190, 9—198.

AUSTRALIA – First Innings: 1—55, 2—65, 3—88, 4—94, 5—122, 6—136, 7—162, 8—165, 9—178.

AUSTRALIA – Second Innings: 1—20, 2—58.

Umpires: C. Hoy and M. J. McInnes.

Australia won by 8 wickets.

# Australia's 'Snatch and Grab'

This momentous day was calamitous indeed from the England angle despite a superb innings by Dexter. It was however a deserved triumph for Australia and in particular for those excellent all-round cricketers, Benaud and Davidson. One's recollection evokes the sharpest contrast of emotions: admiration for Benaud's 'snatch and grab' on the one hand, exasperation on the other at the way in which England were outmanoeuvred.

ENGLAND V AUSTRALIA, Old Trafford, final day: August 1, 1961
*Score at start:* Australia 190 and 331 for 6; England 367
*Score at close:* Australia 190 and 432; England 367 and 201

The Ashes were won and lost this afternoon in a few overs bowled by Benaud to either side of the tea interval. In four overs before it he had four wickets for nine, in half an hour afterwards two more. It was fine bowling, and in many ways this has been a magnificent game of cricket. It is better to concentrate on this aspect, just as it is only proper to offer due congratulations to Australia, rather than to dwell unduly on a glorious English opportunity thrown away by misjudgment and plain poor batting.

At two moments today Australia were, in all human probability, a beaten side. First when, after 20 minutes, play, they were 334 for nine England needed only the last wicket with the long day stretching before them and a mere 150-odd to get.

Davidson and McKenzie in a last-wicket partnership beyond praise brought their side right back. Yet thanks to Dexter's great batsmanship England, as 4 o'clock approached, needed only 102 runs more at one a minute with nine wickets left. All seemed set fair.

But Dexter left for 76, and the age-old bogey of accurate, teasing leg-spin suddenly knocked this unsound, relatively inexperienced England middle batting right off balance. Australia fielded finely, they took every catch, and suddenly we were left with the prospect of our three fast bowlers needing to hold out for the best part of an hour.

Little did they look like doing so. Trueman stayed for 40 minutes, alternating solid defence with a few safe hits. Then he lost patience, and when all hope of victory had gone aimed a wild swing against a leg-spinner from Simpson very much as in the first innings – when it had mattered so much less.

At the end Australia, I daresay, could scarcely believe their luck. With little enough bowling in the first place, and strains to Davidson and Mackay to deplete them they snatched – thanks to their captain – a game that was three-parts lost.

Davidson this morning and Benaud afterwards, two great cricketers, played the decisive part, and however disappointing it may be to English followers to have got so near and had victory snatched away it is appropriate that Benaud should achieve the ambition of every Australian captain and successfully defend the Ashes in this country. From first to last on this tour he has sought to play cricket in an enterprising and sporting way. England, indeed, have met him in this, and have contributed – until the last sad phase – no mean part in this fascinating and extraordinary match.

It would be hard to imagine a morning's cricket wherein fortune shifted so excitingly, where collapse and recovery were so clear-cut and the saving act more admirably done. At twenty minutes past eleven, with nine Australian wickets down, England had the game all but won. When they came in at one o'clock, 98 runs later, the job had multiplied in difficulty 10 times.

The last-wicket stand had lasted only a quarter of an hour when May brought on Close for Statham. The pitch was still as good as gold (apart from the wide rough areas made by the bowlers) but the ball could be turned a little and the pace had gone out of it for the faster men.

It was a reasonable change, but unfortunately Close could not fill the bill. In his two overs were five full-pitches and 15 runs. Australian morale rose many points and now with McKenzie playing so safely that he had no need of protection Davidson launched forth at Allen. The first ball of Allen's 38th and last over Davidson drove magnificently over extra-cover for six. The third he drove like a bullet between bowler and long-off to the screen. The fifth Allen dropped a little short and it sped to the cover boundary. The sixth was dismissed with a tremendous blow over the crowd into the top row of the open stand at long-off – 20 sweet runs.

The last wicket put on 98 excellent runs. Australian common sense and cool-headed aggression have never been better blended.

England made 20 solid, sensible runs in the 20 minutes before lunch, and the temper of the batting afterwards made it clearly apparent that the target had seemed to the captain to be a proposition. As, of course, it was. Benaud shared the bowling with Davidson who, apart from nursing a strained side, was no doubt feeling his morning exertions. Pullar punished him with unwonted freedom; but at 40, hooking early at a very short one, he merely ladled it off the splice to square-leg.

There followed the glorious episode of Dexter's innings. It lasted 85 minutes wherein he and Subba Row made 110. The latter's share was only 32, but all Dexter needed in this mood was an anchor-man at the other end. Apart from two sudden, savage pulls for four apiece, and a dab or two through the slips, this was the part Subba Row played.

Dexter took the Australian bowlers apart one after the other, with supreme confidence and literally not a dangerous false stroke. The narrow shave came when Subba Row drove Davidson hard into the pit of Benaud's stomach at short-leg very near the bat. Technically a chance, it might possibly have stuck.

Dexter first put paid to Davidson with a series of powerful off-side strokes off both front and back foot, with a couple of hooks thrown in. He also hit Benaud resoundingly for four over mid-on. Benaud tried McKenzie for Davidson. Having begun with two wides he was driven and hooked for 14 in the over and promptly relieved. Simpson was on next, and Dexter alternately smote the ball through the off field or tingled the fingers of those who got in the way. He also reminded us what a fine cutter he is.

If I dwell awhile on Dexter it is to make the less of what followed. Simpson was succeeded by Mackay, who found himself straight-driven with a stroke that all but split the sight-screen, hooked, and finally deposited, with a blow that propelled the ball with the trajectory of a brassie-stroke down-wind, into the open stand at mid-wicket.

At 150 for one, shortly before four, England had scarcely a care in the world. The change came when Benaud came round the wicket to the right-handed Dexter. He had been keeping Subba Row quiet bowling into the worn places well outside his off-stump. Now he used them for Dexter, and looked like bowling him a maiden.

The last ball Dexter leaned away from to cut, and snicked into Grout's gloves. May's steady entry looked reassuring enough, but after he had seen Subba Row play a maiden from Mackay he swept at Benaud leaving the leg-stump uncovered, and the ball spun in off the rough to tickle off the bails.

To describe Close's innings taxes charity beyond endurance, as indeed it taxed credibility to behold. To Benaud's first ball, a yard wide of the off-stump, he aimed a sweep, legs askew, which sent the ball skirling over backward short-leg off the shoulder of the bat for two. Close had 10 balls, all from Benaud.

He played this stroke, if such it can be called, five times, mostly without connection. The fifth time he scooped a catch to the man waiting to receive it some 20 yards behind the square-leg umpire. Midway through this nightmare Close had stepped down the wicket and, aiming straight for the only time, driven Benaud grandly for six. Could irony stretch farther?

Close's loss was irritating, but not irreparable. Subba Row was different. He went to drive the last ball before tea, hitting with Benaud's spin but not perhaps quite getting there. He was bowled, and suddenly the shocking possibilities were nakedly exposed.

After tea five wickets remained, 85 minutes were left for play, and the fact of 93 runs being required had become more or less irrelevant. It was not that they could not possibly be got – only that the risk involved was incommensurate with the reward. A draw would still give England a chance of winning the Ashes at the Oval. Defeat was final.

The England tactics after tea left some doubt in the mind as to the objects of the exercise. Murray and Barrington each hit a clipping four, each was out to a defensive stroke. Thereafter Australia were always snatching their wickets ahead of the clock. Allen, after half an hour's watchfulness, was caught at slip. Trueman and Statham succumbed in turn. Twenty minutes from time it was all finished and Australia gave themselves over to celebrating their first Ashes' win in England since 1948.

## Australia

| | | | |
|---|---|---|---|
| W. M. Lawry lbw. b. Statham ... ... | 74 | — c. Trueman b. Allen... | 102 |
| R. B. Simpson c. Murray b. Statham ... | 4 | — c. Murray b. Flavell ... | 51 |
| R. N. Harvey c. Subba Row b. Statham... | 19 | — c. Murray b. Dexter ... | 35 |
| N. C. O'Neill hit wkt b. Trueman ... | 11 | — c. Murray b. Statham | 67 |
| P. J. Burge b. Flavell ... ... ... | 15 | — c. Murray b. Dexter ... | 23 |
| B. C. Booth c. Close b. Statham ... | 46 | — lbw. b. Dexter ... | 9 |
| K. D. Mackay c. Murray c. Statham ... | 11 | — c. Close b. Allen ... | 18 |
| A. K. Davidson c. Barrington b. Dexter... | 0 | — not out ... ... | 77 |
| R. Benaud b. Dexter ... ... ... | 2 | — lbw. b. Allen ... ... | 1 |
| A. T. W. Grout c. Murray b. Dexter ... | 2 | — c. Statham b. Allen ... | 0 |
| G. D. McKenzie not out ... ... ... | 1 | — b. Flavell ... ... | 32 |
| B. 4, l.b. 1 ... ... ... ... | 5 | B. 6, l.b. 9, w. 2 ... | 17 |
| | 190 | | 432 |

## England

| | | | | |
|---|---:|---|---|---:|
| G. Pullar b. Davidson ... ... ... | 63 | — | c. O'Neill b. Davidson | 26 |
| R. Subba Row c. Simpson b. Davidson... | 2 | — | b. Benaud ... ... | 49 |
| E. R. Dexter c. Davidson b. McKenzie... | 16 | — | c. Grout b. Benaud ... | 76 |
| P. B. H. May c. Simpson b. Davidson ... | 95 | — | b. Benaud ... ... | 0 |
| D. B. Close lbw. b. McKenzie ... ... | 33 | — | c. O'Neill b. Benaud... | 8 |
| K. F. Barrington c. O'Neill b. Simpson... | 78 | — | lbw. b. Mackay ... | 5 |
| J. T. Murray c. Grout b. Mackay ... | 24 | — | c. Simpson b. Benaud | 4 |
| D. A. Allen c. Booth b. Simpson ... | 42 | — | c. Simpson b. Benaud | 10 |
| F. S. Trueman c. Harvey b. Simpson ... | 3 | — | c. Benaud b. Simpson | 8 |
| J. B. Statham c. Mackay b. Simpson ... | 4 | — | b. Davidson ... ... | 8 |
| J. A. Flavell not out ... ... ... | 0 | — | not out ... ... | 0 |
| B. 2, l.b. 4, w. 1 ... ... ... | 7 | | B. 5, w. 2 ... ... | 7 |
| | 367 | | | 201 |

## England Bowling

| | O. | M. | R. | W. | O. | M. | R. | W. |
|---|---:|---:|---:|---:|---:|---:|---:|---:|
| Trueman ... | 14 | 1 | 55 | 1 | 32 | 6 | 92 | 0 |
| Statham ... | 21 | 3 | 53 | 5 | 44 | 9 | 106 | 1 |
| Flavell... ... | 22 | 8 | 61 | 1 | 29.4 | 4 | 65 | 2 |
| Dexter... ... | 6.4 | 2 | 16 | 3 | 20 | 4 | 61 | 3 |
| Allen ... ... | | | | | 38 | 25 | 58 | 4 |
| Close ... ... | | | | | 8 | 1 | 33 | 0 |

## Australia Bowling

| | O. | M. | R. | W. | O. | M. | R. | W. |
|---|---:|---:|---:|---:|---:|---:|---:|---:|
| Davidson ... | 39 | 11 | 70 | 3 | 14.4 | 1 | 50 | 2 |
| McKenzie ... | 38 | 11 | 106 | 2 | 4 | 1 | 20 | 0 |
| Mackay ... | 40 | 9 | 81 | 1 | 13 | 7 | 31 | 1 |
| Benaud ... | 35 | 15 | 80 | 0 | 32 | 11 | 70 | 6 |
| Simpson ... | 11.4 | 4 | 23 | 4 | 8 | 4 | 21 | 1 |

### FALL OF WICKETS

AUSTRALIA – First Innings: 1—8, 2—51, 3—89, 4—106, 5—150, 6—174, 7—185, 8—185, 9—189.

AUSTRALIA – Second Innings: 1—113, 2—175, 3—210, 4—274, 5—290, 6—296, 7—332, 8—334, 9—334.

ENGLAND – First Innings: 1—3, 2—43, 3—154, 4—212, 5—212, 6—272, 7—358, 8—362, 9—367.

ENGLAND – Second Innings: 1—40, 2—150, 3—150, 4—158, 5—163, 6—171, 7—171, 8—189, 9—193.

Umpires: John Langridge and W. E. Phillipson.

Australia won by 54 runs.

# CHAPTER FOUR

# PROPHECIES, CONCLUSIONS—AND A FEW MIS - HITS

I seem to have spent the last twenty-odd years 'a-prophecying avay like clockwork', in the words of Sam Weller. Likewise post-mortemizing. There is room here for just a few of the hundreds of items of this kind, beginning with the first words I wrote on cricket after the war, not very long after my return from the Far East. The commentator, by the way, was Rex Alston.

## Getting Back to it (1946)

*The Field*, April 27, 1946

A little more than eight months ago several British officers walked, one evening, out of a camp that lay beside the Burma-Siam railway. In another place much might be written regarding the emotions, at that moment, both of those who walked out and of the Japanese guards who, still armed, continued to occupy an ambiguous position at the gate. For the prisoners had waited just three and a half years for their walk, and their hearts were full.

When they reached the village cafe the patron politely, and with many smiles, tuned in his wireless to the British programme. Next moment we were at Old Trafford, and the commentator, using the familiar technique (which we had heard irreverently parodied at a camp 'sing-song' shortly before!), was apparently much enamoured of an Australian cricketer called Cristofani . . . England, it seemed, was in the throes of a Victory Test Match.

During the days of waiting that immediately followed, long news bulletins shortened the time for the prisoners, who had to remain in the camp; news of ultimatums from great commanders, of emissaries flying hither and thither, of instructions and arrangements for the release of prisoners-of-war. But no item was awaited with so sharp an interest as the cricket scores. The occasion emphasised a conviction towards which almost every day as a prisoner provided evidence: that among all types and ages of Englishmen a deep-rooted affection and interest for cricket persists.

No deep psychological exercise is needed to predict that, for all the grave issues overhanging us, cricket is going to be in the fore-front of attention this summer. All over the country clubs have used the winter in preparation – from the great Yorkshire club, with its many thousand adherents and its fat bank balance, down to the most modest village. The fighting ended at a convenient time of year, for there has been much for faithful hands to do. To those who say, 'Cricket is not what it used to be,' the stock answer suffices, 'It never has been.' But though we may have no fears for the spirit behind it all, it will be astonishing if the general technical level does not reflect the gap of six summers that separates us from the last season of peace.

So far as the counties are concerned they have no alternative but to recruit their teams very largely from among those who were the 'stars' of seven years ago; no alternative because the generation that has grown up in the interval, or rather the surviving part of it, has had no chance of developing its powers, and the great bulk still remains in the Services, for the most part abroad. A British crowd generally surveys its 'old 'uns' with a warm, nostalgic eye, and it will be splendid to see once more the heroes of the 'twenties and 'thirties.

But even the greatest of them cannot cheat nature indefinitely, and as some of the names have been announced in the Prospects Columns I have thought of the remark made, and accompanied by an indulgent smile, when Mead was batting in his later years, 'He plays from memory now!' There will be more than a few of them 'playing from memory' in 1946, and I dare say they may play uncommonly well.

I see that in his latest book (*English Cricket:* Collins) Neville

Cardus stresses how eloquent is cricket at any time of the English mood and temper. In the tired and disillusioned 'twenties, 'beautiful and brave stroke-play gave way to a sort of trench warfare, conducted behind the sandbag of broad pads . . . A shrewd professionalism decided on a compromise; enough of pace, pitched just short of a length, and a suggestion of spin and more of swerve, the attack directed on the leg stump – the main idea being to obtain a reasonably good bowling analysis every season at the expenditure of a minimum of risk and physical endurance.'

On Mr Cardus' analogy our immediate cricket future would seem somewhat depressing, for a certain weariness there is in the air, and must be. But if the cricket of the 'twenties reflected the trench battles of Flanders, maybe that of 1946 will be conditioned by the spirit of the commandos and the paratroopers. And if Mr Cardus is right, as I think he certainly is, in putting much of the blame upon a new genus of post-Great War county captains who, like the Duke of Plaza Toro, 'led their regiments from behind', we may certainly take heart from the present. For there has probably never been a better collection than those who have been appointed for this year; better in the sense of having a truer notion of the essentials of a cricket match, of whatever kind.

There will be a lively note of conflict engendered right enough. To sustain it there must be bowling of quality – and a fair wicket. To a large degree the former depends upon the latter. The captains indeed can do much, but not everything, to set first-class cricket (from which all other in some degree takes its tone) going on the right lines. Much the most important factor affecting the success or otherwise of the coming season is the wicket. A wicket with *pace*, however 'plumb', makes for a fair issue between bat and ball. The 'doped' wicket puts an impossible disadvantage on the bowler, and though this has been proclaimed often enough, it is, I think, particularly worth stressing just now, when the prospect as regards English bowling looks desperately thin.

Indeed, now that we have come face to face with the everintriguing business of discussing the new England XI that is to take the field in Australia in October, let us at least begin on a note of optimism by a brief survey of our batsmen. W. R.

Hammond will be 43 in June, and I have found no one who suggests that he is not every bit as good as ever. If he goes to Australia, as he surely must, he will be a good three years younger than Jack Hobbs, when he went for the fifth and last time, and, incidentally, averaged fifty in the Test Matches.

There is no need to emphasise how lucky it is that, in a transition period, such as the next year or two must be, the figurehead of English batsmanship is a player of such style and proportions. Hobbs and Woolley and K. S. Duleepsinhji have gone, but Hammond remains as a model for all young cricketers to be brought to see.

Of the two young men already touching greatness when the war came, Compton is unaltered, and has been playing beautifully in India. Hutton's misfortunes with his left arm have left it appreciably shorter than the right, but, though it may be a source of weakness if damaged again, it does not, apparently, affect his batting at the moment. I like the story that when a critic remarked recently in print that he was no longer able to cut, he went in next day and proceeded to cut *everything*. One was reminded of the newspaper article wherein one of his most distinguished opponents was rash enough to cast doubts on Larwood's speed. The production of this cutting when his colleagues thought the medium-paced bowler needed a touch of the whip used to have magical results.

Add Hardstaff to Hammond, Compton and Hutton, and there are four whom the Australians can hardly better, even if (as I hope and believe) Bradman is one of them. Of those who come next, Washbrook and Edrich are said to be batting well. Washbrook has it in his favour that only R. W. V. Robins compares with him at cover-point, while Edrich of course fields more than well, and is a dangerous 'occasional bowler.' P. A. Gibb and H. T. Bartlett have emerged safe from specially adventurous wars, and both are palpably close to the best side. R. T. Simpson, of Notts., is said to be reminiscent of C. F. Walters, and if that is even a moderately near estimate it is to be hoped he will not need to spend the summer in India with the R.A.F.

The one heartening item regarding possible bowlers for Australia is that, at 36, Voce is apparently still in his own high class, the one bowler of pace who consistently moves the ball away from the bat. The tiresome thing is that so many of our most effective bowlers in England happen to be either in-swingers or leg-spinners. Both are types that the Australians must be praying for. A 'seam' bowler as such is next to useless in Australia, where the shine lasts only an over or two; nor are any records more depressing than those of the successive leg-spin bowlers sent since Braund and B. J. T. Bosanquet had their successes more than forty years ago. Oh, for an E. R. Wilson, a Verity, or a J. C. White!

## Prospect in Australia

There is a vein of optimism no doubt proper to the occasion running through these remarks which events did not unfortunately bear out. Having had evidence of Wally Hammond's limitations as a captain on the M.C.C. South African tour of 1938–39, I had certain mis-givings which do not come through in print.

I was not the only one with doubts. On our way to Australia – a very leisurely way on a government-controlled, crowded, one-class, DRY *Sterling Castle* – I remember George Duckworth saying quietly one evening as we gazed over the rail: 'You know, the chap who ought to have been bringing this side out is Bryan Valentine.' A few months later there would have been scarcely anyone in the English party, players and press, who would have disputed his judgment.

August 30, 1946

When the 17 cricketers selected by the M.C.C. board their steamer at Southampton tomorrow, they will be following in the wake of nearly all (though not quite all) of the foremost English cricketers of every generation over little short of 100 years.

Just as it is the height of every Australian cricketer's ambition to play at Lord's – and it is always arranged that all who come over do play there once, whatever the measure of their success – so the fulfilment of the dream of an English player is to go to Australia with the M.C.C.

The historically-minded perhaps may contrast the palaver of tomorrow's departure, with the array of journalists and all the impedimenta of modern publicity, with the pioneer journey of 1861. In that remote year, even before Bismarck had begun to alarm the chancelleries of Europe, 12 bewhiskered heroes stepped aboard a paddle-boat at Liverpool on their precarious journey.

They arrived in Melbourne on Christmas Eve, and it is interesting to observe that then, as now, the enthusiasm and glamour of cricket was set in a higher key in Australia than over here.

It was W. G. Grace who aroused the national consciousness of England for cricket, and in 1861 the triumphs of that great man were still confined to the apple orchard at Downend, with the dogs and his mother and Uncle Pocock scouting out.

Yet at Melbourne the obscure company from Liverpool were met by 10,000, and, as Mr H. S. Altham tells us, were driven off for their first practice to a secret destination in the bush in order that they might have some peace from their admirers.

Twelve years were to pass after the first Englishmen had landed in Australia to play cricket until W. G. himself appeared there. He found in his antagonists a tough combativeness exceeding even his own and that of his brother 'E. M.'. It may perhaps be said that he set a standard in that direction of which Australians have rarely fallen short.

From W. G.'s visit to our own day the series of battles has gone on, and the heroes of 'the Golden Age', MacLaren, Jackson, Fry and Jessop on the one side, Noble, Hill, Gregory and the immortal Trumper on the other, are still household names.

Were these old players any better than those whom we watch and admire today?

Comparisons are difficult, not to say superfluous. What is certain is that the game is always changing. There are developments of technique and developments of tactics, not all of them sound, and not all, indeed, calculated to enhance the attractiveness of the play to the onlooker. Only the first principles in the separate arts of batsmanship, bowling and fielding remain the same.

The question which exercises the followers of cricket at present is the measure of skill of the team which Hammond leads from home tomorrow. There are some factors which are better set down now than when the battle is joined.

The most important is that this tour, undertaken relatively so soon after the close of six years of war, takes place specifically because the interest of millions of Australians and Englishmen seemed to the authorities to demand it.

There is no need to disguise the fact that many would have liked to see our cricketers tuned up for the business by the full dress series of the Test matches due to be played over here against the South Africans next summer. The gap of six seasons has prevented a whole generation from showing its mettle, and the older players from keeping their skill from going to rust.

The English golfers, one may note, have declared a two-year truce before continuing engagements with their enemies from America. But cricket's spotlight has a brighter and more powerful beam. It must be added that Australia, too, have had their losses and their interruptions. Further (what we often overlook) their source of supply is a small fraction of ours. The population of Australia can still be contained within that of Greater London.

Where the selectors of the present side have been particularly handicapped is in the generally low standard of our cricket this summer. It is an inevitable thing, but none the less tiresome, that long scores made against many of the counties in 1946 have been valueless from the point of view of appraising the likelihood of a batsman's success against Australian bowling on Australian wickets. Equally, it is little criterion that a bowler may have taken eight for 45 against Blankshire, or even captured 100 wickets and be sixth in the averages.

On the face of it, as many have written to point out, it must seem strange that few of the bowlers chosen are anywhere near the top of the averages. What the selectors have insisted on is good fielding, and wherever possible batting ability as well. I doubt if any side to visit Australia has had fewer real passengers in the batting line.

As for the fielding, there are several fine natural athletes in the party and few real weaknesses. But they will have a tremendous standard to live up to. A. P. F. Chapman's team did not miss a catch in Australia until the rubber was won. I believe that D. R. Jardine's missed only one. In two series Ames missed only one chance behind the wicket. Here, in his Kentish successor, Evans, I think we are still well provided.

One thing is quite certain: the captain himself demonstrates a sense of chivalry on the field which will make utterly impossible another such situation as threatened to spoil these great matches 14 years ago.

We like to think that our batsmanship is powerful, and I believe it to be reasonably so, though Jack Hobbs, who knows better than any man, has just issued a timely warning against the facile assumption that our side is worth 500 runs a time. Batting in Australia has its differences.

Runs have been desperately cheap in England this summer, and before the first Test match starts at Brisbane on November 29 there will be not over-many chances for the newcomer to adapt his ways. It is safe to say that our batting will be built round three great players, Compton, Hutton and Hammond himself, now at the age of 43, embarking on his fourth visit.

There are six other batsmen probably to contest four places, and their admirers can hope for the best as regards one and all of them. It is well to remember that with batsmen, even more than with bowlers, temperament plays a tremendously large part, and Australian crowds are not apt to take their pleasures silently. I remember a young Australian cricketer playing under the shadow of Worcester Cathedral who told me that he was badly put off. 'By what?' I asked. 'By the calm of everything,' he replied.

Our bowling, as all the world knows, or thinks it knows, is weak. It will be better time to judge that when our men have turned their arms over Australian pitches. A vast deal depends upon Voce, who has already proved his high quality down under. At the age of 37 can he do so again?

Bedser has done great things in his first summer of English cricket, and Wright, unsuited by the heavy rains of the last few months, may well take to the quick Australian turf. The development of Edrich as a bowler improves our prospects vastly, for we shall need to bat strongly right down the order.

The English team can perhaps hardly be compared in point of all-round efficiency with that which A. E. R. Gilligan took over in 1924, Chapman's in 1928, or Jardine's in 1932. But I do not know that it compares ill, man for man, with G. O. Allen's team of 1936, and how very nearly Allen came to winning the Ashes is known to all but the youngest.

A vast deal depends on the following-through of a sound plan of campaign. Indeed, there are in Test cricket subtleties of strategy and tactics impossible to convey in print to the layman.

## The 1948 Australians Assessed

*The Field*, August 28, 1948

When the wireless commentators were each saying their valedictory pieces after the stumps had been pulled up at the end of the Fifth Test Match, Mr Arthur Gilligan observed that we had lost not only the Ashes but our sackcloth as well. That, perhaps, was a fair way of expressing the utterness and completeness of Australia's victory in the series. No team before has won four Tests in an English summer, and if that in itself is not extraordinarily significant because this is the first time they have stretched over five days, the figures are conclusive indeed.

But if English cricket is left naked and maybe just a little ashamed, the rubber might well have ended just as drastically in our favour in the old days under the new arrangement. To anyone in need of a little sustaining I recommend a study of the Australian tour of England in 1905. A strong case can be made for England winning the series by five matches to none if time had allowed. Jackson, Fry, Tyldesley, Rhodes, Spooner, MacLaren, Hirst, Arnold, Lilley and Brearley – these were almost, perhaps not quite as much, better than an Australian team beginning with Trumper, Duff, Hill, Noble, Armstrong and Darling as Bradman's Australians were better than the England of 1948. It is pretty poor consolation in a sense, but one is at least reminded that success comes in cycles. In any case it is more pleasant, as well as fitting, to end the season by setting the emphasis on the excellence of the Australians.

How good are they? Better than Warwick Armstrong's side of '21, or Joe Darling's of 1902? The inevitable question can demand only one answer. A game that is perpetually in development and change no more allows comparisons of this sort to be made, than does a study of warfare the relative merits of armies. This time, too, there is the important and conclusive factor that we can hardly know the Australians' strength because they have not been properly tested. 1902 was a vintage year for England, as well as Australia; even in 1921 our team had been pulled together fairly successfully by Lord Tennyson by the time of the last Test. This year, the first day at the Oval was the sorriest of all, with the fight virtually all over when England's last wicket rattled down for 52.

Taken by itself the performance that followed, of bowling out Australia for 389 on a pitch which never gave the bowlers very much, was a perfectly good one. But the heart was really out of the match, and though Hutton and Edrich and Compton, especially Hutton, batted thoroughly well in the second innings we never seemed likely to have the pleasure of watching Bradman bat again in a Test.

The Australian heroes were Lindwall and Johnston in the bowling, and Morris, once more, in the batting. Lindwall has, from first to last, been the main danger, and it was on the last day but one of the series that he brought his total of wickets level with the twenty-seven which McDonald took against England in '21. Three English wickets remained on the fourth morning, and Lindwall thus might have gone one better than Grimmett's twenty-nine in '30. But it was Johnston who, by taking all three, brought his own number equal with Lindwall, a fact which, in the general wind-up, escaped much notice.

I mention it because Johnston himself has rather been obscured by the more spectacular efforts of Lindwall, and, when he has bowled, of Miller. Johnston, as the stock bowler, equally happy bowling fast-medium over the wicket, or medium-pace round it, swinging the new ball or cutting the old one across from leg, and always keeping it straight and well up, has been the success and surprise of the tour. Outside these three, Toshack and Johnson have had a good deal of bowling to do, mostly in a more or less defensive rôle, and have illustrated the virtues of control of length and direction that one looks for in all Australian bowlers, without often threatening great danger.

Incidentally, what Australian bowler has not been notably accurate above all things? I can recall only Arthur Mailey, that erratic genius, and the left-arm googly bowler, Fleetwood-Smith, whose style of attack has never been adopted economically by anyone since it was first practised by C. B. Llewellyn, of Hampshire and Natal.

The fielding in support of this formidable band was scarcely ever anything but adequate, and often it was extremely brilliant. Tallon, behind the wicket, generally was magnificent, and some of his catches, such as the one from a full-pitch off the inside-edge, standing up to Toshack, which sent back Washbrook at Lord's, and the low one, diving left-handed at Hutton's snick off Lindwall at the Oval, will be pictured in many memories. There was no great first slip, of the quality of Gregory or Chipperfield, but Miller at second slip or gully, in this respect if no other, was showing his genius all the time.

On the subject of Miller it would need much space to sift out the reasons for his not bulking larger in this series, but perhaps the main point is that he seems to need the spur of danger and responsibility. His influence was greater than his figures would suggest, but, however you look at it, his batting was the one Australian disappointment. Other fielders who must be mentioned are Harvey, probably the finest of long fielders, Loxton, Lindwall, and, of course, Barnes close up on the leg-side.

The Australian batting was only slightly less devastating than in some recent years by the measure of Bradman's more modest achievements. Morris, Barnes, Bradman, Hassett, Miller, Harvey, Loxton was an order which, against contemporary English bowling, could hardly go wrong, and the proof of its strength is that Brown, averaging sixty and playing almost as well as ever, could be safely excluded. Add to all this virtue the calculated skill of Bradman's captaincy, and the result is a most formidable side – formidable, and singularly attractive.

One last thought; one wonders whether, collectively, the team has yet reached its best. When Bradman took the new Australian team on to the field at Brisbane less than two years ago he had only two cricketers, Hassett and Barnes, who had ever played in a Test Match. The rest have made good in the two series, and there is not one who does not owe much to his captain's influence. Don Bradman's great career is over, but his hand will be seen on the Australian teams of many years hence.

# Five Years Later

The Ashes are now in England's hands. Perhaps this moment marks the high peak of post-war cricket zeal. At any rate when *The Daily Telegraph* collected my Test reports into paper-back book form, with a Foreword by C. B. Fry, sales approached 60,000 in a few weeks.

September 19, 1953

When I summon to my mind memories of the Australian tour which winds finally to an end at Edinburgh today I sometimes find myself thinking of that Saturday afternoon of the first Test at Nottingham wherein Alec Bedser once again sheered his way through an Australian innings, and in so doing seemed to be setting England's batsmen on the road to victory.

In the end rain settled the argument at Nottingham, and, as we like to think, saved Australia from defeat. The particular picture that occurs to me, though, is of one Australian batsman after another, as each walked back in a situation made even more anxious by his own departure, summoning some sort of a rueful smile: Morris, Harvey, Miller, Benaud, playing against England for the first time, Lindwall . . .

I begin my appreciation of the Australians of 1953 with this illustration, because whereas Hassett's was such a pleasantly cheerful team, there yet exists a notion that dies hard in England of Australian grimness on the cricket field. Perhaps the legend derives from the egregious Armstrong and the poker-faced Herby Collins, and the first impact, many years ago, of those sinister, long-peaked green caps.

Perhaps it stretches back further, even to the very first great Australian cricketer, Spofforth, a starkly hostile figure if ever there was one. It is nourished today, no doubt, by the habit the Australians have always brought with them from home of putting into their appeals a loud, aggressive fervour that sometimes struck harshly on English ears.

However it may be, the common idea – at least, so far as post-war Australian teams are concerned – is a misconception. There is a resilient toughness about our old enemies of the cricket field. They fight hard, and, pray Heaven, always will. But their whole approach is the antithesis of dourness and gloom, and it is a point well worth getting straight if we are not to be in danger of being thought humbugs. For it is English cricket, or at any rate county cricket, which tends too often to suffer from a canny, defensive over-seriousness.

If the Australians have brought anything to our fields this summer it is a zestful enterprise, rising frequently to gaiety, whether they have been batting, bowling or fielding. And for that spirit alone they deserve all the bulging money-bags they are taking home for the nourishment of cricket in their own country.

How good were Hassett's team? Or, as some would put it who cannot conceive of England beating anything but a thoroughly weak Australian side, how bad were they?

There was less concrete in the batting than in Bradman's 1948 side, which, after two Tests and despite an average in the fifties, could even dispense with the services of W. A. Brown. There was less sustained speed and venom in the bowling, and slightly less variety, too. (It is hard to think that Ian Johnson would not have been well worth his keep these last few months.) Nor for all Hassett's virtues has he quite the tactical and strategical grasp of Sir Donald Bradman, than whom probably neither country has produced a shrewder captain.

Australian cricket was at its peak in '48, and to find a side to offer comparison with it one needs to go back at least 20 years to A. P. F. Chapman's M.C.C. team of 1928–29. Yet, even by comparison with the best, Hassett's team does not emerge discreditably, if contemporary English cricket be taken as the yardstick.

Bradman's 1948 team, outside Tests, won 19 first-class matches and drew seven. Hassett's team, in a distinctly wetter summer, have won 16 matches and drawn 11. They have won 12 times by an innings, and the cause of most of the drawn matches has been the weather. Of their 20 county fixtures, they failed to win 11, but most of their opponents were in all probability saved by rain. Warwickshire had a remarkable moral victory, and the only other counties that lasted out over three fine days were Yorkshire in the return match, and Sussex.

Their ascendancy over the counties, in fact, has been almost as complete as their predecessors', and it is doubtful whether the county standard has shifted very much. I am inclined, in fact, to think it is slightly lower now than five years ago; but the difference is not appreciable.

Looking back, then, to the achievements of previous Australian sides, one finds the advantage lying with Hassett's forerunners right the way back to 1926. But the exceptional strength of those four sides between 1930 and 1948 can be explained by the presence of one man – Bradman. He not only broke every batting record during his four tours here, but scored an unprecedented number of runs at an unusual speed. By his own achievements he made runs infinitely easier to come by for his companions at the other end.

Anyone who questions this should compare the Australian totals during Bradman's career, which spans 20 years and 37 Tests against England, with the totals in the 10 Tests since his retirement. The drop in runs is fantastic. With his departure, in fact, the predominance of the bat in Test matches ceases at present to be a problem.

However, compare Hassett's side with the last Australian touring side pre-Bradman – that of 1926, captained by Collins – and the picture is very different. Collins's team had one batsman greater than any present Australian, Macartney; but the batting generally seems scarcely stronger, and in other departments Hassett's team look to have the advantage every time.

Hassett's team will be remembered first, I think, for the splendour of the fielding. While most of them could distinguish themselves anywhere, one thinks specially of Harvey in the covers and of the young brigade close to the wicket – Davidson, Hole, Archer and Benaud. There has probably never been a better fielding side than that which played in the Fourth Test.

There was just one occasion, at Leeds, when – not without provocation – some of the Australians had to clutch pretty hard at the last remnants of their good humour. But, considering the issues involved, and the strain and ardours of a long tour, the side have maintained the serenity of their outlook in a way that has been the admiration of all in close touch with them.

Certainly no defeat could have been better taken, and it is significant that since August 19 the Australians have played perhaps some of the most effective and attractive cricket of

*Administrators.* TOP LEFT: S. C. Griffith of Cambridge, Sussex and England: Secretary of M.C.C. since 1962.    TOP RIGHT: J. H. Nash of Yorkshire. The oldest serving County Secretary. Joined the office staff in 1922 and has been Secretary since 1930. BOTTOM LEFT: A. E. R. Gilligan, President of M.C.C. 1967/68. Former England captain at home and in Australia 1924/25. BOTTOM RIGHT: Gilbert Ashton, the oldest of the brotherhood who from 1921/23 inclusive captained Cambridge. Formerly Chairman and now President of Worcestershire

PATRICK EAGER                                    PATRICK EAGER

*Four colleagues in the press and commentary boxes.* TOP LEFT: Michael
Melford. Joined *The Daily Telegraph* in 1950 and was posted to *The
Sunday Telegraph* as Cricket Correspondent when that paper was
founded in 1961. TOP RIGHT: Richie Benaud. Captain of Australia
from 1958/63; was, like Jack Fingleton before him, at once a Test
cricketer and a professional journalist. Chief interests are now *The
Sun* (Sydney), *News of the World* and the B.B.C. BOTTOM LEFT: John
Woodcock. Since 1954 has been 'our cricket correspondent' of *The
Times.* His identity was officially disclosed with the change in
policy in 1967. BOTTOM RIGHT: John Arlott. Broadcaster, author and
journalist. In words spoken and written possibly runs neck-and-neck
with E.W.S. over the period 1946/68

PATRICK EAGER

their tour. The whole party will leave a multitude of friends behind when they sail for home: all of them, but especially the one and only Lindsay Hassett.

## Odds on Australia?

When the 1958–59 team under Peter May left England there was a lot of extravagant prophecy. It was even described as the strongest team ever to set sail under the colours of M.C.C. When the side failed to live up to such an estimate there were a lot of words to be eaten, and in some cases they came to be garnished with a bitter sauce. I never saw the picture in such glowing colours, and concluded this prospect piece by saying that the odds seemed to be slightly on Australia. Well, we lost the Ashes, and (at the moment of writing) have yet to recover them almost ten years later.

September, 1958

For the fourth time since the war ended an M.C.C. team is leaving for Australia. Each such tour – and the first was launched all but a century ago – has its own distinct background, and its own problems, and to compare thoughts this morning with those on the similar occasions in 1946, 1950 and 1954 is to trace in outline the development of Test cricket over this period in the two countries.

When W. R. Hammond's team sailed for Australia after the first post-war English season the mood was one of reunion and goodwill. Dr Evatt had come over and pleaded at Government level the quickest possible resumption of Test matches. M.C.C., generally quick to respond to an emotional appeal of this kind, accepted the invitation, somewhat against the better judgment of several of the foremost players.

The tour fulfilled its hopes from the Australian point of view better than the English. Under Bradman was quickly built a fine side which established an unrelenting ascendancy, while M.C.C., potentially as formidable so far as batsmanship was concerned, failed under cool, disappointingly remote leadership, to show the best that was in them. Moreover, friendliness soon gave place to friction.

The team F. R. Brown took out four years later was substantially weaker than the one before, and no one gave it a

F

possible account of itself. In the event it exceeded expectation. But the pace bowling was all on one side, and the balance of power still patently belonged to Australia.

In 1954 Len Hutton's team, by contrast, sailed to defend the Ashes which had been most narrowly won at the Oval the previous year. The greater speed belonged now to England, who, after an extraordinary series, returned victorious, thanks largely to the efforts of four young members of the present party, May and Cowdrey, Statham and Tyson.

The keynote of the first tour was Reunion, of the second a Quest against Odds. Grim Challenge perhaps best expressed the third, and I suggest that a sense of Mission is an appropriate keynote to the fourth.

Every captain wants to win. Peter May at least as much as most, and it may be safely assumed that he will imbue his team with a proper sense of antagonism, neither asking for quarter nor expecting it. It is, however, even more true of this tour than of most to say that its success should be rightly judged less by a balance of wins over losses, than by the reaction to it of the ordinary cricket public in Australia.

Precisely the same is true of course, as regards spectator requirements in England. But we at least have a full programme, and Test visitors every summer. Apart from the infrequent appearances of South Africans and West Indians, Australia can look forward to the glamour of a Test series only when M.C.C. are with them one year in four. Hence it is not hard to credit the opinion that the future of the game in Australia depends to a considerable extent on the popularity of this tour.

May's fellow-selectors have presented him with a party of specialists, the teams from which must be chosen to a rigid pattern. The emphasis is on fast bowling to a greater extent than in any team sent overseas by any country at any time.

By contrast, no M.C.C. side has before gone to Australia with only two spin bowlers. The wicketkeeper will be standing back to five bowlers out of seven. It will be exceedingly hard to keep the game moving at an acceptable tempo, and it will be remarkable if the sameness of the scene does not tell on the spectators, to say nothing of the critics.

From the strictly playing point of view, what, now, are the

prospects of M.C.C.? To get as full a picture as possible of the battles ahead we had best try and take a look, so to speak, behind the enemy lines.

Just two years ago Ian Johnson's Australians were making their farewells from England after a tour which, however many allowances were made on the score of weather and wickets, had been from the purely cricketing angle all but disastrous. Apart from the Lord's Test, the Australians were heavily outpointed in the rubber. The Test averages made the most woeful reading. They won only nine first-class matches in all out of 31, and of the five counties they beat, four ended the season at the foot of the Championship.

This was the barren inheritance which Ian Craig took over, when only 12 months later, in October last year, the Australians set off on their tour of South Africa.

The tour was a triumph for Craig, the youngest captain in Test history, and scarcely less so for the senior men who supported him so admirably, Harvey, Benaud – both of whom must have been hoping for the captaincy – and McDonald.

Now Craig is under the doctors, and although the latest reports are reasonably hopeful, there must be a doubt as to his health and form. Craig may make the new Australian side, or he may not. But in either case he has instilled a spirit into the leading players which is likely to make the proposition more difficult from the English aspect this winter.

The Australian selectors will be acting with much less than their usual sagacity if they do not regard their 1957-58 team to South Africa as the nucleus of the one that is asked to present itself at Brisbane in early December.

There is, though, one potential reinforcement of whom so much has been said that one can scarcely wait to see him. Just as the Australian crowds are looking forward to watching for the first time the three bowling celebrities, Laker, Lock and Trueman, so the English party are thinking about the youthful New South Welshman, Norman O'Neill. What they know is that O'Neill is a strong, athletic six-footer who in State cricket has been punching his way along at a rate of 50 an hour.

Last season, while the Australian side were in South Africa, he averaged 83, and headed not only the batting but the bowling averages as well. (He spins leg-breaks and googlies.)

He actually scored 1,000 runs, and although the best bowlers were certainly away from home, the fact is that only two men before him, Ponsford and Bradman by name, have ever reached four figures in an Australian first-class season.

On the day before sailing, it might be as well to stress what an exacting job is likely to lie before May and his team in the Test series. People have come very much to expect England to win Test matches nowadays, and it is true that *at home* we have lost only two Test rubbers since the war.

This is an excellent team in several respects. But Anglo-Australian form in this country is only a very hazy guide to what may be expected overseas. It is a stark fact that on the last three tours abroad, to West Indies, Australia and South Africa, England have won seven Test matches, lost five and drawn four.

There is no conclusive story of superiority in hard-wicket conditions to be drawn from these figures, and one's feeling is that if they bring home the Ashes once more, May's team will probably have done extremely well.

A great part of English hopes must rest on Bailey as the one all-rounder. If he can come off again in both departments the tail will not start too early. Otherwise, in what is sure to be a much higher-scoring series than last time, Australia will have an important advantage in the presence of Benaud, Davidson, and possibly Archer, in the lower part of the order.

If pressed for a view I would say that the proper odds at this stage may be just a shade in Australia's favour.


## A Troublous Tour Surveyed

As is predicted here, after England's 4-nil defeat, this M.C.C. Australian tour of 1958–59 marked the end of the road for several. Five of the side, Bailey, Laker, Loader, Tyson and Watson, did not play again for England. There were seven survivors, May, Cowdrey, Dexter, Subba Row, Statham, Trueman and Swetman in the M.C.C. side with which May won the rubber in the West Indies in the following winter.

February 20, 1959

The last chapter of one of the most surprising of all Anglo-

chance of doing more than fighting hard and giving the best Australian rubbers was written this morning when Australia made short work of scoring the 69 runs needed to win.

I describe the outcome as surprising only because of the extent of Australia's success. England were always likely to be extremely hard pressed.

What is extraordinary is that not after even a single day's play in the series have we been able to say that England were in the stronger position. The good phases, the better days, have only cancelled an Australian advantage which Benaud's team have been quick to snatch back.

It is this which has made the series so disappointing to watch and describe from the English viewpoint – and no doubt also to read about.

Only a few of the England players have lived up to their reputations: May, of course, as a batsman, Cowdrey, Statham and Laker. Graveney began and ended the tour well, but lost form in the middle. Evans kept very well when he was fit and others had their days of success.

But while several of the older men have probably played against Australia for the last time no single young one has marked out a definite position for himself.

One can scarcely write down as many as half a dozen in all who are certain members of the side that is due to go to West Indies at the end of the year.

The satisfactory aspects of the tour boil down more or less to two. In the first place the admirable performances of Benaud and of his team have helped a great deal to restore interest in and respect for the game in Australia, which, of course, is an important matter in itself, both to English and Australian cricket.

Also, thanks to the higher gate charges rather than an overall increase in attendances the tour has made a record profit both for M.C.C. and the State Associations. It seems as though M.C.C. will hand over something just short of £30,000 for distribution among the counties, major and minor, and the two Universities.

There are certain respects in which the tour has been particularly unsatisfactory, but this is not, I think, the time for recriminations and I believe those who have followed in these columns the happenings as they unfolded will have conjured a fair picture of events.

Another is the delicate issue of doubtful actions. The law has always seemed clear enough on the subject, even if umpires throughout history have been shy of invoking it. Nor is it always easy from the square-leg position to say at precisely which point in the swing of the arm the elbow either bends or straightens – as I discovered the other day when standing umpire in the amiable atmosphere of the Prime Minister's match against M.C.C. at Canberra.

It might be worth considering some clarification for the benefit of umpires, perhaps on the lines of Ian Peebles' suggestion. He would like the Law amended, or a note added to the existing wording, to the effect that the arm must be straight from the moment it reaches the horizontal coming up until after the ball is released.

While there are four or five doubtful Australian bowlers, excluding Burke (whose action is surely indefensible), let us not forget that there are several counterparts in English cricket also.

Judging by a recent pronouncement by the South African authorities, there are also men not above suspicion in South Africa. This would seem a matter for next summer's Imperial Cricket Conference, and, if necessary, as part of the agenda for private talks over the table between M.C.C. and the Australians.

There has been, I believe, far too much diplomacy by letter as between England and Australia, with consequent opportunities for misunderstanding, and also for delay, seeing that something around 3,000 miles divides Perth from Brisbane, and that the Board meets only twice a year. It takes little longer nowadays to fly between London and Sydney.

If I conclude with a word on umpiring it must not be thought for one moment that I attribute England's defeat in the rubber either to throwing or to bad decisions. That is not the case at all. The Ashes and the rubber were won by a side incontestably better in batting and bowling, and with the more positive tactical plan: one might add also, with the fresher and more zestful approach to the game.

It has not, however, been a particularly happy series as

regards the umpiring, and I dare say that England this time may have had the worst of the breaks.

The losing side is generally the one that is inclined to feel that the decisions have gone against them, as one knows from the confessions of various visiting sides to England over the last several years.

Perhaps in this series there have been more than the usual number of awkward decisions to give. My impression is, however, that the Australian umpiring standard is a little below that of the other three post-war tours.

It is, of course, much more difficult to come by first-class umpires in Australia than in England, where there is sufficient work to make it worth the old cricketer's while to take it on as his summer employment.

In Australia, with its restricted programme, there is little money in umpiring, and no State player ever thinks of embracing it when he retires.

The consequence is that though some umpires have been grade cricketers they tend as a bunch to be theoretical adjudicators. They need not necessarily be the worse for that, but they have to earn the confidence of the players as distinct from being automatically accorded it.

This is one of the directions which Australian authority must watch with some care, for if the umpiring is indifferent the whole conduct of the game is in danger. Some may well say that it is in even greater danger from what is being written by former Test cricketers and others, who umpire the game from the Press box and see every debatable decision as a blunder and a scandal.

Here, indeed, is another of the problems of cricket, perhaps in the long run the most menacing one of all.

## The Tied Test

It is my chief cricket regret that I was not in Australia for the best of all series. All I could contribute in writing were certain envious reflections from afar, beginning with this one on the great tie at Brisbane in the First Test.

The Solomon referred to is the little Guyanese who with the scores level, and only the last ball of the last over to follow, ran out Meckiff by hitting the single stump from square-leg.

December 15, 1960

As our correspondent remarks in his cable from Brisbane, yesterday was a wonderful day for cricket: not only for Test cricket, and not only for the teams led apparently so bravely and so well by Benaud and Worrell. If ever the game needed some revivifying event to remind the world of its unique dramatic possibility and of its capacity, *when played in the right spirit*, to sustain an enthralling appeal over the full length of a match, this indeed was the moment.

The fact of this First Test ending in a tie of course, inscribes its fame in history with a capital letter. A tie, need one say, is a glorious fluke, having some analogy with a hole in one, or a dead heat in a Boat Race.

To imagine the odds against it one need only reflect that in around 500 Test Matches played since Tests began this is the first tie. (Among the many thousand games of first-class cricket played since the 1914-18 war only 19 have ended in ties.)

But, if one weighs the matter as properly as is possible, looking on enviously from afar, it would seem – as Benaud afterwards remarked – that in a tie poetic justice was perfectly served. The course of the game was certainly such that either side could have counted itself desperately unlucky to lose.

Australia especially must have felt so when late on the fifth and last afternoon their captain along with that magnificent cricketer, Davidson, were pulling the game round so gallantly after Hall's great burst of fast bowling. Yet Benaud, despite the obvious fallibility of those due to follow, kept his sights fixed on victory. Thus he maintained at the last the challenging spirit set by the West Indian batsmen on the first day.

Bearing in mind the West Indies' caution against the England bowling last winter one naturally wondered whether the attacking approach of their early games would extend to the Tests. Sobers' tremendous 100 – in two hours! – on the first day did a good deal to provide the answer.

The West Indian effort did not maintain this key, which was not surprising, and indeed Worrell seems to have had several moments of tactical indecision. But, taking the game as a whole, no one will say that he and his side did not earn a fair share of the glory.

Nothing is more sure than that Sobers, still a mere 24, will be one of the great cricket figures of the 'Sixties. It is scarcely less obvious than that an equal focus of attention will settle on O'Neill.

Cricket urgently needs personalities with the stamp of such genius as these two possess, and it was perhaps a good augury for England next summer, as well as for the series just begun, that O'Neill should have made his highest Test score.

Of course, however obliging are the great players in producing an outstanding performance, however prepared the two captains to promote a full-blooded match, only once in a life-time will events conspire to produce an epic.

What we may well hope for, though, is a rubber waged by two sides each of which is persuaded that a rational measure of attack is not only a paying proposition, but indeed more often than not in cricket the safer course.

Inevitably odious comparisons are being made between this West Indies tour and the last to Australia by M.C.C. It was in Brisbane just two years ago that England were ingloriously beaten in just about the worst game ever played, and Bailey made 68 in seven and a half hours of the most misguided effort ever perpetrated in the name of cricket.

The contrast is astonishing: 665 in the one game, 1,474 in seemingly very similar conditions and only a few hours less in the other; frustration and recriminations in the first place, today a joyful echo of courage and excitement that penetrates to us at home through the cold murk of winter.

But this is a good moment to remind ourselves that the recent M.C.C. tour of West Indies gave evidence of a welcome change of heart on the part of a rejuvenated England team. Brilliant though much of the batting was at Brisbane, it cannot have been much better than that of Cowdrey at Kingston, or of Dexter at Bridgetown and Port-of-Spain.

All eyes and ears now will be trained on the next Test that begins at Melbourne on December 30.

But whatever occurs it will not dim the recollection of a game fit to rank with Manchester and the Oval, 1902, or Melbourne, 1908, or Durban, 1948 (when England won by two wickets from the last ball of the last over), and other tight-run classics of the past.

The nearest parallel probably was that Melbourne game wherein Barnes and Fielder put on 39 together to win for England by one wicket. With the scores level they embarked on an apparently suicidal run, but scrambled home as Hazlitt threw a wide return.

When the scene was re-enacted yesterday, more than half a century later, the West Indian concerned kept his head a good deal better: at the climax his side owed all to the judgment of Solomon!

## West Indies

| | | | | |
|---|---|---|---|---|
| C. C. Hunte c. Benaud b. Davidson | ... | 24 | c. Simpson b. Mackay | 39 |
| C. Smith c. Grout b. Davidson ... | ... | 7 | c. O'Neill b. Davidson | 6 |
| R. Kanhai c. Grout b. Davidson | ... | 15 | c. Grout b. Davidson | 54 |
| G. Sobers c. Kline b. Meckiff ... | ... | 132 | b. Davidson ... ... | 14 |
| F. M. Worrell c. Grout b. Davidson | ... | 65 | c. Grout b. Davidson | 65 |
| J. Solomon hit wkt b. Simpson ... | ... | 65 | lbw. b. Simpson ... | 47 |
| P. Lashley c. Grout b. Kline | ... | 19 | b. Davidson ... ... | 0 |
| F. C. M. Alexander c. Davidson b. Kline | | 60 | b. Benaud ... ... | 5 |
| S. Ramadhin c. Harvey b. Davidson | ... | 12 | c. Harvey b. Simpson | 6 |
| W. Hall st. Grout b. Kline | ... | 50 | b. Davidson ... ... | 18 |
| A. L. Valentine not out ... | ... ... | 0 | not out ... ... | 7 |
| Extras ... ... ... ... | ... | 4 | Extras ... ... | 23 |
| | | 453 | | 284 |

## Australia

| | | | | |
|---|---|---|---|---|
| C. C. McDonald c. Hunte b. Sobers | ... | 57 | b. Worrell ... ... | 16 |
| R. B. Simpson b. Ramadhin | ... | 92 | c. sub b. Hall ... | 0 |
| R. N. Harvey b. Valentine | ... | 15 | c. Sobers b. Hall ... | 5 |
| N. C. O'Neill c. Valentine b. Hall | ... | 181 | c. Alexander b. Hall... | 26 |
| L. Favell run out ... ... ... | ... | 45 | c. Solomon b. Hall ... | 7 |
| K. D. Mackay b. Sobers ... ... | ... | 35 | b. Ramadhin ... ... | 28 |
| A. K. Davidson c. Alexander b. Hall | ... | 44 | run out ... ... | 80 |
| R. Benaud lbw. b. Hall ... ... | ... | 10 | c. Alexander b. Hall... | 52 |
| A. W. T. Grout lbw. b. Hall ... | ... | 4 | run out ... ... | 2 |
| L. Meckiff run out ... ... | ... | 4 | run out ... ... | 2 |
| L. F. Kline not out ... ... | ... | 3 | not out ... ... | 0 |
| Extras ... ... ... ... | ... | 15 | Extras ... ... | 14 |
| | | 505 | | 232 |

## Australia Bowling

| | O. | M. | R. | W. | | O. | M. | R. | W. |
|---|---|---|---|---|---|---|---|---|---|
| Davidson | ... 30 | 2 | 135 | 5 | — | 24.6 | 4 | 87 | 6 |

| | O. | M. | R. | W. | | O. | M. | R. | W. |
|---|---|---|---|---|---|---|---|---|---|
| Meckiff | 18 | 0 | 129 | 1 | — | 4 | 1 | 19 | 0 |
| Mackay | 3 | 0 | 15 | 0 | — | 21 | 7 | 52 | 1 |
| Benaud | 24 | 3 | 93 | 0 | — | 31 | 6 | 69 | 1 |
| Simpson | 8 | 0 | 25 | 1 | — | 7 | 2 | 18 | 2 |
| Kline ... | 17.6 | 6 | 52 | 3 | — | 4 | 0 | 14 | 0 |
| O'Neill | | | | | | 1 | 0 | 2 | 0 |

### West Indies Bowling

| | O. | M. | R. | W. | | O. | M. | R. | W. |
|---|---|---|---|---|---|---|---|---|---|
| Hall ... | 29.3 | 1 | 140 | 4 | — | 17.7 | 3 | 63 | 5 |
| Worrell | 30 | 0 | 93 | 0 | — | 16 | 3 | 41 | 1 |
| Sobers | 32 | 0 | 115 | 2 | — | 8 | 0 | 30 | 0 |
| Valentine | 24 | 6 | 82 | 1 | — | 10 | 4 | 27 | 0 |
| Ramadhin ... | 15 | 1 | 60 | 1 | — | 17 | 3 | 57 | 1 |

### FALL OF WICKETS

WEST INDIES – First Innings: 1—23, 2—42, 3—65, 4—239, 5—243, 6—283, 7—347, 8—366, 9—452.

WEST INDIES – Second Innings: 1—13, 2—88, 3—114, 4—127, 5—210, 6—210, 7—241, 8—250, 9—253.

AUSTRALIA – First Innings: 1—84, 2—138, 3—194, 4—278, 5—381, 6—469, 7—484, 8—489, 9—496.

AUSTRALIA – Second Innings: 1—1, 2—7, 3—49, 4—49, 5—57, 6—92, 7—226, 8—228, 9—232.

Umpires: C. Hoy and C. J. Egar.

# Worrell - and Partner

The quiet part played by Gerry Gomez, the manager of Frank Worrell's team in Australia, is noted here by Ron Roberts, that most dedicated of cricketophiles, writer and organiser of Commonwealth tours, who contributed with such distinction to the sporting pages of *The Daily Telegraph* in the decade prior to his early death through a brain tumour in 1965.

February 17, 1961

The series in Australia has drained everyone of superlatives; the administrators and statesmen of cricket, the Press, and not least the most important people of all, the players.

It has been the most intriguing and longest-sustained newspaper sporting story in my experience, from the first moments in Brisbane in November to the last palpitating exchanges in Melbourne.

In a sense it has been a freak (just as the Brisbane tie was a glorious fluke) since however willing two captains may be to throw out and accept challenges the resulting exchanges will rarely make such a perfect balance.

Obviously, the moral answer was a shared rubber. But it was no doubt hoping far too much that Providence should intervene a second time, and since the West Indians are being feted like conquerors I shall be surprised if their sunny temperaments have not already shrugged off the disappointment of defeat.

The prime moral for all concerned with the welfare of cricket – and I am sure its point will not be lost on the Rait-Kerr Inquiry Commission whose first sitting takes place next week – is, of course, that the game is as fascinating a pastime as it ever was. The crucial thing is the attitude of the players. The basic laws don't need fiddling with when a five-day match, without the benefit of any sort of public holiday, can attract 270,000 people.

It is hard to overpraise Richie Benaud's contribution to the series. He has always been an intelligent and courageous, as well as a highly-talented, cricketer. He has acquired during the last two years a fully-developed sense of the responsibility for the well-being of cricket that goes properly with the job of Test captaincy.

A professional journalist – and therefore, need it be said, a shrewd, dispassionate observer of the human scene! – he spent last summer in English Press boxes and I feel that his outlook was broadened by his experiences – not least among them his coverage of the Imperial Cricket Conference.

However, it is not the Australian side of the picture that is the extraordinary one. With few exceptions – and their 1956 English tour was one – Australia's cricket has generally been virile and combative. Above all, they have rarely failed to take up any gage thrown down by the enemy.

The really significant thing is the over-all performance of the West Indians. Their cricket virtues have been admired by all, over the years, but certain apparently intrinsic limitations of temperament have too often counter-balanced them.

Brilliant, yes – but are they 'stickers'? If you get on top of them can they fight back? In a crisis won't they lose their heads? Such questions have always surrounded West Indian cricketers. They have been asked so often that they must have doubted the answer themselves.

It is the measure of the achievement of this team that in Australia, before the toughest (but not the least generous) public of all, they have dissolved all such doubts. They have met adversity with brilliant counter-attack, they have 'stuck it' when necessary, they have kept their heads in critical situations at least as well as their opponents.

What lies behind the new approach? Frank Worrell, of course, has been the architect on the field, and I would not take away an iota from his triumph. But he has had behind him a manager whose name has scarcely been mentioned, G. E. Gomez.

R. A. Roberts, whose accounts have so enlivened our winter, has thus summed up for me the complementary contributions of these two:

'Worrell has immense natural dignity. No cricketer since Hammond has had such sheer presence as he takes the field. The petty things of cricketing life seem to be below Worrell. The will to win at all costs is somehow distasteful to him. The game, not the result, means more.

'Worrell has been the producer and master-mind of this show but he has also had in the wings a most able director. Gomez, with that jutting jaw like the prow of a battleship, has not tried to run the party. For all his own deep knowledge and feeling for the game he has tactfully let Worrell take care of the cricket. But his presence in the background has been extremely reassuring to his captain.

'Gomez, in his handling of public relations, has been equally good. "We have nothing to hide," said Worrell and Gomez to the Press on their arrival. Indeed together they have everything to show with pride.'

In other words success derived from the partnership between captain and manager, and the fact that the latter has kept to the background scarcely means that his part was the less valuable.

It should be emphasised to a public even wider than that of cricket that here was a perfect blending in harmony between the two predominant races forming the West Indies nation. Could the point be noted even in Cape Town and Pretoria?

What do the immediate gains add up to? In the first place Australia, whose cricketing economy has been nearly as rocky as our own, have now the prospect of another regularly stimulating visit besides that of M.C.C. Before this they had not considered the West Indies as serious Test opponents.

On the £ s d side, the Fifth Test produced a record turnover of £39,000 and the West Indies – who actually lost money on their last visit to Australia – will this time take home more than £25,000.

As a revivifying influence on cricket the tour has been priceless, and I will not weary our English cricketers by reiterating the obvious. For them this indeed is the moment of truth.

## The Benaud Invasion

*Richie Benaud, as befits a cricketer-journalist professional in both spheres, had a knack of expressing the right sentiment in an appealing phrase. He does so here on the threshold of the 1961 tour wherein Australia retained the Ashes.*

April 22, 1961

The Australians have arrived not merely with the usual peal of bells but something if possible even more penetrating: a trumpet blast, one might say, comparable to that which greeted Sir Donald Bradman when he brought over the first post-war team in '48. Now the spotlight plays just as strongly, not on the old master, but on Richie Benaud who, in little more than two years, has made so notable a mark as captain of Australia.

Yesterday on board the *Himalaya* as he handled his Press conference with the understanding that derives from his being a journalist as well as a cricketer, one wondered whether either he or any of his questioners recalled that he was appointed quite out of the blue as Test captain in November, 1958.

The choice was unexpected and by no means well received. Yet since that day, Benaud's stock has risen without pause from the first overwhelming victory over England at Brisbane to the deciding Test against West Indies last winter in that series which will be recalled and written about so long as cricket is played.

Now here he is, having done so much to rehabilitate cricket's good repute in his own country and expected to play the leading part in boosting it here. The accent everywhere is on the game rather than the result. Yet, of course, once issue is joined what happens will seem to most people rather more important than how and why: at least it will to those who merely read and listen and look in on their screens.

The captain, knowing this as well as anyone, seemed to strike the right note when at Tilbury he said: 'We want to win very badly but if we lose, we want to lose playing attractively.'

That is fair enough, and it might be as well to add on his behalf that there are inevitable moments of consolidation at cricket which will only be absorbing to the connoisseur. Also, no one has yet gone so far as to suggest that, if a game cannot be won, in the interest of 'brighter' play – that over-used, misleading word – it should be gaily flung away.

A grim rearguard can be good cricket, indeed, some of the best. Who will forget Lord's, 1953?

He has struck a good note, too, by remarking: 'It doesn't concern us what the opposition does. We have our policy and will stick to it.'

In fact, up to a point, it takes two sides to make a game. But much has been lost in English cricket of late through one captain watching the other with the greatest intensity lest his own generous outlook (as he supposes it) is not swiftly reciprocated (in his own estimation) by his opposite number.

Advance forecasts have pictured the Australians as being strong in batting and, in bowling, over-reliant on the mature Davidson – who at nearly 32 will need some nursing – and, of course, the captain himself. Obviously they will be hoping that McKenzie fulfils the high hopes held out for him and that the other two new-ball men, Gaunt and Misson, learn how to use English wickets.

Since these are to be covered over-night, the wrist-spin of Kline and Simpson may have more scope than the orthodox left-arm of Quick. It is to be noted that the side contains no off-spinner: in Australia such creatures scarcely exist. Thus, so far as the bowling is concerned, we must wait and see. Strangely enough Australian bowlers have quite often failed in England, where it might be supposed that the friendlier pitches would have suited them.

Paradoxically, Australian batsmen seem to come straight off their own shirtfronts and deal with the more variable English conditions with the least possible demur. Very few Australian batsmen have failed to make plenty of runs over here and one both hopes and expects that there will be many big scores this summer.

Harvey and McDonald are old favourites, Burge is seemingly much improved, Simpson is now very much a force, and we hear well of Booth and Lawry.

The man who must attract most attention, however, is O'Neill, a natural athlete, strong and full of talent. On the evidence of several of his innings in Australia in 1958-59 – and notably his 71 not out in the Brisbane Test – few heights are beyond him.

How powerful the 1961 Australians prove to be can be assessed as time goes on. What is sure is that they will make the most of themselves under an extraordinarily shrewd and enthusiastic captain.

## Post-mortem 1962-63

Because the last Test ended in stalemate, this tour has often been denigrated. In my view it was one of the happier and more successful of post-war M.C.C. enterprises, as I indicate from the spot.

February 22, 1963

No Test tour is complete without its post-mortems. The song is over but the melody lingers on. What sort of a melody? How happy are one's recollections?

Well, the Ashes are left in Australia or, as I prefer to put it, they remain in suspense. In a sense this is unsatisfactory and for some the sterile ending leaves a taste of ashes in the mouth. But now is the time surely to try and see a tour in perspective and if one can adjust the focus at such a short distance the good, it would seem, more than counterbalances the bad.

Upwards of a million people have watched M.C.C. since they landed at Fremantle four and a half months ago – in days of falling attendances in all sports that is a bare quarter of a million fewer than the highest ever figure of a quarter of a century ago – and the memories of most of them will I expect be satisfying ones.

Glamorous individual things are, of course, too numerous to count. But certain items stand out at random; Dexter's hundred, for instance, against the Australian XI at Melbourne, one of the finest pieces of forcing batsmanship I have ever seen; the prolonged felicity of Cowdrey's 307 at Adelaide; the composite effort by Sheppard, Dexter and Cowdrey that won the second Test.

Most of England's batting in the Brisbane Test was effective and satisfying. Graveney had his moments of quality and the prolific Barrington, cast in a more sombre role, was by no means always quiet and restrained. The English out-cricket, certainly, was generally less satisfying.

Trueman's fire in the second innings at Melbourne was one conclusive performance, while Titmus, surely the find of the tour, had several, Allen, except for one bad day in the State match at Sydney when some odd notion or other was being put to the test, usually showed the arts of slow bowling at their best, while if many, too many, catches were missed some beauties were taken by Cowdrey, Graveney, Titmus, Barrington, Smith and others. Let no one forget the effort of Statham who, at the age of 32 and on his fourth tour of Australia, did much more work than any of the other faster bowlers, got most wickets and as far as I can recall was never off the field for a moment.

The disappointment in the cricket lay chiefly in the climax. Brisbane was a fine match and a proper draw in that the bat was in the ultimate account a little too good for the ball.

Melbourne and the first Sydney match were clear-cut and deserved victories for the respective sides. Then came the draw at Adelaide. It could be said there that the wicket was too good for the bowlers but no one can be sure that either side might not have won but for the injury to Davidson at the beginning of England's first innings and equally but for the half-day lost in the middle to the weather.

This last Sydney Test has been analysed enough already. It was unfinished because of England's tactical misappreciation on the first day, which I thought the most unsatisfactory episode of the tour, because of the sluggishness of the wicket and, indeed, the whole field which surely needs the urgent attention of Australian cricket officialdom, and not least because the fact of their holding the Ashes persuaded Benaud's team to wage defensive war from the beginning of the England second innings.

From the broad English viewpoint, granted certain reservations, the picture is not unsatisfactory. Few people expected Dexter's side to escape with a halved series. They have done so against more mature opponents for whom with the retirement from touring of Benaud, Harvey, Davidson and Mackay this marks the end of an era.

What now of the captain? He is an arresting figure of course and my belief is that both as leader and batsman the best of him lies immediately ahead. He has made a lot of mistakes of a tactical kind but he has the intelligence to learn from them.

A certain combination of impulsiveness and a wayward concentration has prevented his making quite such an impact as a batsman as he promised in the first two Tests. Yet he ranks with Sobers as one of the two most exciting batsmen in world cricket today. It is characteristic of the modern hypercritical attitude to those at the top that his supposed limitations are stressed and his virtues taken for granted.

Dexter, it seems to me, has the constitution and the temperament to withstand the strong tensions surrounding the leadership of the England XI at home and abroad. Not least he can combine toughness on the field with amiability towards the enemy off it.

It may seem trivial to mention but it will not be so to those who have had close connections with touring teams that on the eve of the final Test the two captains and their wives should have been seen together happily enjoying the performance of Nat King Cole.

So far as the off-field impression of his team is concerned Dexter could hardly have been luckier than to be surrounded as he was. Not many cricket visitors to Australia will have left behind more friends than the Duke of Norfolk, Alec Bedser, Colin Cowdrey and David Sheppard.

## "World Decider"

Having missed Australia v West Indies 1960–61, I was determined if possible to see the return engagement. Here are some thoughts from the spot before battle was joined. It is history now that the highest expectations were not realised, though after their ill-fortune in Australia there was compensation in West Indies winning the rubber and so becoming what they still remain (at the moment of writing) – World Champions.

*Sunday Telegraph,* February 28, 1965, Bridgetown

It will surprise no one at home to hear that the West Indies-Australia Test series, which begins at Sabina Park, Jamaica, on March 3, has enthused this corner of the cricket world to no ordinary degree.

For once the issue of supremacy as between the foremost cricket countries is apparently clear-cut. In successive summers first the West Indians and then the Australians have come to England and gone home with the honours.

Whoever win the rubber here can fairly claim to be cocks of the walk and if that should prove to be the West Indies it would be for the first time in cricket history.

Every man here knows this. He also knows that his side are probably better equipped all round than they have ever been, while Australia have bowling limitations, on paper at least, that ought in theory to let the strong array of West Indian batsmen in for some mighty tall scores. But Australia's batting list is also long and formidable, and aside from individual technical comparisons, West Indians are uncomfortably aware at the bottom of their hearts that though they have won several series against England, Australia have always been too much for them.

There have been four rubbers altogether, and though Frank Worrell emerged with the greater share of the glory from the last great battle in Australia, the fact is that the home side squeezed home to bring their Test victories to 13 against the West Indies' three.

The only time the Australians have previously visited these islands, 10 years ago, the power of their batting on wickets that were on the whole a slightly more perfect version of their own, swamped the West Indians. Australia made two scores of 500, one of 600.

In those days, however, West Indian cricket was to the same extent suffering certain growing pains which one hopes do not afflict it today. Over and above island rivalries – still strong – it took a long time for the administrative leaders to accept the idea of a professional captain.

The first time I came to the West Indies in 1947/8, the Board of Control, as a concession to contending interests, nominated three different captains for the four Tests before the series started. Although the great George Headley was one of them, on this occasion the prejudice against professionalism meant in practice that the most experienced men were apt to be overlooked and this was widely interpreted as a snub to colour.

There was therefore a sharp social significance to Worrell's outstanding successes, and the old order, thankfully, has passed.

Today the West Indies stand on the threshold of a new playing era, with Gary Sobers, their most distinguished cricketer, made captain and with Worrell, now Sir Frank, seconded from community development duties with the Trinidad Government to serve as team manager for all five Test matches.

This latter appointment is a great step forward which increases West Indian chances from evens to somewhere around five or six to four on. At the same time an enormous amount is being asked of Sobers as tactician, batsman, bowler in two styles, and fielder extraordinary, and one can scarcely open the paper here without either the captain or the manager emphasising what a big job lies ahead.

It is wonderful to be surrounded by such faith and moral support, but there comes a moment when it must be terribly difficult to live up to. As to island rivalries, it remains to be seen whether a selection committee comprising G. E. Gomez, J. D. Goddard, A. F. Rae and B. Gaskin, plus the captain and manager, can forget origins altogether.

For instance there are gathered now in Kingston seven men from Barbados, four from British Guiana, and one from Trinidad, and from these and also from the Jamaicans engaged against the Australians the first Test team will be picked.

Is there a Jamaican good enough? If not, will they stretch a point and give the home crowd at least one here to cheer on?

There is no great brotherly love between islanders born 1,000 miles apart. In this hotbed of Barbados they have little doubt that their own kith and kin could do the job best, though if pressed they might more or less willingly co-opt the services of Kanhai and Gibbs.

But however the selectors decide, there is no doubting the strength of a side the basis of which will be Sobers, Kanhai, Hunte, Butcher, Hall, Griffith, and Gibbs assisted by four from Solomon, Davis, McMorris, Nurse, White, King and either Allan or Hendriks as wicketkeeper.

I have pictured the scene from the West Indian angle, since the Australian potential will be appreciated pretty accurately in the light of their doings in England last year. Simpson is radiating confidence and he must be highly pleased with the early form of his batsmen.

At this range it looks rather a matter of whether even the West Indian attack can bowl them out twice.

# CHAPTER FIVE

# SOME FIRST IMPRESSIONS

This chapter, I fully realise, might well be criticised as being more 'bitty' than most. Sometimes one was unlucky in that the first few times one saw a great player he made no special impact on the game; or one's space was unusually tight. Though my records have been carefully kept I suspect that in one or two instances the cuttings may have gone astray. I am sorry that nothing emerges about Brian Statham, Tom Graveney, Ken Barrington, Wes Hall, Lance Gibbs or Neil Harvey, to name a few of the post-war 'greats'.

In one or two cases – notably Ted Dexter and Graeme Pollock – my first real look has coincided with a really outstanding innings, so that the length of the entry is in no way a measure of the eminence of the subject as compared with others equally famous.

I begin, without apology, with what was very far from a first impression, since I saw all but one of Don Bradman's great innings of 1930. When, however, we sailed for Australia in 1946–47 one question dominated all others: would he, the greatest of all cricketers since W.G., play again? After reading this report from Adelaide, *Daily Telegraph* readers knew the answer.

## Genius Revived

October 24, 1946

I have just been watching Don Bradman bat. The little group of Englishmen on the Adelaide ground this evening were seeing him for the first time on a cricket field since that dramatic day at the Oval eight years ago, when, within a few hours of Hutton breaking his record, he was carried in with a broken ankle.

It is possible, I feel, that the everlasting reports relating to the probability or otherwise of Bradman (who captains South Australia against the M.C.C. in the match beginning on

Friday) playing in this coming Test series may have aroused some impatience at home.

In case that is so, I should say at once that in civilian clothes the greatest cricketer of his time looks a frail little man, full of good spirits but struggling with ill-health.

The impression, indeed, lasted while he indulged gingerly in some fielding practice at the range where he has achieved especial fame, deep-mid-off. But then in an English March wind and with the nets in deep shadow he went in to bat.

The pitch was slow – roughly an inch of rain has fallen this last 24 hours. The bowlers were those who will comprise the South Australian attack against the M.C.C. on Friday.

Bradman played quite beautifully. Although he used the bowling merely as a vehicle for trying out one stroke after another, he was never beaten nor even put under the necessity of departing from the smooth pendulum of his swing.

Whatever are the secrets of genius in batsmanship, the secrets which among modern batsmen Bradman shares in like measure with Jack Hobbs alone, they seem to be operative still: the exceptional speed of eye, that automatic reaction in the brain called 'reflex action' that is to within a minute fraction of time instantaneous and which when translated into action, produces the most perfectly rhythmic stroke.

From a distance of 30 yards Bradman might have been having a brief knock before continuing one of his great innings at Leeds or the Oval. But it is one thing to test one's skill for 20 minutes in private and another to embark on a six-day Test match.

It is obvious that he could have made no announcement regarding his availability for first-class cricket until he had tried himself out, and equally clear that he must have been physically incapable of doing so until now.

One might add he will have his work cut out to become as hard and resilient as he will wish by the time of the first Test at the end of November.

## The "W" Triumvirate

There was no doubt of the impression created in my mind by the

young West Indians, Clyde Walcott, Everton Weekes and Frank
Worrell, who in their first innings against the M.C.C. team of
1947–48 made respectively 120, 118 not out, and 97. This, however,
was the worst period of the newsprint restriction when even a Test
Match might only rate half a column. So rich descriptive prose was
at a premium!

January–February, 1948

Walcott looked a most dangerous batsman. He is a tall, powerful young man with beautiful wrists which he uses for a squarish
drive after the manner of Compton. He is strong on most of the
leg-side strokes too, and altogether a horrible person to bowl
to on these pitches.

So we thought until Weekes arrived, and then it was soon
clear that here was another cricketer with all the characteristics
of the very best West Indians. Scarcely bigger than Headley,
Weekes is wonderfully nimble on his feet and quick to judge
the length of the ball.

\*          \*          \*

The most significant happening of the day was an innings
from Worrell ending three short of his hundred, which proclaimed him in his first Test to be a very fine player. Here
seems to be a tremendously good batsman. To have time to
spare is a common sign of ability, but I can remember no one,
not even Bradman or Duleepsinhji, who seemed to be a more
leisurely stroke-maker than this new West Indies Test player.
There may be flaws in his method that these conditions did not
disclose. Today, at any rate, he was the complete batsman, an
adept at every stroke, and none more than the straight drive
played with a full follow through that engendered remarkable
power considering he is quite a slight young man. In the
evening Gomez showed an unusual power and variety of stroke,
and Worrell went on briskly to a seemingly inevitable hundred
until late-cutting a wide one he snicked a catch to the wicket-
keeper.

# Harvey at Headingley

Harvey's first innings against England ranks among the greatest of its kind, comparable (within my recollection) with Duleep's 173 in 1930 and Doug Walters' 155 in 1965. But fourteen paragraphs was not a lot in which to describe such tremendous cricket as the third day's play in this Fourth Test at Headingley.

July 26, 1948

The cricket touched the heights, with the classic partnership of Miller and the 19-year-old Harvey as the culminating point.

I have never seen a better short innings than Miller's 58, not even Woolley's 41 at Lord's in 1930, and Harvey must have owed something to his elder's example at the critical time they came together. At any rate, a beginning more confident and certain than Harvey's has hardly been made in my recollection. It is clear that Australia have found a left-handed stroke-maker of the style and order of McCabe and Kippax.

Harvey will make many more excellent hundreds, but he may never play a better innings than this, just as Washbrook may never bat more finely, though in a manner very different, than he did on the first day.

# A Great New-Zealander

It was a nice point in the first years after the war whether Arthur Morris, Martin Donnelly or Bert Sutcliffe was the best left-handed batsman playing.

May 2, 1949

The New Zealand cricketers have made an admirable beginning, and in a single day thoroughly established the strength of their batsmanship, at least in the early numbers.

Sutcliffe, the young left-hander, played a convincing and delightful innings. He has several unfailing hall-marks: a long, straight back-lift, and oceans of time, and his body is always over the line of the ball. Yesterday his strokes were mostly on the on, because the bowlers tended to pitch short and to leg-ward. His hook is violent in effect, but smooth and controlled, and he swings on to the ball surely when he is executing all the variations of the pull off the front leg.

He had scarcely put a foot wrong when a flick off his toes flew round the corner to where Hutton and others stood so profitably for Bradman. He seemed to have his hundred already written in the book, but as it was, his 72 in a hundred minutes could hardly have been more impressive.

Scott's christian name is Verdun, and *ils ne passeront pas* probably described aptly enough both the ambitions and limitations of his batsmanship. His back-lift is often scarcely discernible, but his phlegmatic concentration seems an ideal counterpart to Sutcliffe. It is significant that Scott has been in first in only one previous match, the last trial before the team was announced. In that Sutcliffe and he put on a double hundred in each innings. They fit, and, not least, they run quickly and easily together.

Three old friends must be more cursorily noticed. Wallace, after he had got his bearings, played a confident attractive innings, in which he used all the strokes, tuning up one after the other. Hadlee batted with characteristic soundness, and if Donnelly made a few mistakes when the whole burden of the scoring fell upon him, his first 23 in a quarter of an hour was the gem of the day.

# May-Time at Cambridge

Peter May, after serving as a National Serviceman in the Navy, went up to Cambridge in the autumn of 1949, as did David Sheppard. The Cambridge XI of 1950 thus contained in the first four places men who either then or within a twelvemonth were Test batsmen: Dewes, Sheppard, Doggart and May. Add such names as Subba Row, Warr, Alexander (all Test cricketers) and Marlar, and the quality of the cricket at Fenner's in the early fifties cannot be difficult to imagine.

I first played against Peter in 1947, his last year at Charterhouse (and even by some unusual mischance took his wicket). This was my first sight of him – the first of oh! how many – in senior company. This comment was what an innings of 39 in an hour seemed to rate in two-thirds of a column describing a big Cambridge score.

May 11, 1950

After a dismal succession of wet days Fenner's, looking its green and lovely best, basked in sunshine this morning. There was a keen edge to the cricket, with the University naturally anxious to make up for their many lost hours and a singularly young set of Lancashire bowlers striving to win their stripes.

Dewes's 125 was his second highest score in first-class cricket and it was stretched over $4\frac{3}{4}$ hours. He seemed to be conscious during most of his stay at the wicket that he was not timing the ball well, but it is a virtue just to go playing on hoping the touch will come. The saving graces of his innings, from a spectator's viewpoint, were an occasional fine clumping hit past mid-off and his running between wickets, which was, as usual, excellent. In fact, I am inclined to think that only a quick-footed batsman would have pushed the game along really quickly against accurate bowling on this wicket, for the ball was keeping even lower than usual.

Alas! I can contribute no information about the promising Sheppard, for he was promptly bowled by a ball well up that swung in late, always a good one, in the first over.

Several distinguished judges have committed themselves to glittering opinions about May, and he seemed, during his hour at the wicket, to have all the marks of a batsman of extremely high quality. There are three striking things about his play: he is remarkably quick down the wicket to slow bowling, he plays back with oceans of time in hand, and he is always right over the line of the ball. What better foundations for batsmanship could there be?

## Eight for Trueman

This notice would be more properly described as an early Test impression since Fred Trueman had made his mark in the two Tests against India prior to this one. But after the fast bowling drought, when Australia had had all the fire and speed and England none, here was a young fast bowler suddenly ripping out the stumps and establishing himself within a few weeks as the long-awaited prodigy. Trueman has often bowled better in the 64 further Tests he has played since this one, but neither he nor any fast bowler in

Test history has had a better return than his analysis here of eight for 31.

July 21, 1952

No England bowler has taken eight wickets in an innings, as Trueman did, since Verity bowled out Australia at Lord's on a sticky dog. And though everyone remembered how Tom Richardson, heroically unavailing in one of the classic pieces of fast bowling, took all seven Australia wickets that fell in the Old Trafford Test of '96 no one could quote a case of an English fast bowler getting eight.

If it came to the point, nor could anyone remember such suicidal batting in a Test match from accredited batsmen, as that of Umrigar and Phadkar. So bowling comparisons, on the strength of figures, if not odious, are at any rate valueless.

Nevertheless, make whatever reservations you like and Trueman still performed an impressive and highly encouraging feat. He bowled down a strong wind, blowing from about mid-off, and he had the stimulus of the occasional ball that kicked.

The rain that had held up the game over the first two days was mostly drizzle that did not penetrate very deep. Nor far below the surface the earth was still firm, and so the ball was apt to rise to different heights.

It was certainly not a thoroughly spiteful wicket: nothing like that, for instance, on which Hutton and Ikin stood and took a battering from McCarthy this time a year ago. However, it had enough life to raise apprehension and worse in several of the batsmen, and such a state of mind causes only one sort of reaction in the fast bowler.

Trueman bowled faster than at Headingley, when the wind also blew stiffly behind him, and he bowled straighter. Furthermore, thanks to the combination of a native shrewdness and the quiet advice of his captain, he bowled very sensibly.

Trueman knows that to the batsman whose legs stray to the width of the return crease the best of all balls is a fast half-volley. He has the good sense to vary his pace, and so conserve his energy, and he also has the most useful of all balls for a fast bowler, the yorker.

All comparisons with famous fast bowlers may be discounted

at the moment. For all his 24 wickets in this series the real
testing is yet to come. In these two respects, however, he does
distinctly resemble Lindwall.

## The Young Cowdrey

When Colin Cowdrey in 1953 made Oxford's first hundred in the
University match for five years, I was moved to compare him at the
wicket with Walter Hammond. Colin was then only 20, and before
the summer was out he hit two notable fifties for the Gentlemen
against the Australians at Lord's which made me rue the fact – in
late August – that he had not been given the chance to mature in
the West Indies that winter. He of course went to Australia with
Len Hutton's side a year afterwards and fully justified any praise
that might up to then have seemed extravagant.

July 6, 1953

Cowdrey's century was the bright jewel of the day, the best
piece of batsmanship perhaps in the University match since
H. E. Webb's 145 not out put Oxford on the road to victory
five years ago. (What a sad thing that, outside the circle of
hospitals cricket, nothing has been seen of Webb since!)

Cowdrey had just one major piece of luck, and it was a very
vital piece. Before he reached double figures slip missed a low
catch off Marlar. When he was in the 60's Marlar himself
failed to take what would have been a wonderfully good catch
off his own bowling. Early in his innings Cowdrey once or
twice was in trouble against Marlar, apparently playing for
the off-break to balls that came straight on. But while these
items are mentioned in justice to Marlar the general impression
was of a fine, mature piece of batsmanship in which two strokes
predominated, the off-drive and the forcing hit wide of mid-on.

There is a picture taken of Cowdrey at the age of 18 making
a stroke that was the very image of Hammond. Extravagant
predictions seldom help anyone, and more often than not they
recoil on the heads of their authors. All I will say then is that
Cowdrey, who is now only 20, has two important points of
resemblance with that great batsman: poise and balance.

When he is hitting the ball he is usually steady as a rock,

head still, and the feet firmly planted. Some of his off-driving was a joy to see, and to at least one distinguished old player added pleasure was given by the sight of Lumsden and Hayward, one from West Indies, the other from Australia, standing at short-leg applauding the stroke.

## Sobers' Début

There had to be something about Sobers, but unfortunately I can discover only these brief, if flattering, references on the occasion of his first Test Match, at the age of 17, against England at Kingston. The accent there was on Trevor Bailey's seven for 34, followed by Len Hutton's 205, which together won the match and halved the series.

March, 1954

Before Ramadhin went, Sobers had been able to show several wristy left-hander's strokes and to make it clear furthermore that nothing Trueman could send down was too fast to ruffle him.

\*          \*          \*

Sobers made an excellent impression. He is a slim young man who runs lightly up to the wicket and the arm almost touches the ear as it comes over. On what might serve as a model action for a slow left-hand bowler, he builds changes of flight and spin in the classical manner. It will be surprising if we do not come to know his name well in the years ahead.

## Dexter Rampant

Ted Dexter on top of a fine school record at Radley did his National Service in the Far East, had a reasonably good but not scintillating first year at Cambridge, and really burst on the cricket world in 1957. The power and quality of this innings in the Fenner's sunshine strikes very clearly in the mind. He played for the Gentlemen at Lord's – taking five wickets for 8 – and within a year had his first cap for England, as will be seen.

May 23, 1957

Walcott, Sobers, Close, and now, to complete a quartet of fine
innings seen within a few days, Dexter, who made 185 for
Cambridge here today. The Lancashire bowling, with Statham
and Tattersall looking on, was not terribly strong. The Fenner's
wicket, as usual, was a beauty. The difference in the circumstances prevents a comparison as between Dexter's batting
today and that of the other three at Lord's. But in the power
and cleanness of his hitting Dexter gave as much pleasure as
any of them.

It is safe to say that no undergraduate has dealt so forcibly
with a county attack since M. P. Donnelly was wreaking
destruction in the Oxford Parks just after the war. What added
to the value of Dexter's innings was that examinations had
taken away at least four key players from the University side,
and in consequence it seemed only he stood between Lancashire and an inconsiderable total. Two wickets were down for
a handful when he went in, and a third fell with only 27 on
the board.

Having reached his 50 inside the hour, Dexter was always
ahead of the clock in terms of 100 before lunch, and he duly
got it with quarter of an hour to spare. The game began at
11 a.m. (in order to give Lancashire an easier journey on the
last day), but since Dexter had not gone in until 11.20 the
distinction can be granted him without any qualification.

The older habitués were harking back to E. T. Killick to
remember the last undergraduate century before lunch. The
occasion apparently was a match in 1929 against Essex wherein that great cricketer took his second double hundred within
a fortnight, hitting, strangely enough, exactly the same number
of boundaries as Dexter today, three sixes and 27 fours.

A score of 180 for four at lunch was an extraordinary transformation. The new ball soon afterwards quietened things a
little. Dexter going to some pains to play himself in again and
to iron out a fault which apparently had been getting him out
recently, playing across the line of the fast good-length ball on
the off stump.

When he got going again he hooked one six to long leg,
another to mid-wicket, and off-drove a third, the last a soaring

blow to the far end of the field, hit full into the breeze and landing on the running track.

The last stage of Dexter's innings was played in the company of Swift, an Australian Freshman from St Peter's, Adelaide, who later showed himself a good workmanlike wicket-keeper. For a No. 10 he is no duffer, it seems, with the bat.

Dexter was bowled at last, hooking, and both the crowd and the Lancashire players applauded him all the way home for an innings that has established his stature as a university batsman without any fear of argument.

## Success - And Yet

Rain so interfered with play in the Old Trafford Test of 1958 against New Zealand that at the week-end, when the M.C.C. team for Australia was due to be picked, one of the candidates, Dexter, had not been in to bat. The team was nevertheless chosen, and he excluded, though called for later from Paris. Though not strictly a first impression this notice seems therefore to have some historical interest.

The selectors' decision seems just as foolish retrospectively as it did at the time – even though when called upon to fly to Australia in mid-tour Dexter could not at once find his feet. If he had gone with the original party the story might possibly not have been such a sombre one.

July 29, 1958

The England captain signalised the announcement of the M.C.C. team for Australia by making a brilliant 100, his 10th in Test matches, while Dexter, in his first Test innings, made 52 in 80 minutes, scoring practically run for run with his famous partner.

One could scarcely over-praise May's innings, for hard though he hit the short and over-pitched ball, the basis of it was the soundest possible defence. He saw the ball so early that he seemed able almost to glance up and decide on the direction of the stroke to a matter of a yard or two.

The more important performance, however, bearing the

*Four County Captains* – and good ones. A. C. D. Ingleby-Mackenzie of Hampshire, Captain 1958/65 (TOP LEFT); D. Kenyon of Worcestershire, Captain 1959/67 (TOP RIGHT); M. J. K. Smith of Warwickshire, Captain 1957/67 (BOTTOM LEFT); D. B. Close of Yorkshire, Captain 1963/68 (BOTTOM RIGHT). Ingleby-Mackenzie led Hampshire to their first Championship in 1961, Kenyon led Worcestershire to theirs in 1964 and won again in 1965. Close has had three Championships in 1963, 1966 and 1967, and has also led Yorkshire to the Gillette Cup, seen here. Warwickshire under Smith won the Gillette in 1966, and were Championship runners-up in 1964

PATRICK EAGER

ABOVE: Modern Score Board. Herewith the only English Australian-style score board (and electrically operated), at Trent Bridge. BELOW: Canterbury Week. Friendly informality and family watching, two of the chief ingredients of the oldest of all cricket weeks (founded 1842), are well captured in this picture

PATRICK EAGER

future in mind, was Dexter's. I have already lamented his absence from the M.C.C. team. I dare say if Sir Donald Bradman, or any other of the Australian experts, had been here this afternoon, they would have been both extremely surprised, and also somewhat relieved, that they would not be seeing him this winter.

Equally, he would certainly have aroused the most disquieting thoughts among the M.C.C. team selectors, most of whom, their job accomplished, had already left Manchester.

It was a sorry irony that his batting had come just a day too late. I have little doubt that if he is able to play with sufficient regularity, Dexter will take an important part in English cricket very soon.

The point is, though, he might so well have done so in Australia, for his method of batting is better suited to the wickets there than that of any of the new batsmen chosen.

## O'Neill Arrives

When M.C.C. landed at Perth in October, 1958, England had won three Test series running and Australians were hoping fervently for some new star to help bring the honours back, and to re-enthuse the public. Norman O'Neill had had a tremendous build-up, and expectation was correspondingly high when he took the field for the Combined XI in the second game of the tour. There were thus all the ingredients for a first impression, of one sort or another. We were not disappointed.

October 21, 1958

The manner of O'Neill's appearance had a dramatic touch. McDonald, presumably at the instigation of the captain Rutherford, made the sign, 'O'N,' to the dressing room.

Apparently Mackay would have come in No. 3 had a wicket fallen quickly. No sooner was this done than Cowdrey, in May's absence, called up Laker for his first bowl in Australia, and Laker's fourth ball, floating seductively away, had McDonald picked up low by Cowdrey at slip.

So it was O'Neill v Laker and, at the down-wind end, first Trueman and then Statham.

The play that followed was worthy of the build-up with which O'Neill's appearance had been preceded, and it became progressively more evident as the afternoon wore on that this time, at least, those who have been heralding the arrival of a new Australian star have scarcely been claiming too much for him.

O'Neill began quietly, but with the most mature confidence. He was content to take a long look at Laker, who deserved all the watching anyone could give him, and he attempted no liberties with the speed.

He played out at Laker, and the ball trickled for a single to third man. Statham tried him with a fast bouncer, and O'Neill only avoided it by falling in the crease on his back. In a later spell by Statham he aimed a late-cut and missed, and when Trueman in the evening came on up-wind there was a slash which might have been a chance had there been a second slip.

These were the only false strokes until just before the close O'Neill made rather a hash of a hook and took a knock on the fingers. He had once previously attempted the stroke and nearly given a catch. Might this be an Achilles heel? The evidence is extremely slender, but it could just possibly have given the M.C.C. captain an idea. It ought also to be emphasised that this was a wicket of the easiest possible pace. It is highly improbable that O'Neill would have had such a comfortable ride on the Perth wicket of four years ago.

With this qualification made, however, I must say I cannot remember when a young cricketer announced himself with such certainty. There are the seeds of greatness in O'Neill, and his natural attributes are clearly such that the future will be largely what he chooses to make it.

It is a reserve of character, tenacity, courage, calm detachment, other moral virtues too, perhaps, which divides the Bradmans, the Huttons and the Mays from others of their kind. Whether O'Neill can remain undazzled by the arc lights remains to be seen.

The physical equipment is obviously there. He is all but six feet tall, but the impression one has is of breadth rather than height. He is big in the thighs, thick across the shoulders and wonderfully strong in the fore-arms and wrists.

He played all the strokes (the hook off the fast bowlers

excepted), but it was the power off the back foot which impressed one most. Here he showed glimpses of Walter Hammond, and the nearest resemblance I can suggest is to Hammond when young, even down to the thick dark thatch of hair.

In the stance the blade is held shut, but the back-lift is pretty straight, especially for an Australian, and if the ball is only slightly short he is back on the right leg, and the stroke is made with a punch which as often as not beats the in-field.

In forward play he is inclined to be more deliberate, but when he is 'there' he clips the ball as hard off the left leg as the right.

This is a sufficient general analysis for the moment. There will certainly be plenty of opportunities for adding to the picture. Perhaps I shall need to subtract something.

Subtract something? Not immediately. His Test career began brilliantly at Brisbane, and O'Neill for the next seven years was as exciting a batsman as any in the game. Consistency of achievement, however, eluded him. 'Calm detachment' was something he could not command. His nerves were tightly strung, and when he retired at the early age of 30 it was with his high promise only partly fulfilled.

## Pollock at Trent Bridge

I grant myself a little poetic license here since this innings of Graeme Pollock's was played in the Second Test, and I had seen him make 56 and 5 in the First at Lord's. However, if not exactly a 'first impression' it was near enough – and as one of the most memorable pieces of batting since the war it obviously had to have a place in this book.

August 6, 1965

An innings was played here today by Graeme Pollock which in point of style and power, of ease and beauty of execution, is fit to rank with anything in the annals of the game.

Pollock came in when after 50 anxious minutes South Africa's score stood at 16 for two. Between this point and lunch he batted easily and without inhibition or restraint while two more wickets fell, and his companions struggled in every sort of difficulty against some very good swing bowling by Cartwright.

When the afternoon began the scoreboard showed 76 for four, Pollock 34. An hour and 10 minutes later it said 178 for six, and Pollock was walking back with 125 to his name, and the crowd standing in salute to a glorious piece of batting which must have carried the minds of the older ones among them to Stan McCabe's great innings here against England in '38.

In cold fact this young man of 21 had made then 125 out of 162 in two hours and 20 minutes, and in the 70 minutes since lunch 91 out of 102. In his whole innings were 21 fours, and the two of these that came off the edge from Cartwright's bowling were the only false strokes of any kind that I saw.

The other 19 were either hit with a full, easy swing of the bat, or glanced or cut to every point of the compass. No one could find any way of containing him because (like E. R. Dexter, G. Sobers and R. Kanhai, perhaps alone among modern players) he uses every stroke.

He saw the ball so early that if it were of good length or more he met it with an almost leisurely movement, and drove off the front foot with a freedom and certainty that left the field standing.

When the length faltered, as it did of course under such assault, he lay back and clipped the short stuff with a crack that must almost have echoed the other side of the river.

It may perhaps be said by anyone trying to evaluate this innings that to have deserved the label of greatness it would have needed to be confronted by bowling of a higher quality than much that was seen. Well, when South Africa were at their worst pass, at 43 for four, with Bland just gone, he made three strokes to the cover boundary inside a few minutes, two off Cartwright and one off Titmus, and all three from balls that would have looked a good length to anyone else, with a precision of timing and consequent speed over the field that had everyone gasping.

With these strokes the moral balance shifted dramatically, and South Africa must have begun to see the vision of recovery so long as their young hero could stay. It may be that after lunch as his assault reached its climax the bowling began to look somewhat ragged. The fact is, though, that until Pollock got into his stride almost anyone on the ground would have estimated South Africa's probable total at around 120, and there would have been a great many words spilt about the difficulty of getting modern bowling away, the impossibility, indeed, in conditions which allowed the ball to move as much as it did today.

Pollock has been spoken of in the same breath as Frank Woolley, and so far as the multitude of admirers of that great man are concerned such words are close to blasphemy.

There is no one who holds Woolley in greater esteem than myself, and I believe that he would have been proud, at his best, to have played as well as Pollock did this afternoon. Indeed, in the left-handedness, in the height and reach, and in the clean-cut simplicity of his striking of the ball, the comparison with Woolley is the obvious one that applies. And if any young cricketer asks how the very best of the pre-war players batted he could be safely told: 'Just like Graeme Pollock did against England at Trent Bridge.'

## Enter Douglas Walters

Walters in '65 was hailed in Australia almost as enthusiastically as O'Neill had been in '58. Like O'Neill, Walters responded with a hundred in his first innings against M.C.C. The background in this case was an English score of 527 for six, declared, which was about the best composite batting performance I have seen by an M.C.C. side in six tours of Australia.

November 29, 1965

I must hasten to applaud the old master on the New South Wales side (Booth) and to salute the new one. Walters joined his captain directly before lunch with New South Wales facing M.C.C.'s huge total at four for two.

Behind him Walters had two dropped catches and a rough handling as a bowler. He must have known how sadly he had disappointed those who see in him the obvious recruit for the Australia XI at Brisbane. A young cricketer is not insensitive to such a predicament. It is just that some react better than others.

I can only say that from his very first scoring stroke, a late cut to the fence, Walters batted beautifully. He sees the ball early, he has a nice sense of timing and he is very straight, apparently happiest when driving the fast bowling.

Booth's batting, of course, is in the classical mould and one cannot pay Walters a higher compliment than to say that often it was only by noting Booth's extra height that one could tell one batsman from the other.

For Walters, Booth's smooth technique at the other end while he was playing probably the most important innings of his life up to date must have been a tremendous encouragement. Together they made 142 for the third wicket in a shade under two hours, the rate comparing with all but the purple patches in the M.C.C. innings.

# CHAPTER SIX

# TOPICAL ESSAYS

The pieces which follow are taken some from the leader page of *The Daily Telegraph*, one or two from general articles, but most from the Cricket Commentaries in which these many years I have been allowed to range over a wide variety of subjects. They can mostly be allowed to speak for themselves without much in the way of additional comment. The first was published in *The Field*, for whom I was very glad to write in the first five years after the war when space in daily papers was such a problem. Contraction is no doubt a valuable discipline for a writer, and I have often been accused (and with good reason) by less fortunate colleagues of having had to submit too little to considerations of length. Looking back, I am surprised at the space I used to fill once papers grew larger. But at least the subjects here have been pruned to a tidy length.

## W. G.'s Day, This

*The Field*, June 11, 1949

It is fifty years to within a few days since W. G. Grace played for the last time in a Test match. Captain C. B. Fry has told exactly the manner of his going out: how he was late for the Selection Committee meeting that was to choose the team for the Second Test match of 1899; how, on his arrival, the Doctor, who was in the chair, put to him the point-blank question, 'Should Archie play at Lord's?': and how thus, unknowingly, he gave the decisive opinion which involved the great man himself standing down. Few eminent figures have found it easy to leave the stage, and we know that W. G. did not do so without a pang, but that he felt in his heart that the decision was the proper one.

The crowd at Trent Bridge, perhaps irked at England's rather moderate showing – they did not achieve their draw with much to spare – had been critical of his fielding, and to be barracked was an experience he neither understood nor appreciated. He was too slow now, too slow and too heavy, and perhaps, at fifty, his eye was not quite quick enough to cope with Ernest Jones. This, by the way, was W. G.'s last year with Gloucestershire, too, before the unfortunate misunderstandings that caused him to leave the West Country, and to launch his London County project. Thus, it could be said, we celebrate now the anniversary of a landmark in the county sense, for the Graces made Gloucestershire, and Gloucestershire were among the sponsors and founders of the County Championship.

But 1899 was the beginning and end of an era in several senses. It was the first year in which the Tests, instead of being the concern and responsibility of the various County clubs on whose grounds they took place, were brought under the management of the newly-formed Board of Control. Again, it was the first year in which their number was increased to five. The googly, too, with its revolutionary effect on the technique of batsmanship, was only a year or two ahead. It was the closing both of a century, and of one of the cricket ages.

I hardly think the average modern enthusiast can conjure any closely-detailed design of the cricket of fifty years ago. He knows from the photographs and the prints what the players looked like, he may have seen the short simple skeleton pads, the fashionable batting-gloves of the period, the caps with short peaks, and so on. He can imagine, perhaps, from the pictures the actions of some of the bowlers: of Tom Richardson, for instance, with his bounding, swinging run-up, and the dainty, slanting approach of Colin Blythe. But what of the batting? I confess that my own imagination, at least, is not equal to any clear impression of how W. G. went through the motions of batsmanship, or J. T. Tyldesley, or Victor Trumper.

In a more general picture certain features seem fairly well established. If an early film showing the action of a match could be brought to light I suppose the first thing that would strike the modern eye would be the direction of the bowling and the more formal disposition of the fielders. The faster bowlers, especially, kept their attack going at the off-stump or outside, and mid-on and square-leg had no assistance in guarding the on-side. Off-side play was the thing, though there were, of course, famous exponents of the various leg-hits, from Charles Fry downwards, and no one presumably bowled to 'Ranji' without a long leg. The leg-break, too, was coming into fashion, developed by C. L. Townsend, and practised, at its best, by Len Braund.

The off-theory itself, incidentally, was of no great antiquity. Mr Altham records how, according to W. G., a Gloucestershire amateur, R. F. Miles, who bowled slow left-arm with no particular skill, threw up an innocent-looking barrage of wide half-volleys to Surrey one fine day on the Oval wicket with notable effect. The theory, apparently, extended gradually to the right-arm bowlers, causing, it may be added, much slow play, particularly on the part of the northern professionals.

It is a common cricket weakness to eulogise the past, and perhaps difficult, in these days of in-swingers and leg-slips, not to sigh for the old off-side play. But a conscientious comparison with fifty years ago must note that period as the one of pluperfect pitches, when marl and liquid manure were applied with more liberality than discretion, and the bowler's lot was harder than at any time in history. Within two years of W. G.'s last Test came Alfred Lyttelton's famous proposal to amend the law of l.b.w., the proposal that won the day at a full meeting of M.C.C., but failed to obtain the two-thirds majority needed to change the *status quo*.

As to what W. G. would think of modern cricket, a great deal might be hazarded, particularly by those who knew him and his generation. No doubt many things would appeal to him; the general skill of the wicket-keepers, which by all credible account exceeds those of the 'nineties, the scientific placing of the field, and, of course, the complicated art of the googly. How W. G. would, himself, have enjoyed ensnaring his victims with the one that went the other way!

Equally surely, some things would have mystified him; chiefly, I think, the decline of length in bowling, with all the inevitable consequences of that defection, which has so lowered the batsman's art. The cricket of 1899 was more formal and stereotyped, less flexible and ingenious. There was certainly a more implicit adherence to first principles, both in batting and bowling. More attractive? As to that, there are many whose views are worth very much more than mine.

## "Better Cricket"

Like most such sentiments this piece could have been written yesterday. The point is, it was appropriate when the post-war cricket boom was at its peak.

May 12, 1952

What's in a word? The answer frequently is that there is a great deal. I am not conscious of ever having written the phrase 'brighter cricket'; at all events, I can safely promise not to use it in future. For, as describing the movement to which the county clubs have committed themselves, with the enthusiastic approval of their patrons, it conveys a false idea.

Some writers, appreciating this, have cast about for different adjectives: more enterprising, more attractive, more virile cricket, and so forth. But there is surely a simpler, unambiguous word covering all one wishes to imply. What is wanted is merely *better cricket*.

The real condemnation of so much of the county play of recent seasons has not primarily been that it was dull, although it was dull, but that it was bad. It is dull, for instance, to watch batsmen pushing away at a slow left-arm bowler without anyone in the deep field, and making no effort to hit the ball over his head.

I have been haunted all winter by a fantastic analysis which Middlesex allowed Wardle to produce at Lord's one day last June when, from first to last, he scarcely turned the ball an inch and had no fielder further from the bat than deep mid-off. It is dull watching but it is also essentially bad batting.

It is equally dull to watch an in-swing bowler slanting his attack at the batsman's legs with a covey of fielders lurking round the corner to pick up the snicks, the glides and the tickles. It is dull watching, and it is bad bowling. The opposite of dull is bright: hence the phrase. Yet, it must be recognised that there are circumstances dictated by tactics, or by the wicket, when slow play may be good play. Cricket is not a circus.

A few days ago a distinguished player asked me with a distinct touch of scorn in his voice, 'And what do *you* think of this brighter cricket caper?' He affected to believe that everyone was now expected to go in and start thrashing the ball to the boundary or over it, and he concluded, reasonably enough that 'it's all very well to talk.' His sentiments were roughly on a par with those of the famous cricketer who cynically remarked, 'Brighter cricket! I only hope they try it out against us!'

The Indian manager, Mr P. Gupta, may or may not have had a similar thought in his mind when, speaking after the dinner to the Indians at Worcester, he remarked that, in the cricket sense, his countrymen had always been our pupils. 'You give us the lead in this brighter play and we will follow you.'

Of course, when one pins down the average cricketer in discussion he will admit that much modern county play in recent years has been flaccid, unimaginative and bad. He will admit as much in theory. He may not, however, see in its true light the situation in which his own innings or his own bowling is involved. And that is precisely why in cricket, with all its shifts and changes, and its rich and frequent tactical opportunities, the most important single factor is captaincy.

There will be plenty of occasions in the next few months when the county captain, who makes every effort to put energy and initiative into the play, will be deserving of sympathy.

He will be dealing, in many cases, with men who have been brought to accept a counterfeit standard: bowlers who are happy to be prodded and dabbed square of the wicket for ones and twos for hours, but whose pride is at once assailed if anyone hits them straight: batsmen who regard a score of 70 for one at luncheon on the first day as infinitely more satisfying than 140 for three. To such men it will naturally follow that a brave scheme which misfires is the proper penalty of tempting providence.

## A Throwing Case

The no-balling of Cuan McCarthy in 1952 was only the second case in half a century of a bowler being called in English county cricket. It was followed later the same season by the no-balling of Tony Lock, just after the first of his 47 appearances for England. Note the detached view one took of the incident. Throwing was soon to be seen in a more sinister light.

June 30, 1952

The no-balling of C. N. McCarthy at Worcester last week for throwing has occasioned a deal of talk among cricketers, but all of it seemingly on a detached and friendly plane. While there is naturally general respect for Corrall, the umpire, in having had the strength of mind to take an unwelcome course in answer to his conscience, I find also much sympathy for McCarthy, an extremely popular young cricketer and the last person to seek to take an unfair advantage.

The atmosphere has changed markedly since the grumblings of many years came to a head at the turn of the century, with the famous meetings of the county captains and the subsequent *cause célèbre*, Phillips v Mold, wherein umpire Phillips no-balled Mold, Lancashire's fast bowler, 16 times during a match against Somerset at Old Trafford.

There were many doubtful actions in the eighties and nineties, or at least many bowlers concerning whom there were dark whisperings. The Australians were strongly critical of certain English bowlers, and apparently were moved eventually to retaliate.

Middlesex and Nottinghamshire declined to arrange fixtures with Lancashire, and Kent once went so far as to refuse to fulfill their return match, Lord Harris being intent on persuading the authorities to take some action.

The recorded reactions of other cricketers matched their temperament. A. C. MacLaren, for instance, having had his stumps hit by M. A. Noble, is said to have remarked as he passed him: 'Well bowled, Monty – and dammit, you threw that one!'

'W.G.,' playing at Fenner's against Cambridge, once dropped the bat, received the ball deliberately somewhere on his ample person, and cried out: 'Now then, young so-and-so, that was a throw.' This agreeable tale would have had a cloudy ending,

I dare say, if the undergraduate had thereupon had the temerity to appeal for l.b.w.

Lord Harris, always a great stickler for the law, was an active campaigner against throwing, as was Sydney Pardon, the famous editor of *Wisden*, whose words for so many years carried vast weight in the councils of cricket.

On the practical side the chief executioner was Jim Phillips, an Australian who played awhile for Middlesex. After a stormy umpiring career in Australia, during which he called Ernest Jones, Phillips returned to England and promptly no-balled C. B. Fry. He also no-balled Mold and the very slow left-arm Tyler, of Somerset, in the season before the captains' meeting of December, 1900. This meeting, incidentally, condemned Mold's bowling by 12 votes to one, the one presumably being that of MacLaren. Lancashire continued to play Mold in face of the decision until he was given the final *coup de grâce* by Phillips, while other counties with bowlers whose actions were considered dubious dispensed with their services.

The present mood among many cricketers tends to be that the legitimacy of an action is something about which it is generally not possible to be definite, and that, in any case, it is no easier to throw than to bowl. This, I think, may be a dangerous conclusion, and it is not difficult in these inflammatory days to conceive a situation in an important match wherein success by a bowler with a doubtful action led to ill-feeling and a disagreeable palaver. In Australia, for instance, where no law can safely be trifled with, each Sheffield Shield state has a bowler of whom some say he throws at least the occasional ball.

It is, of course, difficult to be positive as to the distinction between a bowl and a throw, and although Law 26 categorically says that either umpire must call no-ball if he 'be not entirely satisfied,' in practice he will certainly not call on vague suspicion.

It makes it no easier that a bowler may be unaware of throwing, or unaware of it until the particular ball has left the hand. Captain Fry, who was no-balled by three different umpires who disliked what he calls 'my slightly-bent arm action,' vehemently denied he ever threw a ball; yet Pardon described his being no-balled as an example of 'long delayed justice.'

After being no-balled by Phillips at Brighton, Captain Fry

came out with his right elbow encased in splints and bandages under the sleeves of his shirt, which was buttoned to the wrist; but to his chagrin the Sussex captain W. L. Murdoch would not put him on to bowl and so bring Phillips's judgment to the test.

Although Gilbert was seemingly no-balled for a jerk of the wrist, the crucial point is generally agreed to be the elbow. Indeed, the M.C.C. Coaching Book advises bowlers to cock the wrist, and some movement of the wrist is necessary to produce life off the wicket, as well as all forms of spin and swerve. Yet many bowlers have bowled fairly with a bent elbow, particularly off-spinners.

A ball surely becomes a throw when there is a straightening of the elbow at the moment of delivery. The law does not seek to define a throw, and there seems a case for an explanatory note which presumably would be to the effect that any movement of the elbow joint during the final swing of the arm constitutes a throw. In McCarthy's case, incidentally, it must be remembered that since he is double-jointed at the elbow the forearm is straight, so to speak, when it is bent backwards.

I feel that Corrall's action at Worcester after virtually half a century's silence from English umpires may sound a note of salutary caution. No-balling from square leg should obviously not be taken as necessarily implying anything against the individual's sense of fair play. Nonetheless, it should help to make the bowler who bends the elbow during the later stages of his run-up scrupulously careful.

## The First Test Covering

A reactionary view on Australia's historic decision to cover wickets in Test Matches. But at least I offered a practical alternative which, retrospectively, has its points.

December 17, 1952

Australian authority is naturally much exercised just now to keep the pot boiling, and their latest moves particularly are to be interpreted to that end. Thus it has been decided, with the concurrence of M.C.C., to cover the wickets in Test matches the next time an English side go to Australia, which is in 1954–55. On the surface, as it is not difficult to see, there is a fair prima facie case for covering. On recent tours there have been a lot of ruinous wet Saturdays, and in some instances there probably could have been cricket if the whole wicket area had been effectively covered.

When, in response to a direct request from Australia to agree to the covering of the wickets over there, M.C.C. sought the opinions of many famous English players and discovered that they were pretty well equally divided for and against, there seemed little alternative but to concur, at least for the next tour.

M.C.C. have held on as far as they could, out of respect to the views of many of their most experienced and distinguished members, by agreeing to the coverings as an experiment.

One must admit the plausibility of the case for covering, though personally I abominate the idea on principle, and on practical grounds distrust it. As to the latter objection experience has shown that when it really rains in Australia all forms of wicket covering so far devised are futile. At Brisbane six years ago when the heavens opened the tarpaulins might well have been found wrapped round the boundary pickets.

Covering when it is effective must tend to destroy that prospect of variety and hint of chance to which all the cricketing philosophers ascribe the game's unique appeal. And in my view it is the very sameness of the scene which is tending to limit interest in Australia. In other words in the long run I believe covering to be against Australia's best interests.

The argument of those in favour of covering, that no batsman has a fair chance on a real Australian 'sticky', I would neutralise by taking away the crease covers which under present regulations in Australia v England Tests give the quicker bowlers, as it were, a firm firing platform.

They bowl straight half-volleys, or should do, and the wicket more or less does the rest for them. That at least is the theory, though certain eminent batsmen led by Hobbs and Sutcliffe, in their day, have upset it.

If neither the creases nor the rest of the wicket were covered, the bowling, when play became possible after rain, would have to be done at first by the slow bowlers, who could get a firm footing. Under present arrangements they do not get put on. That solution conjures prospects of an infinitely fascinating battle – and surely a fair one.

However, there it is, the deed is done, temporarily at least, artifice has triumphed over nature, and we must accept what is certainly the most fundamental difference there has ever been in the laws and match regulations as between Test matches in England and in Australia.

## A Defence of "G and P"

July 15, 1957

If there is one hardy annual that never fails to flower, whatever the weather, it is the old argument as to whether the match between Gentlemen and Players is or is not outmoded. The latest phrase describes it as 'the nuisance match.' Has it out-lived its popularity and its prestige? Is it, in fact, an anachronism?

Certainly this game can never again be the classic event of the season, for apart from other considerations every season now is heavily over-loaded with Test matches. By an evil decree the Board of Control a few years ago ordained five per season irrespective of the touring team concerned, all of five days: twenty-five days' Test cricket against Australia, twenty-five days likewise next summer against our friends from New Zealand, who have been playing Test cricket twenty-six years and who a year ago last March celebrated their first Test victory in history.

Again, the distinction between amateur and professional has grown hazy, to say the least, both socially, which no doubt is all to the good, and in point of amateur definition, which is a much more vexed subject. There are some, too, who find offence in the traditional title – which, I suppose, is neither more or less inappropriate than many another ancient form of words handed down by history.

It was half-a-century ago that the matter of the title was explained to the schoolboy. This was the match, he was told, in which all the Players were gentlemen, and all the Gentlemen were players. Enough said surely.

Whereas before the war the average paying gate for the match was 15,000, it is now, taking an average over the years since 1946, 23,000. Where there is so much Test cricket, with all its stresses and magnified importance, and so much county cricket, a good deal of it sadly indifferent, it seems that people look forward to a game complete in itself to which hang no Ashes, or Championship points, or other weighty matters whatever.

Naturally, it is of value to Test and tour selectors. So also is it to the professionals who get a fee of £56 over and above expenses. They are not so rich, most of them, as to be indifferent to the amount. It may be that in due course the match will dissolve itself, as it were, by a redefining of the terms 'amateur' and 'professional', or even by the abolition of the distinction.

The next few years may see many changes. Whatever happens, though, there ought to be room for what might be called a command performance – in the domestic sphere. It would be foolish, surely, to abandon something of past associations and present value – certainly for the sake of a name.

## Amateurism in the Balance

August 12, 1957

The points mentioned as being among those to be examined when the subject of amateurism is tackled at Lord's in the autumn should not be allowed to obscure the fact that the Committee called together by M.C.C. will report on the matter of amateur status from all angles.

The looseness of the amateur definition in cricket has always been a source of surprise, not to say amusement sometimes, with players of other games. The rules governing, for instance, athletes and rugby footballers are both strict and rigidly applied. The cricketer can write articles and books (and even, if his conscience permits, allow himself to be 'ghosted'), he can coach, lecture, advertise drinks, razors, tobacco, and other things unconnected with the game as well as signing bats and the other items of cricket equipment. He can change his status without the slightest difficulty, as many have done.

Cricket authority has allowed an elastic interpretation of amateurism partly because, in M.C.C., at any rate, there has generally been a strong dislike of regimentation and bureaucratic control; also there is the considerable practical difference that what might be reasonable in the case of a man playing once a week on a Saturday afternoon, or at most twice, is not necessarily so as regards a game which goes on all the summer six days a week.

Indirect perquisites, however, are one thing. The suggestion now put forward in some places that selection for tours and in Test matches should be directly rewarded is, however, quite another. If a man is paid for playing as such he simply is not an amateur, and there is an end of it. If he requires payment there is nothing to stop his turning professional and getting what he is worth.

Many people see a possible solution in the abandonment of the terms 'amateur' and 'professional'. Everyone would be a cricketer and would be paid for his services automatically by his county. The difficulty here, though, is that many who now play as amateurs would be dragged into a new category quite against their will.

Receiving a wage involves responsibility to one's employers. This would be a system that had no place for the man of talent who wanted to take part in first-class cricket and still remain independent, free to play or not as he chose.

The Committee which is to sit has surely a complex job on hand. It will recognise that no one will want to make things more difficult for the existing amateurs, least of all those who are playing such a valuable part in county and Test cricket.

Whatever may be said English cricket without the products of Oxford and Cambridge would have sunk to a low ebb in this post-war age. At the same time there is a limit beyond which, if it were passed, the matter must sink into pure hypocrisy.

# Lock Reforms His Action

May 11, 1959

There seems little doubt that the most important event of this new season so far as it has gone – and we must be duly grateful for the loveliest warm, sunshiny start – is the effort being made by Tony Lock to so amend his action that, like Caesar's wife, it is beyond reproach.

The story behind this decision by Lock is both interesting and instructive. During the M.C.C. visit to New Zealand he saw two strips of film, one taken in Australia by a member of the M.C.C. team, of the Tests in which he was not engaged, the other by H. B. Cave, the New Zealand vice-captain, of some of the Tests in England last summer.

The chief attention of the audience was directed at the actions of certain of the Australian bowlers. But Lock was also portrayed, and he himself was much shaken by seeing his 'broken arm' from front and sideways on, and also reduced to slow motion.

He determined then and there to straighten his arm at the elbow and, with rather discouraging results, put this into effect right away in New Zealand. Since his return to England he has been working regularly on what is a quite new and unfamiliar action. It has been said that his knee has been giving him trouble, and indeed it is a recurring source of worry. But the chief reason why he has not yet played for Surrey concerns his change of action more than his physical fitness.

The first point to be made is that Lock determined to change his action on his own initiative, before the Advisory County meeting at Lord's on March 17, as a result of pictorial evidence.

The second point suggests strongly what I am coming to believe; namely, that a bowler may throw and not realise that he is doing so.

In Lock's case many people, including two West Indian umpires and also one, F. Price, on the English list, have thought that at different times he threw the extra-fast one.

It is, however, at least two years since he gave vent to that ball, and I believe the ball he has also decided to cut out is the stock slow one when he has looked to uncock the arm at the moment of rotating the wrist in an effort to impart greater spin.

Lock is a great fighter and also a great trier. And in England, though not abroad, he has been a tremendous match-winner, both in Tests and for Surrey. It seems to me to redound very greatly to his credit that he should have acted in advance of cricket opinion, as expressed by the counties, rather than perhaps load on some unhappy umpire the responsibility of calling him.

In the old days – and it must be recalled that the last major throwing controversy happened more than half a century ago – a man convicted usually found himself excluded, and so passed from the scene. In most cases, however, it should be possible to change the action as, for instance, Pearson of Worcestershire is endeavouring to do. How successful Lock will prove to be is still to be awaited, but that is what he also is endeavouring to do.

One's thoughts turn in this connection to the suspect Australians. I am quite sure that Rorke and Slater can bowl within the Laws.

Burke with the most blatant action I have ever seen anywhere (apart from a coloured man with a red fez in Trinidad, who was allowed to perform only in nets), has announced his retirement, and so is no problem. About Meckiff I am not quite so certain.

It would be interesting to know responsible Australian reaction to Lock's gesture. No one of good will wants to see England and Australia at odds on the issue of fair and unfair bowling, and I suppose there must be exchanges on the subject soon between the governing bodies.

I understand the Cricket Committee of M.C.C. is to consider late in the month the tour reports of their captain and manager. If these reports contain the criticisms they may be expected to contain, it is a certainty that the interpretation of Law 26 will be on the agenda at the Imperial Cricket Conference at Lord's in July.

## Throwing an International Issue

This essay preceded the famous Imperial Cricket Conference (as it was then called) to which Sir Donald Bradman flew from Australia, and at which the full implications of the threat were recognised.

July 13, 1960

Certain meetings at Lord's in the past, called to resolve problems of the moment, are a part of the history of cricket. Such was the famous meeting of members in 1901 whereat it was sought, unsuccessfully, to alter the Law of leg-before-wicket.

There were the committee meetings of 1933 wherein the angry body-line cables from Australia were debated and answered. The late Lord Hailsham, then Secretary of State for War, was in the chair as President of M.C.C., and no situation more bellicose was he called upon to handle during his term of office.

There has been a deal of inflammatory stuff flying over the wires these past few weeks from Australia and South Africa implying all sorts of chicanery and base motives to English cricket authorities on the subject of the throwing Law, while in the English Press, Sir Donald Bradman and his Board of Control Chairman, Mr Dowling, have been portrayed (in some quarters) as tough, tight-lipped Khruschevian characters, arrived here for the express purpose of defending their suspect bowlers right or wrong, thus ensuring Australia's retention of the Ashes here next summer – and presumably, risking a first-class Commonwealth upset into the bargain.

The pre-Summit atmosphere, indeed, could with advantage be calmer. Yet I think it is reasonable to hope that the meeting of the Imperial Cricket Conference at Lord's tomorrow will be conducted more in the spirit of 1901 than of 1933. The character and integrity of those concerned should ensure that the propaganda and ballyhoo fall on deaf ears.

What is the Imperial Cricket Conference? First formed half a century ago when the only Tests were those played between England, Australia and South Africa, it consists nowadays of representatives of all the governing bodies of Test-playing countries within the Commonwealth. Its function is to agree the programme of future Test tours, and to resolve other matters relating exclusively to Test cricket.

Otherwise its role is strictly consultative, and until this year countries saw no necessity to send their delegates across the world to attend its deliberations. Their views on the previously circulated agenda were conveyed by proxies on the spot.

This year things are different, and it may be that, with cricket generally in a state of such uneasy transition, there may be regular meetings in future between heads of government, despite the time and expense involved, rather than weighty exchanges of correspondence without the benefit of first-hand discussion.

Certainly there will be value this time from discussions between the delegates, whether inside the Conference or out, on the broad question: what can we do to increase the tempo of Test cricket and so restore its appeal? The state of Test cricket in general is an even more important matter than the proper observance of the throwing Law.

However, this is the special issue of the moment and we have seen from the repercussions of the unhappy Griffin case how dangerously explosive national feelings can render it. If the situation is to be put right some national prejudices and short-term interests may have to be set aside.

This present epidemic of throwing and the blitz thereon, prosecuted this summer and last in England and fully approved in principle by all the other countries at the corresponding I.C.C. meeting a year ago, is no new thing.

Throwing became prevalent in the early eighteen-eighties and at first those closely concerned were inclined to wink at it. Not so the late Lord Harris. Not so a forthright Australian umpire, by name Jim Phillips. Not so successive editors of *Wisden*, the famous Charles and Sydney Pardon, who campaigned long and vehemently to purge the game of throwers.

The fact that the battle in the end was won was due chiefly to these men. Lord Harris declined to lead Kent into the field against two Lancashire throwers and cancelled the match, and it was he who ultimately brought together the county captains, who agreed not to play men with illegal actions.

Phillips, who umpired all the year round, travelling to and from Australia to catch the cricket seasons, called both the English throwers, notably Mold and C. B. Fry, and also, in a Test match at Sydney, his fellow Australian Ernest Jones.

The climax came in the late 'nineties. The greatest Australian bowler of his day 'the Demon' Spofforth, retired and domiciled in England, publicly accused of throwing his fellow-countryman M'Kibbin. Sydney Pardon, while agreeing, remarked that 'Australian bowlers never threw in England until we had shown them over and over again that Law X could be broken with impunity.'

In 1900 the captains named six illegal bowlers and the counties undertook not to employ either them or any other whose action was suspect. That did the trick and, apart from one solitary man who was no-balled in his first match and promptly disappeared, no English bowler was no-balled for throwing for half a century until G. A. R. Lock was called by F. Price in 1952 at the Oval.

Moreover, with one possible exception, the whole considerable company were, over this long period, above suspicion. In Australia doubts surrounded perhaps two or three, none of whom was ever sent to England.

Over the past few years – say five – there has sprung up an alarming crop of bowlers of whose actions it must be said, in the words of the most recently worded note to the Law 'there has been a sudden straightening of the bowling arm, whether partial or complete, immediately prior to the delivery of the ball.'

We saw at least half a dozen deeply suspect bowlers in Australia in 1958–9, while in county cricket six Englishmen have been called already this season. Opposing players have condemned bowlers in the West Indies and India, while in South Africa, G. Griffin has been twice called, both within his own province and outside. Such is the recent story.

The conclusions I arrive at in the light of history and recent observation can be summed up as follows:

(1) The bowler who straightens (i.e., jerks) the elbow in the act of delivery, thereby gaining an unfair advantage, must be eliminated without regard to personal feelings. Otherwise imitators will multiply, and the abuse will spread beyond the hope of checking.

(2) Quibbles regarding the wording of the Law take the matter no further. In practice the thrower can be detected at close range, most easily of all by the opposing batsman.

(3) Throughout history umpires, as old cricketers themselves, have been understandably reluctant to pass sentence of death on offending bowlers. Note that in the 'nineties only Phillips steeled his heart.

Thus it does not exculpate, for instance, I. Meckiff to say that he has never been called. Both in South Africa and New Zealand, when he toured with Australian teams, umpires in private denounced his action. So have the broad body of old Test cricketers who have seen him, both English and Australian.

Since so sinister an interpretation has been put on the Griffin no-balling as a threat aimed particularly at Meckiff and G. Rorke if they come here with the Australians next year, it is worth mentioning that urgent representations about the enforcement of the Law were first made to English umpires by the Cricket Committee of M.C.C. in the spring of 1958, that is to say, before the last English tour in Australia and before these two names meant anything in this country.

(4) No country's hands are pure white. For instance, England's selectors turned a blind eye to Lock's action for several seasons after he had been no-balled in the West Indies. If this conference is going to get anywhere confession rather than recrimination must be the keynote.

(5) The English umpires this summer, assured in the most emphatic terms of the support of the authorities, have named certain men. Yet I feel the various Boards of Control and counties must collaborate with them to the extent of not selecting or employing those with suspect actions. The maxim must always be that 'the game is greater than the player.' The whole responsibility cannot be honestly passed to the umpires.

(6) Anyone who seriously suggests that throwing should be allowed ought to be obliged to bat, at the requisite range and without additional protection, against, say, Hall, Watson, Statham, Trueman, O'Neill (no better 'arm' in the world than his) and Meckiff – the whole battery *throwing* – not bowling – all out. Batting, like bowling, would cease to be an art. The result would be a highly dangerous game vaguely similar to baseball.

Writing in 1897 Spofforth said: 'In conclusion, if nothing is to be done in this matter, the best way is to legalise throwing, and in one season it would bring its own cure.' But those were the days before TV and humming Press boxes a hundred strong. Such a 'cure' today would be prohibitive in terms of Commonwealth relations and the good repute, tarnished as this is, of the game of cricket.

It is, indeed, the good repute of cricket that the various eminent administrators of England, Australia, South Africa, West Indies, New Zealand, India and Pakistan have to safeguard and embellish this week.

## G. O. Allen's Retirement

August 28, 1961

His work now done the moment is ripe to acknowledge the remarkable services as chairman of selectors of G. O. Allen, who is firmly resolved after seven long years of office to hand over the job.

No one with close knowledge of what Test and tour selection involves will question the value of what Mr Allen has done. He has taken endless pains, and he has impressed those with whom he has been in regular contact, players, administrators, and cricket writers, with an open-mindedness and an analytical flair which cannot perhaps have come particularly easily in the first place to one who, if he will pardon my mentioning it, is by nature inclined to be dogmatic.

Hence the misguided charge recently made that he had too much 'influence' in affairs on the field. For myself I hope his successor strives as hard and cares as much.

With 18 home Tests won during his time, seven drawn and only five lost, Mr Allen's record is secure against criticism, even if in two years out of the seven the opposition was not quite worthy of England's mettle.

The cricket world will be reconciled to a fresh brain tackling the chairman's job only if it is a really good one, with the necessary background of experience at Test match level. I personally believe also that the chairman and preferably one other of his quartet should have first-hand knowledge of the game pre-war.

It may be a sign of my own approaching senility, but other things being equal, I put a higher value on the views of those who knew cricket in the '30s than on the exclusively post-war cricketer whose experience is limited first by a period of very weak English bowling and latterly by that of the so-called sporting wickets which gave birth to so many false doctrines and put a bogus value on batsmen and bowlers alike.

Happily there seem grounds for hoping that Mr Robins might be prepared to stand. His views regarding the proper approach to all cricket are well known, and if he took on the job he could be relied on to put into it the necessary effort and zest.

Walter Robins did succeed to the job for the following three years, 1962-4 when ill-health caused his retirement.

## Death of the Amateur

Five years after the setting up of an investigation into the status of the amateur noticed a few pages back, the Advisory County Cricket Committee voted (not by a wide margin) in favour of the abolition of the traditional categories of amateur and pro. The news came to the M.C.C. party in Brisbane on the eve of the First Test Match of 1962-63. I deplored the decision, and M.C.C.'s endorsement of it, and nothing that has happened since has shifted my view. Incidentally, I believe that if the matter had been put to the vote of the members of M.C.C. and of the seventeen first-class county clubs the resolution would never have been passed.

November 28, 1962

In the context of history the 535th Test match (as I judge it to be), which in a day or two will be making quite a stir in these parts and at home, must seem a small matter compared with the news contained in my breakfast-time cable this morning.

'Amateurs abolished' it announced laconically, and behind the words one saw 'finis' written to the oldest of all the traditional rivalries of the cricket field. Not only that, of course. The evolution of the game has been stimulated from its beginnings by the fusion of the two strains, each of which has drawn strength and inspiration from the other.

English cricket has been at its best when there has been a reasonably even balance between those who have made the game their livelihood and those who have played it, with whatever degree of application and endeavour, basically for relaxation and enjoyment. It is easy to wax romantic over the disappearance of the amateur, and I imagine the change will be regretted instinctively by all with any knowledge of the background.

On first thought, it is perhaps hard to separate sentiment from practical reality. I can only say, having made the effort, and having regarded the possibility of the decision for some while, that the change strikes me as not only unnecessary but deplorable.

Cricket professionalism has been an honourable estate ever since the first-class game took more or less its present form in the middle of the 'nineties. But it is, of its nature, dependent, and the essence of leadership is independence.

To some extent one must see the change in terms of leadership. This is not to say there have not been some admirable professional captains. Tom Dollery showed the way with Warwickshire, and all know how much the 1962 champions and their runners-up owed respectively to J. V. Wilson and D. Kenyon. Equally, there have been some indifferent amateur captains, and anyone can elaborate this remark according to taste.

Yet other things being roughly equal, there are obvious advantages, especially to the players themselves, in the control of an independent agent with only a season's tenure. The alternative is control by a player from a staff whose members have served their apprenticeship, and graduated together.

A county club have always been able to sack their amateur if he has not given satisfaction, as we have seen. It is by no means so easy to demote a professional captain, as we have also seen.

It has been said, of course, that the word amateur is an anachronism, that to preserve the status is mere humbug. I wonder. As soon as the broken-time principle was sanctioned, and advertising restrictions removed, a distinction was created between the few who cashed in on various perquisites of their fame, and the Simon-Pure amateur.

But the latter category was far from extinct. What services in this last decade and more have not D. J. Insole and J. J. Warr rendered respectively to Essex and Middlesex! Each preferred to make a personal sacrifice in order to maintain his independence.

It is doubtful whether either would have been elected a county captain when he was, under the new dispensation. It is equally unlikely that my friend, henceforward to be known as Mackenzie (A. C. D. Ingleby-) would have emerged at the age of 24 to captain Hampshire. He would have been lost to the City, or more probably to the Turf, and if half the personal tributes to him are to be believed, Hampshire would never have enthused the cricket world last year by gaining their first championship.

I recall a young schoolmaster-cricketer who, a summer or two ago, got a term's leave and travelled the country with his county in a battered old car. He gave pleasure alike by his play and by his company. The spirit of the adventure would surely have been lost if he had been paid for it.

In future, such a man might opt out: but who will be the odd man? Is not the pattern likely to be one of the suppression of individuality in favour of a somewhat colourless uniformity? Counties will be inclined to take the safe course when vacancies occur, and appoint the senior man rather than run the risk of jealousies.

With the disappearance in due time of such characters as I have named, will there emerge some system of non-playing managership in order to sustain the captain and help impose discipline? This could happen, and it might even work well. But one is apprehensive of the effect of more control from the committee room.

Again, although I disliked the amateur anomalies as much as the abolitionists, the time when the future structure of the first-class game was precariously in the balance was surely the wrong one to introduce a classless society on the cricket field.

If a six-day-a-week championship is on the way out, might not the future pattern have involved smaller staffs and an inflow of unpaid talent operating mostly at week-ends? The amateur can scarcely be revived now. That section of the history book is closed tight for ever.

Finally, one questions the moral authority of the Advisory County Cricket Committee to have made the decision. (The first word of their title is now apparently a euphemism, and M.C.C., like a constitutional monarch, merely confirms).

The backbone of the game, without whom there would be no first-class cricket, is composed of the members of M.C.C., of the 17 first-class counties, and of the University clubs. There are, in round figures, 100,000 of us, and we, broadly speaking, pay the bill. No one has canvassed our opinion on something that must fundamentally affect the future of cricket.

The decisive votes have been cast, after much heart-searching no doubt, by a majority from among two representatives apiece of each of the county committees. These committees are largely self-perpetuating, and are confined to men with the interest, industry and not least the leisure, to administer. They are not necessarily representative from the cricket angle.

The record of the various ACCC decisions over the last decade certainly does not encourage the hope that they have got the answer right in this case, which has more important repercussions than any other.

When, last summer, a Yorkshire administrator was advocating what has now come to pass, he was asked the question: 'If amateur status were to be abolished, would a single player be brought into the county who could not now be considered?' He could not say so. That, surely, is an acid question.

Whom will the change include? Whom will it exclude? I only hope that time proves me a pessimist as well as, patently, a crusted reactionary.

As to the inclusion and exclusion I believe that few young men of first-class ability have been attracted who would not have played under the old order either as amateur or pro, whereas the fact that county sides are now in the nature of 'closed shops' from which only those under contract are normally considered, means that a considerable potential is, to all practical purposes, excluded. The independent player is being missed not less but more as county cricket pursues its stereotyped way.

# The Twin Tour Plan

July 13, 1963

When the Imperial Cricket Conference meets on Wednesday next at Lord's it will come face to face with a matter of some delicacy, the eventual outcome of which is of great moment to cricket followers in this country.

I mean, of course, the annual Test programme, which is the focus and centrepiece of the English season.

The subject has been made acutely topical by the great boost given by the current West Indies tour. As happened when the West Indies toured Australia a couple of years ago, everyone is asking: 'When are they coming again?'

In Australia they are still inquiring for the next visit is not yet fixed. For the English cricket world the melancholy answer, according to present plans, is: 'In eight years' time – and again in seven years after that.'

Why? Because in 1960 M.C.C., with the approval of the counties, laid down a programme extending to the dim mists of 1978 which ordained a roster of tours to England based on the principle that Australia should come every four years, South Africa every five, and the West Indies, New Zealand, India and Pakistan approximately every seven.

When the ICC (which meets annually at Lord's and is confined to the Test-playing countries) approved this list, South Africa were members both of the Commonwealth and of the Conference. Since then withdrawal from the first has brought about automatic exclusion from the second.

In the cricket sense South Africa have excommunicated themselves. Nevertheless, the Board of Control (made up of delegates from all the counties with a good leaven from the Committee of M.C.C.) lost no time in saying that they would stand by the home dates already arranged, while M.C.C. promised to honour the plans to tour South Africa, even though the Tests would be unofficial.

The white countries, I believe, would like to change the ICC rules to bring South Africa back into the fold, but this the dark-skinned ones, for whom the apartheid policy is an even greater anathema than it is in the minds of liberal Englishmen, are not at present prepared to allow.

That is a political side to the picture, in which there is room for honest men to differ. But there is a cricket side on which most fair-minded cricket followers agree, and it is that an English season which has as its highlights five 5-day Tests against New Zealand, India and Pakistan is, as playing standards are and have been, unbalanced and embarrassing to all parties.

Since five 5-day Tests against everyone 'regardless' were very short-sightedly agreed to in 1955, each of these three countries has played one series here. Of the 15 matches England have won 13, all by very large margins both in runs and time, and the weather has won the other two. Out of 40 Tests in England against these three, the home country has lost once only, narrowly and with a weakened side, to Pakistan.

Results in themselves are not the chief consideration, and no one would deprive any of our visitors of the chance of playing in England, nor English crowds of watching them. There is no telling that India, say, where there is boundless enthusiasm for cricket, may not have England fighting just as hard for their lives as the West Indies are doing this summer.

Nor will the West Indies necessarily be as attractive to English crowds as they are today. At the moment, though, long drawn Tests from which the weaker countries can scarcely hope ever to escape unless rain comes to their aid are as deflating to the spirits as such a series as this against the West Indies is stimulating.

In other words, the present programme is unsatisfactory in every particular, except in so far as it concerns the Australians, and English cricket is that much the worse for it.

Yet while this is generally realised by the hierarchy at Lord's, they obviously cannot default on their undertakings, however ill-advised such long-term plans may have been in the first place. The programme could be modified only by general consent.

The solution, as I see it, lies in shorter tours which, at least so far as the visiting side is concerned, are generally desirable anyway. Recently there appeared in these columns a letter from Mr T. J. R. Dashwood, which has occasioned much sympathetic comment.

The Dashwood plan has a beautiful simplicity in that it comprises a four-year cycle wherein England play Australia and the West Indies once each and the other two years are taken up, one with South Africa and New Zealand on shorter but overlapping tours, the other similarly with India and Pakistan.

Three Tests would be played against each, preferably of four days, and if they wished, the visiting countries could also play at least once against one another. Such an idea would involve no hardship to New Zealand, India and Pakistan, who would, I believe, prefer a shorter tour of say three months and three or four Tests every four years rather than one of five months and five Tests every seven. Nor, I think, would it be any less likely to pay its way.

The only country which would be slightly the worse off would be South Africa which could be compensated, I think, to mutual advantage, by more frequent, and again shorter, M.C.C. visits to the Union. Incidentally M.C.C. have already accepted the principle of brief tours and have also tacitly admitted that their programme is not inviolable by contemplating a short tour this winter to India, although they were last there only two years ago. Other countries (such as the West Indies) might well be saying next week: 'What about us?'

This, in brief, is one of the most pressing problems which will overshadow next week's Conference held as usual under the chairmanship of the President of M.C.C. He, this year, is Lord Nugent, who will be supported by Mr H. S. Altham and Mr G. O. Allen as the other English representatives.

These experienced statesmen of the cricket world will know full well how bored the English public is with protracted minor Tests, how spontaneous is the reaction to the calibre of cricket that Australia and the West Indies can provide, how much harm the one sort does, how much good the other.

They have to reconcile their position as the trustees of English cricket, representing the interests of the players, the spectators (not least) and the health of the game at large, with the natural ambitions and agreed rights of the various countries.

These, of course, include South Africa, from which must be hoped some gesture of friendship towards the West Indies, India and Pakistan that would lead to their return to the Con-

Worcester. Beside the Worcester ground flows the Severn; beyond the river is the Cathedral, from the tower of which comes this unusual view of the field and environs

PHOTOGRAPH: PATRICK EAGER

TOP LEFT: Fenner's. The inimitable home of Cambridge cricket since 1848. TOP RIGHT: 'Cricketer' Cup, for Public School Old Boy teams was successfully inaugurated in 1967. A game in the first competition, between Radley Rangers and Uppingham Rovers at Radley. BELOW: Two great fast bowlers in their delivery stride: Fred Trueman and Keith Miller

ference of which they were originally members. Certain practical possibilities occur in this direction which space precludes my mentioning here.

I feel that so long as the possibility of a suspension of the future schedule is accepted, and the idea of shorter tours is sympathetically examined, a solution need not be despaired of, because I believe that by careful adjustment all interests could be served. As air travel becomes faster, and the world accordingly contracts, flexibility in sporting tours is imperative. More often, but shorter, is the watchword.

Here, according to present plans, are the fixtures to England over the next eight years:

| 1964 | ... | ... | ... | Australia |
| 1965 | ... | ... | ... | New Zealand |
| 1966 | ... | ... | ... | South Africa |
| 1967 | ... | ... | ... | India |
| 1968 | ... | ... | ... | Australia |
| 1969 | ... | ... | ... | Pakistan |
| 1970 | ... | ... | ... | South Africa |
| 1971 | ... | ... | ... | West Indies |

Readers, unhampered by the diplomatic considerations that will tax the ICC members, will perhaps amuse themselves by making their own adjustments.

The upshot of this meeting was the adoption of the twin-tour plan whereby England were to receive two opponents in alternate years. Australia was to come alone and, as before, one year in four. The other countries could come singly on a roster system in the remaining year of the cycles of four.

The programme therefore was so re-arranged that the West Indies came again in 1966; but it also meant that if the other countries all took up their options there could not be another full West Indian tour until 1986. That is still the position.


# Cricket's World Parliament

July 15, 1965

The annual supra-national cricket meeting, attended by the representatives of England, Australia, the West Indies, New

H

Zealand, India and Pakistan, takes place at Lord's today.

By its constitution the Imperial Cricket Conference confines itself to members of the Commonwealth, but the probability is that at last the countries concerned are ready both to amend the anachronistic title and to open their doors a little wider.

The constitution in fact has been under review these past 12 months. The Conference is due, I expect, to become International in name. The question is whether, with this change, it is about to become more up-to-date in its consultative machinery and more comprehensive in its terms of reference.

Cricket, that 'beautiful, complicated' game as C. B. Fry called it, is by its nature never free from problems. It has not, however, often been beset by so many as surround it at the moment.

Some are of purely domestic English concern, but most are in some degree international, common to all countries where the game is widely played and highly competitive. All, according to long custom, are considered the affair of Marylebone Cricket Club, on whose shoulders the counties pile every matter that needs dispassionate inspection. So, equally, as regards the international affairs that come under their notice, do the members of the ICC.

But M.C.C., though willing enough to undertake anything that might be of benefit to the game (and the record of voluntary – and honorary – service by its leading members is impressive enough), is nowadays greatly overworked. As a non-elective body, 'a private club with a public function,' it is sensitive to the anomaly of its situation.

The government of cricket (like all forms of government) tends to become more complex and more difficult. M.C.C., by the consent of cricketers from ancient times, acts as the lawmaker, but it administers directly only its own affairs as a club and English tours abroad.

The Advisory County Committee (on which M.C.C. is represented and whose president normally takes the chair) runs English county cricket: the Board of Control (much the same body under another name) runs Test cricket at home. The Imperial Cricket Conference, with its annual one-day gathering, has a somewhat woolly function, and it needs some considerable event, such as the throwing crisis in 1960, to rouse the countries to real action.

It may be that the present highly unsatisfactory throwing situation may impel the ICC to formulate a change in the law and issue some sort of plea to the world's umpires. It might also decide on the number of overs for the taking of the new ball and ask M.C.C. to alter the law accordingly. Limitation of the leg-side field could probably have been agreed already but for the intransigence of the West Indies.

But the fact is that the other Test countries have never shown much inclination to play a part in the government of cricket; nor, if it comes to that, have they been invited to share the burden to any greater extent than the provision of a couple of ICC delegates. These, by the way, are often Englishmen appointed by the countries concerned. Australia's representatives this year, for example, are to be B. A. Barnett, the former Test cricketer, long domiciled in this country, and R. W. V. Robins. With all possible respect to them, they cannot carry the authority of Sir Donald Bradman or of some other members of the Australian Board.

Consider just a few contentious topical matters which would benefit from a general consultation at top level:

1. The bowling law.
2. The preparation of pitches.
3. The restriction of the bowler's run-up – advocated at the ICC meeting of 1963 by Sir Frank Worrell.
4. The artificial shining of the ball.
5. The limitation of the leg-side field.
   On what might be called the political side there would be:
6. The itineraries of Test tours.
7. Sunday play, tried by two States last season in Australia, and now mooted in England.
8. The activities of player-writers.

There is at present no machinery for a regular interchange of views, nor a procedure for making and implementing decisions, other than these surely inadequate annual meetings of the ICC. In brief it would seem that the moment has come when the international body should have its own secretariat and standing committee, its members in close touch with their separate Boards of Control.

Lord's would be the natural headquarters, and M.C.C. would continue, as for almost 200 years, to be the law-maker. But each Test country in turn might be host to the full annual conference, which would be attended by the leading administrators of each.

As a result of this meeting the first word of the title was changed from Imperial to International, but that was the extent of reform. The Conference remains, if the mixed metaphor be allowable, a talking shop without teeth.

## The "65-overs" Folly

The 1966 season was spoiled by surely the most foolish of all the counties' experiments, the restriction of the first innings in certain matches (12 per county) to 65 overs. The restriction was not repeated in 1967. One *hopes* the idea is dead – but it would be premature to say so.

October 27, 1966

Some significant figures relating to the 1966 championship matches have just emerged from Lord's, the respective over and run rates per hour achieved by each side, and also the overall average for the 17 counties.

Briefly, the counties bowled 19.2 overs per hour as against 18.9 in 1965. They scored 41.1 runs per 100 balls as against 40.2 in 1965. So the increase of runs in a day is almost exactly 10, and the average in a full six hours, less an interval between innings, is around 285. In other words almost 'no change'.

Optimists may gain some comfort from the fact that, low as the scoring rate is, both it and the over rate have shown a modest reversal of the trend of the previous five years, which was downwards in both respects.

The chief interest is in the comparison between the figures in the first innings of 65-over matches and the rest. It will be recalled that this basic experimental change in the Laws of the game was justified in advance, as heralding a new age of scintillating play on first days, instead of on third.

The Glamorgan captain, O. S. Wheatley, in a long letter to

*The Daily Telegraph*, ended thus: 'And just a little wager for Mr Swanton – I'll bet more runs are scored on the first day in the matches operating the 65-over limit than in those played under the old rule. And surely this won't be such a sad thing. Even the diehards must enjoy seeing the ball hit.'

Well, no actual wager was made, but if it had been the accountants, according to my modest arithmetic, would have declared Mr Wheatley winner by eight runs a day: two snicks off the edge! The run rate for '65 overs' was 45.8 per 100 balls, but, as was easily predictable, the over-rate was down to 18.1 – because nearly all the work was done by the faster bowlers.

The Assistant Secretary of M.C.C. notes that but for '65 overs' the overall average would probably have been approximately 19.6 overs per hour. On this figure the customer saw a run and a bit more per hour in '65 overs.' The fact that fielding captains bowled to contain rather than to get the other side out confined the difference to that.

So all the artificiality, the denial of the fundamental purpose of cricket, which is to dismiss the opposition by positive means, has been in vain so far as any brightening of the scene is concerned.

All those middle and lower-order batsmen whose development has been arrested by this latest playing of the game round the committee-table, all those frustrated spinners, all those budding slipfielders banished to the middle distance to save one in the magic circle, have suffered for a summer in vain.

Ah well, let it be hoped that this prostitution of cricket, expensive though it has been in terms both of the progress of individual players and of the game's repute, has taught some people something.

# CHAPTER SEVEN

# THE SEAMY SIDE

In the cricketer's dream-world there could be no such title as this in relation to the game. But cricket can only reflect the mood and nature of the times, and it would be astonishing if it were to exist in a blessed calm, an oasis of peace in a turbulent world.

In fact cricket throughout its history has engendered strong emotions that have often over-spilled – if there is a warm fellowship among cricketers and followers of the game there have also from time to time been sharp animosities.

Since the war the thing that has provoked most friction has been the written word, sometimes the extravagant outpourings of the professional press, sometimes – indeed more often, until recently – the flamboyant 'revelations' by players themselves, or, more usually, by their 'ghosts', in books and articles.

It is this development that caused the counties in 1959 to draft a disciplinary rule whereby cricketers became obliged to submit for approval any writing intended for publication – under threat of loss of registration.

## Australian Umpires Under Fire

This cable was slightly cut in *The Daily Telegraph*, but by arrangement with *The Argus* of Melbourne appeared in that paper as follows.

January 6, 1947

Australia lead in their second innings by 307 runs, with six wickets in hand and two days to go, in the third Test. But before a day's play from which the English team generally emerged with much credit can be briefly described, or the implications of it on the match and rubber be discussed, a matter of more

230

importance and interest calls for attention. It is the tendency which has shown itself on this tour towards public criticism of the decisions of umpires, both by cricketers on the field and critics beyond the boundary.

It is a tradition in all sport that the findings of the umpire or referee are final and binding, and we cricketers are apt to claim, with not too conspicuous modesty, that specially noble virtues are inherent in and derivable from cricket. We must seem to many a hypocritical breed when the great question of the hour seems to be not whether England can win or save the match, but whether Edrich or Compton was or was not l.b.w.

There would be no point today in the classic reply of the late Bill Reeves to the batsman who, as he passed him, observed that he was not out: 'Weren't you? Well, just you look in the paper in the morning.' Nowadays apparently the matter would depend upon which paper he looked in!

There is, perhaps, a special irony in the fact that the press-box in Melbourne, which is beyond midwicket and third man, is further from the play and at a worse angle than any in the world. It is sometimes possible, from a position directly in pro-longation of the wicket, to form a private view as to whether the luck may have gone for or against a batsman in the case of l.b.w. or a catch, but the views of anyone looking from a slant are worth precisely nothing.

It follows that the only 'evidence' in such a case is the gestures or demeanour of the players on the field. Unfortunately both Edrich and Compton, in the heat of the moment, were unable to avoid giving the impression of being surprised when given out. Indeed, Compton has been read a little lecture in print by that striving, red-blooded cricketer W. J. O'Reilly, who, incidentally, until possibly the arrival of Toshack, exposed his inmost feelings to the public gaze with greater emphasis and frequency than anyone who ever stepped on to a field. The fact that there are certainly not two players more widely or deservedly admired in Australia for their buoyant and cheerful attitude towards the game than Edrich and Compton, is just an indication of what the stress and strain of a Test match means to all concerned.

Nor is the onus for restraint confined to batsmen. When Toshack, for instance, has an appeal answered against him, it seems as though he can hardly bring himself to the point of bowling the next ball. Again it is surely indefensible to appeal unless the bowler or fielders concerned are reasonably confident that the batsman may be out. There are degrees of probability in these things that have sometimes been raucously ignored out here in this series, perhaps rather more by the Australians than by the Englishmen. These things tend to make the job harder for the two wretched humans who have to stand up to the racket.

It is one of the fascinations of cricket that it is so clear and open a test of character, and no one wants to see the natural humours of a man subdued to the point of dull anonymity; but the truth is that these tremendous sporting affairs on which it might be thought the prestige of nations rested, can only be kept in any remote degree of perspective if all concerned, players, Press, and public, do our best to see the 'other fellow's' point of view, and, frankly, mind our manners.

To instance the present match again, there have been probably three decisions (of which Compton's is not one), in which, among those in any way qualified to judge, the umpire expressed a minority view. Two favoured Australia, but it can never be established that those two had a more weighty bearing on the contest than the one favouring England had the other way.

In the England-Australia Test match at Lord's in 1930, with the great Frank Chester standing umpire, Hammond was given not out when all the Australians near thought he had been caught and bowled by Grimmett. But I can remember no commotion by Australian journalists. Nor when, in the second innings of the same match, K. S. Duleepsinhji was considered by his opponents to have been caught at slip, did an Australian writer claim to have detected the mark on his bat that had been made by the ball . . .

Comment of this description is analogous only to that of a person who claims to have been hit by a poker, and adds, 'If you don't believe me, here is the poker.'

Having written so much, it is fair to add that irrespective of whether or not the rub of the green has so far gone against the English side in this series, the opinion of Australian cricketers generally is that the standard of umpiring in Australia is less admirable than it might be. There is, of course, vastly less first class cricket in Australia than in England, and the choice of the best must be from a small number. But what probably matters more is that umpires in Australia are rarely drawn from the ranks of the old players, as is the almost invariable custom in England. As a visitor one would respectfully suggest a reform in that direction.

This commentary would not be complete without a sidelight on the general attitude of the Australian public to this series. Everywhere one finds a genuinely sympathetic understanding of the grave handicap under which the M.C.C. side was collected. There has been absolutely no barracking. Indeed, one of the embarrassing things has been that the English side has not been able to live up to the hopes of the majority, who clearly wish it to win. I have watched this third Test from two places: the Melbourne Cricket Club pavilion and the non-members' stand. In both, exactly the same spirit has been apparent. Nor, so say the English fielders on the far boundary, who after 12 days' cricket here are on close terms with the outer habitués, are the sentiments any different in the outer. Such a setting makes English cricitism of Australian umpires when England is having the worst of it especially distasteful.

The reference to 'the mark on the bat' concerns a comment made on the dismissal of Bill Edrich, who was l.b.w. to Lindwall for 89. One of my colleagues of the press-box (not himself a cricketer!) maintained that Edrich had snicked the ball, citing as evidence that he had seen the mark on the bat. Duly cabled back to Australia, this phrase became something of a national joke. In the public mind we were all, to some extent, tarred with the same brush!

## Compton Makes a Stir

This no doubt was one of the books that ultimately impelled the counties to pass their disciplinary writing rule.

April 30, 1958

Denis Compton is a legend in cricket. He has stood always for adventure and good fun, and for courage, whether in ill-health or in adversity, at the wicket.

As a batsman he was a genius, obeying no laws, a cricketer of instinct and humour. And he has just published a book *End of an Innings* (Oldbourne, 15s), which has created a stir far and away beyond its real merits or intrinsic interest because a good deal of what he has said seems to contradict the general idea of his character, and particularly because he has written in strongly critical terms of his distinguished contemporary, Sir Leonard Hutton.

It will be appreciated, of course, that the serialised excerpts of the book contain what the newspaper concerned no doubt regarded as the spice. 'The day Hutton lost his nerve' is not a heading that quite reflects the content or the temper of the whole book. But Compton has nothing complimentary to say about his fellow-cricketer and erstwhile England captain, apart from certain references to his batting skill.

Hutton's captaincy, according to the author, had no redeeming merit, and it is clearly implied that both in the West Indies and in Australia – to say nothing of the last evening at Leeds in '53 – Hutton had little grip either of himself or of his side.

It should be said at once that Compton's picture, even if at many points it touches the truth, lacks balance and perspective: this quite apart from the ethical issues involved as to whether conversations in dressing-rooms and hotel bedrooms should be committed to print.

At one point we are told how the tour selection committee of 1954–5 voted in regard to whether or not Alec Bedser should be dropped. In this particular case I am satisfied that Compton has given the correct version of the matter, and Hutton in his own book an inaccurate one. But that is a detail, and, for that matter, Compton's book has all the slips and mistakes to be looked for in books written in a hurry.

I never review a book written by a player unless first satisfying myself that it was substantially written by the man himself. That means that very few of such books are mentioned in these columns, for it is an exception if the name on the cover is that of the actual author. Writing a book is very hard work, and most modern cricketers (amateurs as well as professional) quickly call in a 'ghost' even if, as generally happens, they do not engage one in the first place.

In this case I am assured by Compton that the book was

spoken by him into a tape-recorder, and was afterwards only sub-edited by a professional hand – and this apparently not the hand of a man close to the world of cricket. That perhaps is why in the finished version the game takes second place to the gossip.

There will be those, including some post-war Test cricketers, who welcome what he says in regard to Hutton's unduly grim, adventureless attitude to Test cricket. For so long as the results were all right there was scarcely such a thing as constructive criticism of a way of playing cricket which had first been given a trade mark by D. R. Jardine, and, in *riposte* some years later, by Sir Donald Bradman.

The West Indian tour, from the point of view of good sportsmanship and British prestige in the Islands, was a disaster. Hutton, as captain, had at least to share the responsibility with his manager, though the original fault undeniably belonged to the M.C.C. committee of the day which failed to provide their first professional captain with the manager he wanted and the man who could have both helped from the disciplinary point of view with his own team, and in his relations with his hosts.

From that one M.C.C. decision much ill has sprung. But before the West Indies Hutton had led his team to the first successful rubber against Australia for 20 years. And in Australia 18 months later he won again. Handsome is as handsome does.

Neurotic and not physically strong, Hutton was thrust into the England captaincy by an irresistible combination of circumstances. There was a large pressure of public opinion behind the appointment. He fulfilled his job conscientiously, to the best of his ability and with a considerable degree of success.

In any case, a disquisition on Hutton's captaincy in the West Indies does not come well from a man who had had a prior taste of authority as vice-captain of M.C.C. in Australia, and who had scarcely distinguished himself in the job.

It is a rarity, anyway, for a great batsman to make a gifted captain, least of all probably a professional whose success has depended largely on a single-minded concentration on making runs. It should be remarked, too, that though in the writings under his name Hutton may sometimes have seemed less than generous to some of England's opponents, he has not to my knowledge ever expressed criticism of his fellow England players; certainly not of Compton. The fact that temperamentally they are poles apart has not made him unappreciative of Compton as a cricketer.

Compton's admirers will hope that the storm will blow itself out, and that his reputation over the years will stand the strain of present feeling.

In a wider sense, some good may come from the furore in the long run, for the good name of cricket cannot survive the recent spate of 'sensational revelations' purchased for huge sums by agents and publishers.

## The Wardle Story

The Wardle story dragged on for three weeks. The brief facts are that on July 30, 1958, three days after he had been chosen to go with M.C.C. to Australia, Yorkshire announced that they would not be calling on his services after the end of the season. M.C.C., on being asked, said that Yorkshire's decision would not affect their invitation.

Early in August, however, a series of articles appeared in *The Daily Mail* under Wardle's name wherein in unbridled terms he attacked the Yorkshire captain, J. R. Burnet, his fellow-players and the committee. Thereupon, on August 11, Yorkshire dismissed him 'forthwith', issuing a statement which said that it was felt that the recent articles 'fully justify the Committee's decision.'

This made a new situation for M.C.C. who, incidentally, had had every right to be aggrieved in the first place in that Yorkshire had no sooner informed them of Wardle's availability for the tour than they announced the termination of his contract. Nor were M.C.C. helped by Peter May, their captain and a member of the M.C.C. Committee, announcing that he still hoped and expected to have Wardle with him on the tour. On August 19 Wardle appeared before the Committee of M.C.C., who afterwards issued the following statement:

'The Committee of M.C.C. have considered certain articles contributed by J. H. Wardle to a national newspaper since the date of his selection for the forthcoming Australian tour.

They have also considered a report received from the Yorkshire County Cricket Club, many of the details of which were not available to the Selection Committee at the time when the team was chosen.

The Committee considered that the publication by Wardle in the Press of the criticisms of his county captain, his county committee and some of his fellow players, in the form and at the time that he published them, did a grave disservice to the game.

They believe that the welfare of cricket as a whole in terms of loyalty and behaviour must override all other considerations.

After an interview with Wardle, and after very careful consideration of all aspects of the question, the M.C.C. Committee have reached the decision that the invitation to him to go with the M.C.C. team to Australia must be withdrawn.'

August 20, 1958

M.C.C. said after their Committee meeting at Lord's last evening that they must withdraw their invitation to J. H. Wardle to tour Australia this winter. The above statement gives their reasons for the decision, to which Wardle's comment on being interviewed was: 'It's my own fault, and I asked for it. I am not going to say any more.'

Thus ends this sorry matter, and it remains only to debate whether M.C.C. will invite another player, or whether they will restrict themselves to 16, which was the number generally thought sufficient in the first place.

When big issues are in the balance, M.C.C. endeavour to have the benefit on their Committee of distinguished men outside the immediate politics of cricket, who see the game in its broadest perspective, and who, one might almost say, represent the views of the averagely intelligent and informed sportsman with a love for cricket. The present Committee has a leaven of such men, headed by the president, the Duke of Norfolk. It contains also a company of cricketers, ex and present, of various generations, from Sir Pelham Warner down to the England captain, P. B. H. May.

This body has seen and heard the evidence. Above all it has listened to and questioned John Wardle, and it has given its verdict, which probably has been awaited with more widespread interest than any one single decision by M.C.C. or any other cricket body since the body-line series a quarter of a century ago. The result has gone against Wardle, and it has gone in support, as the M.C.C. statement says, of 'the welfare of cricket as a whole in terms of loyalty and behaviour.'

These considerations must override all else. They must certainly override convenience and 'patriotism' in terms of prospects of success in a Test series. They must equally be independent of a captain who not unnaturally wants to be able to face Australia with his best side.

The prospect of Wardle being allowed after all to go depended on his being prepared to make a complete apology, both for what he had written, and for having broken his contract by writing at all. The M.C.C. statement makes no mention of his having broken contract, and I believe it is the weaker for that since the honouring of such obligations must have been in the forefront of the Committee's mind. How far Wardle was able to go one does not know, but apparently it was not far enough.

I daresay the mood of the Committee was such that he would have needed to touch the depths of abject apology. For there can be no doubt that the general temper of cricket at the moment, with players attacking one another in print and offering every sort of ill-considered comment, conditioned the feeling of the meeting.

Whether the man in the street agrees with the findings or not, he must recognise that M.C.C. have put their foot down with all possible firmness, and said in effect that the old standards of sportsmanship and good manners must be preserved, insofar as they have it in their power to preserve them.

The statement also says nothing on the general question of the moral obligations of cricketers regarding what they write, or what appears under their names. In this respect the findings are disappointing, since it is natural that people should say: 'They have condemned Wardle, and they have condoned others, who have been equally indiscreet and unprincipled.' Maybe this aspect of the matter is merely postponed, in which case the point could well have been made. One thing is certain. The general writing about cricket will tend to reflect its seamier side so long as 'big names' are exploited as they are at present.

To those who may still wonder what sort of right Wardle may have had on his side so far as his dismissal with Yorkshire was concerned, one might now add that, however illtimed the Yorkshire action was, it had the approval of the present members of the county XI.

I understand that the players offered to sign a unanimous statement confirming their complete faith in their captain J. R. Burnet, and their agreement with the action taken by their committee. They were told that their gesture was much appreciated, but that the document was unnecessary.

While the Committee of M.C.C. were in session this afternoon and evening, with a screen in front of the doors to guard them from prying eyes, and a company of news reporters and photographers deployed inside and outside the ground, a remarkably fine game of cricket was being contested out in the middle between Middlesex and Surrey.

It was well worthy of the notice that was being focused elsewhere. Yet everyone was talking about and debating 'The Case' rather than the match.

Even Compton, in the infinitely welcome guise of a cricketer rather than a writer, and May, who brought victory to Surrey in a superb flourish of high-class batsmanship, commanded only incidental attention.

Let us hope that there will be plenty of fine and chivalrous cricket this coming winter to take our minds off current scandals, and that the decision reached in regard to Wardle will have a salutary effect on the world of cricket.

The hope of 'fine and chivalrous cricket' in Australia was, unfortunately, doomed to disappointment. But though player-writing has given offence since, it has never done so on such a scale and with such dire results.

## Laker's Apologia

In 1960 a book under the name of Jim Laker entitled 'Over To Me' had caused such a furore that both Surrey and M.C.C. withdrew the honorary membership they had accorded him. The following year came a second book, 'The Australian Tour of 1961', which, unlike the first, he wrote himself. Herewith an excerpt from my review of the second book. This story has a happier ending than the last, since both his county and M.C.C. have since restored Laker's privileges, and the cricket world accords him the respect due to a man who has been big enough to say he is sorry.

November 22, 1961

Mr Laker's book has, of course, a special significance, apart from its own considerable merits, coming some 18 months after his previous one, received by the cricket world with a hostility that culminated in the withdrawal of his privileges at the Oval and Lord's.

He begins now on a note of contrition, regretting that, instead of sticking to his original intention to write the other book himself, he allowed himself to be ghosted, and while he admits that he had not time to correct the final proofs, he realises that the responsibility for what appeared under his name was manifestly his, and no one else's.

Nowhere, perhaps, has the contemptible system of the sporting book, cooked up in sensational form and sold by an agent for big serial fees, been more strongly and consistently condemned than in *The Daily Telegraph*. It has done the greatest harm to the reputation of the English professional games-player in the eyes of the ordinary sporting follower and patron who likes to see his hero as a man to be respected for himself as well as admired for his skill.

How satisfactory, then, to read now from Mr Laker his repudiation of the whole business and his concluding comment: 'I feel I can now offer this advice to future cricket-authors. Complete your career before going into print and most emphatically take your time to publish a book which will truly be the work of the author's name on the cover.'

## Trueman Fined—

Shortly after the return of the 1962–63 M.C.C. team from Australia came the news, presumably 'leaked', that Trueman had had £50 deducted from his bonus money. 'Fred' was 'furious', and at one moment the cricket world was rocked by the possibility of his declining to play against the West Indies in the following series.

May 29, 1963

As a result of the following statement issuing from Lord's yesterday it may be assumed that F. S. Trueman will take his appointed place in the first Test at Old Trafford tomorrow week, the team for which is to be announced on Sunday.

'On consideration F. S. Trueman has decided to accept the
decision of the M.C.C. with regard to the bonus awarded
to him for the recent M.C.C. tour of Australia and in so
far as he and M.C.C. are concerned the matter is therefore closed.'

The important point to make before this particular storm
dies the death is that the magnanimity is at least two-
sided.

Trueman has decided, under the guidance, he says, of Sir
William Worsley, the Yorkshire president, to accept the £50
deprivation about which no one would have known but for
what was apparently an 'inspired leak' to the newspaper for
which he writes. M.C.C., it seems, for their part are prepared
to look no further into the origins of a story which has led to
their receiving a great deal of adverse publicity. This has
characterised M.C.C. as high-handed despots in the minds of
the public, most of whom can have little idea of what international sporting tours involve.

Test cricketers away from home live as a rule in expensive
hotels. Hospitality is showered on them and can be hard to
decline. Casual acquaintances often embarrass them with their
attentions. The tour management have the difficult job of
reconciling this sort of social life with the chief object of the
journey: in other words to keep their players in the best possible
state of fitness. To help managers and captains in this, M.C.C.
very wisely apportion part of their player's fee in the form of a
bonus which can be regulated according to each member's
contribution to the general discipline and team spirit.

This is a confidential matter and individual instances are
never divulged by M.C.C. It can be taken, however, that on
recent tours there have been numerous cases similar to Trueman's. It would probably be the majority view of accompanying
camp-followers, Press and others, that if several have not been
mulcted they well might have been.

This is not a general reflection on touring cricketers by any
means, still less on E. R. Dexter's side which was one of the
most popular and likeable off the field I have travelled with.
In the nature of the enterprise, however, they want a great deal
of 'looking after' to get the results for which those at home are

hoping. The greater players must obviously be on exactly the same basis as all the rest.

# —And Reprimanded

Two years later! Articles, due to be followed by a book, centring partly around the 1962–63 tour, were announced with a great fanfare in *The People*. 'Fred' was due to 'lash out' – but without having got Yorkshire's permission. Herewith the outcome.

*June 4, 1965*

At a meeting of the cricket committee of Yorkshire held at Bradford yesterday, under A. B. Sellers' chairmanship, F. S. Trueman was called upon to answer for a breach of discipline in relation to writing due shortly to appear under his name.

Afterwards J. H. Nash, the Yorkshire secretary, issued this statement: 'Trueman was interviewed by the Committee and he expressed his regret at having broken his agreement by contracting to write a book, newspaper and magazine articles without obtaining prior consent to do so. He has been severely reprimanded and warned that any future breaches of his contract will result in instant dismissal.'

The first thought that will probably occur to most lovers of the game on reading these terse words is that the day when the most famous of counties deems it necessary to issue so severe a public rebuke to their most distinguished player is a sad one for cricket. So indeed it is, but that is not to say that the county's action may not have been well considered.

Yorkshire could have spoken as strongly as they pleased in private to a member of their staff and announced the outcome in a brief and formal way. Other cricketers before today have been given a last chance. But no one before Trueman has ever been required to bear the additional stigma of a statement of this sort.

There may well be some sympathy on this account in the minds of the general public for Trueman, whose impulsive, sometimes tempestuous, nature has tended to make him a popular 'bad boy'.

Those familiar with the inner workings of cricket will, however, be much more inclined to applaud Yorkshire for grasping
the nettle so firmly. To them it will seem a welcome blow for
discipline, especially in this particular direction of player-
writing. It is worth stressing again, as regards the necessity
placed on all registered players to submit their writings to the
counties, that the rule was not made with the idea of muzzling
honest opinion.

Cricketers have always been allowed to express their views,
even if heterodox, so long as they were genuine. There has
never been in cricket the veto that exists, for instance, in Rugby
Football and some other sports.

The present regulations – which, incidentally, apply for two
years after a man has stopped playing – were designed to
protect players from the temptation of allowing 'ghosts' to blow
up 'revelations' out of all perspective, for the sort of sums that
might properly reward the reminiscent pieces of a retired Prime
Minister or a great military commander: in short, to check the
growth of a disreputable racket.

Even after pruning at the county's demand, these articles caused
hard feelings between Sussex and Yorkshire, the former considering
that their President, the Duke of Norfolk, manager of M.C.C. in
Australia, had been unjustly maligned.

## Benaud Accuses Griffith

Richie Benaud published his condemnation of Griffith's action
before the last day of the First Test between the West Indies and
Australia at Kingston, when his countrymen were on the verge of
defeat. In the view of West Indians the timing of the article compounded the offence.

March 9, 1965

Australia's former captain, Richie Benaud, has raised a hornet's
nest about his ears here by denouncing Charles Griffith's action
in an article on the front page of the *Daily Gleaner*. His criticism
appears under the heading 'Charlie Griffith a "Chucker".' He
begins: 'West Indian Charles Griffith throws. I am quite con-

vinced of this, having watched him in action in the first Test match of the series against Australia. Photographic evidence supports my view.'

The article is illustrated by one of the many photographs taken by Benaud from the Press-box situated behind the bowler's arm. It shows Griffith's arm, shortly before delivery, indubitably bent in towards the head. The body is leaning outward and the ball (strangely, since the camera was behind) is clearly visible. Benaud comments: 'Like most bowlers of suspect action, he has splayed his left foot out towards point and is beginning to open his body to the batsman.'

The article has been syndicated throughout the West Indies and in India in addition to appearing in Benaud's own paper, the *Sydney Sun*. It is challenged in the *Daily Gleaner* by their cricket correspondent and sports editor, L. D. Roberts, who points out, fairly enough, that this 'outcry' at the crucial stage of the match 'may well produce an adverse psychological effect on the West Indies team.'

This is the aspect which, I expect, will first occur to most people. The matter of throwing has implications of honour and national prestige which loom far larger than a technical consideration which rests, according to No. 26 of the Laws of Cricket, on the personal opinion of the umpires.

I might add that if either of the umpires here in the fervid, hot-blooded atmosphere of Sabina Park had agreed with Benaud's opinion and no-balled Griffith, the consequences would have been incalculable.

I must repeat what I wrote a fortnight ago from Barbados – that he seems to be making a scrupulous effort to keep the arm straight, to bowl from near the stumps with a full follow-through, and to avoid the exaggerated arching of the back and falling away towards the offside that, with him, are the danger-signals. Watching him carefully through glasses, I have not felt any dubiety here, though I certainly did on occasions in England in 1963.

Benaud's picture looks bad, but stills can be dangerous evidence. The slow-motion film camera is the fairer test. Benaud's experience when, as captain of Australia, he saw I. Meckiff no-balled out of cricket at Brisbane against South Africa two seasons ago, has fired him with a determination to see that no other offender escapes. Hence, he has blurted out his opinion as soon as he thought he had the evidence regardless of consequences.

## Dexter Suspended

This (to date) is the last of the player-writer cases, and it is the only one which has resulted in suspension. I wonder if it is too much to hope that by the machinery that has been set up, including the practical deterrent of suspension, the authorities have finally got on top of this taxing problem.

July 20, 1966

E. R. Dexter, the former England and Sussex captain, has been disqualified from playing for a month, as between July 20 and August 19 inclusive, by a decision of the Executive Committee of the Advisory County Committee which controls county cricket in this country. They acted, as is explained in the following statement, because M.C.C. were dissatisfied with the admonition and warning given by Sussex a month ago.

M.C.C. are entitled under the Discipline Section of the rules in such a case to refer the matter to this Executive Committee. The statement reads:

At a meeting of the M.C.C. Committee on July 5, it was decided to refer the publication of Mr E. R. Dexter's book, *Ted Dexter Declares*, to the Executive Committee as provided for in the rules of the Advisory County Cricket Committee.

The Executive Committee met at Lord's on July 20 and decided that Dexter had failed to conform to the rule of the Advisory County Cricket Committee concerning public pronouncements, to which he had agreed, in that he had published a book without the prior consent of the Sussex County Cricket Club.

The Executive Committee in considering this matter noted Mr Dexter's recent public apology, but decided to suspend his qualification for Sussex for one month (July 20 to August 19, 1966 inclusive) and have directed the Registration Committee accordingly.

The elaborate procedure which has been followed was laid down several years ago to protect players from the spate of highly spiced and equally highly rewarded 'revelations' of their colleagues which often disregarded the confidence of the dressing-room and tended generally to bring the game into disrepute.

This book was not 'ghosted', as were the great majority of those which gave offence. The bulk of it, as I wrote at the time of the Sussex announcement, is unexceptionable. There are, however, at least two passages which would certainly have been amended, I imagine, if Dexter had complied with the regulations and given Sussex the opportunity to see the book in time.

Would the book have attracted ripe syndication fees without these contentious references? Where such indiscretions involving such large financial considerations are concerned, is it acceptable for the player to 'forget' and say sorry afterwards? No, the committee seem to have decided, especially when a similar offence has been committed before, as in this case.

This is the first instance of a player being suspended under this rule, though it will be remembered that F. S. Trueman was given a 'last warning' by Yorkshire. From the practical point of view it cannot be said that the decision will affect the immediate composition of the England XI, for since Dexter announced that he proposed to play and to make himself eligible for selection he has scarcely appeared, except in light-hearted games before the television cameras on Sunday afternoons. At the same time it is indeed highly distressing that a sportsman of Dexter's fame and talents should have attracted the limelight in such a way.

## Close in the Dock

August 23, 1967

It would be ridiculous to pretend that this is a happy day for cricket. On the eve of a Test match Brian Close, the England captain, is called to Lord's to answer charges of unsportsman-like conduct (for that is what time-wasting amounts to) in the handling of his county side, as a result of reports from the umpires and of his opponents.

The meeting of the counties' Executive Committee gains in interest, naturally, because of Close's position, and because his claims to the leadership of M.C.C. in the West Indies are at stake. Yet, this Warwickshire-Yorkshire match is the third to be put under post-mortem by the counties this summer, and there must have been other border-line cases.

The tactics of both Leicestershire and Notts have been called into question (their opponents having been Sussex and Somerset respectively), and while it was found that the evidence was 'insufficient' in the Nottinghamshire case, the committee took the opportunity to remind the umpires of their powers – not to mention their firm duty.

By inference, it can be accepted from the statement issued that time-wasting *was* proved in Leicestershire's case, and I understand that a caution was given.

In these days, when almost every first-class player plays for his livelihood, the temptation is becoming the greater to overstep the line that separates the utmost keenness – which is the essence of all good cricket – from sharp practice, which is a different thing altogether. A cricketer knows the difference all right – and so do about 99.9 per cent of those who watch the game and follow it. So, certainly, do those whose unwelcome task it is to pronounce today's verdict.

The Executive Committee, formed under the rules of county cricket to deal with disciplinary matters, comprises the president of M.C.C. and the chairman of the cricket sub-committee or their nominees, two members from counties unaffected by the dispute, a representative of the club concerned, and, if thought advisable, one from the Board of Control selection committee. Under these regulations A. E. R. Gilligan, of Sussex, president-elect, will take the chair with D. G. Clark, of Kent, as the M.C.C. delegates, C. G. A. Paris (Hampshire), E. J. Gothard (Derbyshire), A. B. Sellers (Yorkshire) and D. J. Insole (Essex) for the selectors. In addition, C. C. Goodway, of Warwickshire, will be in attendance to give evidence, though not to vote. Nor, of course, have Mr Sellers and Mr Insole a vote.

All six members of the committee are ex-county captains,

and I imagine that their experience and fair-mindedness would be accepted by any cricketer who found himself before them.

I say that 999 cricketers out of a thousand respect the distinction between keenness and whatever exceeds it – call it gamesmanship, or sharp practice, or just plain cheating as you will. But, as always, there is a tiny 'lunatic fringe' supporting the win-at-all costs philosophy. I wonder how far in cold practice, such misguided folk would go? For example there are, perhaps, six minutes of a game remaining, time for at least a couple of overs, with the batting side within sight of victory.

There is nothing in the laws to prevent the bowler going back to the sight-screen to start his run, and to repeat the manoeuvre until the over is completed, throwing in a no-ball or a wide or two maybe – or even losing his step and starting again – if the hands of the clock still showed a half-minute or so to the time for drawing stumps. Is that all right, or is it going too far? Only two-thirds of the way back perhaps?

Even the recent first-class regulations, which give the umpire powers first to warn and then to ban the bowler, specify that they can take the latter course only at the end of his over. By that time, in this hypothetical case, the damage would have been done, and the discreditable draw perhaps achieved. Would the win-at-all-costs school approve?

Supposing – just incidentally – such a manoeuvre were tried in a Test match in the West Indies, or South Africa, Australia, India, or Pakistan, and a riot ensued, what would be their attitude then? Would that be just part of the fun?

If one remarks that cricket has always been synonymous with fair dealing there will be no doubt those who ridicule such a 'square' notion on principle (if that be the word). The fact is, however, such is its leisurely character and such the opportunities to evade the law, that if cricket is to flourish it must so continue to be synonymous.

It is difficult in any game to legislate for cheats – rugby football is a conspicuous example of the truth of this. In cricket you simply cannot eliminate all the loopholes: which, of course, is why the powers-that-be must insist on a strict code of self-discipline, and must retain the right to reprimand or ban those who contravene it. It follows, in particular, that the authorities at all levels must repose their confidence in the captains: which brings me back to the Close case.

What everyone will want to know is how the selection is affected of the captain and team for the West Indies if, unhappily, he is not completely exonerated.

The situation is that a meeting of the full M.C.C. committee has been summoned for tomorrow, at which the selectors' final nomination for the captaincy will be received and a decision reached.

The captaincy settled at last, the selectors can then set about their choice of the 16 men. According to present intentions, however, it is unlikely that anything will be announced until the Oval Test is concluded, whatever is today's outcome. It is needless to stress how unsatisfactory a position this is – unavoidable though it may be. However, there it is: cricket will survive.

The outcome of the enquiry was that by unanimous vote Brian Close was severely censured, and under this slur led England in the final Test against Pakistan. The M.C.C. did not disclose their decision regarding the leadership of their team to the West Indies until the Test was over. When they did, and announced Colin Cowdrey as their captain, Douglas Insole, the chairman of the selectors, ended an embarrassing incident on the sorriest note by saying that his committee had voted for Close notwithstanding the decision, but that their nomination had not been accepted by the M.C.C. Committee. In such circumstances Cowdrey took on the job amid the sympathy of all, whatever their feelings on the Close issue.

# CHAPTER EIGHT

# TRIBUTES TO THE GREAT

I have restricted myself in these notices, written at the time of death or shortly before, to a few men – eleven in all – whom I both knew well and (with one exception) saw play. Thus such heroes as Sydney Barnes, George Hirst and R. H. Spooner are not included because their cricket preceded my time and I could only write their obituaries at second hand. The exception is Frank Chester who, of course, is included as the greatest of all umpires rather than as a player.

Apart from Harry Altham, whose services in all branches of the game qualify him for the title of 'the compleat cricketer', all here mentioned were Test stars of the brightest calibre. They were also without exception men who adorned the game for what they were as well as for what they did. One thinks back on them all with affection as well as respect. More could well have been found who fulfilled these requirements – Bill Woodfull, for instance, Ernest Tyldesley, J. W. Hearne and Maurice Tate. But this chapter, like the rest of the book, has had to be an exercise in compression. I should add that the death of George Duckworth occurred when I was with the 1965–66 M.C.C. side in Australia. Hence the all-too-brief piece cabled twenty-four hours later.

One further point about obituaries. I have never written one of a famous cricketer without receiving in due course letters from readers on the subject of my notice. Nostalgic chords always seem to be touched to the point of putting pen to paper – which, as every journalist knows, means that they have not been touched lightly. This being so, I felt that this sort of book would not be complete without this sort of chapter.

## F. Chester (1896-1957)

Frank Chester was by common agreement the best of all umpires, and furthermore one whose ability raised the whole standard and standing of his craft. But his personality, which communicated itself unfailingly to the crowds, and the story of cricketing promise cut short which led to his becoming an umpire, combined to make the man a sporting institution.

On the recommendation of Alec Hearne, Chester, at the age of 14, went to qualify for Worcestershire. At 16½ he won his county cap, and by the time the Great War came after less than three full seasons' play he was acclaimed an England cricketer in embryo.

As a bowler he was an exponent of both sorts of spin, as a batsman a free stroke-maker who in an innings of 178 not out against Essex hit the late 'Johnny' Douglas (then just about the best opening bowler in England) for four sixes.

Having survived the second battle of Loos, Chester was transferred to Salonika where, when guarding ammunition, he was hit in the arm by a piece of shrapnel. Penicillin being then unknown, he endured various operations and ultimately amputation.

He began his first-class umpiring in 1922 at the age of 26, and made his mark so rapidly that two years later he was standing in a Test match. In all he stood in 48 Tests, and for 28 years as an umpire.

He described the three chief requisites of an umpire as 'hearing, eyesight and knowledge of the laws.' But that leaves out of account concentration and strength of character, both of which Chester commanded in full measure, and also something intangible which Mr Aird perhaps expressed when, on hearing the news yesterday, he said: 'He was an inspiration to other umpires. He seemed to have a flair for the job, and did the right thing by instinct.

The best epitaph to his skill comes from the greatest of all modern cricketers, Sir Donald Bradman: 'Without hesitation I rank Frank Chester as the greatest umpire under whom I played. In my four seasons' cricket in England he stood for the the large percentage of the matches and seldom made a mistake. On the other hand, he gave some really wonderful decisions. Not only was his judgment sound, but Chester exercised a measure of control over the game which I think was desirable.'

Latterly, before he gave in to persistent ill-health, Chester now and then fell into mortal error, and he neither appreciated, nor was appreciated, by the Australians, who were irked by his apparently dictatorial manner.

But he often umpired when he should have been in bed. Until the last few years he was as nearly infallible as a man could be in his profession, and by his conscientiousness and zeal served as an example to all.

# K. S. Duleepsinhji (1905-1959)

K. S. Duleepsinhji was a great cricketer, one of the most gifted as well as most graceful, who ever played for England.

Considering that his health allowed him only seven full seasons, his achievements are memorable enough. But news of his death has aroused a pang as well as a distant echo, both among those who played with him and those who watched him play, because of the man he was.

When the old heroes are talked about and his name is mentioned people will say 'Ah, Duleep!' – and the pause tells of affection as well as respect, for he was a most modest, gentle person. One almost recalls the charm of his character before his merits as a cricketer.

As a batsman he was unquestionably the best amateur between the wars. Indeed, he had no technical superior among the professionals, and it is only the extreme brevity of his prime that prevents comparison with Hammond, Hutton and Compton. Most of the great batsmen have been at their best between 25 and 35. 'Duleep' was finished at 27.

Only Hammond rivalled him as a slip fieldsman, while in two summers his intelligent, persuasive leadership left an indelible mark on Sussex cricket. The county would not still be looking for its first Championship if he had been spared to play another year or two, perhaps a bare fortnight more.

Duleepsinhji learned his cricket at Cheltenham, and he duly crowned his career as a schoolboy with a hundred for the Lord's Schools. He was lucky in his teachers, at school W. A. Woof, a household word in Gloucestershire to this day, and afterwards the incomparable Aubrey Faulkner. They for their part had unique natural gifts to work on, plus the magical tradition of his uncle 'Ranji'. If anything was certain it was that 'Duleep' was born to greatness on the cricket field.

His career was divided into two phases by the first onset of the tuberculosis which later caused his retirement. After two auspicious years in the Cambridge XI he began 1927 at Fenner's with a hundred against Yorkshire. He followed it with a fabulous 254 not out (wearing two sweaters!) against Middle-sex, and was taken that same night into the Addenbrooke Hospital. The end of this prelude to greatness was a year in Switzerland.

Five seasons more, as it turned out, were left to him. During that time he made nearly 10,000 runs for Sussex with an average of 50, scored three hundreds at Lord's against the Players, two of them in the same match, toured New Zealand and Australia with A. H. H. Gilligan's team, and, of course, took his rightful place at number four for England following Hobbs, Sutcliffe, and Hammond.

The 173 against Australia in the classic Lord's Test of 1930 was the peak of his achievement. Holding the innings together, he yet scored his runs in four hours and three-quarters. An element of tactical indecision may have helped his end. When he was caught at long-off off Grimmett at quarter-past six, and his uncle, the Jam Saheb, was remarking 'the boy was always careless,' A. C. MacLaren, an oracle of awesome resonance, was deploring Percy Chapman's criminal folly in not having declared already. The truth was no one then knew quite how to wage a four-day Test. Bradman was soon to show them.

In this innings against Grimmett at his best, and in many others against the foremost bowlers of his day, Larwood and Voce, McDonald, Tate, J. C. White, Freeman and the rest, 'Duleep' showed himself the complete artist. He had all the strokes, but as with an earlier aristocrat, William Beldham, his special glory was the cut.

He was as lissom and keen of eye as was to be expected from his race. But he did not presume upon his gifts to flaunt the book. He, if anyone, put a bloom on the orthodox. And what a bloom! One day he was cutting McDonald to smithereens at Old Trafford, the next, silk shirt a-flutter, he was dancing out to Freeman at Hastings and reducing that tormentor of the slow-footed to utter impotence.

Freeman! I only heard once of 'Duleep' getting angry, and Tich Freeman was the sufferer. In dry weather Sussex got caught on a most suspiciously wet wicket at Maidstone and were promptly spun to destruction. 'Duleep' said ominously: 'Wait till they come to Hastings.' Kent came and he murdered them to the tune of 115 in the first innings and 246 in the second. In these innings he scored at more than 70 an hour off his own bat, and gave in all two hard chances.

Once, against Northampton, on the first day of the season at Hove he made 333, and was out by six o'clock. No wonder he swiftly became, and still is, a legend in Sussex.

In mid-August, 1932, Sussex and Yorkshire were fighting out the Championship toe to toe. At Taunton against Somerset, 'Duleep's' 90 won the match. It was his last innings. His illness had returned, Sussex lost their leader, and M.C.C. had to find a replacement to send with D. R. Jardine's team to Australia.

But that rancorous tour, in retrospect anyway, 'Duleep' would have been thankful to miss. Cricket to him was not that sort of game.

# A. P. F. Chapman (1900-1961)

A. P. F. Chapman was one of the most successful of England Test captains. He was also, in the view of the more reliable judges among his contemporaries, one of the best.

I stress the point early in this appreciation because the popular conception of Percy Chapman in his heyday was only partly true. He was debonair, generous, carefree in character as in his cricket, and as such the sporting world took him to its heart.

Yet underlying the boyish facade was both a shrewd cricket brain and the good sense to ask advice from those of greater experience. With Jack Hobbs at his side Chapman had not far to look. He showed too, a sympathy for people which naturally in its turn brought the very best out of them. His sides were happy sides.

Chapman's cricket was marked for distinction from his days at Uppingham at the end of the first war. As a schoolboy he played at Lord's with G. T. S. Stevens, D. R. Jardine, C. H.

Gibson, L. P. Hedges, C. T. Ashton, and N. E. Partridge: that was the best of all school vintages.

His adventurous left-handed batting and fielding won him a Cambridge Blue as a freshman. He was one of A. C. MacLaren's legendary side that beat the 1921 Australians at Eastbourne, and in 1922 made 102 not out in the University match, followed the next week by 160 in Gentlemen and Players. This latter innings against the cream of the professional bowling perhaps marked him out as a coming Test cricketer. Eight years later he completed an almost unique trilogy with 121 at Lord's against Australia. M. P. Donnelly is the only other man to have scored centuries at Lord's in the two classics and also in a Test Match.

Chapman played first for England in 1924 against South Africa and went that winter to Australia with A. E. R. Gilligan's side. Thereafter he was practically a permanent member of the England XI until the end of the M.C.C. tour of S. Africa in 1930–31. He led England in 17 Tests, of which nine were won and only two lost, including the Lord's Test already referred to against Australia.

In his career Chapman made 16,309 runs including 27 hundreds with an average of 31.97. But with no man were figures less significant. Too venturesome to be a consistent scorer, he could turn a game by his hitting as quickly and as thoroughly as any cricketer of his generation or since.

Not least he was a superb fielder, in the country in his undergraduate days, but for England and Kent close to the bat, mostly at gully and silly mid-off.

Hail-fellow-well-met with everyone, he became towards the end of his cricket career the victim of his popularity and from the war onwards his life went into sad eclipse. In the last few years his health grew so bad that he could not get to Lord's. The elderly and the middle-aged will recall him rather in his handsome sunlit youth, the epitome of all that was gay and fine in the game of cricket.

# E. Hendren (1889-1962)

It is probably safe to say that no more popular cricketer ever played than E. Hendren (christened Elias but universally known as 'Patsy'), who has died aged 73.

His technical record with the bat between 1907 and 1937 was remarkable enough, with 170 centuries and a total of more than 57,000 runs, figures which rank only slightly behind those of Sir Jack Hobbs and Frank Woolley. But though his deeds for England and Middlesex can be read about in books, the statistics of his career convey no impression as to the kind of man he was.

His short figure, his happy and sometimes wistful smile, his most obvious likeableness, and his facility for enlivening even the most serious situation with some perfectly-timed and never overdone piece of clowning – all these endeared him to everybody, as much as did his flashing square-cut, his favourite lofted on-drive, his mighty hook off the fast bowlers, and his nimble footwork against the slow ones.

Everywhere he went he was persona gratissima – in the West Indies the affection for him developed almost into a cult – and West Indian streets and children were christened 'Patsy'.

Nobody who was present will ever forget the scene, when in his last match at Lord's in 1937, he scored a century against Surrey. As soon as he got his hundredth run the crowd of some 17,000 rose to its feet and after repeated cheering sang 'For he's a jolly good fellow!' There has seldom been a more genuine tribute.

Hendren did not burst with sudden brilliance on the cricket world. He was 24 when, after a long apprenticeship, he became indispensable to Middlesex. Only then began his famous association with J. W. Hearne – 'young Jack' – that meant so much to the county for so long.

He was equally slow to develop as a Test cricketer, and until his mid-thirties was in danger of being regarded as a first-rate county player rather than an essential part of the England XI. He was not the only one to fail against Gregory and McDonald, the Australian fast bowlers, in 1921, but the parrot cry of 'temperament' arose.

A century against Australia at Lord's in 1926, and an even more valuable one at Brisbane for A. P. F. Chapman's team in the winter of 1928, showed how wrong his detractors were, and he became indispensable to England too. Altogether he played

ABOVE: Ken Barrington in flow. He is batting at Arundel against the 1966 West Indians. Sobers is at short leg, Hendriks is the keeper. BELOW: Wesley Hall, in action and repose. At the age of 30 probably nearing the end of his career, Hall has taken more Test wickets than any other West Indian: the fire and fury of his bowling have been one of the unforgettable sights of the 'sixties

Fateful moment. P. B. H. May b. Benaud 0 at Old Trafford 1961. The ball which in all probability settled the rubber. England were beaten by 54 runs with twenty minutes to spare

Compton's Swan-Song. In his last Test in England, Denis Compton returning to the team after the removal of a knee-cap the previous winter, made 94 and 35 not out at the Oval in 1956. England, who held the Ashes, won the rubber. He pushes past Johnson. Langley is the keeper, Archer at slip

48 innings against Australia, 18 against South Africa and 17 against the West Indies. He made 3,525 runs in Tests with an average of 47. As a member of a touring side his personality counted for almost as much as did his performance on the field.

Among his great feats may be mentioned his 301, not out, for Middlesex against Worcestershire in 1933, the scoring of more than 2,000 runs in every season between 1920 and 1929, including a total of 3,311 in 1928, a third-wicket partnership of 375, still an English record with Hearne, his colleague in many a productive stand, against Hampshire in 1923, and his 206 at Trent Bridge in 1925, when Middlesex, who were set to make 502, got the runs in six and a quarter hours. Hendren and F. T. Mann hit off the last 271 in 195 minutes.

In his prime he was among the best of outfields, and later became an adept at short-leg, where his work on the 1928-29 tour in Australia was invaluable.

His opinion on any matter was always worth asking; and the younger Middlesex professionals, especially Compton and Edrich, owed much to his advice and guidance. In his last playing years he was an invaluable lieutenant to the youthful R. W. V. Robins.

His own contribution to the 'body-line' controversy was the typical one of providing himself with a specially-made helmet, which he occasionally wore at Lord's when the wicket was bumpy. When he retired from first-class cricket in 1937, at the age of 48, he was appointed coach at Harrow in succession to Wilfred Rhodes.

In 1939 Harrow beat Eton for the first time since 1908, and in the rejoicing afterwards Hendren was called out to the balcony and cheered again by the Lord's crowd. He retired from Harrow in 1947 and was first coach to Sussex and then scorer with Middlesex until 1959.

In his younger days he was a good Association footballer, and as outside-right for Brentford played for England against Wales in the 1919 'Victory' series.

# Sir Jack Hobbs (1882-1963)

Sir Jack Hobbs, who has died aged 81, was the greatest English

I

batsman since W. G. Grace, a supreme master of his craft, and
the undisputed head of his profession. Born on December 16,
1882, the son of the groundsman at Jesus College, Cambridge,
he made his way to the Oval at the age of 20. Half a century
later, long after his retirement but when his name was still a
household word, he accepted the honour of knighthood.

John Berry Hobbs learned his cricket as so many Cambridge
men have done before and since, on that sublime stretch
between Fenner's and the Town, called Parker's Piece. Tom
Hayward was his mentor there, and it was Hobbs' luck, after
Hayward had persuaded him to qualify for Surrey, that he
should serve his apprenticeship at the Oval as opening partner
to that great batsman.

There have been three men, as one surveys the history of
cricket as a whole, whose genius and influence have transcended
all others: W. G. Grace, Jack Hobbs and Don Bradman. Like
most of the truly great – it was the same with Hutton and
Compton, Hammond and Woolley – Hobbs proclaimed his
promise beyond all argument more or less right away.

He made 155 in his second match for Surrey, scored 1,300
in this first season of 1905 and improved considerably on that in
his second. The next year he was chosen for the Players and
also won a place in the M.C.C. side to Australia of 1907–8. It
was then already said of him that there was no better professional batsman in England bar Hayward and Johnny
Tyldesley.

It was the second of his five visits as a player to Australia that
brought him right to the top of the tree. In that series he
averaged 82, scored three Test hundreds and with Wilfred
Rhodes made 323, which is still the longest opening partnership
for England against Australia.

Noting the consistency of his scoring and the speed with
which the runs generally came in those days, one can appreciate
the remark of Frank Woolley's: 'They can say what they like
about him, but only those of us who saw Jack before 1914 knew
him at his very best.' However that may be, he was and remained the world's premier batsman until when nearer 50 than
40, his gradual decline coincided with the advent of
Bradman.

The long span of Hobbs' career made it probable that he

would corner most of the aggregate records. Thus no one can match his number of runs, 61,221, any more than they can compete with his 197 centuries. No doubt he was lucky in his opening partners – compared with, say, Hutton. Nevertheless, his figure of 166 stands of a century or more for the first wicket sets an almost unassailable target. Even more conclusive may seem the consistency of his performances. He averaged just under 50 in England over his whole time, stretching from 1905 to 1934. In Australia his average was 51, in South Africa 68, and in Tests alone it stood at 56.94.

Hobbs had two great Surrey partners, Hayward and Sandham, two even more famous for England, Rhodes and Sutcliffe. It was he and Sutcliffe who decided the Oval Test of '26 that brought back the Ashes, after many crushing defeats, by their wonderful partnership of 172 on a bad wicket.

In the next series in Australia these two paved the way to the victory that kept the Ashes safe by scoring 105 together on a Melbourne glue-pot – one of the classics of bad-wicket batsmanship. On A. E. R. Gilligan's tour of 1924–5 Hobbs and Sutcliffe, going in against a score of 600, batted the entire day for 283.

If one summer marked his peak it was perhaps 1925, when, at the age of 42, he scored 3,000 runs, including 16 centuries, and with two hundreds in the match against Somerset at Taunton, first equalled and then surpassed the 126 hundreds made by 'W.G.'

Early recollections of Hobbs are confined in my own case to inessential things like the frequent spinning of the bat in his fingers before he settled into his stance, and the way he pulled down the peak of his cap, so that it slanted almost parallel with his slightly beaky nose.

Before I knew enough to admire his batting it was his fielding which fascinated most. He would walk about at cover in an innocent pre-occupied sort of way in between times, hands often deep in pockets. If the ball were pushed wide of him, and the batsmen made to run, he would usually move at a quite leisurely speed to cut it off. Then suddenly an apparently identical stroke would be repeated, and this time the relaxed figure would spring into action with catlike swiftness – there was a dart, a swoop, and the quickest of flicks straight at the stumps, with the batsman pounding to the crease as if for dear life. Australians as a rule are good between the wickets, but on one tour Hobbs at cover point ran out upwards of a dozen of them.

It has been written of him often enough that he was the bridge between the old batting and the new. When he entered the scene it was the age of elegance, and the best professionals absorbed and were caught up in the classical style based on the swing of the bat from the shoulders, driving, and the off-side strokes.

There were, of course, strong back players, notably Fry, and more and more men came to practise the art of working the ball to the on-side. Hobbs was quickly identified with this school. Then, when he was still climbing to the top, came the revolution in technique that was made necessary by the arrival of the googly and the advance of the wrist spinner. At the same time the faster bowlers were exploring the possibilities of swing.

Neville Cardus has described him as 'the first batsman really to master the new bowling.' He combined with the classic freedom of forward play and full swing of the bat the necessary adaptation to defeat the googly and late swerve – legs and pads over the wicket with the hands held loosely on the bat in order to scotch the spin and bring the ball down short of the close fieldsmen, virtually in the crease.

But enough of technique. In the last resort the difference between talent and mastery is a matter of character. Hobbs brought to his cricket an ascetic self-discipline which in tight corners expressed itself perfectly in his play.

He was a man of conspicuous personal modesty; but his pride in his position as – in every sense – England's No. 1 gave to his batting an aura of serenity equally communicable to his opponents and to his fellows. No one ever saw Hobbs rattled or in a hurry. And if he was anxious it never showed.

There was a quiet dignity about him which had its roots in mutual respect: for others as for himself. He had the natural good manners of a Christian and a sportsman, and the esteem in which, in his day, his profession came to be held owed much to the man who for the best part of a quarter of a century was its undisputed leader.

# H. S Altham (1888-1965)

Harry Surtees Altham, who has died aged 76, was president of M.C.C. in 1959 and had been Treasurer of the Club since 1950. He captained Repton for two years in 1907 and 1908, and won his Blue at Oxford in 1911 and 1912.

He played for Surrey when an undergraduate and later while a master at Winchester appeared for Hampshire in the August holiday.

Though he won a Blue in his third year and played a valuable innings of 47 against Cambridge at Lord's, his cricket did not perhaps come on quite as well at Oxford as his reputation at Repton had suggested.

As befitted a devoted disciple of C. B. Fry, whose 'Batsmanship' was his Bible, his batting style was based closely on the text-book. This, of course, served him well when, as a don at Winchester, he began in 1913 the teaching of cricket to boys, which is not the least of his many-sided contributions to the game.

He went to Winchester, as his great friend and contemporary, Rockley Wilson, wrote, 'with a knowledge of cricket beyond his years, and a style ideal for boys to copy.' For nearly 50 years he spent countless summer hours infusing boys with a knowledge and love of cricket, and he still bowled on at the nets at New Field, when nearer 70 than 60.

Altham's activities at Winchester between the wars were such as to satisfy even *his* restless energy. He taught, he coached cricket, he became a devotee and patron of rackets, and he took over Chernocke House, whose honours list grew second to none. He also wrote 'A History of Cricket,' which originally appeared in serial form in *The Cricketer*. It was published in 1926, and in 1938 he paid me the compliment of inviting me to collaborate with him in a new edition. Thanks to Altham's industry and research the book remains the standard work.

In the first war he served as a major with the 60th Rifles and emerged with the D.S.O., M.C., and three mentions in despatches. When the second war ended he was within a month or two of his 57th birthday – a time when most people think of lightening their shoulders gradually of work and responsibilities. So far as Winchester was concerned his career followed the

natural order of things. In 1948 he gave up his house and a few
years later retired officially from the staff, although he continued to assist as Careers Master.

But the lessening of one branch of activity coincided with the
taking up of another, just as taxing, if not more so – the
essential difference being that the new one was honorary work
– for cricket.

In 1947 Altham was elected to the M.C.C. Committee. Less
than two years later he was taking the chair at the first Inquiry
meeting into the state of English cricket, the upshot of which
was the national movement for the encouragement of youth by
means of improved facilities and coaching. The M.C.C. Youth
Cricket Association, with its ancillaries throughout the counties,
the coaching courses, at the Central Council for Physical
Recreation headquarters at Lilleshall, and the whole broad
scheme for bringing the game to the ordinary youth of England
– all this was the rich fruit of his enthusiasm and indefatigable
work.

There are many cricket milieus of which Altham seemed an
integral part, but those who were present said that at Lilleshall
during these courses, whether bowling at the nets or enthralling
his audience by a talk on the history of cricket, he seemed at
his very happiest and best.

In this field we must likewise remember an organisation
equally beholden to him, and fulfilling a parallel function for
younger boys within the schools, the English Schools Cricket
Association. Mr Altham during his Presidency put the E.S.C.A.
on the map. Many county and some Test players have been
through its hands, and its representative team now appears
annually at Lord's.

Finally, in the field of cricket administration he was Chairman for one significant year of the Test selectors. The knowledge gained under his Chairmanship enabled the M.C.C.
Selection Committee to choose at the end of the season a side
to bring back the Ashes from Australia for the first time for
more than 20 years.

Such in brief was Harry Altham: the school, University, and
county player; the coach; the historian; the founder of a
national youth movement; the administrator, the speech-
maker, the senior legislator and fountainhead of Marylebone.

He was a man of deep and abiding loyalties, with a wonderful facility, which his wife fully shared, of inspiring the friendship and affection of the young. As to which was the most valuable of all his contributions to the game of cricket there might be several answers. But there can be but one response surely when it is asked, have M.C.C. ever had so 'compleat' a cricketer in their seat of honour? In 1957 he was made C.B.E. For such multifarious services it was by no means, his friends felt, an extravagant recognition.

## W. R. Hammond (1903-1965)

There has been nothing like the calm serenity of Hammond advancing to the crease, and surveying the field after taking guard. If he made a duck he did so like an emperor, but of course, ducks were not his speciality.

Between 1927 and 1947 (six years being lost by war) he made more runs in Test cricket than any other man: 7,249, averaging 58, and including more hundreds (22) than anyone bar Sir Donald Bradman.

With 110 Test catches, most of them in the slips where he scarcely had a superior, he far and away heads the field. He was also a more than usually useful change bowler, of about the pace of Maurice Tate, with, as might be supposed, an action that mirrored all the virtues.

It was said, probably with truth, that he might have played many times for England had he never made a run, for his bowling was capable of reaching the heights had he needed it to. He was in fact, as may be imagined, a superb natural games-player who could make himself almost equally at home on the golf course, or on the squash and lawn tennis courts.

The basis of his batting was the massive power of his driving, straight and to the off, but he used every stroke, except the hook to fast bowling. O'Reilly aimed to peg him by attacking his legs, but this only curbed his speed of scoring. He averaged 51 against Australia.

In Test cricket he never played better than in his first Australian tour under A. P. F. Chapman when he scored the record aggregate of 905 with an average of 113. But the innings that will specially be remembered by English followers will be his masterful 240 against Australia at Lord's in 1938.

His first-class record was as imposing as his figures in Tests. With 50,493 runs to his name he had a higher aggregate than all save Hobbs, Woolley, Hendren, Mead and Grace, all of whose careers were substantially longer. His centuries, numbering 167, have been bettered only by Hobbs and Hendren. Only two men, Woolley and Grace held more than his 819 catches. No one exceeded his 78 in a season, or his 10 in a match, achieved in 1928.

His unique value to Gloucestershire was never shown more scintillatingly than in a certain five days in the Cheltenham Festival of that year. In the same match against Surrey which contained the 10 catches, he made a hundred in each innings, 139 and 143. Next came Worcestershire who were bowled out before lunch by Hammond, who took nine for 23, went in and made 80 and followed up with six more wickets to give his side victory by an innings in two days.

His skill on bad wickets should be specially noted. One recalls an innings of more than a hundred against Sussex at Horsham after a thunderstorm when everyone else got out as soon as they reached the batting end. In 1946-7 also on the terrible wicket at Brisbane, after another and greater thunderstorm, he gave Australia an object lesson in batsmanship on a wicket where the ball lifted and turned in a way impossible to predict. His exceptional speed of reaction here stood him in marvellous stead.

Was there then no flaw, no Achilles heel, in this truly wonderful cricketer? Technically his batting was only less than excellent against the fastest bowling. He could be discomposed by a Constantine or a Larwood, although the innings which greatly helped to bring him to fame was one of much splendour against McDonald at Old Trafford.

The only limitation concerns his captaincy. On changing status from professional to amateur in 1938 he became captain both of his county and of England, but in Test cricket at any rate, the glamour that surrounded his own cricket found no reflection in his leadership.

He was in particular too much of an individualist to make a good touring captain, and the failure of the 1946-7 side in

Australia, despite the warmest of post-war welcomes, and an abundance of surrounding goodwill, brought about his immediate retirement. But if the end was thus clouded nothing could seriously dim the memory of one of the greatest cricketers – perhaps one of the greatest half-dozen – who ever played for England.

## G. Duckworth (1901-1966)

The news of the death of George Duckworth, three times a tourist with M.C.C. in Australia and baggage-master as lately as 11 years ago, has made a stir here in Australia.

All the world loves a cheerful sportsman and the tributes paid in the Australian Press today underline the regard in which he was held by his opponents as well as by his countrymen.

Duckworth was a magnificent wicketkeeper of the more aggressive kind, always prepared to throw himself at half-chances and never chary of opening his mouth in an appeal that split the heavens.

He was a 'keeper in the Evans mould rather in that of Ames (who succeeded him in the Test side) or of Oldfield. In a crisis he could sell his life dearly with the bat and one recalls the 30-odd spread over several hours, that helped successfully to fight off Australia in 1930 at Leeds.

Whether in later years he was functioning on the Lancashire committee or taking Commonwealth sides to India – which he did three times – or writing in the Press Box or talking on radio or television, George's dry Lancashire humour and his warmth and friendliness towards all cricketers, especially young ones, endeared him everywhere.

He was one of the great North-country pros, rich in character, whose memory will not quickly fade.

## M. Leyland (1900-1967)

Maurice Leyland, after several years of sickness most stoically borne, has died at Harrogate, aged 66.

There are certain games-players whose qualities of character are such that they are, from early days, marked out by the crowd and hailed as friends. Such a one was Leyland, of Yorkshire and England, a great batsman of the between-wars period, and a great sportsman, whose stocky figure, with cap slightly a-tilt, was hailed with warmth and respect wherever cricket is played.

Leyland was born at Harrogate on July 20, 1900. He won his county cap in 1922, and so was brought up in the strongest of all Yorkshire schools with Rhodes and Kilner, Robinson and Macaulay, Sutcliffe, Holmes and Oldroyd.

From early days his left-handed batsmanship was shaped in a more fluid mould than that of most of his northern contemporaries. His play was effective rather than graceful, and quickness of eye and foot made up for the fact that the bat sometimes strayed a longish was from the perpendicular. Yet he was a magnificent cover-point driver. He cut well too, and altogether made more runs than most of his kind on the off-side.

As a young man he was a remarkably fast outfielder, and with a side less well-served could have become a useful slow left-arm bowler of the orthodox kind. As it was he amused himself when occasionally called upon by bowling 'chinamen' (left-arm off-breaks) – a phrase he is generally credited with inventing.

The first of his six M.C.C. tours was to India in 1926–7. Two years later, amid something of a furore, he was chosen for Australia in preference to Woolley, who, in 1928, scored 3,352 runs, an aggregate then exceeded in an English summer only by Tom Hayward.

England's batting was so strong that Leyland did not play in a Test match until the fifth at Melbourne, where he distinguished himself by making 137 and 53 not out on his first appearance against Australia. This was the first of his 41 matches for England. He made 2,764 runs, including nine hundreds, in 65 innings, averaging 46.06. His career record, between 1920 and 1947, was as follows:

| Inns. | N.O. | Runs | Highest | Aver. | 100's |
|-------|------|--------|---------|-------|-------|
| 932   | 101  | 33,660 | 263     | 40.51 | 80    |

These figures bear out the accepted idea that he was a better Test than County batsman. In 1932, by the time August came he had made only about 700 runs. Just in time he collected

1,000 inside a month, went out to Australia after all, and played his full part in the Test series.

A third time he went to Australia, four years later, and with Hammond supported a weak batting side so admirably that England went astonishingly near repeating the victories of the previous two tours. It was on this tour that his moral ascendancy over O'Reilly, at that time the greatest bowler in the world, was fully established and acknowledged.

Maurice was a modest man (like most of the very best performers of his generation), but he was not above exploiting a bit of gamesmanship in the cause. 'Ah've got him skinned,' he was reported as saying. A pause, and then: 'and he knows it!'

Besides his three tours to Australia, one of which also involved New Zealand, and the one to India he went also with M.C.C. to South Africa and West Indies. His biggest Test score was his last: 187 at the Oval in 'Hutton's Match' in '38.

It was scarcely a characteristic innings, for it was scored on a wicket of pluperfect ease against somewhat ordinary bowling – apart from that of his old antagonist, O'Reilly. His best self was seen when the going was tough. Indeed no more courageous or determined cricketer ever buckled on pads for England.

# Sir Frank Worrell (1924-1967)

Sir Frank Mortimer Maglinne Worrell, who has died with such tragic suddenness at the age of 42, will be remembered as a cricketer of the highest attainments, as a great captain and not least as an outstanding citizen of the West Indies.

Born in Barbados on August 1, 1924, his cricket came to light in the war years. He made 308 not out against Trinidad at the age of 19.

When the West Indies re-entered the Test scene in 1948 he was a natural choice along with the other members of the trinity of 'W's' from the same island, Clyde Walcott and Everton Weekes. Thereafter the achievements in concert of these three are legendary. Walcott and Weekes had, however, retired from Test cricket when at the age of 36 Worrell was faced with his sternest trial.

In 1960 he assumed the captaincy of the West Indies in

Australia for what turned out to be in all respects the best, as well as the most exciting, series of modern times. The climax of it was a motorcade through the Melbourne streets amid a cheering throng of half a million people.

Three years later he led the West Indies to their famous 1963 success in England.

Announcing his retirement at the end of this tour, he was knighted the following year. By this time he had assumed high responsibilities first with the University of the West Indies in Jamaica and then as a worker in social fields with the Trinidad Government.

However, he had one further contribution to make to West Indies cricket. When in 1965 Australia visited the Caribbean, Worrell undertook the management of the West Indies team, now under the captaincy of Garfield Sobers. Thus fortified and advised, Sobers led his men to success in the rubber. Thanks to the pair of them, for the first time the West Indies now indeed bestrode the cricket firmament as undisputed champions.

Worrell was a magnificent cricketer, as elegant a batsman as ever walked to the wicket, and on his day a dangerous bowler, but it was as a leader of serene temperament who commanded the loyalty and affection of his men to an extraordinary degree that his name will shine with a special lustre in the game's history.

It was, of course, his high personal qualities which gave him such a valuable influence with young people. In the developing countries of the West Indies he seemed to have a special part to play and I believe nothing was more certain than that a Governor-Generalship would have been offered him had he lived to full maturity.

Worrell's rise as a cricketer, remarkable though it was, is simply the story of a man of much natural talent making the most of it. His development in the broader sense is even more interesting. As a young man he was considered too outspoken for the local cricket authorities of the day and on this account his services were not utilised for the first post-war West Indies tour, that to India in 1948–49. Worrell, however, set his sights on other targets besides cricket.

He forthwith began a long career in the League, first with Radcliffe and latterly with Norton, making his home in

Lancashire and when not pursuing his living as a cricketer preparing for his degree at Manchester University. It was his experience of living in the north that made him such a strong anglophile and so generous a host to English visitors to the West Indies. He was a hero in Jamaica and also in Trinidad. Strangely and sadly, he was slightly less of one in his native Barbados, where there is so strong a pride of island.

Frank was a federalist who saw the many diverse elements of the West Indies as a homogeneous whole. It was this outlook that led to his frowning on what he took to be the presumption of Barbados challenging the rest of the world. Time no doubt would have brought a complete rapprochement, for he had bought land in Barbados with an eye to his distant retirement.

Turning back specifically to his cricket he made 3,860 runs in 51 Test matches with an average of 49 and took with his left-arm bowling 69 wickets at 38 apiece. These are all-round figures that only Sobers among his countrymen can exceed. He made nine Test hundreds, six of them against England, who almost invariably found him at his best.

As a batsman he was conspicuously correct in method, his bat as near to the vertical as the stroke made possible. Sir Neville Cardus has written of another and earlier great batsman that he added a bloom to the orthodox. The same could be said of Worrell. He was slim and lissom, a stylist who could not do an ugly or ungainly thing in any department. It was common talk that he should have been made captain of the West Indies before he was, though in fact he had twice been offered the leadership but had put his university career first. When the chance came in Australia it was accepted by the rest of his side, if not by him, as a challenge to his race. The result was a personal triumph of character and a spontaneity of performance on the part of his team that will never be forgotten in Australia.

# A. A. Mailey (1886-1967)

Arthur Mailey, of New South Wales and Australia, who has died within three days of his 82nd birthday, was a great leg-spin bowler of the 20's, the man who, complementing the fast attack of Gregory and McDonald, helped first Armstrong and then Collins to establish an era of ascendancy in their country's cricket.

In the series of 1920–21 he had 36 wickets, including nine for 121 in the second innings of the Fourth Test at Melbourne; both are 'records' as regards Australian achievements against England. In all, he took 99 Test wickets in his five series and seven years of Test cricket.

But Arthur Mailey was a good deal more than a gifted cricketer: he was a man of diverse and uncommon gifts, and as such invites an unusual obituary.

When first chosen for Australia he was a labourer, and once accepted to play in a Test though not truly fit. But his captain was in the secret, won the match without using his bowling, and Mailey was able to collect the match fee that meant much to him without any awkward questions. Otherwise that tally of 36 would no doubt have been higher.

Mailey, self-taught, became both writer and artist, whose whimsical and independent nature was communicated equally by his pen and his brush. Having taken all 10 wickets against Gloucestershire on the tour of Collins' team for a lucky number of runs, he called his autobiography 'Ten for 66 and All That.' It is perhaps the best reminiscent book yet written by a cricketer.

Though he could talk knowledgeably about the philosophy of spin bowling he never knuckled down seriously to criticism, amusing himself rather by advancing his theories of the moment which were directed generally against pompous administrators, stodgy batsmen, and medium-paced bowlers, whom he thought boring.

Writing for an evening paper, he once forecast an England Test team forgetting to include a wicketkeeper, and diverted the flood of letters by saying that the bowling was such that no keeper was necessary.

Latterly he took to painting in oils, and numbered Sir Robert Menzies as a patron as well as a friend. He was wont to travel in England in a small car with an easel in the boot calling on friends both famous and obscure, and turning up at Australian matches or not, as the mood took him.

When, in failing health during the last M.C.C. tour of Australia, he was reproached for not coming up to the First

Test at Brisbane, he excused himself by saying: 'I make it a principle not to enter the State of which Mackay is a resident.' He no doubt liked Mackay as a man – who would not? – but deplored him as a cricketer.

Mailey is the only bowler whom I have heard make the ball buzz as it left the hand – and that was in his 60s. He had a wonderfully rhythmical, rocking delivery from a wheeling action that began, so to speak, at the hip pocket. Probably no bowler in any age spun the ball more.

He was a famous figure in some of the great sides of history; but it was as a man of kindly wit, solitary and romantic, a 'character' impossible to classify, that he will be affectionately remembered by the cricket world in which he moved for so long.

# CHAPTER NINE

# ODDMENTS FROM EVERYWHERE

These last pieces help, I hope, to justify the title of the book. They begin with a substantial one, in the form of an interview accorded me by Don Bradman at the conclusion of the 1946–47 Test series in Australia which started in a double column on the front page of *The Daily Telegraph* and was syndicated throughout Australia by *The Sun* of Sydney. It contains no earth-shaking revelations but it reflects that maturity of judgment and breadth of vision which have since done so much to guide and direct Australian cricket. Note that he favoured the extension of the law of l.b.w. then – as, I believe, he still does. He did, of course, come to England after all in 1948, and led one of the strongest all-round teams in Test history.

My particular form of cricket-writing does not lend itself to major exclusives though one likes to think it is sprinkled with minor ones. This piece however was definitely rated of scoop proportions. I was by then a warm friend of Don's, and am glad to say we have been on close terms ever since.

March 10, 1947

On the conclusion of the Test matches I have been able to obtain from Bradman in an exclusive interview his opinion on England's performance and some of the major lessons to be learnt from the tour. In his comprehensive survey of the game Bradman, widely regarded as the greatest batsman of all time, spoke with the authority of an elder statesman in the world of cricket.

His personal position as a player after the close of this season has been widely discussed, and no definite pronouncement has yet been made as to whether he will play again. It seems, from what he told me, to be very unlikely that the British cricketing public will see him in action again. In his own words:

'It must be apparent that I was only able to see out the Tests just ended by a careful husbanding of resources. I doubt my physical capacity to go through a tour.' [The Australians are due to tour England next year.]

In what follows I quote the point of my questions [in italics] and the full reply by Bradman to each:

Q: *What is your view of England's cricket future?*

A: Despite the result of the Test series just played I think England has only one or two gaps to fill in order to have a very fine team. The batting is capable of better things. Hutton, Compton and Edrich are a formidable trio around which to build.

The new wicket-keeper, Evans, is of the highest class. In bowling I consider Wright the best of his type England has sent to Australia for at least 35 years, and Bedser is undoubtedly the finest medium-pace bowler seen in Australia since Tate.

In fact, in my opinion, Bedser in 1946 was a better bowler than Tate was in 1928. I do not refer to Tate in 1924, because I did not play against him that year.

I am the only cricketer who has played against both Tate and Bedser in Australia and therefore am in a unique position to express an opinion. I think Bedser should be an even greater bowler in England.

Wright and Bedser were most unlucky throughout the tour, but principally they were overburdened with work, which reduced their effectiveness beyond measure.

What England needs is a really fast bowler, and a good left-hand bowler of the Verity type.

Australians fully realise the handicaps largely resulting from the war which face the English counties in their future efforts to encourage and produce young players of Test calibre. These difficulties may be largely economic and connected with national matters beyond county control, but England must make the effort.

*And Australia's?*

Before this season started I privately expressed the view that Australia would have a strong team, but it has actually turned out stronger than I anticipated. The batting is sufficient to meet any demands and the bowling has the great advantage of variety, but particularly important is the fact that almost every bowler is capable of making a century, and the same may be said of the wicket-keeper [Tallon].

Australia's batting strength at the moment may, I think, be fairly compared with that of the great Test teams of earlier years. Moreover, these players are imbued with a natural aggressive spirit which under most circumstances enables them to play attractive cricket. I feel sure our opponents this season, no less than ourselves, admired, for instance, the sheer artistry, the classical style and power of an innings by Miller.

Then Arthur Morris, the young opening left-hander, gave positive proof that his early successes some years ago in first-class cricket were not an accident. His century in each innings at Adelaide was a performance which few players of any era could have equalled.

It seems to me that from the batting angle the Australian players are destined to provide some delightful performances here and in England in the years ahead.

It would be foolish nonsense to suggest that we developed a bowler of the superb qualities of O'Reilly. However, we did find bowlers possessed of considerable skill endowed with good temperaments who were splendid fieldsmen and batsmen, able to rise to the occasion, and fitting very well into the pattern of the attack.

Most of our bowlers were comparatively inexperienced and their place in history is not to be judged on this season alone. To sum up, I think we may look forward with confidence to Australia being represented by a team of great ability for some time to come.

*It is well known that you sacrificed lucrative Press contracts and took risks with your health and reputation to play this season. Why?*

I felt that I might be able to play some part in the rehabilitation of cricket after the war, and that if I could it was my duty to do so. I realised that there would be tremendous public interest – that tens of thousands of people would pay homage once again to the greatest of all games.

Cricket lovers have been very kind to me through the years, and it was mainly to pay my debts to the game and the people who support it which prompted me to try and give of my best.

I am well aware that a few jealous critics have seen nothing satisfactory in anything I have done. The persistent direction of some of the criticism made the writers' intent so obvious as to be laughable. However, I believe the public in general have appreciated that I have at least sincerely tried to help cricket.

*What are the prospects of your coming over with the Australian team next year?*

It would be premature to say yes or no. However, it must be apparent that I was only able to see out the current series by a careful husbanding of resources. At the moment I doubt my physical capacity to go through a tour, and so, while not finally committing myself, I should say it is unlikely.

There is no reason to decide such a question so far in advance. Needless to say, I would love to go to England again, but there are limitations in all things, and only time can provide the answer.

*Would you consider managing the team if you cannot play?*

Under no circumstances.

*Do you think present Australian pitches give a fair chance to the bowler?*

If you refer only to the pitches for Test matches, then I would answer that the dice in both England and Australia are loaded too heavily in favour of the batsman. Pitches, in my opinion, should be as true as possible, but they should be reasonably natural and amenable to some fair degree of wear.

The spectacle of only one wicket falling on the sixth day of a match, as at Adelaide, is bad for cricket, and I definitely think this aspect of the game requires urgent attention.

While on this subject, it may be of interest to say that I have found the best pitches in England easier to bat on and less helpful to the bowlers than those in Australia.

My preference for batting on English wickets is not shared by most players, and apparently it is a matter of individual style.

*In the* 1939 *'Wisden' you favoured amending the l.b.w. law so that the batsman could be out to the ball pitched on the off-side, even though the part of his person which had intercepted the ball were not between wicket and wicket. Would you vote for an experimental change made now to this effect?*

For many years I have been in favour of amending the l.b.w. law in this direction. One of the worst features in batting is to see a player go across and cover his stumps with his pads – bat held over shoulder – when the ball is pitched outside the off-stump. It is negative, unattractive cricket, heartbreaking to bowlers and mainly indulged in by less competent batsmen. I would like to see the suggested change adopted immediately as an experiment.

Batsmen, who are greatly in the majority, oppose alterations to the l.b.w. law which would assist the bowler, but the laws should be framed to make the game as attractive as possible, not to please the batsmen.

*Are there any other ways in which you think cricket might move with the times?*

I still think the first consideration is the mental outlook of the individual, who can if he chooses spoil any game by his interpretation of its character. Then I think attention must be given to the laws of the game, such as the l.b.w. law and the preparation of pitches, so that matches remain a contest of skill rather than endurance.

I have already advocated that in England modern score boards should be erected on the main grounds. They are a great attraction. In both countries the installation of a loud speaker system at the grounds similar to that in use at Adelaide would prove helpful and entertaining.

*Which of all your innings do you regard as your best?*

My 254 at Lord's in 1930, the reason being that I did not make a mishit of any kind until I was dismissed. I cannot say this of any other innings. Moreover, we were chasing a winning score by England, yet scored fast enough to catch up the leeway and win.

*Whom do you consider the greatest bowler you ever batted against?*

To my mind there has never been a bowler to equal O'Reilly. To play with him was an education – to play against him usually a lesson.

From every conceivable angle, theoretical, technical and practical, he stands supreme. Moreover, his figures are a monument to his skill and they were achieved in an era of high scoring and good wickets.

His control of length was marvellous, his direction always designed to use his fieldsmen to the utmost, and his subtle variations of break and flight were so admirably handled as to be constant source of mental hazard to the batsman.

In support of his natural talents was an outstanding cricket brain which enabled him to achieve a perfection beyond that of any contemporary.

*Do you consider the Tests just ended have justified the quick resumption?*

Undoubtedly. Apart from the psychological benefit which has been derived from the early resumption there are direct tangible benefits.

One is the financial aid which will reach the English Counties and the Australian States. Another is that the way has been paved for a more speedy return of an Australian team to England. A third is the benefit the game itself has derived and the consequent lifting of the standard of play.

## Points from the Post-bag

This article, which appeared on the leader page of *The Daily Telegraph*, brings one to wonder how many readers' letters have been written and answered since 1946. (I always do acknowledge if name and address are given). The answer is certainly well into five figures.

August 2, 1947

There is no quotation more familiar than Andrew Lang's praise of cricket talk. The reminder he gives that, for every cricketer, there are several whose pleasure in it can only derive from reading and reminiscence, is regularly fortified in the case of a Cricket Correspondent by his daily post.

Everyone prefers receiving letters to answering them, and I confess to finding the pile a little quelling sometimes. But few people trouble to write to a newspaper unless their interest (or perhaps their indignation!) is considerable, and one realises, of course, how valuable a means they provide for discovering public opinion.

There are those with schemes and suggestions for improving cricket – and there are still many, even this year, when more people have been seen on the county grounds than ever, who seem convinced that, if the game is not changed, it will die.

Among the radicals must be placed my friend from Luton who wishes to see the captains empowered to announce their teams after they have tossed up, and to change them as they wished after each innings. It is an idea which, I feel, would cause some complications for the score-card printers and the caterers, to say nothing of the wages bill.

A comparatively small adjustment is that proposed by the reader from Kettering who, as in golf, would like to see non-playing captains, who 'could wear the club blazer and stand by the bowler's umpire.'

Some, at least of the older school, will perhaps have more than a hint of sympathy with the writer's further thought that 'this suggestion would give some of our county clubs the opportunity to appoint better captains than they appear to be able to do now.'

The eternal search for all-rounders prompts the notion from Weston-super-Mare that there should be a match between the Batsmen of England and the Bowlers of England.

Then a current note from Churchdown, Gloucestershire, echoed elsewhere, recommends that the England selectors should omit Middlesex and Gloucester players from the Fifth Test, so that all could take part in the great match between the two counties at Cheltenham which coincides with it.

A brief comment on this is that the clash is, I am afraid, unavoidably tiresome. A Test Match is a Test Match, and the South Africans have done fully well enough against us on hard pitches to deserve this last chance of beating the England XI.

Most of us from time to time push our pet theories and reforms. On the way to Australia I remember listening, I hope patiently, to a complicated and highly revolutionary method of playing county matches. Its sponsor was one of the M.C.C. cricketers, and it seemed to last through the Red Sea and half way across the Indian Ocean.

Letters about cricket can be put roughly into three categories: those that have something to put forward – and I have dealt with one or two of them; those that require information, generally about the laws or records; and lastly, the biggest proportion, those that offer comment on topical events, usually with particular reference, favourable or otherwise, to one's notices and reports.

This summer the composition of the England team has provided the best matter for talk and for letters. Many readers, I
find, bring to the subject a skilled judgment and power of
reasoning worthy of the selectors themselves.

I would say, though, as a generalisation to which there are
many exceptions, that the amateur selector has two common
weaknesses. He tends to disregard or under-estimate the value
of fielding, and to put far too much faith in averages.

Thus, when Barnett was chosen, there came more than one
letter from Bristol and Gloucester reminding me that he was
sixth in the bowling averages. But since then that admirable
batsman has fielded through six South African innings, and has
been required to bowl only 10 overs in all, and it is safe to say
his bowling bore no weight in his selection.

I would remind the correspondent from Thorpe Bay who
wrote some time ago that 'the mere matter of current form
should be the deciding factor if we wish to regain our confidence by beating South Africa,' of the dictum of one of the
shrewdest England captains. In assessing a player's claims, he
looked up his record over the years against Yorkshire and
Lancashire and ignored all else.

Figures can be dangerous witnesses, especially now when the
standard of county play is so sadly low. Time, of course, can be
a harsh judge of all our words, but I find in the same bunch of
letters the lament, 'why the selectors still play Hutton and
Washbrook is difficult to understand.' I fancy that 'Old
Scottish County Amateur' from Oxford might have compre-
hended a little better if he had been at Leeds last Monday.

The enthusiasm of the young is always appealing, as, for
instance, that of the cadet from Dartmouth who ends a paean
of praise of his hero with the heart-felt plea: 'I beg you to set
my mind at rest by telling me why this sudden disregard of
Bedser.'

I think I detect signs of hero-worship, too, in the gentle
rebuke of the lady from Southsea who reminds me that M. P.
Donnelly is not the only cricketer to whom the members at
Lord's have recently risen in tribute. It seems that this happened
to Joe Hardstaff in last year's Test against India.

Just occasionally it is not easy to turn the other cheek. But
abuse is usually anonymous, and when one reads: 'Sir – you

d— Southern sports writers are the most biased and vindictive – not to say selfish – sports writers in the world . . .' it is a relief but hardly a surprise to find that at the end of his tirade the author signs himself 'Tyke and Proud of It,' and apparently is of no fixed abode.

After that some morsel of comfort must be snatched from the Birmingham reader's strictly qualified eulogy: 'I must state that I always enjoy your stuff – it is at worst grammatically English and at best quite a vivid and usually reliable report.'

To hear that one may have given some small degree of pleasure to people who have sterner tasks than watching cricket is happiness indeed.

For profit to be added is perfection. Thus the best of all letters is this from the young cricketer at his preparatory school. I had remarked that the essence of batting was concentration. 'During the next match (against a side rather weak in bowling) I tried to concentrate more, and I got 84.'

## Cricket Writers' Dinner

The Cricket Writers' Club was formed in Australia in 1946–47, and the idea has since been followed by writers on other games. Our first dinner was one of welcome to the 1948 Australians. Don Bradman's speech hit the perfect note and brought a record mail care of Broadcasting House. His remarks inspired the four who followed – all men of much distinction, both inside the game and beyond, and all, alas! now dead. Here is Peterborough's note on the occasion in *The Daily Telegraph* next morning.

April, 1948

Cricket last night was the subject of as brilliant a series of after-dinner speeches as I have ever heard.

The occasion was the Cricket Writers' Club dinner in honour of the Australian team. The speakers were Mr E. W. Swanton, Mr D. G. Bradman, Mr H. S. Altham, Canon F. H. Gillingham, Mr Justice Birkett and Mr R. C. Robertson-Glasgow.

As one at the studio end, as it were, of Bradman's broadcast speech, I can testify that he approaches the microphone not much less skilfully than he approaches the wicket.

Mr Swanton, *Daily Telegraph* cricket correspondent and chairman at the dinner, had bowled a perfect opening over. Bradman played after him under film arc lights with a short smile, a coolness and ease which the most polished after-dinner speaker might have envied.

He said this would be his last tour in England and he did not intend to play any more in Australia.

Mr Altham, welcoming the Duke of Edinburgh, believed that he was due to make 167 speeches between now and the end of October. He thought this might exceed the score of the Australians on a sticky wicket.

Canon Gillingham said that after hearing Bradman speak to substantially the same congregation not once or twice but several times, he felt sad – sad that he had joined the Stock Exchange and not the Church.

## An Illustrious XI

The centenary of the birth of W.G. inspired thoughts on other great ones from his day onwards. I name eleven of indisputable lustre and personality, without specifying it as the greatest XI. (For instance there is no wicket-keeper). There are six Englishmen and five Australians. The names should stand the test of time without loss of stature, though any such piece today must recognise the emergence of the West Indies. One could not ignore Garfield Sobers – or, perhaps, Frank Worrell.

*The Field* July 17, 1948

W. G. Grace enjoyed honour and fame enough while he lived. Was it not said that he was the best-known man in England, and did not the station-master at Paddington, none less, open his carriage door when he set off home to the West? But there is perhaps no more remarkable indication of his powerful influence on the game of cricket than the interest shown in the great man this centenary summer of his birth by the generations to whom he is a legendary figure, and nothing more.

For myself I feel I have come to know 'W.G.' quite intimately from the reading and re-reading of Bernard Darwin's delightful picture of him in the Great Lives series, and the likeness of him that seems the most expressive is not the famous Wortley portrait in Lord's Long Room, or that resplendent bust that commands the corresponding position at the Oval, but the photograph, often reproduced, showing him in mufti with Stanley Jackson.

There is affection as well as appreciation in the expression of 'the Old Man,' in mufti, with the thick, silver-banded blackthorn stick, the watch-chain, the stout boots, the long cut-away coat, and the 'Churchill' hat, as he looks down on the flannelled figure of the man who was his most distinguished successor as captain of England, and of the Gentlemen. Thus he smiles out on all members of M.C.C. who climb the last flight leading to the top of the pavilion, giving perhaps a spring to the stride of the elderly.

There was one champion, and one only, and the tyro among cricket historians knows why there can never be another, for he 'made' cricket, brought it from the amusement of rustics and the business of the shrewd colony at Trent Bridge to the status of an English institution. But great figures have followed the greatest, and the present perhaps is an appropriate time to recall some of them. By the time W. G. clumped up the Oval steps on his fifty-eighth birthday in July, 1906, and flung down his bat for the last time after hitting the Players for 74, a young man named Hobbs was firmly established among the coming cricketers, his play, as *Wisden* tells, more than bearing out the promise of the previous summer.

In modern times three batsmen have been transcendent in turn, and it is a tidy arrangement of providence by which W. G. was just overlapped by Hobbs (they played against one another on the Oval in bleak April weather in 1905), while Hobbs had the two Test rubbers of 1928–29 and 1930 in company with Bradman.

The Edwardian Age was full of excellent cricketers, and it is not in any equivocal spirit that, among the portrait-gallery accompanying these notes,* I have picked out Sir Stanley Jackson to represent the Englishmen. It was reasonable surely to choose an amateur, for, so far as batsmanship was concerned,

---

*The Field* article was illustrated by the following cricketers: V. T. Trumper, Sir Stanley Jackson, W. G. Grace, J. B. Hobbs, M. W. Tate, D. G. Bradman, W. J. O'Reilly, W. R. Hammond, W. H. Ponsford, D. C. S. Compton and K. R. Miller.

it was predominantly an amateur age; and if there were others who, playing more regularly, scored more runs and took more wickets over the years his achievements in the great matches were second to none. It is pleasant at the moment, too, to ponder on the deeds of a cricketer who saved up his most shattering performances for the confusion of the Australians. As for Victor Trumper, he has a place as prince of Australian batsmen that none of his countrymen will ever dispute. When has the batting art been more brilliantly shown than by Trumper, with his eleven centuries, in the wet summer of 1902? It is, incidentally, a paradox worthy of some analysis, that the Australians, so often pictured as 'hard-boiled' practitioners whose yard-sticks are averages and analyses, in retrospect venerate their stylists beyond all record-holders.

This is not the place for an essay on Hobbs, who spanned the old cricket and the new, fusing in his own batsmanship the best of both. As he gradually declined Hammond's star rose, so that the classic method was perpetuated in the England XI. Hammond's play, while firmly subordinated to the stern purpose of winning Test Matches which now, in the late 'twenties, had become so weighty a national question, had about it a fine natural poise and dignity.

Undeniably great was he, and equally so in his own sphere was Maurice Tate, whose bowling for England in Australia in the middle 'twenties first revived hopes that the old enemy might be beaten again. Tate, the cartoonist's delight, with the broad grin and the impossible boots, was the stout back-bone of our attack during the climb to equality and finally supremacy that began in 1924 and ended with the ripening of Bradman's power in 1930.

The name of Ponsford does not perhaps strike quite so clear a note today as that of some other more spectacular Australians, but if that is so it is because Bradman put all other record-makers out of business. Time was when Ponsford was a scourge beyond equal, with a strong predilection for going on, if he could, to make two hundred, or three, or four. Ponsford indeed bears a heavy responsibility, for Bradman (who knows?) might not have thought in terms of such indecent totals if Ponsford had not set up the figures for him to beat.

O'Reilly needs no other claim to fame than that Bradman

considers him the finest bowler he ever played against. All the virtues were there, the wonderful control of length, with the co-ordination of brain and muscle which generate 'flight,' the strength of finger-spin and the affectation of stark hostility.

And so to Bradman, greatest of modern batsmen, and each country's heroes of the new generation, Compton and Miller. The time will be soon upon us when a final appreciation of Australia's captain comes due, and his praises will wait until then. Compton is our champion, and it is true that if he were to be out of the England XI, this would hardly be a Test rubber at all. And it is enough to say of Miller that if he were on the other side England might well be the favourites.

## Wooing the Ladies

There has been a big increase in feminine cricket interest since the war. However it expresses itself it must be warmly and intelligently encouraged.

*The Field*, June 10, 1950

Everyone is putting his or her shoulder to the wheel of English cricket, and urging it forward, so to speak, through the treacherous byways of matted, uneven turf to the broad smooth high road of artificial wickets and a general state of Utopia. Two ladies have been assisting the deliberations of the Cricket Enquiry Committee, and it was perhaps their presence thereon that reminded a reader of this paper to give an airing to what he describes as an old theory of his. Womanhood, he says, and he is not, of course, thinking of the experts, must be coached into a new version of the polite, unvarying question: 'How many did you make, dear?'

Small boys home from school, adolescents returning from their first club cricket, married men, young, mature, and elderly, as they sit down to supper, must thus in answer submit a brief, incomplete account of their day to satisfy the conventions. No department of the game save batsmanship is recognised, with the result, says my friend, that the male of the species, from childhood to old age, bends his energies to batsmanship at the expense of all else. His family prestige as a cricketer depends on his score. Surely it is high time to start coaching mothers, wives, and sweethearts in an alternative catechism whereby they may do their bit to restore the vital balance between bat and ball, indeed to encourage the bowlers who are needed to bring back the Ashes. How many wickets did you get? That should be the stock enquiry.

Nor should it be impossible to persuade the truly co-operative to extend their interest to the fielding. Did you hold any catches? Did you run anyone out? And possibly, for the more advanced, how many runs did you save? The imaginative cricketer with an otherwise hollow tale to tell is given scope for a distinct rising of morale and the spirits here. The lady who catches on to the idea, to the length of exploring the psychology of cricket, may even have recourse to the Gamesmanship of Mr Potter, and then it will be perhaps a matter of: 'How many did you *talk* out?' But for the majority a more romantic conception of cricket will probably be more safely encouraged.

I know a young bowler who is conducting the cricket education of his *fiancée* in a most enlightened manner. Not for her the drudgery of learning the places in the field, the difficult distinction between a cover-drive and a square-cut. Her knowledge is to be confined to that aspect of the game which particularly concerns her, the art and, especially, the philosophy of the bowler. Already, I understand, she appreciates the elementary fact that an analysis of one for 60 may well conceal a heroic and skilful performance. She knows that figures, which tell every sort of cricket lie, are never so fallacious as when they refer to the bowler. I predict (for she is as intelligent as she is beautiful) that before the knot is tied, this girl will be launching her solicitous enquiries with some such subtle opening as: 'Did those ghastly slips catch anything for you today, darling?' An evasive or unsatisfactory answer to this will make any reference to an analysis merely gauche and uncalled-for. And no doubt the remembrance that he is returning to such loving understanding will brace the bowler to a final noble effort under the blistering sun, all aches, missed catches, and blind umpires forgotten.

I have been considering, of course, the cricket reactions of women who are not conspicuously games-minded. One well knows that there is a highly-knowledgeable element, not only among those who are or have been players themselves, and who are represented at the Lord's Enquiry by the two members of the Women's Cricket Association. The letters of a Cricket Correspondent contain many from women, nor are they by any means the least enlightened. I am sure that the influence of wireless, and now of television, has played a notable part in stimulating an intelligent interest in what, for many, was hitherto an incomprehensible and mysterious rite. It is impossible of proof, but I take it to be true that the rise in cricket attendances since the war is partly accounted for by the increased interest of women.

There is no doubt of the pull cricket has for women in Australia, where life is distinctly easier for the housewife, and where she has a little more leisure for open-air amusement during the day. At Melbourne the players have to run the gauntlet of many young girls who salute their heroes in the most high-spirited and uninhibited way. At Adelaide they go a step further than anywhere else in the world in encouraging the fair sex, for the middle of the big main stand is their preserve, and the 'men only' sections are at either end. In South Africa too, at the Cape, Durban, and Johannesburg, the stands seem almost half full of women, and their adoption of Test matches as social occasions calling for gay frocks and luncheon-parties undoubtedly adds to their atmosphere, as well as to their glamour.

We welcome feminine inspiration in whatever forms it presents itself, whether from those who sit in the stands, from those who follow our deeds at home, and, not least, from those, never to be forgotten, who in every town and village club serve the cause so admirably by 'doing the tea' and presiding at the feast. In short, in all the talk of the charm of cricket we must be careful to recognise the debt we owe to the ladies.

## Hutton Retires

Len Hutton was never strong, either physically or constitutionally. A long innings took a lot out of him. His innings as England's captain from 1952 to 1955 took much more. When he returned home after winning the Australian series of 1954–55 – thus retaining the Ashes he had regained in 1953 – he must have felt there were no worlds left for him to conquer. He played little in 1955, Peter May taking on the England captaincy and scoring a narrow success over South Africa. It was a disappointment but no great surprise when Hutton announced his retirement early the following year.

January 18, 1956

The cricket world had the most unwelcome possible news yesterday when L. Hutton announced his retirement from first-class play. Only the optimists, perhaps, were expecting him to take part, after the recent bulletins about his health, in another Test rubber against Australia.

Speculation beforehand, however, scarcely blunts the shock of reality when the worst is known. The loss to English cricket is indeed a great one: more serious, of course, because of the lack of young professional batsmen of a stature comparable to that of Len Hutton and Denis Compton when they burst into the limelight more or less together 20 years ago.

Hutton, in publishing his decision, says he has taken it on medical advice, and mentions particularly the risks to his health attendant on playing six days a week. In this latter remark may be found, I think, the clue to his state of mind.

In an age when pressures on great sportsmen were less onerous he would probably have decided, in similar circumstances and still just on the right side of 40, to have had done with the burden of five-day Test cricket and to confine himself to a certain number of matches for Yorkshire.

That probably is what Hutton would have chosen now if he were not such a closely-prisoned victim of his fame. But in 1956 it would need only a hundred or two from him, coupled with the failure of one of England's opening pair in the first Test, to start up a loud cry for his return.

The additional strain of the captaincy has already been responsible for his one and only indifferent Test series as a batsman.

Since he brought England to victory over Australia all else was naturally forgotten. But Hutton is predominantly a batsman, certainly one of the three greatest, in many views the very finest since Hobbs.

In face of doctors' warnings, uncertain how his health and

form would stand up to a full summer in an Australian year, who can blame him for deciding to quit at the top?

One thinks inevitably of Hutton in relation to Sir Jack Hobbs, and the fact is, of course, that his famous predecessor, himself somewhat frail in physique, went on serving England and Surrey far longer.

Hobbs was still batting in Tests against Australia when he was 47. He was 51 when last he played for Surrey, and he scored 100 first-class hundreds after he had passed Hutton's present age.

The life of a famous player in Hobbs's day was, however, much less exacting, just as, incidentally, it was less rewarding. Apart from the M.C.C. Australian tours, Hobbs spent his winters at home. He did not return to South Africa after the First World War: he never went to West Indies. There were Test series in England only every two or three years, and the matches lasted three days.

Hutton in the last 10 years has sustained 16 cricket seasons. He has been three times to Australia, twice to West Indies, and once to South Africa. Moreover, he has never gone into a Test match, since the war, without knowing that if he got out the England batting was horribly vulnerable. The onus of facing the best bowlers in the world at the start of the innings was inevitably his.

Hutton was a few weeks short of his 18th birthday when, at Cambridge in 1934, he played his first innings for Yorkshire. He began, like many a famous cricketer, with a duck, concerning which he quotes Maurice Leyland's characteristic comment: 'Never mind, you've started at the bottom.'

Herbert Sutcliffe had already made the most flattering predictions about the future of the slight young man from his native town of Pudsey, and Hutton was not long in justifying them, even though Yorkshire were so strong that they could afford to introduce him gradually.

Hutton was 20 when he made 1,000 runs for the first time. A year later, just 21, he played the first of his 138 innings for England.

Again, and at Lord's, he began with 0, but he went on to Manchester and there, against New Zealand, made the first of his 19 Test hundreds.

P. B. H. May hitting straight and apparently over the bowler's head: a characteristic sight of the 'fifties when, following Sir Leonard Hutton's retirement, he dominated the England batting

Len Hutton. Knighted in 1956, the most prolific English batsman since Hammond. He plays the late-cut, the keeper being McIntyre of Surrey

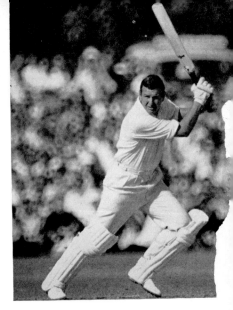

ABOVE: Sussex Strokes. Ted Dexter (ON LEFT) and Jim Parks in full cry. No county partnerships sparkled more than theirs in the early sixties. BELOW: Two of the best of the younger school: Majid Jehangir (LEFT), son of Jehangir Khan, whose hitting for the Pakistanis in 1967 won him a contract with Glamorgan; and Alan Knott, who follows the Kent and English tradition of wicketkeeper-batsman

I had the pleasure of seeing this hundred – and indeed, for that matter, all but some half-a-dozen of his Test innings from first to last – and one's impression is that thus early the youthful Hutton was generally recognised as one at any rate of the long-awaited successors to the immortal Hobbs and Sutcliffe. His technique was so admirable, his application so complete.

By the time the war came Hutton's position was unchallenged and his fame made secure by the fabulous 364 which stands as a wonderful monument to his concentration as well as to the folly of timeless Test matches. When Hutton's deeds and figures are examined it has to be remembered that he had just reached the pinnacle when war broke out. Who can tell what punishment the bowlers, not least the Australian bowlers, were spared in the years 1940–1945?

When Hutton returned to cricket it was with his left arm inches shorter than his right, as a result of a gymnasium accident which threatened for some months to prevent his playing again. His deeds in the last decade form too large a slice of modern history to need detailed recalling.

His batsmanship reached its peak of mastery, utterly responsible and mature, in the Australian series of 1950–51 and 1953, wherein both his aggregate and his average, taking the two series together, were virtually twice as large as those of any other man on either side.

The last phase is that of his captaincy, which began in 1952 with a victory against India and ended three years later, also with a victory against New Zealand. In what turned out to be his last Test it is worth noting that the captain made top score, and saw his bowlers get rid of New Zealand for the lowest Test score in history.

Hutton captained England in 23 Tests over this period of concentrated activity, which is one more than any other man has led England. In more leisurely days A. C. MacLaren led England 22 times, but spread over 12 years. England won 11 Tests under Hutton, lost four and drew eight, and Australia were beaten successively, at home and in Australia, for the first time in a quarter of a century.

To those who knew Hutton well, who were aware how the game monopolised his thoughts, and who realised the nervous effort involved in all he did, both as a player and as a captain,

K

it seemed clear two years ago that he was being taxed beyond his strength.

Whether, if his responsibilities then had been lightened by the appointment to the captaincy in Australia of a younger man, he would now be looking forward to another series against the old enemy, whether in that case, with all the commotion such a decision would have caused, England would have brought home the Ashes, are imponderable questions which, however earnestly they continue to be discussed, can never be answered with any certainty.

What is without doubt is that Hutton captained England with much tactical shrewdness, with the conscientiousness that has always been the prime key to his actions on the cricket field, and, not least, with a quiet dignity that would have befitted any and all his predecessors.

## Coconuts and Centuries

Such was the heading on *The Daily Telegraph* leader page to this article, above an announcement that I was taking a team captained by Colin Cowdrey for a six-week tour of the West Indies. We were also speeded on our way by a friendly reference in a leading article in *The Times*.

March 3, 1956

One cannot travel for long in a West Indian island without meeting the signs of cricket. It is the common bond of interest with Englishmen to an intense degree not to be found elsewhere in the Commonwealth.

To the average Barbadian and Trinidadian, I suppose, England tends to mean the place where the Queen lives and the place where the cricketers come from. English teams of one sort or another have been arriving at irregular intervals for 60 years.

The first amateur parties contained such distinguished names as Warner, Stoddart, Woods, Leveson-Gower, and 'the Odysseus of cricket,' Lord Hawke. At the time of these early visits, in the 'nineties, coloured men first found their way into representative colony teams, hitherto exclusively white.

The roots of cricket in the West Indies go back at least twice as far as this. When one sees a group of barefooted boys playing on a rough plot with a coconut husk for a ball and a stump of palm branch to hit with, they are imitating the grandees, the Weekes, the Walcotts and the Worrells, just as boys were aping the garrison players and the planters who first sowed the seed soon after Trafalgar had made the islands safe under British rule.

The West Indian is a natural cricketer if ever there was one. I remember on my first visit to the Kensington ground at Bridgetown, Barbados, where G. O. Allen's M.C.C. team were preparing for their tour, shaking hands with young Everton Weekes. John Goddard explained how Weekes, having joined the West Indian Regiment as a boy, was spotted as a likely cricketer, and when the war ended was given a job under the groundsman which would afford a chance of practice on good wickets. 'We hope he's going to make some runs against you.'

How many has he got! And what great pleasure have 'the three Ws' given to crowds all over the world these last eight years.

Weekes, Walcott and Worrell, all are Barbadians born and bred, though Frank Worrell has since migrated to Jamaica and Clyde Walcott now coaches in British Guiana. It is remarkable, to say the least, that these three heroes should have sprung, in the same vintage, from an island just about as large as the Isle of Wight.

Unlike the other islands, Barbados since its colonisation in 1627 has always been British, and its inhabitants naturally perhaps took most thoroughly, in the early days, to the English game introduced by the Army and Navy. Since the Challenors and Austins first laid the basis of the West Indies' cricket reputation Barbados has occupied a position corresponding in some way to that of Yorkshire, in the cricket world, in relation to England.

When Hutton and Compton, late in their careers, played for the first time in Barbados each, as he came in to bat, was applauded and cheered all the way to the wicket, just as an artist of world reputation would be received on a first visit to Covent Garden. The crowds are noisy but fair-minded, and they like to see batsmen taking advantage of their beautiful wickets by hitting the ball.

In Trinidad, which contrasts in almost every way with Barbados, cricket needed longer to take root. The island is ten times as big, hilly and largely covered with luxuriant tropical vegetation. Where Barbados is almost aggressively British, Trinidad with its mingling of the blood of former conquerors, Spanish, French and Portuguese, with its East Indians, Chinese, and those of African descent, is utterly cosmopolitan.

Thus in Trinidad sides are to be found names like Stollmeyer and Gomez, Asgarali and Ganteaume, Tang Choon and Achong. Yet the Constantines, father and son, and Pascall, uncle of the great Learie, had helped, before these men came to notice, to found a cricket tradition at least comparable to that of Barbados and British Guiana, and stronger than that of Jamaica some thousand miles to the north-westward. (Caribbean distances are not always appreciated; people sometimes speak of the British West Indies as though they were clustered like the Channel Islands.)

Today at the week-end you may see 30 matches at a time in progress on the Queen's Park Savannah in Port-of-Spain, while at colony and Test matches there may be crowds of 25,000. Though he has long retired, the magic name in Trinidad is still that of Constantine, and as one rides to the golf course the driver will point with awe to the little field at Maraval where, according to legend, father and son practised together.

The team which I have the honour to be taking on a short tour to the West Indies next week is treading where famous men have trod in the main centres at Bridgetown and Port-of-Spain.

We are also, in three minor matches, breaking fresher ground. At Pointe-a-Pierre there is a match against South Trinidad, where we will be in the hospitable hands of Trinidad Leaseholds. There is also to be a brief visit to the reputedly enchanting island of Tobago, a dependency of Trinidad, and the legendary scene of the adventures of Robinson Crusoe.

And as we fly home, we stop for a day to play in Bermuda, where one understands the American influence has not weakened the islanders' zest for cricket.

# Big Hitting

This proved a fascinating subject to readers, some of whose reminiscences I included one Monday morning – which, of course, elicited many more.

June 16, 1958

My notes a fortnight ago on big hitting seem to have tickled the memories of a large number of readers, many of whom have put their reminiscences to paper, as may be seen from the following list. These first-class cricketers, many past and a few present, have all been mentioned in letters, the most notable among them several times:

Alletson, F. R. Brown, G. J. Bonnor, Barnett, H. T. Bartlett, A. W. Carr, Lord Cobham, 'young' George Cox, J. N. and V. F. S. Crawford, L. G. and A. M. Crawley, H. B. Cameron, A. P. F. Chapman, Constantine, G. F. Earle, P. G. H. Fender, N. M. Ford.

C. B. Fry, J. M. Gregory, Rev. F. H. Gillingham, G. L. and the Rev. G. L. O. Jessop, Hammond, K. L. Hutchings, E. P. Hewetson, Hitch, Percy Jeeves, J. J. Lyons, C. G. Macartney, K. R. Miller, K. G. McLeod, F. T. Mann.

A. W. H. Mallett, Peach, Rev. J. H. Parsons, J. S. Ryder, Jim Smith, Trott, C. I. Thornton, Tunnicliffe, Wardle, Wellard, T. B. G. Welch, Whittaker (Surrey), Woolley, Col A. C. Watson.

All these have done great deeds, surely, and I will pass on the recollections of readers for Mr Gerald Brodribb's verification – if he can get it. He will not need to be reminded that fishing stories are not the only ones wherein facts become elongated by time and imagination.

For sheer length there is no claim approaching the hit of the Rev. W. Fellows, who a century ago while at practice at Oxford hit the ball 175 yards from hit to pitch, an authenticated feat annually recorded until recent years in Wisden.

In fact yardage is seldom mentioned, though it seems that a certain P. E. Warhurst, an Oldham Athletic footballer weighing (presumably rather later in life) 17st, at Glossop in Derbyshire, made a stroke which 'first landed 147 yards from the crease, clearing the ground and then bounced clean over a row of houses and finishing up in the market square a quarter of a mile away.'

Several people record hits that have had unusual destinations, chiefly connected with trains. Thus G. L. O. Jessop, son of the greatest of all hitters, when a boy at Weymouth College hit a ball underneath a passing train.

Kenneth McLeod, more famous as a Rugby footballer, playing for Lancashire at Old Trafford, is credited with hitting through the window of a railway carriage, while a Swiss gentleman writes to say that on the same ground Keith Miller landed the ball in a railway wagon which transported it to London, whence it was ultimately recovered.

If Mr Brodribb can unravel the various shuntings and uncouplings necessary to establish this tallest of stories he will be a genius.

On the other hand Glamorgan may help to identify the owner of the high flat overlooking the Cardiff Arms Park who, returning home and finding a window broken, summoned the police, suspecting a robbery. The Law, is seems, discovered a cricket ball under the sofa. Again in the same part of the world, Emrys Davies might be able to say whether a ball bowled by him at Swansea was actually hit into the sea.

Yet another reader from Wales, S. Shipton, proudly mentions a hit by his son when aged 16 at Llanelly. Playing for Briton Ferry, the lad deposited the local bowler over the adjoining Rugby stand, the ball landing against the fence at the farther side of the Stradey Park football field.

Visualising the scene at Llanelly with my mind's eye, this seems a colossal blow.

Another hit of 'several miles' is attributed to a famous character from County Durham, Jack Carr. 'An extremely tall man, the bat was a child's spade in his hands,' says a correspondent. He hit great distances, the ball in this instance finishing up in a coal truck, which promptly moved off.

When 'Jock' Cameron hit his famous 30 in an over off Verity at Sheffield – three sixes and three fours – one of the sixes was lost in the pavilion roof and not recovered until the following year.

Tony Mallett (now a schoolmaster in Rhodesia), when a boy,

is reputed to have hit the ball out of the ground at Lord's, and I myself saw it done twice in an over a few years ago by P. R. H. Anderson, of Marlborough, playing for the Public Schools against Combined Services.

The wicket was high up the square, and both hits cleared Father Time stand and landed in the gardens behind.

Mr B. G. Whitfield, safest of recorders, describes how Macartney stood up in the players' box on the first storey of the Canterbury pavilion and caught a vast six hit by Ryder. He also recalls two remarkable strokes by Lord Cobham, then Charles Lyttelton, now Governor-General of New Zealand.

Playing for the Butterflies against St Lawrence, Lord Cobham cleared the concrete stand at Canterbury, next to the pavilion, which I believe even Frank Woolley never did.

For the Band of Brothers against the Bluemantles at Tunbridge Wells he cleared the pavilion, and laughed heartily at the sound of broken glass. At lunch he discovered he had smashed his own wind-screen.

Equally credible no doubt is the witness of a Roman Catholic priest who saw P. G. H. Fender, batting at the Vauxhall end at the Oval, square-cut a ball clean into the Harleyford Road. (I seem to remember Fender making a similar stroke out of the ground off a Northamptonshire bowler from the pavilion end.)

This reader ends with a panegyric on 'one of the craftiest captains there has ever been – very knowledgeable, adventurous, encouraging, dynamic.'

In club cricket of various degrees some picturesque detail is available. A reader born at Hampstead used in his youth to divide his watching time between Lord's and Parliament Hill Fields. He had a hero there named 'Ginger' Horton, whose best hits exceeded anything seen by him at Lord's.

The deeds of 'Ginger' are related in lyrical prose, culminating in a stroke of some 130 yards from hit to pitch which ran on down the slope – a slightly steeper gradient than that at Lord's – so that he and his partner ran 12!

A Lincolnshire reader can rival this with a memory of a hit at Western Park, Leicester, by a certain David Birkett, playing for South Wigston Mutual Cricket Club. This man was a tremendous hooker, and he once hit a 12, too, a relay of fielders being needed to return the ball while the batsmen finished almost at a walk.

Further north a notable hitter used to operate on the ground of an old Yorkshire captain, the late Sir Archibald White, at Tickhill, near Doncaster. This was a squat, tremendously strong miner, one Samuel Harper.

Here Harper and C. R. Elwis, opening the innings, put up the hundred in 14 minutes, Harper having taken 32 off the first over. They were playing, believe it or not, for the Thorne Colliery Nightjars, and I believe the testimony to be unimpeachable, for my informant is Harper's partner, who himself while this was going on apparently made 2!

The oldest contributor to this saga, writing from Taunton, sends a cutting from the County Gazette describing a one-day match there in 1911 between the Somerset Clergy and the Somerset Stragglers. 'A feature of the match was the heavy scoring of both sides,' remarks the report, which concludes with the full score, but no bowling analyses!

The reverend gents made 453 for nine declared – another instance of the clergy seeing the Devil in a red cricket ball – whereupon the Stragglers, having been left two hours and a half, made 458 for one with nearly half an hour to spare.

H. W. Hodgkinson (229 not out) and O. C. Riddell (183 not out) scored at around four runs a minute, and if we may reasonably assume that the clerical bowling may have been not quite up to the level of the batting they themselves had to get their runs against S. M. J. Woods, whose first-class cricket was only just finished, and a 20-year-old farmer named J. C. White.

Again the evidence is first-hand, for though he modestly does not say so I suppose my 87-year-old reader to be the same Rev. J. F. Turner, who set the pace with an innings of 137.

## "Wine, Women and Song"

Colin Ingleby-Mackenzie, aged 24 and in his first season as county captain, sows the seed which is to bring the championship to Hampshire three years later.

August 11, 1958

The topic of the moment among cricketers seems to be the

television interview given the other day by the Hampshire captain. When asked whether there was any special recipe behind the championship leaders' success, Colin Ingleby-Mackenzie replied: 'Yes, wine, women and song.'!

And to a question about training methods, he said Hampshire had a fixed rule that everyone must be in bed by breakfast time. These remarks were expurgated, perhaps wisely, from the children's version next day!

This sort of stuff is not only in refreshing contrast to the stock platitudes so often served up on such occasions. Behind the banter was a moral, which is simply that games, even county cricket, are played to be enjoyed.

A reader contrasts the Hampshire spirit as he has observed it this summer with that of other sides, with whom 'the manner of winning has been grim. A battle rather than a game. It is true that the connoisseurs – genuine and otherwise – have sought some virtue in this, and written of tactics and strategy. But there has been little for spectators to appreciate or admire, or for youngsters to emulate.'

The enjoyment of the players, he says, 'does communicate itself to the spectators, just as, conversely, boredom does.'

All this is true and obvious enough. The sad thing is, though, that for a side to be obviously happy in its cricket has become NEWS. Before the war I honestly believe that most county sides approached their cricket in much the way that Hampshire do today. May their spirit prove quickly contagious!

## Cases of Heredity

Since this note was written Charles Fry gained his blue and played three years for Oxford, and also followed father and grandfather by appearing in the Hampshire XI. Johnny Townsend at Oxford completed the cycle of four generations of first-class cricketers, but just missed his blue.

June 29, 1959

C. A. Fry, who is competing for the last batting place in the Oxford side, is a son of Stephen Fry, a Hampshire player of the early thirties, and grandson of C. B.

L

J. R. A. Townsend, who is having a successful season at Winchester, is son of D. C. H. (Oxford and Durham), a member of the M.C.C. team to West Indies in 1935, grandson of C. L. (Oxford, Gloucestershire, and England) and great-grandson of F. (Gloucestershire).

So both the Frys and the Townsends can claim three generations of first-class cricketers in the direct line, and if young J. R. A. carries on as he has started the Townsends may before long have a fourth.

The Lytteltons, as might have been expected, earn inclusion in this category. The eldest of eight brothers, C. G., afterwards the 8th Lord Cobham, played three years for Cambridge, the 9th Lord Cobham played a little for Worcestershire, and the 10th of the line, now Governor-General of New Zealand, was, of course, as C. J. Lyttelton, captain of Worcestershire in the thirties.

These three Lord Cobhams, by the way, son, father, and grandfather, were all Presidents of M.C.C., a distinction certainly without precedent and likely to remain so.

A certain amount of research suggests that the case of these three families, Lyttelton, Townsend, and Fry, has no counterpart. At least Roy Webber, that voracious historian of facts and figures, cannot find a parallel, and neither can another notable repository of cricket knowledge, Miss Diana Rait Kerr, curator of M.C.C.

Nine Lytteltons in all played first-class cricket – I don't think any more slipped in a game or two – while the latest Edrich, John, of Surrey, brings the representation of that family to five, associated, incidentally, with seven counties.

Diving into relationships in these and other cases one finds a rare accumulation of brothers, sons, uncles and cousins.

There were seven Walker brothers of Southgate but none of the seven married. (There were also seven daughters, all of whom married.)

Seven Fosters played for Worcestershire and one for Kent, while five Crawleys have spread their favours over both Universities and six counties.

The first-class Graces numbered five. There have been four Gunns and as many as 11 Hearnes, not all, however, related.

When one gets down to three of a kind the list is almost

unmanageable. Here are a few of the names: Parks, Lee, Langridge, Doggart, Mann, Gilligan, Studd. These have it in common that at least one cricketer of the three played for England.

Truly cricket has unique claims to being called 'the Family Game.'

## Miniature Cricketers

Little but good: I give a few examples for a father's benefit.

August 24, 1959

A hopeful Suffolk father wonders whether I can write something about the prowess of very small men on the cricket field to encourage his son who is, apparently, abnormally short.

So many small men have touched the heights in the cricket sense as to confute any idea that lack of inches is a bar to success. Did England or Surrey have a better batsman at the dawn of the Golden Age – 'W.G.' apart – than little Bobby Abel? Have Warwickshire ever had an all-rounder who gave better service than W. G. Quaife?

Who but 'Tich' Freeman ever went as many as three seasons, let alone six, taking more than 250 wickets a year? From 1928–33 inclusive Freeman's bag varied from 253 to the 'highest ever' total of 304.

Wicketkeepers are specially inclined to be short, and the job is the easier for that. Strudwick comes to mind, and Evans and 'Tich' Cornford. Today we have Swetman climbing towards the top of the tree.

There is no figure, so far as I know, exactly recording the shortest first-class cricketer. But several have been barely over 5ft. Johnny Briggs was 5ft 2in., a great slow left-arm bowler, and a comical fellow who, among other eccentricities, chose the day after his wedding to make 186, the top score of his life.

Talking of 'characters' calls to mind Lindsay Hassett, captain of Australia, and the neatest batsman in a generation. Without mentioning more than a few I hope I have said enough!

# Most Before Lunch

I have told elsewhere the story of how L. P. Hedges, of Tonbridge, was taking off his pads at Vincent Square just before lunch when the headmaster of Westminster looked in. 'Just out?', he said, 'bad luck. How many did you get?'

'A Hundred and Ninety-three, sir', came the reply.

The year was 1919, and Lionel Hedges fulfilled his schoolboy promise for Oxford and Kent.

May 16, 1960

'A hundred before lunch' is a feat achieved with a fair degree of frequency in cricket of all kinds. But what is the most runs made by a batsman before lunch?

Without suggesting it is by any means 'a record,' I think some details of a recent innings by Major J. M. H. Roberts deserve notice. Playing for the Brigade of Guards against Household Cavalry at Burton Court and going in to bat at 10 minutes to 12, he was 170 not out when lunch was taken at half-past one.

The Guards' side declared early in the afternoon at 311 for two. Roberts being then 200 not out, and 2nd Lieut M. Cannon-Brooks, who had gone in first, having just been bowled for 100. After such an onslaught it may be thought that the Household Cavalry did by no means poorly to reply with 252 for seven.

Burton Court has short square-leg boundaries, and at each side, though not at either end, the ball has to be hit clean out of the ground to count 6.

On hearing about all this my own thoughts turned to the feats of I. P. Campbell when a schoolboy at Canford. The Wisden of 1947 records that he made 222 not out against Marlborough in two hours and a half, and 237 against Old Canfordians in one hour 46 minutes. Assuming normal hours of play the likelihood is that Major Roberts may have been outdone.

## Frank and Wilfred

It is one of the pleasures of advancing age to try to convey to the younger generation something of the achievements of the great men of the past. In 1967 Frank Woolley reached his 80th birthday, Wilfred Rhodes his 90th. What better ending than to reprint these brief tributes to them?

## Frank Woolley

May 26, 1967

In a lifetime of watching cricket even the most sensational things need some prompting to recall. But a few memories are old familiar friends, and one of them centres upon a brief gesture, no more, that happened at Lord's all but 30 years ago. As the tall, familiar figure made his way to the wicket a large crowd got to their feet and warmly applauded. On his arrival at the crease he stood momentarily to attention with his bat at the 'order arms'. Stationed thus, he raised his cap to the company in a gesture of much dignity before asking the umpire for guard.

Frank Woolley, aged 51 and captaining the Players in his last first-class season, then turned his attention to Kenneth Farnes and made 41 of the most felicitous runs on a hard and slightly fiery wicket against what, according to *Wisden*, was 'the best fast bowling in this match since Arthur Fielder dismissed all the Gentlemen at a cost of 90 runs in 1906.' Farnes took eight for 43, but the eight did not include Woolley who played him, and *leaned* on him, and cut him and drove him with much of the authority he had shown in his two legendary innings of 95 and 93 against Gregory and McDonald when they were routing the England batting at Lord's away back in '21.

On both occasions great fast bowling had been countered by a bat of rigid straightness, a readiness to drive when the ball could be safely reached, to cut or force to leg when it was pitched short, and in general by a determination to wrest the authority and to retain it.

This sounds a suspiciously simple formula, a technique almost too obvious to be true. Woolley's batsmanship was, of course, compounded of other factors, and notably that unusually swift liaison between eye and brain that is one of the essential hall-marks of the great.

His batting was however essentially clear-cut and uncomplicated, both in design and execution, as for that matter has been that of all the classical players. Think of Hammond (if you can), of Hutton, of May, of Dexter, of Graveney today. But this short essay must not devolve into a disquisition on the use of the feet – when going back as well as forward – and on the virtues of swinging (rather than merely pushing) the bat into and through the line of the ball, though our subject gave a prime object lesson in these respects.

My task is to offer congratulations and best wishes, on behalf of all who ever saw him play, to Frank on his 80th birthday which falls tomorrow, to assure him that his deeds will never be forgotten, and at the same time, perhaps, to try and inspire the young with an impression of what he did and what he stood for.

As to his all-round record, it can be matched by only two men in the game's history, W. G. and Wilfred Rhodes, who by the way will be 90 in October. Only Sir Jack Hobbs has exceeded Woolley's 58,969 runs, a mere 23 bowlers have got more than his 2,068 wickets, and no one can come near his bag of 913 catches.

As to his cricket philosophy it is summed up as well as could be in 'My Happy Cricket Life', the article he wrote on his retirement for the 1939 *Wisden*. His life and soul, he says, were in cricket. He was before the public for 29 seasons, excluding the war years, and every year after the first he made a thousand runs – or two, or three. 'We were never allowed to play for averages in the Kent side or take half an hour or more to get the last 10 runs' – this in reference to his having got out 35 times in the nineties. 'We always had to play the game and play for the team.'

It is a warming thought that three of the immortals of the Golden Age are yet with us; Sydney Barnes, still, I believe, at 94 exercising his wonderful handwriting on behalf of the Staffordshire County Council; Wilfred Rhodes, blind but mellow of mind and rich in reminiscence; and the junior of the

trio, Woolley, as straight and spare as in his playing days, with
the mien and gait of a retired bishop. In the language of the
day the Wisden of 60 years ago made the laconic comment:
'the colt Woolley deserves more than passing notice.' He still
does.

## Wilfred Rhodes

October 28, 1967

In the course of nature the household names of The Golden
Age pass on. Ten years ago C. B. Fry was still writing and
talking, 'Plum' Warner was regularly to be seen at Lord's, Jack
Hobbs was positively sprightly both in look and conversation.
The list shortens, but Sydney Barnes, at 94, is still exercising
his fine, flowing hand for the Staffordshire County Council,
Herbert Strudwick, a mere 87, lives quietly at Hove, while
Wilfred Rhodes is looked after by his daughter and son-in-law
farther down the coast at Bournemouth.

Tomorrow, Rhodes, the cricketer with the most prolific
all-round record in the game's history, will be 90, nimble of
mind still, though his sight has quite gone, a reservoir of cricket
wisdom and reminiscence without compare.

Let me dispose quickly of the facts. In a career that spanned
33 years, including those of the First War, he took more
wickets (4,187) than any other bowler before or since. He
made 39,802 runs, with an average of 30, and did the double
the record number of 16 times, two more than his Yorkshire
twin, George Hirst. He played his first Test in 1899, as a lad of
21, and his last at the Oval in 1926, a couple of months short of
his 49th birthday.

What are the clues to such a tremendous and sustained
record of achievement? I suppose they lie in the combination
of a tough constitution – that he was a careful liver scarcely
needs saying – a shrewd, practical mind, and an unlimited gift
of determined application, an infinite capacity for taking pains.

Among the slow left-arm fraternity there have been more
acute spinners of the ball, though it did plenty for him when
his fingers were young and enough right to the end; but it is

doubtful if anyone has had greater control, or has used the air to better purpose.

As a right-hand batsman, application again. There is a moral for all young cricketers in his elevation from the bottom to the top. W.G. (in what was to be his last Test Match) put him in No. 11 at Trent Bridge in 1899. Twelve years later Hobbs and Rhodes were making their immortal stand of 323 for the first wicket against Australia at Melbourne.

He was the perfect foil for the brilliance of Hobbs, thorough, eminently dependable. That is the key to his cricket, with the natural corollary that always, all the time, he played for his side. It was an instinct derived from Lord Hawke, his first captain and, he says, his best, who led the Yorkshire XI out of anarchy in the 'nineties, and was indeed effectively the founder of the Yorkshire tradition. In this sense the mark of Hawke and Rhodes may still be seen in the teamwork that is still so strongly characteristic of Yorkshire cricket today.

Similarly there derives from them the habit that becomes second nature of playing as hard as may be – but of course, within the laws. (There was never a grosser libel on Yorkshire cricketers, living and departed, than the notion recently spread by ignorant apologists that according to their philosophy it was better to cheat than to lose.)

If anyone had the effrontery to question the old maestro on this subject I imagine the answer would be contemptuously terse. On any more amenable topic his conversation is full of wise observation and marvellously informed. He 'sees' the English cricketers of today as though his eyes had the brightness of youth. The hour I most easily recall last summer was the one spent with him on the balcony at Headingley.

He is an oracle, and an institution, a unique link between ancient and modern. The county championship began with W.G. Wilfred bowled to him and got him out. Bradman is the greatest of modern batsmen. He bowled to him, too, in his last match at Scarborough, and if mid-off had been a better fielder he would have had him for a duck. So one reads in Sidney Rogerson's book, 'Wilfred Rhodes: Professional and Gentleman,' published some years ago. It is a biography full of insight, which none can read without improving his understanding of cricket: a worthy memorial to one of the immortals.

A few days later on a bleak December morning Mr Rhodes paid the Lord's Taverners the honour of travelling up by train from his home at Poole, Dorset, to be chief guest at their Christmas luncheon, and I had the great distinction of proposing his health.

The old hero brought down the house when in reply he said, 'I've always been fond of cricket. It's been a hobby of mine.' That is a sentiment which with all modesty can be echoed by your correspondent, and, I expect, by all readers of this book.

# CHAPTER TEN

# EPILOGUE

*The five pieces that follow – three by C. B. Fry and one each by Lord Birkett and Bernard Hollowood – are extracted from the Introductions or "Prologues" to the paper-back books put out by* The Daily Telegraph *containing Mr. Swanton's day-to-day descriptions of famous post-war series between England and Australia.*

*The descriptions could well have stood on their own, but stature was added to them by the distinction of these names: Captain C. B. Fry, a great England cricketer and captain of The Golden Age, scholar, philosopher and wit; the first Lord Birkett, the famous advocate and judge, who in later life became, as a writer and speech maker, a wonderful protagonist of cricket; and Bernard Hollowood, the Editor of "Punch", artist, essayist and in his day a well-known Staffordshire cricketer.*

*These three individualistic commentaries make generous tribute to Mr. Swanton's work. They reflect the styles and personalities of the respective authors in a way which, even in these necessarily abbreviated versions, seem well worthy of reproduction here.*

P.H.

August 12, 1953

For myself, on what I have seen, I should say that our players have let go of two major principles. Our batsmen seem to have forgotten that good bowling can only be tamed by attack – cautious, if you like, but attack. Our bowlers tend to neglect the ruling need of consistent accuracy, our fielders have been too prone to let catches go begging.

If one writes a prologue one may as well be positive. May I, therefore, submit my own belief that no England captain ought ever be invited to take command of an England eleven, as it were, on approval. If he is 'on appro' where is his prestige with his team? Where, perhaps, is his own confidence in himself? Where is the confidence of his men in him?

Baiting of selection committees is futile; you cannot hook them. Our selectors are always individually first-rate; they command far better information than outsiders; if they appear to be doing something particularly foolish, it is certain that they have some specially good reason for their apparent folly. But in principle I advocate that the captain be chosen first by the Board of Control, or its small ad hoc committee. The Chairman of the Board should then present the captain with the choice of two or three colleagues to form with him a selection committee of three. Three is enough; big committees are a mistake because they scatter responsibility. A small committee can obtain any advice it cares to seek.

No one but the captain can organise and stabilise a team. From internal causes and differences Australia can find her best eleven much more easily than we can, but we should face constructively the avoidance of putting trial teams into the field even in the earlier Test matches.

Principles and policies are easier to come by than the achievement of practical success, but in any case they should be the perpetual foundations of procedure.

Far be it from me to confuse existing confusion. Confusion there has been. The critics have cooked it up with uncommon success. What is the good of blaming the selectors for not trailing about their task as if their jobs were the conferring of Knighthoods of cricket? That is not their privilege; their simple task is to select even in the first match a team that is likely to remain in being. Were I the Chairman of the Board of Control I would forbid my selectors to read newsprint – except perhaps such as where our present author may be enjoying himself.

With him I do most cordially agree that the approach of our batsmen to their hazardous game is too modern to be mordant – they have not all of them properly bitten the bullet. There is only one way for a batsman to do himself justice; it is from the very first ball to play every ball on its merits; to let each ball as it comes lead him naturally into the stroke he would unexcitedly apply to it at the nets in terms of his most skilful self.

For lack of following this elementary rule too frequently too many of our batsmen have been bad starters. They have also been much too imaginative; they have also, some of them, forgotten that every stroke in cricket should be a swing; sometimes a very little swing, sometimes a very full one, but a swing. Not a tentative prod with diminishing acceleration.

The rules of batsmanship remain for ever the same, just as the rules of strategy are the same for Monty and for Ike as they were for Hannibal and Julius Caesar. However, detail of this sort is more within the province of your author than of his protagonist.

But stay a moment. Several of our leading batsmen are rather tentative. When I see fine batsmen like Graveney and Simpson I expect to see them play their true game from the very first ball. No doubt they often do so. Sometimes in Test matches they do not. Remembering that I have made all their mistakes myself over an area of 26 Test matches, they must not mind, they will not mind, what I say. What is the good of being an England batsman if you do not, all the time, early and late, proceed to treat the bowling simply and solely on its merits?

Then again, bowlers of the class who find their way into an England eleven should know that such artifices as swerve, deceptive flight, and even cut and spin, are added graces which become ineffective unless superimposed upon insatiable perfection of length.

Not that our bowlers have not, off and on, done very well. They are, however, England bowlers and should obey the rules that every school coach propounds to his pupil as fundamental. As Ranji said, everything that matters in cricket is elementary. No doubt they would have bowled me out even in my prime, but not with long-hops or even with half-volleys.

C. B. Fry

March, 1955

Incredible as it may appear, quite a batch of would-be authorities are still unaware that whereas Test cricket here at home is ruled by the Board of Control, which is not the M.C.C., Test cricket in Australia so far as we are concerned is arranged and conducted by the M.C.C. The Board of Control consists mainly of delegates appointed by the ten leading counties with a minority of delegates nominated by M.C.C. and minor counties. The M.C.C. strictly speaking consists of some 7,000 members of the club with an Executive Committee of twenty or thirty. For our home Tests the teams are selected by a Selection Committee chosen by the Board of Control which does not meet to consider the teams chosen. For the M.C.C. Australian party it is usual, but not obligatory, for the M.C.C. Committee to invite the Selection Committee already in existence as nominated by the Board of Control to operate co-operatively in the choosing of the players, but the whole M.C.C. Committee, advised by its special Cricket Sub-Committee, is finally responsible for the personnel of the team for Australia and particularly for the appointment of the captain, vice-captain and the manager.

If the reader will recall the various criticisms and comments that exploded in various organs of opinion at the time our present victorious representatives were chosen he will observe what a deal of barking there was up the wrong pine tree.

Then again, and as a matter of fact, the Board of Control Selection Committee was about as strong as it could be; two ex-captains of England with much Australian experience, two leading and experienced professionals, and a chairman who, in addition to having been captain of his University and a county cricketer, is the most eminent historian of the game.

Not only this. It happened that I looked into the Lord's sanctum when the Selectors were sitting and, behold, they had in consultation three other ex-captains of England who had taken M.C.C. teams to Australia.

Well, if five ex-England captains plus two exceptionally wise professionals, all with minute Australian experience, could not do the right thing, who on earth could? I ask you.

That, however, would not prevent any young journalist, recently graduated to London ex-Glasgow via Manchester, from infecting several millions of students of his lore with doubts, ditherings and double-barrelled alternatives and from deeply annoying not only countless others but even such a tough and pachydermatous soul as myself.

In this connection there are two salient points that in general fail to jump to people's minds. The first is that when a carefully appointed body of selectors do anything that is frankly contrary to expectation and apparently extravagantly silly the long odds are that they have a particularly good reason for their action. The second is that no Selection Committee ever invented or discoverable can possibly proceed on any other grounds than probability; in consequence it is erroneous to blame them if events show they might have done better since the event is a totally different thing from the probability.

There is the further and very relevant consideration that any England or M.C.C. Selection Committee is always in possession of information far superior to such as is available to Tom, Dick and Harry. Moreover, such a committee can always obtain private and confidential advice from any and every county captain and county official. In short, it is far better placed than any other person or body for the task it is appointed to perform; and it has no motive whatsoever for being otherwise than entirely impartial.

Impartiality is a gem, of course. Yet one of the hubbubs that occurred was over the question of whom to appoint captain – Hutton or an amateur? On this subject the humpty-dumpty of 'snobbery' was enthroned on the wall. There was supposed to be a party at Lord's so rooted in the feudal past as to object to a professional captain on social grounds. And this, of course, was absolute bunkum. The question is an open one because there is no doubt that, other things being equal, professionals themselves prefer an amateur to a brother professional as captain; and there is the further point that as a rule amateur captains from boyhood upwards have had more experience of captaincy and are free from the handicap of knowing that what they do or do not do may gravely affect the economic career

of a member of their team. Nothing can eliminate the difference between the man who is a paid servant of a club and the
man who is a free agent with no duties as an employee. The
volunteer may not please the equalitarian but the paid man
has been paid in cash for his inequality of status; he must let
the credit go if he elects to take the cash.

Nobody in the know failed to recognise Hutton as a shrewd,
steady, capable captain. He was an almost universal favourite
for the job. But certain arguments in favour of an amateur
captain remained and still remain; they are ineluctable. Not to
burke the issue I am myself in favour of an amateur captain, but
I am fully alive to Hutton's eminent merits which have been
amply retestified. Among other triumphs he has proved very
adroit in glancing to leg the cleverness of his interlocutors at
Press conferences and interviews.

C. B. Fry

March, 1955

I wonder whether it occurs to you now to reckon up why it is
that first-class cricketers of the generation of Sir F. S. Jackson,
A. C. MacLaren and myself have always refused to accept any
other batsman as the equal of Dr W. G. Grace; and why it was
that the generation of our peers before that, and also the one
before that, set so high value on the man who is recorded on the
great gates at Lord's as 'The Great Cricketer.' He never
allowed his exceptional talents and physique to betray him
into unorthodoxy.

During the past tour in Australia we have seen a set of batsmen, with fine averages and aggregates to their names in the
pages of *Wisden* for their performances in our own first-class
cricket, not to mention a parallel set of Australian batsmen. We
have seen them too often floundering about with negligible
success on wickets which happened to be variable in pace and
uncertain in quality.

Well, it was on such wickets that W. G. collected his huge
scores with frequency unexampled till the era of red marl and
plate-glass comfort supplanted the old-fashioned natural turf.

There is no immediate utility in comparing teams of different years but there is some interest since it leads to reflexion on differences of technique and method.

Now of our present England team so sound and experienced a censor of batsmanship as Sir Pelham Warner has said that he feared it is brittle. As for me, to me it seemed that, with due regard to the proved fine capacity for runs in the professed batsmen, too many of them are tentative and uncertain starters. Moreover as to method and technique not more than two of them are, by England standard, free of one or more basic faults. Remember we are concerned with players of proved fertility as run-makers on English grounds in modern conditions of performance.

But consider the men who represented us in Test matches in 1882, 1902, 1907 and 1912. In 1882 we fielded ten men in our team capable of a century even against Spofforth, Garrett, Boyle and Palmer. In 1902 every one of our eleven, every one, was genuinely good enough for a century against any bowling. In 1907 ten of our eleven were similarly capable and in 1912 nine. This I suggest is a thought worth thinking; and it is a good exercise for lovers of cricket to bend their brains to an explanation. It is a solemn thought to recall that in 1882 our captain, A. N. Hornby (of our Hornby and our Barlow long ago), walked in tenth in our first innings but first in our second innings. And, incidentally, our team of 1882 mustered eight bowlers every one of whom would figure as a prime asset in our best possible eleven of 1954. Again a thought worth harbouring. Nor does any quip translating *laudator temporis acti* carry any weight in mitigation of the contrast.

A word is enough to the wise. Let those who fancy that little or no good class cricket was played before 1921, revise their attitude and digest the lesson.

No one appreciates the excellence of heroes such as Hobbs, Hammond, Sutcliffe, Mead, Woolley and such like more than I do. But they made their runs under conditions far more favourable than those which confronted Dr W. G. Grace and his consummate correctitude.

Another consideration is that the era of W.G. was an era of fast bowling. He had to play Tysons and Stathams on natural turf wickets which may have been pleasant enough for the early hours of the first day, quite negotiable on the second day, but almost always showed signs of wear by the second evening and favoured the bowler quite distinctly on the third day.

Do our batsmen now give enough attention to the mechanical correctness which rendered W.G. the type of his period?

A great cricketer, a good candidate as an all-rounder for an eleven representative of all time, namely A. G. Steel, K.C., of Cambridge, Lancashire and England, when I asked him to tell me about the Champion replied succinctly: 'W.G.? W.G. was tremendous. He stood head and shoulders above us. He killed fast bowling, even the best, and he was the best change bowler of his time and a brilliant fieldsman.'

Incidentally (again) I myself had the honour of walking in first with W.G. against Australia when he was fifty-one years of age and at the distance of 20 yards I saw him play with peculiar power and precision for about two hours. I could well believe he was tremendous in his teens, twenties and thirties. The point is that W.G.'s method was the type of all the best batting of his long and undisputed eminence.

C. B. Fry

August, 1956

There has grown up of late a fashion in some quarters to decry the Test match as some kind of huge and unwieldy excrescence on cricket, devoid of the beauty with which the summer game should be invested, governed largely by commercial considerations, and fought out for the most part with a bitterness and ill-feeling that is alien to the spirit of cricket.

This kind of criticism is not new, and it is not true. Long before any Australian tour of England was thought of, Miss Mary Mitford was writing of cricket for our lasting pleasure. Many a cricket writer must have envied her the pleasure of saying for the first time:

'Who would think that a little bit of leather and two pieces of wood had such a delightful and delighting power?'

But Mary Mitford didn't like the 'big matches' even then. She once wrote a letter to R. B. Haydon, that tragic figure of a painter and diarist, and referred to a match between Hampshire and All England. Her scorn was quite withering for the 'ugly old men' at Lord's compared with 'our fine village lads.' That great lover of the game, who wrote so charmingly about it – E. V. Lucas – once wrote in a milder but similar strain:

> 'Cricket is not the county ground . . . cricket is the back-yard, the garden, the playground, the school field, the club and college ground, and, above all, the village green.'

Test matches must be judged in the light of modern conditions, and Mr Swanton, I think, sets the matter in its proper bearings, when he writes of that wonderful Saturday at Lord's in the Second Test Match of the present series. And wonderful it was, wonderful, never-to-be-forgotten! Keith Miller, at any rate, will remember, so long as he has breath, that surge of affection and admiration, for such it was, that accompanied him from the pavilion to the wicket in an unbroken ovation and salutation; and that Saturday evening crowd will always remember, too, that masterly little innings of thirty runs, that little gem that set the seal on Miller's greatness and uplifted every heart. Mr Swanton very properly speaks of 'Miller's match' as one speaks of 'Fowler's match,' and calls Lord's 'the Mecca of Meccas.' It was indeed fitting that it was there that Miller should receive this most moving tribute, and Mr Swanton continues:

> 'The air was charged with an excitement and an enthusiasm more common to Melbourne or to Port of Spain, so that the England bowlers were uplifted to regions of effort and inspiration normally outside their scope . . . Cricket is changing, maybe, and cricket can sometimes nowadays be dull and colourless. But a game between England and Australia on a good fair wicket between well matched sides is still a classic *par excellence*.'

That is the language of soberness and restraint, written down by an eye-witness of the events of that memorable day, and it catches the atmosphere of the Test match at its best, so that forty years on, it may be, when the records are brought out, some youthful watcher of today may say with pride – I was there.

For myself, I do not think that any useful purpose is to be served by praising one form of cricket at the expense of another. Village cricket makes its own enduring appeal because it contains within itself something infinitely precious to English folk, and which is most truly part of their history. It began on the commons and village fields of England, and still carries that incommunicable combination of elements that makes cricket the passionately loved thing it is. The greatest piece of cricket writing in the world – John Nyren's *The Cricketers of My Time* – has survived the centuries largely because it holds the same secret and breathes the same spirit. Hambledon playing All England was the forerunner of Test cricket, but there was a robust quintessentially English flavour in Nyren's descriptions, which were not far removed from village cricket, as when he spoke of 'those anointed clod-stumpers' and described the brothers Walker in homely country phrases.

Thousands of people, perhaps millions, who would not know how to set a cricket field, or explain 'seam' bowling, and who would be quite dumb if asked to explain a 'chinaman,' yet possess a deep-seated, almost instinctive, love of cricket, because it belongs to English ways and English life, and to village as well as national history. But these millions of cricket lovers follow Test cricket with an enthusiasm and an eagerness that is quite astonishing in its intensity. National pride is no doubt mixed up with it, but it is the love of cricket that is uppermost. For that enthusiastic and immense public there must be some guide, some instructor, some interpreter, somebody who will discuss with sympathy and understanding and knowledge the questions that are being debated almost everywhere. Who are likely to be selected to play? That is a question which touches local patriotism in the fiercest fashion. Will they pick Johnnie Wardle? When they leave him out the day is darkened for thousands. Will they dare to drop Tom Graveney with all his grace and his lovely strokes? Isn't Cyril Washbrook too old? Can David Sheppard face the opening Australia overs with so little practice? And what about the Australians? Will Ian

Craig establish himself as a great batsman? Has Lindwall's natural fire in any way abated? How does Benaud compare with Jessop? Are we good enough to beat them this time?

It is quite astonishing with what vigour and feeling these and a hundred similar questions are debated, and with what eagerness the commentaries of the knowledgeable on these questions are read.

In these circumstances, the task of the cricket writer is not easy if he would do his job well, and it is clearly a task of great importance. There are some qualities in the cricket writer that are obviously desirable, but there are some that, in my view, are quite indispensable. I think that the quality to be desired, beyond all others, is to possess a certain integrity of mind and character. It is easy to play to the gallery, to flatter popular prejudice, to make specious excuses, and to win cheap applause. It is notoriously much harder to speak frankly as the facts warrant, and as duty dictates, and to disavow the sensational and the insincere. Those who would wish to see the integrity of cricket writing fearlessly proclaimed might read again the opening chapter of Mr Swanton's book *West Indian Adventure* with its forthright condemnation of manners and conduct which are injurious to cricket wherever they are to be found, and with its wide and considered opinions:

'There were two battles going on, one on the field, where the contestants, despite all the hubbub and remarkable to relate, remained more or less friendly; the other in the Press between the rival camps of writers ... Much that was written certainly lacked restraint. Often, also to one watching day by day from the Press box, it seemed to lack a fair perspective ... I am not concerned to criticise it, except to add a personal and possibly quite erroneous impression picked up over the years. It amounts more or less to this, that 'the average reader', that mythical, intangible creature, is much more interested than some editors think in a fair, balanced picture of the play, and far less interested in an 'angle,' often more or less irrelevant, which puts the spotlight on anything controversial. It seems to me that much of the enthusiasm for cricket derives from the fact of people wanting to take their minds

away from anxieties and the sterner realities. They want
to relax, and merely to watch or hear or read about . . . a
game of skill and quality, played hard and cleanly, not an
all-in battle with propaganda accompaniment.'

It is also to be observed that when Charles Cowden Clarke
wrote his introduction to Nyren's famous book, he spoke of the
skill of the players, but emphasised their qualities of integrity
and plain dealing. Cricket has come to be recognised as a game
where fair play is the all-essential thing, and cricket writers do
well to maintain the same standards. When the Old Trafford
pitch was taking spin in the fourth Test match, and Laker was
taking full advantage of it to set up a standard that will possibly
never be beaten, there were some cricket writers (happily few)
who could not forbear to suggest that the wicket had been
deliberately prepared for the discomfiture of the Australian
visitors. This is to do more than put a 'spotlight on the controversial.' This is to poison the relations of goodwill and good
fellowship which happily exist between Australia and England
and between cricketers of both countries. Nobody could believe
for one moment that there was any truth in the suggestion, or
that anybody connected with cricket could be found to take
part in conduct so discreditable. But the power of the printed
word is great, and it is really very important that the standard
of cricket writing should be kept high, and free from elements
of this kind. It has often been said that the best writing on the
spirit of the game was written by Andrew Lang in the introduction he wrote to Daft's *Kings of Cricket*, and it is noteworthy that
he there says that one of the chief characteristics of cricket
which made it 'a very humanising game' was that 'it binds all
the bretheren together, whatever their politics and rank
may be.'

And with what good sense Mr Swanton disposes of the
matter. He says:

'Laker's first innings performance was phenomenal enough,
but its merit was perhaps clouded by the deficiencies of
the Australian batting, as also by the *palaver* over the
condition of the wicket. There was no room for argument
regarding his bowling today . . . If the wicket had been

such a natural graveyard for batsmen, it is inconceivable that Lock, even below his peak, even with the other arm tied to his side, would not have taken more than one wicket ... As the crowd that had massed round the pavilion dispersed ... one of the Australian party summed up the day by saying: "Well, it was a good scrap after all".'

Sir Norman Birkett

February, 1963

By all accounts, including the excellent one that follows these remarks, the Test series of 1962–63 was somewhat disappointing. To watch. Who would have thought when Dexter's men, nobly chaperoned by the Duke of Norfolk, set foot in Fremantle last October that the Ashes themselves would soon be in disrepute and up for auction? The Ashes! We know that the Empire has more or less gone west, that Moidegaulle sees Britain as an inconsiderable off-shore island, that things are not quite what they were, but ... well ... the Ashes! If they are eventually abolished, or demoted (which, frankly, I find unthinkable) I shall be irrational enough to blame Harold Macmillan. Why not? He's blamed for everything else.

Fortunately, cricket that is dull to watch can be exciting to read about. Given a reporter of eloquence and perception, one as commanding as Mr Swanton, one series is very much like another in its rich appeal. In the best literary cricket there are no barren patches. The author never takes too long a run at his paragraphs, never writes negatively down the leg-side, never commits the solecism of ignoring verbal long-hops and half-volleys. Four hours of Lawry in his Sydney mood (final Test) can be wearing even to the most enthusiastic spectator, but the distant reader can career through such tedium in a few lines. A wonderful invention is literary cricket.

Some critics have suggested that this series was a bore from start to finish. It wasn't of course. It most certainly was not to frozen fans in England. I attended each day's play with high hopes, and with as much equipment as I customarily take along to Lord's or the Oval. Instead of sandwiches, flask, binoculars and raincoat my cricketing gear this past winter consisted of an electric blanket, a transistor radio, all the morning, evening and Sunday papers I could afford, and a flask. My practice was to go to bed reasonably early in order to fit myself for the morning's ordeal by radio. I would tap my forehead six and a half times to remind my chilled wits that I had an appointment at 6.30 a.m. sharp: then sleep, perchance to dream. But sleep punctuated by many rude awakenings and feeble fumblings for my watch on the bedside table. What! Only ten past three! Hell! They'll be at it by now. Dexter and Cowdrey. Davidson and Benaud. Please, God, may Dexter be impelled to play his normal attacking game, and please may his head be kept down when driving through the covers . . .

By five-fifteen I was usually awake again, dog-tired, but afraid to relax anew for fear of oversleeping. By six-fifteen I had memorized a few more pages of *Wisden* and the transistor was at the ready on my pillow. At six-thirty . . .!

I am an old hand at this listening-to-Australia business. Forty years ago my mother used to get us out of bed – my father, my sister and my brothers – by yelling at us from the foot of the stairs. 'Hammond's out,' she would say, 'and Hendren's just been dropped at second slip.' And we would all come tumbling down, bleary-eyed, dressing-gowned and slippered, to gather anxiously round the gothic radio set in the kitchen. Reception seems to have deteriorated somewhat since those days. In my memory the sounds emerging from Australia in the 'twenties, though interrupted from time to time by atmospherics, were always intelligible: now, all too often they are not. And nothing in my experience is more infuriating than a commentary that contrives to mention names at irregular intervals without being able to inform the listener whether Titmus (was it?) is batting or bowling, a commentary that screams static abuse when it should be imparting vital statistics.

It was, need I add, pretty cold work. Three nights in a row a glass of water by my bed froze solid, and once my hair sealed itself to a bedpost. There was a power-cut, too, at a critical moment in the Third Test. That morning, the room and the bed like the tundra, I funked it. The problem of extracting my right arm from the sheets and fumbling in the dark for the transistor was too much for me. I waited for Mr Swanton's report after the eight o'clock *News*. It began, as always, with the right words – 'First, the scores . . .' I was suitably grateful.

Another aspect of the radio vigil occurs to me – the weird reluctance of the human brain to adjust itself to predigested geographical and meteorological facts. I know very well where Australia stands on the globe, its latitude and longitude, and I am familiar with the difference in time between London and Sydney. (We will forget for the moment that I once thought there were *two* Australias – an error arising from the misreading at school of a world map depicting one Australia bottom-left and another bottom-right.) All the same I was never once, during those bitter winter mornings, able to adapt myself completely to the idea of being some twelve thousand miles from the battlefield.

It seemed ludicrous, for example, that bad light could stop play. 'The umpires are conferring, peering down the wicket from the popping crease,' said the radio, and my eye would swivel smartly to the window of my room. They must be crazy. The light was excellent. And then I would remember, piling idiocy on idiocy, that the bright morning owed something to the unnatural whiteness of the deep snow in the garden. 'I'm forgetting,' I'd mutter, 'they have no snow in Sydney.'

Two more minor matters upset me. One was Dexter's lofty disregard for the feelings of people in England, demonstrated in the earlier Tests by his unhappy knack of getting himself out during hours of transmission and almost immediately after the start of the broadcast. (Surely he could have put himself in earlier or later!) And the second was the lack of consideration shown by both captains when they took time off for 'drinks' and cut down our listening time. A thoughtless, monstrous tax on our patience and goodwill.

I am reminded too that there was one morning when the BBC engineers failed to make contact with Australia, and managed with praiseworthy enterprise to pick up a relay of the commentary via Colombia. I am reminded *too* that this relay was broken off, by the BBC, whenever the programme seemed likely to be interrupted by commercials.

I mention these things to support my contention that this, in some ways, was demonstrably a winter of discontent.

From time to time we stay-at-homes were allowed a glimpse of the Tests by courtesy of the BBC Television service. There was nothing dull about these snatches of film: wickets toppled like nine-pins, glorious catches were taken every other ball, and practically every scoring stroke was a lofted drive for four over long-on. Cricket telescoped in this way is of course better than nothing, and indeed is surprisingly funny. 'Another day of crawl at Melbourne,' said a popular daily, and the next evening would bring Mr Peter Dimmock's lot with their fireworks, catapulting stumps and rocketing sixes. Delicious. These films were carefully but unrealistically dubbed with sound effects. Sheppard plays back gingerly to a Simpson leg-break, and the sonic record of ball on bat is a mighty crack through the covers. Then Pullar glances Davidson fine with a terrific willowy thud. Every ball, every shot, evokes thunderous applause. Who said that cricket was tame?

Bernard Hollowood

# Index

*Although a player may have been mentioned once or several times in a particular match report, only one entry, referring to the page on which the full score appears, has been thought necessary.*